NEW HAMPSHIRE
SCENERY

NEW HAMPSHIRE SCENERY

a dictionary of nineteenth-century artists
of New Hampshire mountain landscapes

by
Catherine H. Campbell
with
Marcia Schmidt Blaine

Published for the
NEW HAMPSHIRE HISTORICAL SOCIETY
by
PHOENIX PUBLISHING
Canaan, New Hampshire

Campbell, Catherine H.
  New Hampshire scenery.

  Bibliography: p. 223
  1. Artists — New Hampshire — Dictionaries. 2. Mountains
in art. 3. Art, Modern — 19th century — New Hampshire. I.
Blaine, Marcia Schmidt. II. New Hampshire Historical Society. III. Title.
N6530.N4C36   1985   760′.04436′0922   85-3700
ISBN 0-914659-12-X

April 1986

Printed in the United States of America

CONTENTS

FOREWORD

FROM OUR CURRENT VANTAGE it is extremely difficult to reconstitute the mental and cultural geography of the White Mountains during the nineteenth century. The scarred and abused contemporary landscape, garnished with the sordid remnants of tourism, discloses little of the extraordinary value attached to that once sublime wilderness, at first hostile, then later welcoming, to the incursions of human culture. As the most accessible wilderness in America, the White Mountains afforded urbanites of the last century with a vast repertoire of natural resources, both physical and cultural. The creative exploitation of these resources occupied the Romantic imagination for the better part of the era, inspiring countless poems, stories, sermons and, as the present volume attests, acres of paintings, drawings, prints, and photographs.

As if by design, the vogue for the White Mountains coincided with the earliest sustained efforts at national self-definition during the first decades of the nineteenth century, a confluence of concerns which projected the American-self decisively into the embrace of nature. Fueled by the exhortations of such writers as Emerson to "enjoy an original relationship to the universe," and smarting under European assertions of our perceived cultural inadequacies, Americans sought to discover a past as well as a future in the unique circumstances of our wilderness. As the physical embodiment of our national virtue, nature became one of the dominant values of the period, subsuming art, philosophy, religion, science and leisure, to cite only some of the major institutions of the modern world.

Thomas Cole's reconnaissance of the White Mountains during the summer and fall of 1827 and 1828 marks the beginning of the artistic importance of the region. For Cole, the father of American landscape painting, the White Mountains furnished an abundance of sublimely tragic themes ranging from the recent martyrdom of the Willey family in Crawford Notch to the heroic suicide of the Indian chief Chocorua from the summit of the peak that bears his name to this day. Replete with such terrible "gothick" associations, the White Mountains were for Cole and his contemporaries a rich lode of *angst*-ridden pictorial motifs which, according to Romantic literary doctrine, conferred true significance and dignity upon the land. By way of added cultural valence these morbid and lugubrious historical episodes also helped slake the Romantic thirst for gloom and doom. With the possible exception of the Catskills (equally rich in legend but far less redolent of *angst*) no other wilderness region of the country was as copiously supplied with complex associations as the White Mountains, nor seemingly as alluring to the pen and brush of New Yorkers and Bostonians.

In 1839, at the summit of his career, Cole returned to the White Mountains for a final visit. From this experience, which retrospectively seems to have been an effort at cultural reconciliation with the idea of wilderness, eventuated his great canvas in the National Gallery entitled *The Notch of the White Mountains* which appears on the cover of this volume. In this magistral work, one of the undisputed masterpieces of White Mountain painting, Cole transformed Crawford Notch, the locus of the earlier Willey catastrophe, into a benevolent kingdom of light and color, nurturing and fully sustaining of human habitation and cultivation. The rhetoric of this picture, from the conspicuous man-made stump in the foreground to the dramatic clearing storm, indicates that an accommodation has occurred between man and nature. Where formerly the Notch had been viewed as a place of terror, its topography is now made to function as an emblem of divine imminence, an image of Providence akin to the verbal musings of the great New England Transcendentalists. In this resplendent pictorial apotheosis the "gothick" sublime yields to a benign vision of what one historian has happily termed the "Christianized" sublime. In this connection Cole himself noted in a now famous essay on nature, "the Wilderness is yet a fitting place to speak of God."

In subsequent decades the White Mountains became a magnetic pole for artists in search of sublime themes as a means for providing nature lovers with a way of enjoying the wilderness in the comfort of a heated parlor. Asher Durand's advocacy of the Franconia region in the pages of a well-known art journal of the period, for example, introduced Americans to still further natural wonders such as the Old Man of the Mountain and the curiosities of the Flume. As Hawthorne affirmed in a short story bearing the same name, the Great Stone Face shown in David Johnson's *Old Man in the Mountain* on page 2 denoted God's providential judgment upon Americans, while the boulder miraculously suspended in the Flume depicted in Blakelock's *The Boulder and the Flume* on page 224 evoked Christian ideas of Resurrection and Redemption in the excitable minds of the Romantics. As icons of nineteenth-century nature reverence, these images of the "Christianized" sublime effectively served as a form of religious painting for Protestant America. Buttressed as they were by such influential writers as Emerson and Thoreau, these works afford special insight into the character and quality of the nineteenth-century American religious sensibility.

In a related manner Romantic Science transformed the White Mountains from a repository of hard, ugly granite, and obscure arctic flora, to a glacial and biological theater in which the drama of Creation was played out daily before men's eyes. Such exegetes as Agassiz, Tuckerman, Boot, Bigelow and Oakes addressed in their tracts the natural wonders of Creation, reconciling Science and Theology while glossing the Great Book of Nature, a nature simultaneously viewed as fact and natural Revelation. Botanist William Oakes's *Scenery of the White Mountain*, published in Boston in 1848 with sensitive and sophisticated lithographs principally by Isaac Sprague, was one of the most influential works of the era, conjoining words and images in celebration of nature, as well as providing a new body of knowledge and theory through which to interpret the White Mountains. Certainly no writer before Thomas Starr King was more instrumental in forming the popular perception of the region while explicating its scientific and theological significance.

The artistic discovery in 1849 of the Intervale at North Conway by fellow artists Benjamin Champney and John F. Kensett marks yet another major turning point in the history of the White Mountains. Where formerly artists and scientists had come to the region in a spirit of exploration and adventure, the new breed of cognoscenti began to colonize the landscape on a permanent basis. For Champney, the first painter to reside year-around in the White Mountains, the Valley of Conway represented a kind of pastoral paradise, a harmonious condominium of man and nature. In combination with the exceptional beauty of the site, Champney's immense popularity with his artistic confreres (a modest practitioner in his own right, he seems to have possessed a delightfully avuncular personality) attracted painters in ever increasing numbers to this new "American Barbizon." Here, at the base of the eastern slopes of the White Mountains where verdant valleys abutted the towering summit of Mount Washington, a new world Eden was bathed in a clarified morning light ideal for sketching or painting *en plein air*. Even the bite of the ubiquitous and dreaded black fly — the bane of the nineteenth-century painter — seems to have been less virulent in this placid and ordered corner of America.

From Sunset Hill, Kensett sketched in 1851 the view that was to become canonical among White Mountain paintings as well as the most celebrated vision of natural sublimity during the nineteenth century. Kensett's reknowned work, entitled *Mt. Washington from the Valley of Conway* (Wellesley College Museum of Art), was engraved by James Smillie in the same year for the American Art Union and distributed in the thousands to an appreciative membership. In 1860 Currier and Ives issued its famous lithograph *New Hampshire Scenery* by Fannie Palmer based upon Kensett's view and thereby bestowed upon the topography of the Intervale the status of the best known landscape view of the era.

Writers such as Benjamin Willey (*Incidents in White Mountain History*, 1856) and Thomas Starr King (*The White Hills; Their Legends, Landscape and Poetry*, 1859) further proselytized in behalf of the restorative power of wild nature, their verbal sermons adumbrating the pictorial icons in passionate, empurpled prose: "One feels in standing on the green plain, that he is not in any county of New Hampshire but in the world of pure beauty . . . the *adytum* of the temple where God is to be worshipped as the Infinite Artist." (Willey, p. 174).

ix

Such bold mid-century affirmations surely mark the high tide of cultural interest in the White Mountains, written and painted ideals which in subsequent decades were to structure the wider appreciation of nature in America. The period after the Civil War is assuredly the most complex in the history of the White Mountains. Attracted by the blandishments of nature and culture, and transported on a vast new system of railroads, tourists in unprecedented numbers invaded the region, seeking the experience of transcendent sublimity. Summoned by artists and writers to perceive nature in conformity with prescribed canons of beauty and utility amounting almost to a form of landscape liturgy, they undertook dutiful pilgrimage to the Flume, Eagle Cliff, Diana's Bath, Crystal Cascade or the Emerald Pool to meditate upon the sacred and sacral qualities of Creation. Though Emerson had observed in the early 1840's that "It is in vain that we look for genius to reiterate its miracles in the old mountains," the popular experience of the "Christianized" sublime was never more fervid than in the two decades following the Civil War.

Paradoxically it is at this moment that artistic vision began to deflect away from the face of nature towards a new set of aesthetic and psychological imperatives. Winslow Homer, for example, who executed a number of works in the White Mountains during the summer of 1868 no longer looked directly on nature to sustain his vision but to people, their costumes and accessories and above all to light, color and atmosphere, the decidedly more self-referential aspects of art making. This manifest formalism, which stands in contrast to the Romantic-Realism of the first half of the century, informs in varying degrees all the significant art produced after 1860 under such diverse rubrics as Luminism, Tonalism and Impressionism.

In focusing their vision more upon the processes of art than upon the products of nature, these artists further contributed to demythologizing the landscape, sacrificing its numinous properties upon the altar of formal experimentation. In the softened Arcadian views of such painters as George Innes, William Morris Hunt and John Twachtman, the older landscape of potentiation was no longer capable of bearing its former freight of sublime meaning. Rather in the paintings of this period the White Mountains surrendered their special look to French light, color and brushwork, as atmospherics wrested meaning from form and God yielded to the modern religion of style.

A still further contributing factor to the demise of art and culture in the White Mountains during the later nineteenth century lay in the migration of sublimity to the American West or such exotic locales as the tropics and the arctic. The advent of topographic landscape photography from the great western surveys, as well as the pyrotechnic canvases of the Rockies and Yosemite of such myth makers as Albert Bierstadt, projected a new scale and sense of grandeur into the American consciousness. Photographer William Henry Jackson's discovery of the Mountain of the Holy Cross in Colorado in 1863, for example, released a series of cultural reverberations that echoed throughout the last quarter of the century. His photograph of this remarkable natural phenomenon, clear evidence of God's signature in the western landscape, influenced no less a cultural figure than Longfellow, whose famous elegy to his wife is based upon the photographic view of this unknown, but not unseen, mountain.

By the turn of the century neither nature nor the Transcendental Oversoul were much in vogue in New England while the institution of art had deserted nature in order to explore the city and other issues of modernity. Despite the efforts of the northeastern tourist industry to salvage some vestiges of a rapidly migrating sublimity — even snow crosses began to flourish upon the flanks of the White Mountains — the region had definitively entered upon the long period of physical and cultural decline. The strategy of investing technology with the qualities of natural sublimity, a process interestingly documented by historian Leo Marx, engendered for a brief period a kind of Techno-Sublime, but this effort appears only briefly to have forestalled the inevitable processes of cultural and physical disintegration. Despite these retrograde efforts, or perhaps because of them, public consciousness of the White Mountains as a place of restoration and redemption was all but eclipsed by the turn of the century. Around 1900, a new and unprecedented scale of commercial exploitation of the region, especially logging, precipitated still further the physical, and to some extent the cultural, erosion of the White Mountains. As Oliver Wendell Holmes truculently reported "the mountains and cataracts which were to have made poets and painters have been mined and dammed."

For anyone aspiring to recover the values of the Romantic age in New England there can be no more splendid and insightful record than the works of art recorded in this volume, images of land which in their time and place directly revealed the hand and purposes of the Creator.

Robert McGrath
Professor of Art History
Dartmouth College

Hanover, New Hampshire
December, 1984

PREFACE

A S ROBERT McGRATH POINTS OUT in his Foreword, the art spawned in the nineteenth century by a reverent interpretation of the "visible Hand of God" in untamed nature was buried in the work of the new wave of artists who later experimented with different values. This dictionary deals entirely with the era which began in 1816, when the first crude woodcut of Crawford Notch appeared on Carrigain's Map of New Hampshire, to the arbitrary date of 1900 when painters turned to Impressionist visions and left it to the photographers to capture factual views of the White Mountains.

It is for this reason that a limited selection of early stereoscopic views of the specific areas most favored by artists is included in this volume. Photographers of the period also tried to express the awesomeness of untamed nature and the "sublime" in many of their works such as the series on Mount Washington titled *Frostwork*, the cloud-swathed view of the Old Man, and Bierstadt's extensive recording in his series *Stereoscopic Views Among the Hills of New Hampshire*. The detail in these stereographs, enhanced by the three-dimensional effect so difficult to reproduce with the brush (although many artists came close), makes an interesting comparison with paintings of the period.

The corpus of the dictionary includes the names of some 450 artists and well over 6,000 paintings. Included also are drawings, prints, and other forms of graphic art, for in the case of some artists these are the only examples of extant works which have as yet come to light.

In all, ten years went into assembling this information. Data from standard reference works and exhibition lists and catalogs, and information from a wide range of galleries and knowledgeable individuals were gathered, cross checked, and cataloged in card files, to be later computerized and finally structured into the four sections of this book.

The format of the dictionary provides easy access to specifics on both artists and their works and should be of great value as a primary reference source to all professionals interested in this genre of painting — art historians, dealers, museum and historical society personnel, librarians, teachers, and students alike. It is interesting to note that virtually every major museum in this country has works of this period in its collections, and here for instance, the dictionary would be a material help in developing the criteria for mounting an exhibition by subject, period, or artist.

Beyond the immediate art field, historians and sociologists will find interesting and little-known material concerning changes in public attitude reflected by the shifts in the popularity of subjects and areas painted. Finally, collectors and that segment of the general public interested in nineteenth-century American art will find the dictionary an invaluable source of factual information on both well-known and obscure artists and their works — the vast majority of which is not to be found in standard reference sources.

It is recognized that by its very nature certain of the information contained herein is obsolete even before it appears in print. Despite every effort to ensure comprehensive coverage, it is also recognized that sins of omission must surely exist, and it is hoped that corrections and additions will be forwarded to the New Hampshire Historical Society for validation and inclusion in the next edition of this work.

Although it is impossible to include the names of all who have helped bring this self-imposed task to fruition I should like to note with special thanks The Fine Arts and Print Departments of The Boston Public Library, The Institute of New Hampshire Studies at Plymouth State College, the New Hampshire Historical Society, the New-York Historical Society, The Albany Institute of Art, the Smithsonian Institution, the Frick Art Reference Library, the Boston Atheneum, the Vose Galleries of Boston and S. Morton Vose III, the Archives of American Art, Phyllis F. Greene; and, most important of all, my late husband Crawford J. Campbell, and my research fellow, Marcia Schmidt Blaine.

Finally, we have tried to ensure accuracy, but to err is human.

Catherine H. Campbell

Centre Harbor, New Hampshire
January, 1985

USER INFORMATION

Guide to Use of the Dictionary

Section I of the dictionary is arranged alphabetically by artist and is cross-referenced in Section II by subject.

Locate the name of the artist being researched in Section I. On the line below the artist's name is a series of letters which refer to other standard sources listing the artist. The Standard Source Reference List, which follows immediately below, gives the full title for each of these sources.

The biography which follows the listing of standard sources is generally brief, primarily dealing with known New Hampshire material concerning the artist's life, and is followed by references other than the standard sources. For lesser-known artists all known bibliographical material is listed at the end of the biography. In the case of well-known artists biographical material is generalized and bibliographical material is selected. If a bibliographical source is cited more than once, a full citation may be found in the Location / Source List beginning on page   .

The list of paintings which follows the bibliography contains signature abbreviations immediately after the painting name. A full explanation for each abbreviation may be found at the beginning of the Standard Source Reference List below. The paintings list also includes the location and / or source of the painting. Consult the Location / Source Reference List (Section III) for a complete address or citation.

The dictionary also includes in Section II a list of paintings by subject. In some cases, little-known or less painted areas are listed under the heading of miscellaneous. An index to the contents of this section is listed on page 185.

Standard Source Reference List

Artist signature abbreviations used in the paintings lists

S/D Signed and dated.   L/L Lower left.   L/R Lower right.

Abbreviations used for standard reference books throughout the dictionary

A   Perkins, Robert F., Jr., and William J. Gavin III, eds. *The Boston Athenaeum Art Exhibition Index, 1827-1874*. Boston: Library of the Boston Athenaeum, 1980.

AAA   Archives of American Art (see Location / Source Reference List).

AAU   American Art-Union (see "C").

B   Benjamin, S. G. W. *Art in America*. New York: Harper and Row, 1880.

Ba   Baigell, Matthew. *Dictionary of American Art*. New York: Harper and Row, 1979.

Be   Benezit, Emmanuel. *Dictionnaire critique et documentaire de peintres, sculpteurs, dessinateurs et graveurs de tous les temps et de tous les pays . . .* Nouv. ed. 8 vols., Paris, 1945-55.

C	Cowdrey, Mary Bartlett. *American Academy of Fine Arts and American Art-Union*. 2 vols. New York: New-York Historical Society, 1953.
Ce	Cowdrey, [Mary] Bartlett. *National Academy of Design Exhibition Record, 1826-1860*. 2 vols. New York, 1943.
Co	Collins, J. L. *Women Artists in America*. Chattanooga, TN: University of Tennessee, 1973.
C&H	Clement, Clara Erskine, and Laurence Hutton. *Artists of the Nineteenth Century and Their Works*. Boston: Houghton Mifflin and Co., 1880.
DAB	Johnson, Allen, and Dumas Malone, eds. *Dictionary of American Biography*. 11 vols. New York, 1946.
E	Ebert, John and Katherine. *Old American Prints for Collectors*. New York: Charles Scribner and Sons, Inc., 1974.
F	Carr, James F., compiler. *Mantle Fielding's Dictionary of American Painters, Sculptors and Engravers with an Addendum Containing Corrections and Additional Material on the Original Entries*. New York: James F. Carr, publisher, 1965 (Fielding first published in 1926).
F(sup)	Fielding supplement. See above.
G&W	Groce, George C., and David H. Wallace. *The New-York Historical Society's Dictionary of Artists in America, 1564-1860*. New Haven: Yale University Press, 1969 (first published in 1957).
K	Koke, Richard J., compiler. *American Landscape and Genre Painting in the New-York Historical Society*. Boston: G. K. Hall and Co., 1982.
Ka	Karolik, M. and M. *Collection of American Water Colors and Drawings: 1800-1875*. 2 vols. Boston: Boston Museum of Fine Arts, 1962.
N	Naylor, Maria. *The National Academy of Design Exhibition Record, 1861-1900*. New York: Kennedy Galleries, 1973.
NAD	National Academy of Design (see "Ce" and "N").
PAFA	Pennsylvania Academy of the Fine Arts (see "R").
R	Rutledge, Anna Wells. *Cumulative Record of Exhibition Catalogues, the Pennsylvania Academy of the Fine Arts, 1807-1870; the Society of Artists, 1800-1814; the Artist's Fund Society, 1835-1845*. Philadelphia: 1955.
S	Smith, Ralph Clifton. *Biographical Index of American Artists*. Charleston, SC: Garnier and Co., 1929.
T	Tuckerman, Henry T. *Book of the Artists. American Artist Life*....New York: F. Carr, Inc., 1967 (reprints, first published in 1867).

NEW HAMPSHIRE
SCENERY

SECTION I

Dictionary

of

Painters

Old Man in the Mountain (in Franconia Notch)
David Johnson, 1876
Oil on canvas, 60" x 48" / Collection: State of New Hampshire / Ref. page 100

A

ABBAT, AGNES DEAN
N
Born 1847. Died 1917.
Abbat studied at Cooper Union and the National Academy. When Abbat exhibited at the NAD in 1881, she lived at 337 4th Ave., N.Y.C. She also exhibited at the Boston Art Club. She painted flowers and landscapes in watercolor and oils. She was elected to the NAD in 1902.

INTERVALE ROAD, NORTH CONWAY; THE . . .
    NAD, 1881, #21; NMAA Inventory.
    Signed A., A. D. (probably Abbat, Agnes Dean).

NORTH CONWAY.
    1880. Oil.
    13½ x 9¾ (34.3 x 24.8).
    NMAA Inventory.

ADAMS, WILLIS SEAVER
N
Born 1844. Died 1921.
Adams gave his address as Springfield, MA in 1882 when he exhibited at the NAD.

Bibliography:
American Studies Group. *Willis Seaver Adams* exhibition, Deerfield Academy, Deerfield, MA (1966).

MOOSILAUK [sic] MOUNTAIN.
    Before 1876. Oil.
    Deerfield Academy. *Willis Seaver Adams* (1966); BIAP.

NEW HAMPSHIRE FOREST.
    Before 1876. Oil.
    Deerfield Academy. *Willis Seaver Adams* (1966); NMAA Inventory.

ALEXANDER, MARIA B.
Nothing is presently known of this artist.

WINTER SCENE OF MOUNT MONADNOCK.
    Late 19th century. Oil.
    8½ x 10 (21.6 x 25.4).
    Private collection (1975); NMAA Inventory.

AYER, CLARA DWIGHT MCMILLAN
Born 1841. Active 1864-c. 1875.
Nothing else is known of this painter.

ARTIST'S FALL, CONWAY, NH, FALL.
    C. 1875. Oil.
    18 x 11¾ (45.7 x 29.8).
    Private collection (1975); NMAA Inventory.

ARTIST'S FALL, CONWAY, NH, SPRING.
    C. 1875. Oil.
    18 x 11¾ (45.7 x 29.8).
    Private collection (1975); NMAA Inventory.

PANORAMA OF NORTH CONWAY, NH, WITH MOUNT WASHINGTON IN BACKGROUND.
    1884. Oil.
    16 x 32 (40.6 x 81.3).
    Private collection (1975); NMAA Inventory.

B

BABCOCK, AUGUSTA
Active before 1877.
Nothing else is presently known of this artist.
MOUNT WASHINGTON.
   Pre-1877; Delaware Academy of Design (July 1, 1857) (see Philadelphia Museum of Art Library for information).

BACON, JULIA
Be, S
Born Boston, MA. Died 1901.
Possibly the J. L. Bacon who exhibited at the NAD in 1884, 1885, and 1887 and who gave as his/her address Attleboro, MA, Bacon studied under Edmund Tarbell and exhibited at the Boston Art Club (see American Art Annual 4).
CHERRY MOUNTAIN, JEFFERSON, NEW HAMPSHIRE.
   Boston Art Club (1898), #199.
EAGLE MOUNTAIN.
   Boston Art Club (1897), #29.

BAKER (or BARKER), ANNIE D.
Active 1863.
Painted in the Monadnock region.
MOUNT MONADNOCK, NEW HAMPSHIRE.
   1863. Oil.
   9 x 13 (22.9 x 45.7).
   Private collection; NMAA Inventory.

BAKER, CHARLES
C, Ce, F, G&W
Born c. 1818. Died after 1862.
New York City directories from 1842 to 1862 list Baker as a saddler, gunsmith, and importer. In 1847 he did silverplating. His paintings were in the collections of Cropsey and Leupp. Some of his paintings are copies of works by Thomas Cole, whom he much admired.
Bibliography:
Blum, Betty. "Charles Baker." *Antiques* (Feb. 1981), pp. 366-367.
SCENERY NEAR CONWAY.
   Before 1851.
   NAD, 1851, #197.

VIEW IN FRANCONIA NOTCH.
   AAU, 1848, #451; NAD, 1851, #149; NAD, 1852, #405.
VIEW ON THE SACO RIVER.
   30 x 22 (76.2 x 55.9). Oval.
   AAU, 1849, #219.
Attributed:
UPPER SANDWICH RANGE FROM THE SOUTH (after Cole).
   Oil on cardboard on canvas.
   22⅝ x 19⅜ (57.5 x 49.2).
   Princeton University Art Gallery (1983); *Antiques* (Feb. 1981).

BANGS, MISS
Painted in the White Mountains with Sanford Gifford, Alfred Ordway, Benjamin Champney, and R. W. Hubbard in 1854. See Gifford sketchbook at the Albany Institute of History and Art.

BANNISTER, EDWARD MITCHELL
B, C&H, F, G&W, N, S, T
Born St. Andrews, New Brunswick, 1828.
Died Providence, RI, Jan. 9, 1901.
Bannister studied at the Lowell Institute and the Rhode Island School of Design with William Rimmer. He exhibited at the NAD in 1879.
Bibliography:
Cederholm, Theresa. *Afro-American Artists.* Boston Public Library (1973).
DORCHESTER, NEW HAMPSHIRE.
   1857. Oil on canvas.
   14 x 20 (35.6 x 50.8).
   Kennedy *Quarterly* 10:4, p. 181.

BARROW, JOHN DOBSON (or J. L.)
G&W, N, R, T
Born 1823. Died 1907.
Barrow exhibited at the Boston Athenaeum in 1866-67, the NAD from 1861 to 1888, and the PAFA from 1865 to 1869 while living in New York City and Skaneateles, NY.
MOUNT LAFAYETTE.
   Pre-1877; Chicago Industrial Exposition (1875).
VIEW NEAR LITTLETON, NEW HAMPSHIRE.
   NAD, 1876, #286.

New Hampshire Scenery

BARTLETT, WILLIAM HENRY
E, G&W
Born near London, March 26, 1809.
Died at sea, Sept. 13, 1854.
A prolific illustrator, Bartlett made sepia wash drawings the exact size to be engraved. His engraved views were widely copied by artists, but no signed oil painting by his hand is known.

Select Bibliography:
Arnot Art Gallery catalog, Elmira, NY. *William H. Bartlett and His Imitators* (Oct. 23-Dec. 4, 1966).
Cowdrey, Bartlett. "William Henry Bartlett and the American Scene." *New York History* 22 (Oct. 1941).
Earl, Mary Ellen. "William H. Bartlett and His Imitators." *Antiques* (July 1974), pp. 84-101.
Place, Frank. "W. H. Bartlett, Illustrator of American Scenery." *Appalachia* 25, pp. 25-28.
Ross, Alexander M. *William Henry Bartlett: Artist, Author and Traveller* (University of Toronto Press, 1973).
Willis, N. P. *American Scenery; or Land, Lake, and River. Illustrations of Transatlantic Nature from Drawings by W. H. Bartlett. . . .* Published in parts between 1838 and 1839 and as a book by George Virtue, London, 1840; reprint, Imprint Society, Barre, MA, 1971.

Note: All of the engravings listed below which appeared in *American Scenery*, except *Pulpit Rock*, had the following dimensions: 4¾ x 7 (12.1 x 17.8). Dimensions of *Pulpit Rock* were 7³⁄₁₆ x 4⅝ (18.3 x 11.8).

CENTRE HARBOR.
    1842. Engraving.
    Graham's Magazine (1842), engraved by A. L. Dick.
LAKE WINNIPISGOGEE [sic] FROM RED HILL.
    Engraving.
    Willis. *American Scenery.*
MOUNT JEFFERSON FROM MOUNT WASHINGTON.
    Engraving.
    Willis, N. F. *American Scenery.*
MOUNT WASHINGTON AND THE WHITE HILLS.
    Engraving.
    Willis. *American Scenery; Appalachia* (June 1940).
NOTCH HOUSE, WHITE MOUNTAINS.
    Engraving.
    7½ x 10¾ (19.1 x 27.3).
    Willis. *American Scenery.*

PULPIT ROCK.
    Engraving.
    Willis. *American Scenery.*
RED HILL, CENTER HARBOR.
    Engraving.
    Willis. *American Scenery.*
SQUAM LAKE FROM RED HILL.
    Engraving.
    Willis. *American Scenery.*
VIEW OF CENTER HARBOR.
    1838. Engraving.
    Willis. *American Scenery.*
VIEW OF MEREDITH.
    Engraving.
    8¼ x 11½ (21 x 29.2).
    Willis. *American Scenery.*
VIEW FROM MOUNT WASHINGTON.
    Engraving.
    Willis. *American Scenery; Appalachia* (June 1940).
WILLEY HOUSE.
    Engraving.
    Willis. *American Scenery.*

Attributed:
MEREDITH, NH.
    C. 1840. Oil on canvas.
    8¼ x 11½ (20.6 x 29.2).
    Private collection.
MEREDITH, N.H. S/L/L.
    23 x 32¾ (58.4 x 83.2).
    Oil on canvas. (signature in question).
    Sotheby PB catalog (Oct. 21, 1983), #28.

BATES, MISS M. D.
Nothing is presently known about this artist.
BETHLEHEM, NH.
    Charcoal sketch.
    Boston Art Club (April 1875), #21.

BAYNE, WILLIAM MCPHERSON
G&W, R
Born 1795. Died 1859.
Bayne was a British-American who painted panoramas. While living in Boston in the 1840s he exhibited at the Boston Athenaeum and the PAFA.

AMMONOOSIC [sic] FALLS, NEAR THE WHITE MOUNTAINS.
    Pre-1877; Boston Artists' Association, at Hardings Gallery (1843) (see Boston Athenaeum for information).

BEAL, REYNOLDS

F, N, S

Born 1867. Died 1951.

Illness prevented Beal from working consistently after his late 20s. He exhibited at the NAD from 1895 to 1900 and was a member of the Century Association from 1918 to 1951.

Bibliography:

Archives of American Art. Rolls 278-282, 286.

Vose Galleries catalog (Oct.-Nov. 1973).

Vose Galleries catalog (July 1983).

SUNSET HILL, CENTRE HARBOR, NH, FROM LONG ISLAND.

    1886. Pencil.

    8 x 9¾ (20.3 x 24.8).

    Private collection (1983); Vose Galleries (1975).

WHITE OAK POND, NH (Holderness).

    1886. Pencil.

    5 x 8¼ (12.7 x 21).

    Private collection (1983); Vose Galleries (1975).

BEAMAN, GAMALIEL W.

Died after 1893.

Nothing else is presently known of this artist.

MOUNT MONADNOCK FROM MOUNT WACHUSETT.

    Oil.

    27¾ x 37¾ (70.5 x 95.9).

    Richard Bourne, Inc., catalog (Aug. 16, 1977), #13; NMAA Inventory.

BEARD, WILLIAM HOLBROOK

C&H, DAB, F, G&W, N, R, S, T

Born Painesville, OH, April 13, 1824.

Died New York, NY, Feb. 20, 1900.

Mostly an artist of animal humor, Beard lived in New York City and Buffalo in the 1850s and 1860s. He was the brother of James Beard and married the daughter of portraitist Thomas LeClear in 1863. A member of the Century Association from 1866 to 1900, Beard kept a studio in the 10th Street Studio Building (N.Y.C.) from 1861 to 1900. He was a member of the NAD from 1862 to 1900, and he exhibited at the NAD and the PAFA.

SCENE IN THE WHITE MOUNTAINS.

    Pre-1877; Buffalo Fine Arts Academy (1865) (see Albright Knox Gallery, Buffalo, for information).

WHITE MOUNTAINS (2).

    Pre-1877; Buffalo Fine Arts Academy (1865); Utica (NY) Art Association (1867).

BECKETT, CHARLES E.

C, F (sup), G&W

Born Portland, ME, 1814. Died 1856.

One of the earliest Maine landscape painters, Beckett developed a very linear style. He exhibited at the AAU in 1847, 1849, and 1850 and illustrated S. B. Beckett's guidebooks.

Bibliography:

Maine Library *Bulletin* 13 (July-Oct. 1927), p. 4.

CRAWFORD NOTCH.

    1852.

    Beckett, S. A. *St. Lawrence Guide Book* (1853).

CRYSTAL CASCADE.

    1852.

    Beckett. *St. Lawrence Guide Book* (1853).

GLEN ELLIS FALLS.

    1852.

    Beckett. *St. Lawrence Guide Book* (1853).

GLEN HOUSE.

    1852.

    Beckett. *St. Lawrence Guide Book* (1853).

IMP; THE...

    1852.

    Beckett. *St. Lawrence Guide Book* (1853).

MOUNTS JEFFERSON AND ADAMS, FROM THOMPSON'S MILL.

    1852.

    Beckett. *St. Lawrence Guide Book* (1853).

MOUNT MORIAH FROM LARY'S.

    1852.

    Beckett. *St. Lawrence Guide Book* (1853).

MOUNT WASHINGTON FROM PEABODY VALLEY.

    1852.

    Beckett. *St. Lawrence Guide Book* (1853).

PLEASANT MOUNTAIN HOUSE NEAR BRIDGTON.

    C. 1851. Oil on canvas.

    24 x 34 (61 x 86.4).

    Portland Museum of Art (1983).

VALLEY HOUSE IN CRAWFORD NOTCH; THE...

    Formerly in the Sweat Memorial Museum (now the Portland Museum of Art); Maine Library *Bulletin* 13 (July-Oct. 1927), p. 4.

WHITE MOUNTAINS FROM BERLIN FALLS.

    1852.

    Beckett. *St. Lawrence Guide Book* (1853).

WHITE MOUNTAINS FROM RANDOLPH HILL.
Signed.
> Before 1853. Pencil.
> 7¾ x 10 (19.7 x 25.4).
> Private collection (1983); Pre-1877.

WHITE MOUNTAINS FROM SHELBURNE.
> Pre-1877; Maine Charitable Mechanic Association, Portland (Oct. 4, 1859).

WILLEY HOUSE.
> 1852.
> Beckett. *St. Lawrence Guide Book* (1853).

BECKETT, MARIA (or MARIA J. C. à BECKET or M. G. BECKETT)
Be
Born Portland, ME. Died 1904.
Primarily a watercolorist, Beckett was the daughter of Charles E. Beckett, artist, and niece of S. B. Beckett, publisher. In 1874 John Neal wrote that Charles E. Beckett "has left a daughter with some of the properties he lacked for she really is a fine colorist and her drawings and paintings are full of promise." She exhibited at the Boston Art Club in April 1875 and at the NAD in 1883 and 1888, during which time she lived in New York City.

Bibliography:
Maine Library *Bulletin* 13 (July-Oct. 1927).
Truetner, William H. "William T. Evans, Collector of American Paintings." *Art Journal* 3:2 (Fall 1971) mentions "New Hampshire Woods" by Maria à Becket.

BERLIN FALLS. S/D/L/R.
> 1859. Pencil.
> 5½ x 8¼ (14 x 21). Oval.
> Private collection (1983); Stinson House, Rumney, NH (1973).

BRIDAL VEIL FALLS.
> Present whereabouts unknown.
> Formerly in the Sweat Memorial Museum (now the Portland Museum of Art).

CARTER MOUNTAIN. S/D/L/L.
> July 1859. Pencil.
> 5½ x 9½ (14 x 24.1). Oval.
> Private collection (1983); Stinson House, Rumney, NH (1973).

CONNECTICUT RIVER FROM STRATFORD, NH.
S/D.
> July 1859. Pencil.
> 5½ x 9 (14 x 22.9). Oval.
> Private collection (1983); Stinson House, Rumney, NH (1973).

FOOT OF CARTER MOUNTAIN.
> Oil.
> Boston Art Club (April 1875), #128.

WOODS AT THE WHITE MOUNTAINS (or NEW HAMPSHIRE WOODS).
> *Art Journal* 3:2 (Fall 1971); NAD, 1888, #164.

BELLOWS, ALBERT FITCH
B, C&H, DAB, F, G&W, K, Ka, N, R, S, T
Born Milford, MA, Nov. 27 (or 29), 1829.
Died Auburndale, MA (or New York, NY, in DAB), Nov. 24, 1883.
Apprenticed to a Boston lithographer at 16, Bellows studied architecture in 1845 and even set up an architectural partnership (which he dissolved in 1849). After serving as the principal of the New England School of Design from 1850 to 1856, Bellows studied art in Paris and Antwerp. A pioneer in watercolor, he wrote a book on art. Unfortunately, most of his work was destroyed in the Great Fire of Boston in 1872. He exhibited at the NAD from 1861 to 1883 and was a member of the Century Association from 1865 to 1883.

Bibliography:
Bellows, Albert Fitch. *Watercolor Painting: Some Facts and Authorities in Relation to Its Durability* (1868).

ARTIST'S BROOK, CONWAY.
> Brooklyn Art Association (1882), #3.

ARTIST'S BROOK, NH.
> Watercolor.
> MA. Charitable (1881), #452.

ARTIST'S BROOK, NORTH CONWAY.
> Etching.
> Brooklyn Art Association (1882), #3; MA. Charitable (1884), #80.

AUTUMN ON THE ANDROSCOGGIN.
> NAD, 1862, #146.

FRANCONIA MOUNTAINS.
> Brooklyn Art Association (1866), #53; (1868), #174.

FRANCONIA NOTCH AND MOUNT LAFAYETTE.
> Oil.
> 8 x 13 (20.3 x 33).
> Vassar College Art Gallery (1973); NMAA Inventory.

MOUNT LAFAYETTE.
> U.S. Sanitary Commission (1864), #69.

NOOK ON THE WILDCAT, JACKSON, NH.
> Watercolor.
> Pre-1877; NAD, watercolor show (1873).

NOTCH AT LANCASTER.
  1867. Watercolor.
  C&H.

BIERSTADT, ALBERT

B, Ce, C&H, DAB, F, G&W, N, R, S, T
Born Solingen, Germany, Jan. 7, 1830.
Died New York, NY, Feb. 18, 1902.
*Known for his grand and large paintings of the
American far west, Bierstadt's career in New
England was largely ignored until recently. The
Bierstadt family moved to New Bedford, MA,
from Germany when Albert was about three
years old. Little is known of his basic artistic
training. By 1850 he had mastered enough
technique to advertise instruction in
monochromatic painting. Any formal training
came between 1853 and 1857, when he returned
to Düsseldorf, Germany, to study painting. On
his return to this country, he organized an exhibition of 150 paintings in New Bedford which
included works by all the leading American artists of the day. In December of the same year,
the Boston Athenaeum became the first museum
to buy one of his works, THE PORTICO OF
OCTAVIA, ROME. From then on his career
was assured. Bierstadt always loved mountains
and he visited the White Mountains before he
left for Düsseldorf, for his signature appears in
the register on top of Mount Washington on
Aug. 11, 1852. He returned at various times
from 1858 to 1886. Sometime in 1859 or 1860,
Bierstadt visited New Hampshire with his
brother, Edward, working in the then new
medium of photography (see Section IV). He
stayed at the Conway House in Conway, listing
himself as "A. Bierstadt, New York," on Sept.
13, 1862. He also spent considerable time at the
Glen House in 1869 while at work on
EMERALD POOL, which he considered his
finest work. He exhibited at the Boston
Athenaeum from 1859 to 1864 and at the
Brooklyn Art Association from 1861 to 1881.
A member of the NAD from 1860 to 1902, he
kept a studio in the 10th Street Studio Building
(N.Y.C.) from 1861 to 1879. He was a member
of the Century Association from 1862 to 1902.
Bierstadt became internationally renowned for
his beautiful and enormous paintings of the
newly accessible American west, and his works
found their way into public and private collections at staggeringly high prices. His popularity and wealth rose to tremendous heights, only
to fade as the rise of interest in the Barbizon
School and impressionism turned public taste
away from his highly detailed landscapes, suf-
fused with golden light. By 1895 he declared
himself bankrupt.*

Select Bibliography:
Archives of American Art. Rolls NDA, CAL
I, D5, N4, N7, N56, 439, 847.
Amon Carter Museum catalog. *Albert Bierstadt*
(Fort Worth, TX, 1972).
Byers, William Newton."Bierstadt's Visit to Col-
orado." *Magazine of Western History* 11:3 (Jan.
1980).
Campbell, Catherine H. "Albert Bierstadt and
the White Mountains." *Archives of American
Art Journal* 21:3 (1981), pp. 14-23.
Dwight's *Journal of Music* 23 (April 1865), p. 14.
Heller, Nancy, and Julia Williams. "Albert
Bierstadt: The American Wilderness." *American
Artist* (Jan. 1976), pp. 52-58.
Hendricks, Gordon. *Albert Bierstadt.* New
York: Harry N. Abrams, Inc., 1974.
Hendricks, Gordon. *Albert Bierstadt, 1830-1902*
(Sept. 15-Oct. 10, 1972), Knoedler catalog.
Florence Lewison Gallery, NY, catalog. *Albert
Bierstadt* (1963).
Florence Lewison Gallery, NY, catalog. *Man,
Beast and Nature* (1964).
Lindquist-Cook, Elizabeth. *Art Quarterly*
(Winter 1970), p. 365.
Lipke, William C., and Philip N. Grime. "Albert
Bierstadt in New Hampshire." The Currier
Gallery of Art (Manchester, NH) *Bulletin* 2
(1973), pp. 20-34.
Santa Barbara Museum, CA, catalog. *Albert
Bierstadt Retrospective* exhibition (1964).
Sears, Clara Endicott. *Highlights Among the
Hudson River Artists.* Boston: Houghton Mif-
flin (1947), pp. 143-152.

ASCUTNEY MOUNTAIN FROM CLAREMONT,
NEW HAMPSHIRE. S/L/R.
  1862. Oil on canvas.
  41½ x 70 (105.4 x 177.8).
  Fruitlands Museum (1974); NMAA Inventory; Boston Athenaeum (1862), #26;
  Brooklyn Art Association (1862), #176.

AT THE SUMMIT. S/L/R. (possibly New Hampshire)
  Oil on board.
  15 x 21½ (38.1 x 54.6).
  Richard Bourne, Inc., catalog (1977), #14.

AUTUMN IN NEW HAMPSHIRE. S/L/R.
  Oil on canvas.
  13¾ x 19¾ (34.9 x 50.2).
  Lauren Rogers Library and Museum of Art
  (1978); NMAA Inventory.

New Hampshire Scenery

AUTUMN IN THE WHITE MOUNTAINS.
Oil.
13⅞ x 19½ (35.2 x 49.5).
Private collection; NMAA Inventory.

AUTUMN LANDSCAPE (N.H.). S/L/R.
Oil on canvas.
19¾ x 27¾ (50.2 x 70.5).
Gallerie de Tours.

CATHEDRAL LEDGE. S/L/R.
C. 1860-62. Oil on paper.
9⅜ x 12⅛ (23.8 x 30.8).
University of Notre Dame Art Gallery.

CHICOURA [sic] MOUNTAIN, NEW HAMPSHIRE.
C. 1857-58. Oil.
4⅜ x 13⅝ (11 x 34.6).
Robert Hull Fleming Museum (1972);
Florence Lewison Gallery catalog (1963),
#10.

CHICOURA [sic] MOUNTAIN, NEW HAMPSHIRE.
Oil.
9 x 13½ (22.9 x 34.3).
Stark Museum of Art (1978).

CHOCORUA LAKE.
Oil.
Private collection; Boston Art Club (March
1873), #110.

CLOUD STUDY. S/L/L.
C. 1858. Oil on paper.
6½ x 11¾ (16.5 x 29.8).
Thomas Gilcrease Institute of American
History and Art.

CONNECTICUT RIVER VALLEY FROM CLARE-
MONT, NH. S/D/L/L.
1868. Oil on canvas.
27 x 14 (68.6 x 111.8).
Berkshire Museum, Pittsfield, MA.

CONWAY MEADOWS, HAYING. S/D/L/R.
1864. Oil on canvas.
36 x 58 (91.4 x 147.3).
Private collection; *Archives of American Art
Journal* 21:3 (1981).

CONWAY, NEW HAMPSHIRE. S/L/R.
Oil.
9½ x 12⅛ (24.1 x 30.8).
University of Notre Dame Art Gallery
(1979).

CONWAY VALLEY, NEW HAMPSHIRE.
Oil.
13¼ x 19¼ (33.7 x 48.9).
Old Print Shop *Portfolio* 29:2, p. 71.

DEER ON MOUNT WASHINGTON, WHITE
MOUNTAINS, NEW HAMPSHIRE. S/L/L.
1871 or c. 1858. Oil on sketchboard.

13 x 17 (33 x 43.2).
Kennedy Galleries.

EAGLE CLIFF, WHITE MOUNTAINS, NEW
HAMPSHIRE.
C. 1858.
8¾ x 6¾ (22.2 x 17.1).
Florence Lewison Gallery catalog (1964), #3.

ECHO LAKE, FRANCONIA MOUNTAINS, NEW
HAMPSHIRE (or WILDERNESS LAKE). S/D/L/L.
1861. Oil on canvas.
25 x 39⅛ (63.5 x 99.4).
Smith College Museum of Art; NAD, 1861,
#463.

EMERALD POOL.
Oil on canvas.
27 x 20 (68.6 x 50.8).
Private collection; *Archives of American Art
Journal* 21:3 (1981), p. 23; Anderson Auc-
tion Galleries (1905), #74.

EMERALD POOL. S/D/L/R/Center.
1871. Oil on canvas.
76 x 119¾ (193 x 304.2).
Chrylser Museum, Norfolk, VA; Earle's
Gallery (Jan. 1871).

FIELD, WHITE MOUNTAINS. S/L/L.
C. 1857-58.
19 x 13¼ (48.3 x 33.7).
Kennedy Galleries.

FLUME, WHITE MOUNTAINS; THE… S/L/L.
1869. Oil on academy board.
5½ x 7½ (14 x 19.1).
Hirshhorn Museum, Smithsonian Institution.

FRANCONIA SCENE.
C. 1862. Oil on canvas.
44 x 30 (111.8 x 76.2).
Private collection (1973); *Archives of American Art Journal* 21:3 (1981), p. 23.

GATHERING HAY, NEW HAMPSHIRE. S/D/L/L.
1867. Oil on canvas.
27¼ x 44¼ (69.2 x 112.4).
Sotheby PB (Oct. 17, 1980), #120.

GLEN ELLIS FALLS (formerly WATERFALL). S/L/R.
C. 1869. Oil on canvas.
40 x 30 (101.6 x 76.2).
Rutgers University, Jane Voorhees Zimmerli
Art Gallery.

GREY TEMPEST (WHITE MOUNTAINS, NEW
HAMPSHIRE).
C. 1857. Oil on paper.
6 x 8¾ (15.2 x 22.2).
Hirshhorn Museum, Smithsonian Institution;
Florence Lewison Gallery catalog (1963), #6.

Dictionary of Painters

INDIAN SUMMER IN NEW HAMPSHIRE.
S/D/Reverse.
    1868. Oil on cardboard.
    7¼ x 10¼ (18.4 x 26).
    Private collection; Kennedy Galleries (1974).

INDIAN SUMMER, WHITE MOUNTAINS, NEW HAMPSHIRE. S/L/L.
    Oil on paper.
    19 x 13¼ (48.3 x 33.7).
    Tyler Gallery, Los Angeles, CA.

LAKE AT FRANCONIA NOTCH, NEW HAMP-
SHIRE. S/L/R.
    C. 1860-62. Oil on paper.
    13½ x 19¼ (34.3 x 48.9).
    University Art Gallery catalog, University of New Hampshire (1980); Newark Museum (1944).

LANDSCAPE NEAR CLAREMONT, NEW HAMPSHIRE.
    C. 1862. Oil on paper.
    10¼ x 12¾ (26 x 32.4).
    Buffalo Bill Cody Historical Center, Cody, WY (1974).

LANDSCAPE, NEW HAMPSHIRE.
    C. 1870. Oil.
    11 x 15 (27.9 x 38.1).
    Private collection (1980); Sotheby PB.

LIMPID DAWN, WHITE MOUNTAINS, NEW HAMPSHIRE.
    C. 1858.
    5⅜ x 6⅞ (13.7 x 17.5).
    Florence Lewison Gallery catalog (1963), #1.

MAPLE LEAVES, WHITE MOUNTAINS.
S/Reverse/L/R.
    1862. Oil on paper.
    13½ x 19¼ (34.3 x 48.9).
    Private collection (1981); University Art Gallery catalog, University of New Hampshire (1980), #1.

MOAT MOUNTAIN, INTERVALE. S/L/R.
    C. 1860-62. Oil on canvas.
    19 x 26 (48.3 x 66).
    Currier Gallery (1974).

MOUNT ADAMS BY MOONLIGHT.
    Brooklyn Art Association (March 1873), #29.

MOUNT ADAMS, NEW HAMPSHIRE.
    C. 1857-58. Oil on paper.
    11⅛ x 15¼ (28.3 x 38.7).
    New Hampshire Historical Society, owner. *Historical New Hampshire* 16:4; Santa Barbara Museum of Art catalog (Aug. 1964), #5.

MOUNT CHOCORUA.
    C. 1857-58. Oil.
    4⅜ x 15⅝ (11.1 x 39.7).
    Robert Hull Fleming Museum (1973); *Art Quarterly* (Autumn 1973).

MOUNT CHOCORUA, NEW HAMPSHIRE.
    Oil.
    7½ x 7½ (19.1 x 19.1).
    NMAA Inventory.

MOUNT CHOCORUA, NEW HAMPSHIRE.
    13½ x 10½ (34.3 x 26.7).
    Jim Fowler's Period Gallery West, Scotsdale, AZ (1974).

MOUNT CHOCORUA, NEW HAMPSHIRE
(previously titled WYOMING). Signed.
    C. 1860-62. Oil on canvas.
    19¼ x 26½ (48.9 x 67.3).
    Museum of Fine Arts, Santa Fe, NM.

MOUNT CHOCORUA, NEW HAMPSHIRE. S/L/L.
    C. 1860-62. Oil on paper.
    10½ x 13½ (26.7 x 34.3).
    Private collection; *Archives of American Art Journal* 21:3 (1981).

MOUNT LAFAYETTE.
    PAFA, 1862, #67.

MOUNT WASHINGTON.
    C. 1864. Oil on canvas.
    36 x 58 (91.4 x 147.3).
    Collection of William Nathaniel Banks.

MOUNT WASHINGTON FROM SHELBURNE, NEW HAMPSHIRE. S/L/R.
    1859. Oil on canvas.
    19½ x 29½ (49.5 x 74.9).
    NAD, 1859, #681; Boston Athenaeum (1859), #181.

MOUNT WASHINGTON FROM THE SACO RIVER. S/D/L/R.
    1871. Oil on canvas.
    40 x 60 (101.6 x 152.4).
    Sotheby PB (Jan. 27, 1977).

MOUNT WASHINGTON, WHITE MOUNTAINS, NEW HAMPSHIRE. S/L/L.
    Oil on canvas.
    30 x 22 (76.2 x 55.9).
    Kennedy Galleries (1978).

MOUNTAIN LANDSCAPE, APPROACHING STORM. S/L/R.
    C. 1860-62. Oil on paper.
    19 x 13 (48.3 x 33).
    Private collection; *Archives of American Art Journal* 21:3 (1981), p. 22.

MOUNTAIN MOTIF (Mount Washington).
    C. 1858.

New Hampshire Scenery

Moat Mountain, Intervale
Albert Bierstadt, c. 1860
Oil on canvas, 19" x 26" / Collection: The Currier Gallery of Art,
    Manchester, New Hampshire / Ref. page 10

6 x 11⅝ (15.2 x 29.5).
Florence Lewison Gallery catalog (1963), #9.
MOUNTAIN STREAM ON MOUNT WASHING-
TON. S/L/R.
    Oil on canvas.
    14 x 19½ (35.6 x 49.5).
    Kennedy Galleries.
MOUNTAIN TOPOGRAPHY (formerly TUCKER-
MAN'S RAVINE, WHITE MOUNTAINS, NH).
    C. 1869. Oil on paper on board.
    11⅛ x 11⅜ (28.3 x 29).
    Florence Lewison Gallery catalog (1968), #4;
    Santa Barbara Museum catalog (1964), #6.
MOUNTAINS.
    C. 1858. Oil on paper.
    9 x 13⅛ (22.9 x 33.3).
    Private collection; *Archives of American Art*
    Journal 21:3 (1981), p. 20.

NEW HAMPSHIRE SCENE.
    Oil on paper.
    10 x 13 (25.4 x 33).
    Alexander Gallery catalog (1983), #27.
NEW HAMPSHIRE SKETCH.
    10 x 14 (25.4 x 35.6).
    Private collection.
ON THE PEMIGEWASSET.
    Saved from the 1882 fire at "Mahlkasten";
    Archives of American Art Journal 21:3
    (1981), p. 23.
ON THE SACO.
    NAD, 1886, #721.
RISING MIST, WHITE MOUNTAINS, NEW
HAMPSHIRE.
    C. 1858.
    5½ x 7¼ (14 x 18.4).
    Florence Lewison Gallery catalog (1963), #2.

Dictionary of Painters

ROCKS AND RAVINE, THOMPSON'S CASCADE, GLEN HOUSE, NH.
C. 1860.
11½ x 13⅜ (29.2 x 34).
Florence Lewison Gallery catalog (1964), #15.

ROCKY POOL. S/L/R.
C. 1860. Oil on canvas.
18 x 24 (45.7 x 61).
Denver Art Museum (1982).

SHADY POOL. S/L/R.
C. 1869. Oil on canvas.
22½ x 30 (57.2 x 76.2).
Hirshhorn Museum, Smithsonian Institution (1975); University Art Gallery catalog, University of New Hampshire (1980).

SHADY POOL, WHITE MOUNTAINS, NEW HAMPSHIRE.
Oil.
22½ x 20 (57.2 x 50.8).
Hirshhorn Museum, Smithsonian Institution (1975).

STUDY IN GREY (NEW ENGLAND, WHITE MOUNTAINS).
C. 1858. Oil on paper.
7¾ x 10 (19.7 x 25.4).
Hirshhorn Museum, Smithsonian Institution; Florence Lewison Gallery catalog (1963).

STUDY OF FERNS, WHITE MOUNTAINS, EMERALD POOL.
1869. Oil on paper.
12¾ x 9¾ (32.4 x 24.8).
Florence Lewison Gallery (1964), #11. Archives of American Art. Roll 837, Frames 403-404.

SUNSET NEAR CONWAY, NEW HAMPSHIRE. S/L/R.
Oil on paper.
9 x 13¼ (22.9 x 33.7).
Kennedy Galleries.

TURBULENT CLOUDS, PRESIDENTIAL RANGE, NEW HAMPSHIRE.
C. 1858. Oil on paper on board.
9 x 11 (22.9 x 27.9).
Florence Lewison Gallery catalog (1963), #17.

UNDULATIONS, WHITE MOUNTAINS, NEW HAMPSHIRE.
C. 1857-58. Oil on paper on board.
10⅜ x 14¼ (26.4 x 36.2).
Princeton University Art Gallery (1983); Florence Lewison Gallery catalog (1963), #20.

VIEW FROM INTERVALE [,] MOAT, WHITE MOUNTAINS, NH.
Private collection; NMAA Inventory; Washington County Museum of Art exhibition (1947).

VIEW NEAR NORTH CONWAY. S/L/R.
C. 1860-62. Oil on paper.
18⅜ x 25 (46.7 x 66).
Danforth Museum; Whitney Downtown Gallery, N.Y.C. (June-July 1980).

WHITE MOUNTAIN CONFLAGRATION. S/L/R.
Oil on paper.
11¼ x 15¼ (28.6 x 38.7).
Thomas Gilcrease Institute of American History and Art.

WHITE MOUNTAINS.
Oil on paper.
13½ x 19¾ (34.2 x 50.2).
Argosy Gallery; Santa Barbara Museum catalog (Aug. 1964), #3.

WHITE MOUNTAINS.
Oil.
19¼ x 13⅜ (48.9 x 34).
Hirschl and Adler Gallery (1978).

WHITE MOUNTAINS.
Oil.
8 x 9 (20.3 x 22.9).
Sotheby PB (1969).

WHITE MOUNTAINS.
1869. Oil.
11⅛ x 15 (28.3 x 38.1).
Stark Museum of Art; Hirschl and Adler Gallery (1978).

WHITE MOUNTAINS. S/L/L.
C. 1869. Oil on paper on canvas.
26 x 19 (66 x 48.3).
Tyler Gallery, Los Angeles, CA.

WHITE MOUNTAINS LANDSCAPE.
Oil.
12⅜ x 17⅞ (31.4 x 45.4).
Private collection (1960); NMAA Inventory.

WHITE MOUNTAINS THROUGH THE CLOUDS.
Oil on paper on masonite.
13½ x 19 (34.3 x 48.3).
Hayden Gallery, Massachusetts Institute of Technology (1973); *American Art Journal* (Spring 1973).

WHITE MOUNTAINS, MOUNT ADAMS.
Oil.
11½ x 7¾ (29.2 x 19.7).
Stark Museum of Art (1978).

WHITE MOUNTAINS, NEW HAMPSHIRE.
Oil.

New Hampshire Scenery

13¼ x 10¼ (33.7 x 26).
Kennedy *Quarterly* 1:2 (1960), p. 33.
WHITE MOUNTAINS, NEW HAMPSHIRE.
Oil.
11¼ x 9⅜ (28.6 x 23.8).
Stark Museum of Art (1978).
WHITE MOUNTAINS, NEW HAMPSHIRE.
Oil.
8 x 11¾ (20.3 x 29.8).
Stark Museum of Art (1978).
WHITE MOUNTAINS, NEW HAMPSHIRE.
Oil on paper.
11 x 15 (27.9 x 38.1).
Thomas Gilcrease Institute of American
History and Art (1974).
WHITE MOUNTAINS, NEW HAMPSHIRE. S/L/R.
C. 1858. Oil on paper.
6½ x 10¼ (16.5 x 26).
Kennedy Galleries.
WHITE MOUNTAINS, NEW HAMPSHIRE (or
TWO BEARS IN CRAWFORD NOTCH).
C. 1858. Oil on paper.
3½ x 4 (8.9 x 10.2).
Sotheby PB (Oct. 27, 1979).
WHITE MOUNTAINS, NEW YORK [sic].
Oil.
7 x 9 (17.8 x 22.9).
Sotheby PB (1975).
WHITE MOUNTAINS, STUDY OF FERNS ABOVE
EMERALD POOL.
C. 1860. Oil.
12¼ x 9¼ (31.1 x 23.5).
Robert Hull Fleming Museum (1973).
WHITE MTS, NH.
Oil on paper.
9¼ x 13¼ (23.5 x 33.7).
Alexander Gallery catalog (1983), #33.
WHITE MTS, NH.
Oil on paper.
8 x 13¼ (20.3 x 33.7).
Alexander Gallery catalog (1983), #34.
WOODED LANDSCAPE.
Oil on board.
13¼ x 18⅜ (33.7 x 46.7).
Buffalo Bill Cody Historical Center, Cody,
WY.

BIRCH, THOMAS

B, Ba, DAB, F, G&W, Ka, R, S, T
Born London, England, July 26, 1779.
Died Philadelphia, PA, Jan. 14, 1851.
*Birch came to the United States in 1793 or 1794
and settled in Philadelphia. In 1799 or 1800 he*

*worked with his father at designing, engraving,
and publishing views of Philadelphia. Known
primarily as a marine painter, he also produced
portraits, miniatures, and landscapes. An
honorary member of the NAD, he exhibited at
the Society of Artists of Pennsylvania, the
Apollo Association, the American Art-Union,
and the NAD.*

Attributed:
EAST WHITE MOUNTAINS, ANDROSCOGGIN
RIVER AT SEAGER.
1850. Oil.
48 x 36 (121.9 x 91.4).
Sotheby PB (1974).

BLACKWELL, S. ELLEN

N
Active 1860-67.
*While exhibiting at the NAD from 1861 to 1866,
Blackwell lived in New York City.*

ON THE ELLIS RIVER.
Oil on paper.
3 x 4 (7.6 x 10.2).
Skinner catalog (1977).
CHOCORUA MOUNTAIN, NEW HAMPSHIRE.
Signed B., S. E. (probably S. Ellen
Blackwell).
1875. Oil.
4 x 7¼ (10.2 x 18.4).
Portland Museum of Art (1977).

BLAKELOCK, RALPH ALBERT

DAB, F, N, K, Ka, S
Born New York, NY, Oct. 15, 1847.
Died Adirondacks, NY, Aug. 9, 1919.
*A self-taught member of the NAD, Blakelock
exhibited there from 1868 to 1899, at the
Brooklyn Art Association in 1874, 1879, 1880,
and 1884, and had a studio in the 10th Street
Studio Building (N.Y.C.) in 1884. Of unsound
mind, he spent long periods in an asylum and
finally returned to New York in 1916.*

Bibliography:
Geske, Norman A. *Ralph Albert Blakelock*,
catalog. Nebraska Art Association, 1974.
Young's Art Galleries catalog. *The Works of R.
A. Blakelock and His Daughter Marian
Blakelock* (April-May 1916).

BOULDER AND THE FLUME; THE...S/L/L.
C. 1878. Oil on canvas.
54 x 28 (137.2 x 71.1).
Metropolitan Museum of Art (1975); NMAA
Inventory.

MORNING NEAR DEVIL'S DEN, WHITE MOUNTAINS.
NAD, 1868, #308.

MOUNTAIN ROAD NEAR GORHAM, NH.
Oil.
16⅛ x 24¼ (41 x 61.6).
Flint Institute of Arts, Flint, MI (1978); NMAA Inventory.

BLUNT, JOHN SHERBURNE

A, G&W
Born Portsmouth, NH, 1798.
Lost at sea, 1835.
Blunt was a self-taught artist whose work appears to have been influenced by 18th-century Dutch painting. He named a daughter, born in 1823, after the prominent British artist, Angelica Kaufman. In 1829 he exhibited at the Boston Athenaeum, giving his address as Portsmouth, NH. By 1830 he had removed to Boston. He was a friend of Charles Codman, also of Portsmouth.

Bibliography:
Bishop, Robert S. "J. S. Blunt." *Antiques* (Nov. 1977), pp. 964-971.
Bishop, Robert S. "J. S. Blunt: The Man, the Artist, and His Times." Museum of American Folk Art's *The Clarion*, N.Y.C. (Spring 1980), pp. 20-39.
Little, Nina Fletcher. "Indigenous Painting in New Hampshire." *Antiques* (July 1964), pp. 62-65.
Little, Nina Fletcher. "J. S. Blunt, New England Landscape Painter." *Antiques* (Sept. 1948), pp. 172-174.

LANDSCAPE, NEW HAMPSHIRE.
Oil.
27 x 38½ (68.6 x 97.8).
Private collection (1970); NMAA Inventory.

NOTCH IN THE WHITE MOUNTAINS; THE...
1826. Oil on canvas.
32 x 27¾ (81.3 x 70.5).
New Hampshire Historical Society (1983).

VIEW OF LAKE WINIPISEOGEE [sic].
C. 1826. Oil on wood.
16 x 22 (40.6 x 55.9).
New Hampshire Historical Society (1973); *Antiques* (1948); Boston Athenaeum (1829), #163.

VIEW OF THE SACO. S/L/R.
1826. Oil on canvas.
Childs Gallery.

WINTER SCENE
C. 1831.
27¼ x 26½ (69.2 x 69.9).
Boston Museum of Fine Arts.

BOARDMAN, WILLIAM G.

C, Ce, G&W, N
Born Cazenovia, NY, c. 1815.
Died Providence, RI, 1895.
A member of the NAD, where he exhibited from 1846 to 1871, Boardman was labeled by the American Art-Union *Bulletin of 1848 as "very clever." He was painting in Jackson, NH, as early as 1847. He was a friend of George Inness.*

CASCADE AT JACKSON, NEW HAMPSHIRE; THE...
NAD, 1848, #180.

CASCADE ON WHITEFACE MOUNTAIN NEAR NORTH SANDWICH, NH.
NAD, 1850, #338.

FALLS NEAR JACKSON, NH.
AAU, 1848, #127.

INDIAN MAID'S TOILET (TAKEN FROM KEWASARGE [sic] MOUNTAINS, NH); THE...
32 x 40 (81.3 x 101.6).
AAU, 1849, #266.

SCENE ON THE BEAR CAMP RIVER, NH.
NAD, 1858, #632.

SQUAM LAKE.
60 x 40 (152.4 x 101.6).
AAU, 1848, #121; AAU, 1850, #116.

SQUAM LAKE ROAD, NH.
9 x 10 (22.9 x 25.4).
AAU, 1852, #108.

SUNSET ON SQUAM.
NAD, 1853, #10.

VIEW OF BARTLETT AND NORTH CONWAY FROM IRON MOUNTAIN, JACKSON, NH.
NAD, 1848, #300.

VIEW ON BLACK RIVER, NH.
NAD, 1853, #22.

VIEW NEAR LITTLE FALLS.
AAU, 1848, #436.

WHITE MOUNTAINS, NH; THE...
38 x 28 (96.5 x 71.1).
AAU, 1849, #64.

BOGGS, W. BENSON (or WILLIAM BENSON or WILLIAM BRENTON)

C, Ce, F(sup), G&W, K, Ka
Born New Brunswick, NJ, July 2, 1809.
Died Georgetown, DC, March 11, 1875.

New Hampshire Scenery

An associate of the NAD, where he exhibited from 1839 to 1844, Boggs spent most of his life in the Navy and seems to have had some official duties as an artist during his naval employment.

AN AUTUMN SUNSET, LAKE SCENE, NH.
    NAD, 1844, #136.

LAKE SCENE, NH.
    27 x 18 (66.6 x 45.7).
    AAU, 1850, #351.

VIEW ON LAKE WINNIPISEOGEE [sic].
    NAD, 1841, #162.

VIEW ON THE SACO RIVER.
    NAD, 1840, #144.

BOUTELLE (or BARTELLE), DEWITT CLINTON

A, B, Ce, C&H, G&W, F, N, R, S
Born Troy, NY, April 6, 1820.
Died Bethlehem, PA, Nov. 5, 1884.
An associate of the NAD, Boutelle moved to New York City in 1846 and exhibited widely at the Boston Athenaeum in the 1850s and at the PAFA and the NAD from 1862 to 1874. Influenced by Thomas Cole and Asher Durand, he produced a full-sized meticulous copy of Cole's VOYAGE OF LIFE.

Bibliography:
Ferber, Linda. "Ripe for Revival: Forgotten American Artists." Artnews (Dec. 1980), pp. 68, seq.
Pennsylvania State University Museum of Art catalog. All That Is Glorious Around Us: Paintings from the Hudson River School (Jan.-March 1981), p. 42.

CONWAY VALLEY.
    Boston Athenaeum (1854), #148; (1855), #110; (1856), #210.

VALLEY OF CONWAY. Signed.
    1860. Oil on canvas.
    32½ x 49 (82.6 x 124.5).
    Rensselaer County Historical Society Museum, NY.

WHITE MOUNTAINS FROM NORTH CONWAY.
    Boston Athenaeum (1856), #339.

BRACKETT, EDWARD AUGUSTUS

DAB, R
Born Vassalboro, ME, Oct. 1, 1818.
Died Massachusetts, March 18 (or 15), 1908.
Brackett grew up in Maine and in 1835 moved with his family to Cincinnati where Edward studied art. In 1841 he moved to South Woburn,

MA, and opened a studio in Boston. He was best known as a sculptor, but he also did woodcut engravings and portraits and turned to landscapes in the 1860s. Although no White Mountains views by Brackett have yet come to light, Dwight's Journal of Music (vol. 1, p. 164, Aug. 28, 1852) noted that Champney, Gerry, Hoyt, and Brackett were all doing landscapes at North Conway. He gave up art in 1873 to devote his life to scientific work in fisheries.

BRADBURY, GIDEON (or GIBEON) ELDEN (or ELDON)

Born 1833. Died 1904.
Bradbury lived in Buxton, ME, during his active years. He was a brother-in-law of Benjamin Paul Akers, painter, sculptor, and author.
Information courtesy of Portland Museum of Art and Vose Galleries.

LANDSCAPE, WHITE MOUNTAINS.
    Pre-1877; Art Association of Montreal and Society of Canadian Artists exhibition (April 8, 1872).

MOUNT WASHINGTON FROM CONWAY INTERVALE.
    Before 1850. Oil.
    17 x 23 (43.2 x 58.4).
    New Hampshire Historical Society (1983); NMAA Inventory.

ON SACO RIVER.
    1877.
    8x 12 (20.3 x 30.5).
    Private collection (1975).

SUNSET ON THE SACO RIVER.
    1891. Oil.
    12 x 18 (30.5 x 45.7).
    Private collection (1975).

VIEW ON SACO AT SALMON FALLS, BUXTON.
    1870. Oil on canvas.
    9¾ x 13¾ (24.8 x 34.9).
    Portland Museum of Art (1976).

BRADLEY, SUSAN H. (or F.)

F
Born Boston, MA, 1851. Died 1929.
A landscape painter and watercolorist, Bradley exhibited at the Boston Art Club and studied at the School of the Boston Museum of Fine Arts. She was a member of the Philadelphia Water Color Club, the New York Water Color Club, and the Society of Independent Artists.

MOUNT BARTLETT FROM INTERVALE.
  Boston Art Club (1898) #183.

Signed Bradley.
A NEW HAMPSHIRE SCENE (SACO IN THE NOTCH).
  Oil on canvas.
  13½ x 20 (34.3 x 50.8).
  Private collection.

BRENNER, CARL C.
N, S
Born 1838. Died 1888.
Brenner lived in Louisville, KY, when he exhibited at the NAD from 1877 to 1886.
GLIMPSE FROM WILDCAT MOUNTAIN.
  Pre-1877; Louisville Industrial Exposition (1879).

BRICHER, ALFRED THOMPSON (or ALBERT T.)
A, B, C&H, F, G&W, K, Ka, S
Born Portsmouth, NH, April 10, 1837 (or 1839). Died New Dorp, NY, Sept. 30, 1908.
Largely self-taught, Bricher was a businessman in Boston from 1851 until 1858 when he became a professional artist. In the 1860s Bricher followed his contemporaries to the popular vistas of the White Mountains. There, particularly at North Conway, he studied and painted with Albert Bierstadt, William Morris Hunt, William Paskell, Gabriella Eddy, and Benjamin Champney. Bricher was a prolific artist and in 1860-61 alone his sketchbook records 20 finished paintings. Attesting to his popularity as an artist, as well as to the popularity of his subject matter, are numerous chromolithographs made after his work. In 1868 he moved from Boston to New York where he became a member of the American Society of Painters in Water Colors in 1874 and was elected an associate of the NAD in 1879. During the 1870s he devoted himself almost entirely to marine painting and spent much of his time exploring the coast of Maine, Narragansett Bay, and the Jersey Shore.
Bibliography:
Archives of American Art. Roll D32.
Brown, Jeffrey R. "Alfred Thompson Bricher." *American Art Review* (Jan.-Feb. 1974), pp. 69-75.
Brown, Jeffrey R., and Ellen W. Lee. *Alfred Thompson Bricher, 1837-1908.* Indianapolis Museum of Art catalog (Sept.-Oct. 1973).
Sotheby PB catalog (Oct. 21, 1983).

ARTISTS [sic] BROOK, NORTH CONWAY.
  Oil.
  12 x 9 (30.5 x 22.9).
  Private collection (1976).

AUTUMN ON THE ANDROSCOGGIN, SHELBURNE, NH.
  Leonard Auction (Oct. 18, 1872), #4.

AUTUMN, WHITE MOUNTAINS. S/D/L/L.
  1867. Oil on canvas.
  16 x 12½ (40.6 x 31.8).
  Kennedy Galleries (1977); Indianapolis Museum catalog (1973), p. 43.

DOWN BY THE BROOKSIDE, A CONWAY SKETCH. S/D/L/L.
  Oil.
  12½ x 10½ (31.8 x 26.7).
  Sotheby PB catalog (Oct. 21, 1983), #37.

ECHO LAKE, FRANCONIA. S/D/L/L.
  1868. Oil on board.
  10 x 18 (25.4 x 45.7).
  Unlocated.

ECHO LAKE, NEW HAMPSHIRE. S/L/R.
  C. 1860s. Oil on board.
  14¾ x 22½ (37.5 x 57.2).
  Mead Art Gallery (1973); Hirschl and Adler Gallery catalog (1972), p. 32.

FETCHING WATER (SPRING IN NH). S/L/L.
  Oil on canvas.
  12 x 10 (30.5 x 25.4).
  Richard Bourne, Inc., catalog (1980), #96.

FOREST INTERIOR NEAR THE FLUME, WHITE MOUNTAINS.
  1871. Oil on canvas.
  30 x 25 (76.2 x 63.5).
  Private collection (1973); NMAA Inventory.

HIDE-A-WAY PICNIC ALONG THE SACO RIVER. S/L/L.
  1867. Oil on canvas.
  34 x 27 (86.4 x 68.9).
  John H. Surovek Fine Arts, Inc., Palm Beach, FL (1981); *Art and Antiques* (May-June 1981).

ISRAEL'S RIVER, JEFFERSON, NH.
  NAD, 1873, #168.

LATE AUTUMN IN THE WHITE MOUNTAINS.
  1866. Prang chromolithograph from a Bricher painting.
  9 x 18 (22.9 x 45.7).
  McClinton, p. 172.

LATE AUTUMN, SACO RIVER.
  American Art Gallery sale, N.Y.C. (1892); McClinton, p. 175.

MOUNT ADAMS.
    1871. Watercolor.
    C&H.
MOUNT ADAMS AND JEFFERSON. S/D/L/L.
    1870. Oil on canvas.
    27½ x 50 (69.9 x 127).
    Private collection (1983); Richard Bourne, Inc., catalog (Aug. 1977), #100; Pre-1877.
MOUNT ADAMS FROM JEFFERSON, NEW HAMP-SHIRE.
    Oil.
    20 x 16¼ (50.8 x 41.3).
    Sotheby PB (1977).
MOUNT CHOCORUA.
    Boston Athenaeum (1866), #296.
MOUNT CHOCORUA AND LAKE.
    Chromolithograph.
    4½ x 9 (11.4 x 22.9).
    McClinton, p. 172. Painting for chromo-lithograph sold at Leeds Gallery (March 1870).
MOUNT CHOCORUA, NH. S/L/L.
    1865. Oil on canvas.
    20 x 40 (50.8 x 101.6).
    Richard Bourne, Inc., catalog (Oct. 22, 1976).
MOUNT CHOCURA [sic] AND MOUNT MOAT FROM INTERVALE, NEW HAMPSHIRE.
    C. 1860-65. Oil on canvas.
    8½ x 16 (21.6 x 40.6).
    Los Angeles County Museum; Sotheby PB (1977).
MOUNT WASHINGTON.
    1870.
    Unlocated.
MOUNT WASHINGTON AND THE SACO.
    1864.
    Austin Arts Center.
MOUNT WASHINGTON FROM WALKER'S POND.
    C. 1865. Prang chromolithograph from a Bricher painting.
    4¼ x 9¼ (10.8 x 25.5).
NEW ENGLAND LANDSCAPE ("MOUNT KEAR-SARGE") (really Mount Washington from the Saco). S/L/L/Center.
    1864. Oil on canvas.
    12¼ x 24 (31.1 x 61).
    Austin Arts Center; University Art Gallery catalog, University of New Hampshire (1980), #93.
NEW HAMPSHIRE LANDSCAPE.
    Oil.

16 x 24 (40.6 x 61).
    Richard Bourne, Inc., catalog (Aug. 24, 1971).
NORTH CONWAY SOUVENIR.
    1877. Watercolor.
    20⅜ x 15 (51.8 x 38.1).
    Indianapolis Museum catalog (1973), p. 61.
ON LAKE CHOCORUA.
    Oil.
    9 x 18 (22.9 x 45.7).
    Raydon Gallery (1976).
ON THE ELLIS RIVER, WHITE MOUNTAINS.
    Pre-1877; Utica (NY) Art Association (1871) (see Utica Public Library for information).
ON THE SACO (Kearsarge). S/L/L.
    Oil on canvas.
    19½ x 15½ (49.5 x 39.4).
    Unlocated.
ON THE SACO RIVER, NORTH CONWAY.
    Chromolithograph.
    4½ x 9 (11.4 x 22.9).
    McClinton, p. 172. Painting for chromolithograph sold at Leeds Gallery (March 1870).
SAWYER'S POND, WHITE MOUNTAINS.
    Chromolithograph.
    4½ x 9 (11.4 x 22.9).
    McClinton, p. 172. Painting for chromolithograph sold at Leeds Gallery (March 1870).
SILVER CASCADES.
    McClinton, p. 175; peremptory sale of all Prang's paintings (1875).
SUMMER ON THE SACO.
    Before 1870. Oil.
    18 x 33 (45.7 x 83.8).
    Mead Art Gallery; Indianapolis Museum (1973); NMAA Inventory.
SUNSET IN OCTOBER ON THE ELLIS RIVER.
    1869. Watercolor.
    C&H.
SUNSET, GREEN'S CLIFF, NH.
    Leonard Auction (Oct. 18, 1872), #29.
VIEW IN CONWAY, NEW HAMPSHIRE.
    Leonard Auction (June 16, 1865), #67.
WHITE MOUNTAIN LANDSCAPE.
    Oil.
    8½ x 16 (21.6 x 40.6).
    Private collection (1983); Los Angeles County Museum (1977).

BRISTOL, JOHN BUNYAN

A, B, Ce, C&H, DAB, F, G&W, N, R, S, T
Born Hillsdale, NY, April (or March) 14, 1826.
Died New York, NY, Aug. 31, 1909.
Although Bristol studied briefly under portrait painter Henry Ary, he was primarily self-taught. He exhibited at the NAD from 1858 to 1900 and was elected an associate academician in 1860 and a member in 1875. Though Bristol lived in New York City, he traveled and painted throughout New England almost every summer. He was a member of the Century Association from 1873 to 1909.

A GLIMPSE OF LAKE OSSIPEE.
    NAD, 1884, #29.

CLEAR MORNING IN SEPTEMBER NEAR OSSIPEE LAKE, NH.
    Boston Art Club (1885), #79.

MOUNT WASHINGTON FROM LANCASTER, NH.
    Leonard Auction (Nov. 26-27, 1878), #14.

NEAR FRANCONIA MOUNTAINS, NH.
    NAD, 1878, #541.

SACO RIVER, NH.
    NAD, 1898, #96.

VIEW IN THE WHITE MOUNTAINS.
    Oil.
    24 x 44 (61 x 111.8).
    Kennedy *Quarterly* 6:1 (1966), p. 36; NMAA Inventory.

WHITE MOUNTAINS.
    Oil on canvas.
    14 x 22 (35.6 x 55.9).
    Private collection; BIAP.

BROWN, D.

Nothing is presently known about this artist.
WHITE MOUNTAIN SCENE.
    Pre-1877; Art Association of Montreal (Feb. 11, 1864).

BROWN, GEORGE LORING

A, B, C, Ce, C&H, E, F, G&W, K, Ka, N, R, S, T
Born Boston, MA, Feb. 2, 1814.
Died Malden, MA, June 25, 1889.
Nicknamed "Claude" Brown for the French landscape painter Claude Lorrain whom he admired, Brown was among the most celebrated of American painters living abroad in the 19th century. He began his artistic career as an apprentice to Abel Bowen and received further training from Eugene Isabey in Paris during his first trip to Europe in 1832-33. On his return to Boston, Brown was inspired and encouraged by the aging Washington Allston and exhibited frequently at the Boston Athenaeum. In 1839-40 he went back to Europe and settled in Italy, making a comfortable living for nearly 20 years by painting Italian landscapes to sell to American and European tourists. In 1859 Brown returned to the U.S., and in the 1860s and 1870s he made many sketching trips to the White Mountains. Perhaps Brown's greatest New Hampshire scene was THE CROWN OF NEW ENGLAND, a huge panoramic view of Mount Washington, which was purchased by the Prince of Wales in 1861 (now unlocated, but a smaller version is in the Dartmouth College Art Galleries). Brown exhibited at the Boston Athenaeum, the Brooklyn Art Association, the PAFA, and the NAD. He primarily painted Italian scenes in later life, responding to the public's preference for his European views.

Bibliography:
Archives of American Art. Roll 498.
Robert Hull Fleming Museum. *George Loring Brown: Landscapes of Europe and America, 1834-1880,* catalog, Burlington, VT (Oct.-Nov. 1973).

AUTUMN MORNING, NEW HAMPSHIRE. S/L/R.
    1867. Oil on canvas.
    24½ x 35¾ (62.2 x 90.8).
    Austin Arts Center (1980); University Art Gallery catalog, University of New Hampshire (1980), #94.

CALM MORNING, SACO MILL POND AT WEST CAMPTON, NEW HAMPSHIRE.
    1869. Oil.
    9⅜ x 13 (23.8 x 33).
    Private collection.

CHASE'S AT CAMPTON VILLAGE, NH.
    1875. Oil.
    10½ x 14½ (26.7 x 36.8).
    Parke-Bernet (1955).

CROWN OF NEW ENGLAND; THE . . .
    1868. Oil on canvas.
    15 x 24 (38.1 x 61).
    Dartmouth College Art Galleries (1974); Parke-Bernet (1964).

CROWN OF NEW ENGLAND.
    C. 1860. Oil.
    Sold to the Prince of Wales in 1861. Unlocated. Engraving by George G. Smith, 1868 (Dartmouth, 1974).

View of the Saco
J. S. Blunt, 1826
Oil on canvas, 27 1/4" x 31 1/2" / Private collection. Photograph courtesy of
    Childs Gallery, Boston / Ref. page 14

ECHO LAKE, SUNSET (or FLUME HOUSE, WHITE MOUNTAINS, SUNSET, 1862).
   1862.
   16½ x 22½ (41.9 x 57.2).
   Old Print Shop (1947).
FARMYARD, WEST CAMPTON, NH.
   1870. Oil.
   20 x 48 (50.8 x 121.9).
   Shelburne Museum (1976).
FRANCONIA NOTCH, WHITE MOUNTAINS.
S/L/L.
   Pre-1866. Oil.
   29 x 50 (73.7 x 127).

NMAA Inventory; Shelburne Museum; NAD, 1866, #337.
HAZY MORNING, HEAD OF THE ANDROSCOGGIN.
   NAD, 1837, #62.
MOAT MOUNTAIN FROM GOODRICH FALLS.
   North Conway Library Exhibition (1965).
MOAT MOUNTAIN RANGE; THE . . .
   North Conway Library Exhibition (1965).

Dictionary of Painters

NEW ENGLAND LANDSCAPE. S/L/L.
1866. Oil on canvas.
14 x 21½ (35.6 x 54.6).
Richard Bourne, Inc., catalog (Oct. 1976).
NEW HAMPSHIRE LANDSCAPE STUDY.
1878. Oil.
9 x 13 (22.9 x 33).
Sotheby PB (1970).
NEW HAMPSHIRE SCENE.
1838. Oil.
36 x 51 (91.4 x 129.5).
Mead Art Gallery (1973).
OCTOBER, PEMIGEWASSET VALLEY.
MA Charitable (1881), #567.
OLD WAGON HOUSE, PLYMOUTH, NEW HAMP-
SHIRE.
1876. Oil.
10½ x 14½ (26.7 x 36.8).
Kennedy *Quarterly* 15:2 (1977), #2.
ON THE PEMIGEWASSET.
Brooklyn Art Association (Nov. 1874), #38.
PEMIGEWASSET VALLEY AND FRANCONIA
NOTCH FROM WEST CAMPTON, NEW HAMP-
SHIRE.
1865. Oil.
14¼ x 20⅜ (36.2 x 51.8).
Mead Art Gallery (1973).
STORMY DAY, MOUNT LIBERTY. S/D.
1876. Oil on canvas.
22 x 36 (55.9 x 91.4).
Richard Bourne, Inc., catalog (Aug. 1977),
#24.
SUNRISE IN THE WHITE MOUNTAINS. S/D.
1862.
18 x 24 (45.7 x 61).
NMAA Inventory.
VIEW OF MOUNT WASHINGTON.
PAFA, 1862, #103.
WHITE MOUNTAIN STREAM.
1870s. Oil on paper on canvas.
10¾ x 14¾ (27.3 x 37.5).
Currier Gallery catalog (1973), p. 35.

**BROWN, HARRISON (HARRY or HENRY)
BIRD**
A, B, C&H, F, G&W, N, S
Born Portland, ME, 1831.
Died London, England, March 10, 1915.
*Beginning as a sign and banner painter, Brown
painted in New England until removing per-
manently to London in 1892. He exhibited at*

*the NAD from 1858 to 1875, the Philadelphia
Exposition of 1876, Boston, and London. In
1890 he produced two widely distributed il-
lustrations of Crawford Notch for the Maine
Central Railroad. In 1892 he was elected presi-
dent of the Portland Society of Art. Very soon
afterward, he moved to England to be with his
only surviving child, a daughter.*
Bibliography:
"Harrison Bird Brown." Portland Museum of
Art *Bulletin* (Jan. 1962).
"Harrison Bird Brown, Landscape Painter."
Maine Library *Bulletin* 13 (July-Oct. 1927), pp.
5-6.
AUTUMN IN THE WHITE MOUNTAINS.
Oil.
25 x 42 (63.5 x 106.7).
Portland Museum of Art (1977); NMAA
Inventory.
BIRCHES AT NORTH CONWAY, NH.
Oil.
14 x 10 (35.6 x 25.4).
Portland Museum of Art (1977).
ELLIS RIVER, JACKSON, NH.
Oil.
13 x 25 (33 x 63.5).
Bowdoin College Museum of Art (1972).
FRANCONIA NOTCH. S/L/L.
Oil.
12 ¹⁵/₁₆ x 10 ¹³/₁₆ (32.9 x 27.5).
Colby College (1969); BIAP.
HEART OF THE NOTCH, WHITE MOUNTAINS,
MAINE CENTRAL; THE . . .
1890.
Stinson House (1973).
LAKE WINNIPESAUKEE. S/D.
1867. Oil on canvas.
14 x 26 (35.6 x 66).
Old Print Shop.
MOAT MOUNTAIN RANGE.
North Conway Library Exhibition (1965).
MOUNT JEFFERSON AND ADAMS FROM THE
GLEN, NH. S/L/L.
1861. Oil on canvas.
10 x 18 (25.4 x 45.7).
Baridoff Gallery auction (July 11, 1981), #21.
MOUNT WASHINGTON.
1864. Oil on canvas.
12½ x 22½ (31.8 x 57.2).
Private collection (1982).
MOUNT WASHINGTON AND MOUNT MONROE
FROM CONWAY VALLEY, NH. S/D/L/C.
1867. Oil on canvas.

New Hampshire Scenery

13 x 15 (33 x 38.1).
Private collection.
MOUNT WASHINGTON FROM FRANKENSTEIN, MAINE CENTRAL RAILROAD.
1890.
Stinson House (1973).
NEW HAMPSHIRE SCENE (Carter Notch?).
Oil on canvas.
14 x 23 (35.6 x 58.4).
Vose Galleries (1980).
NORTH MOAT, NORTH CONWAY.
Lion Gallery (1976); North Conway Library Exhibition (1965).
OLD MILL, NORTH CONWAY.
North Conway Library Exhibition (1965).
ON THE ANDROSCOGGIN.
MA Charitable (1878), #22 (won medal for the painting, Boston, 1874).
PASTORAL, SACO VALLEY.
North Conway Library Exhibition (1965).
PRESIDENTIAL RANGE FROM CONWAY MEADOWS. S/L/R.
1867.
25 x 42 (63.5 x 106.7).
Robert Goldberg (1983).
PRESIDENTIAL RANGE, NH.
Private collection (1947); Washington County Museum of Art (1947).
VIEW OF MOUNT WASHINGTON FROM CONWAY MEADOWS. S/L/R.
1866. Oil on canvas.
25 x 42⅛ (63.5 x 107.1).
Portland Museum of Art (1980).
VIEW OF MOUNT WASHINGTON FROM THE CONWAY MEADOWS.
1863. Oil on canvas.
12 x 20 (30.5 x 50.8).
Portland Museum of Art (1977).
VIEW OF NORTH CONWAY, NH. S/D.
1867. Oil.
24¾ x 42 (62.9 x 106.7).
Sotheby PB (1977); Old Print Shop (1973).
VIEW OF WELCH MOUNTAIN, NH.
1863. Oil on canvas.
11⅞ x 20 (30.2 x 50.8).
Portland Museum of Art (1980).
WHITE MOUNTAIN SCENE (after Benjamin Champney).
1880. Oil.
24 x 34 (61 x 86.4).
Portland (ME) Public Library (sold).

BROWN, JOHN APPLETON
A, B, C&H, DAB, F, S
Born West Newbury, MA, July 12, 1844.
Died New York, NY, Jan. 18, 1902.
Brown studied art briefly as a youth and opened a studio in Boston in 1865. He soon found a need for further training and spent a year under the direction A. T. Bricher and two years in Paris with Lambinet. Brown settled in Boston in 1875. He exhibited at the Boston Athenaeum from 1870 to 1874 and at the NAD from 1877 to 1900 and was a member of the Paint and Clay Club in 1885.
Bibliography:
Archives of American Art. Roll 1406.
Robinson, Frank T. *Living New England Artists.* Boston: Samuel E. Cassino, 1888.
CHOCORUA PEAK.
1864. Oil on board.
11¾ x 20 (29.9 x 50.8).
New Hampshire Historical Society catalog (July 4-Sept. 1, 1965).

BROWN, JOHN GEORGE
B, Ce, C&H, DAB, F, G&W, N, R, S, T
Born Durham, England, Nov. 11, 1831.
Died New York, NY, Feb. 7/8, 1913.
Brown started painting portraits by the age of nine despite an early accident which had severely crippled his right hand and left him with only two usable fingers. From a poor family, his early years were a struggle, and he was apprenticed as a young boy to a glasscutter and followed that trade for a while after immigrating to the U.S. in 1853. Through the generosity of his employer in America who recognized talent, Brown was able to study art. He exhibited at the Brooklyn Art Association from 1851 to 1891 and at the NAD from 1863 until the year of his death. He was elected a member of the NAD in 1860, serving as its president in 1869; and to the Century Association in 1864. From 1861 to 1913 he had a studio in the 10th Street Studio Building (N.Y.C.). Though most of his subjects were genre, he was also a fine landscapist and lithographer.
Bibliography:
American Art Gallery. *Finished Pictures and Studies Left by the Late J. G. Brown, N.A.* Public sale (Feb. 9-Feb. 10, 1914).
Ferber, Linda. "Ripe for Revival: Forgotten American Artists." *Artnews* (Dec. 1980).

MOUNTAIN LANDSCAPE (White Mountains?).
Oil.
13½ x 21 (34.3 x 54.6).
NMAA Inventory.

WATERFALLS, NORTH SANDWICH, NH. S/L/L.
23¾ x 14¾ (60.3 x 37.5).
Private collection (1983); Sotheby PB (April
29, 1976); American Art Association sale
catalog (Feb. 1914), #29.

WHITE BIRCH TREE, NH. S/L/L.
20 x 12 (50.8 x 30.5).
American Art Association sale catalog (Feb.
1914), #10.

BROWN, J. S.

Nothing is presently known about this artist.
MOUNTAIN SCENERY OF CONWAY, N.H.
Pre-1877. St. Louis Agricultural and
Mechanical Association (Sept. 1858).

BROWN, WALTER FRANCIS

Ce, F, R, S
Active 1853. Died 1879.
*Painter and illustrator with a bent for caricature,
Brown exhibited at the NAD in 1860 and was
a member of the Century Association from 1864
to 1879.*
OCTOBER IN THE WHITE MOUNTAINS (CAR-
ICATURES OF TRAVEL). S/L/L.
1874. Engraving.
Harper's Weekly (Oct. 31, 1874), p. 892.

BROWN, WARREN W. (or W. WARREN)

Nothing is presently known about this artist.
MOUNT ADAMS FROM THE GLEN HOUSE, NEW
HAMPSHIRE.
Oil.
14¾ x 29½ (37.5 x 74.9).
NMAA Inventory; North Conway Library
Exhibition (1965).

BROWN, WILLIAM MASON

Ce, F, G&W, N, R, S
Born Troy, NY, 1828.
Died Brooklyn, NY, Sept. 6, 1898.
*Brown was first trained as an engraver, and in
his landscapes delighted in careful, pre-Raphaelite renderings of grasses and flowers. He also
was known as a painter of still lifes. He exhibited
at the Brooklyn Art Association from 1865 to
1886 and at the NAD from 1859 to 1891.*

Bibliography:
Pennsylvania State University Museum of Art
catalog. *All That Is Glorious Around Us: Paintings from the Hudson River School* (1981).

AUTUMN, WHITE MOUNTAINS.
Oil.
21½ x 35 (54.6 x 88.9).
NMAA Inventory.

COVERED BRIDGE AT BERLIN FALLS, NH.
Oil.
10½ x 16 (26.7 x 40.6).
Dartmouth College Art Galleries (1974).

WHITE MOUNTAINS, NH, IN THE AUTUMN.
1875. Oil.
6 x 8 (15.2 x 20.3).
Private collection (1975); BIAP.

BROWNE (or Brown), ROBERT

Be
Born Rotterdam, Holland, 1866.
*Browne was obviously a trained and talented
landscapist. Nothing else is presently known of
him.*
ECHO LAKE, WHITE MOUNTAINS. Signed.
Oil on canvas.
26 x 30 (66 x 76.2).
Private collection.

BROWNELL, CHARLES DEWOLF

C&H, F, G&W, N, S
Born Providence, RI, Feb. 2, 1822.
Died Bristol, RI, 1909.
*The Brownell family moved to East Hartford,
CT, when Charles was two years old. He
studied and practiced law in Hartford from 1850
to 1853, when, at age 31, he turned his attention to the arts, never returning to law. He
studied under Joseph Ropes and Julius Theodore
Busch and did many paintings of Cuba, where
he spent seven winters. He lived in Europe from
1866 to 1872. For many years he kept a strange
diary in English words written in the Greek
alphabet.*
Bibliography:
Sheeler, Robert L. "The Strange and Cryptic Picture Diary of Charles DeWolf Brownell." Providence *Sunday Journal*, June 8, 1947.
MOUNT WASHINGTON.
NAD, 1862, #140.
PINKHAM NOTCH, WHITE MOUNTAINS. S/L/R.
1862. Oil on canvas.
28 x 41 (71.1 x 104.1).
Kennedy Galleries (1978).

New Hampshire Scenery

BRUSH, GEORGE deFOREST

Ba, F, N, S

Born Shelbyville, TN, Sept. 28, 1855.
Died Hanover, NH, April 24, 1941.
Primarily a figure painter, Brush studied at the NAD and in Paris with Jean-Léon Gêrome. He was elected an associate of the NAD in 1888 and a member in 1901. He had a studio in New York City and also in Dublin, NH.

MT MONADNOCK. S/D.
  1883. Oil on canvas.
  11 $^{3}/_{16}$ x 35^{5}/$_8$ (28.4 x 90.5).
  Milwaukee Art Center (1983); Berry Hill Galleries.

BULLOCK, JOHN

R

Nothing is presently known of this artist.

MORNING IN THE WHITE MOUNTAINS.
  PAFA, 1865, #667.

BUNCE, WILLIAM GEDNEY

C&H, DAB, F, G&W, N, S

Born Hartford, CT, Sept. 19, 1840.
Died Hartford, CT, Nov. 5, 1916.
After studying under Julius Busch in 1856, Bunce moved to New York City in 1863 where he trained with William Hart. He moved to Paris in 1867 where he opened a studio next to the American sculptor Augustus St. Gaudens. He studied, not only in Paris, but also in Munich, Antwerp, and Venice. He lived most of his adult life in Europe and was particularly noted for his Venetian paintings. He exhibited at the Brooklyn Art Association from 1873 to 1883 and at the NAD from 1871 to 1885.

Bibliography:
Archives of American Art. Rowe Papers.

SQUAM LAKE, NEW HAMPSHIRE. S/L/Center.
  Possibly 1860s. Oil on board.
  14 x 16¾ (35.6 x 42.5). Oval.
  Private collection (1983); Richard Bourne, Inc., catalog (1977).

BURDICK, HORACE ROBBINS

C&H, F, N

Born East Killingsly, CT, 1844. Died after 1925.
Burdick lived in Providence, RI, and worked as a photographer. In 1864 he moved to Boston where he opened a studio in 1865. He studied at the Lowell Institute and the Boston Museum of Fine Arts. He painted portraits and still lifes as well as landscapes.

MOUNT WASHINGTON FROM THE GLEN HOUSE.
  C. 1870.
  Private collection (1982).

BURGUM (or BURGAM), JOHN

G&W

Born Birmingham, England, 1826.
Died Concord, NH, 1907.
A coach and sign painter and decorator, Burgum also painted landscapes. He came to Concord, NH, in 1850. An exhibit of his work was held at the New Hampshire Historical Society in 1981.

MOUNT WASHINGTON FROM SEBAGO LAKE.
  1897. Oil on wood panel.
  6 x 9⅞ (15.2 x 25.1).
  New Hampshire Historical Society (1983).

BURNHAM, THOMAS MICKELL

C, Ce, G&W

Born Boston, MA, 1818.
Died Boston, MA, 1866.
Burnham turned his hand to any lucrative job involving painting, executing portraits, genre, and landscapes. In 1836 he was a sign painter in Detroit, and in 1852 he was in Melrose, MA, copying daguerreotypes of California views. He exhibited at the Apollo Association from 1840 to 1843 and the Boston Athenaeum from 1840 to 1844.

EAGLE ROCK, WHITE MOUNTAINS.
  Pre-1877; Leeds Art Gallery (Feb. 7, 1870).

C

CABOT, EDWARD CLARKE
DAB, N
Born Boston, MA, April 17, 1818.
Died Boston, MA, Jan. 5, 1901.
Cabot, a brother of James Elliot Cabot, began as a sheep farmer and eventually became an architect. He designed the present Boston Athenaeum in 1845, the Boston Theatre in 1852, and the Johns Hopkins University Hospital, and is credited with introducing Japanese art to Boston. He sketched scenes with Winslow Homer during the Civil War and devoted himself to painting after his retirement in 1888; he exhibited at the NAD in 1895 and 1896.

Bibliography:
Information courtesy of Vose Galleries.
Elia, Richard. "Edward Clarke Cabot." *Antiques* (Nov. 1978), pp. 1068-1075.

JEFFERSON, AUGUST, '82.
　　1882. Watercolor.
　　Private collection (1978).

CABOT, JAMES ELLIOT
Born Boston, MA, June 8, 1821.
Died Brookline, MA, June 16, 1903.
Primarily an architect, Cabot was a brother of Edward Clarke Cabot and set up an architectural firm with his brother from 1849 to 1858 and from 1862 to 1865.

Bibliography:
Cabot Genealogy. Vol. 2, pp. 693-696.
Historical New Hampshire (Summer 1968).

AT THE LOWER END OF THE NOTCH, WHITE MOUNTAINS, JULY, 1847.
　　1847. Wash drawing.
　　New Hampshire Historical Society (1983).

LAFAYETTE HOUSE, FRANCONIA NOTCH, SEPTEMBER 1, 18[45].
　　1845. Wash drawing.
　　New Hampshire Historical Society (1983); *Historical New Hampshire* (Summer 1968).

NOTCH HOUSE, AUGUST 30, 1845.
　　1845. Wash drawing.
　　New Hampshire Historical Society (1983); *Historical New Hampshire* (Summer 1968), p. 35.

NOTCH, WHITE MOUNTAINS, JULY, 1847.
　　1847. Pencil and watercolor.
　　9¾ x 11⅜ (24.8 x 28.9).
　　New Hampshire Historical Society (1983); *Historical New Hampshire* (Summer 1968), cover.

OLD CRAWFORD'S-NOTCH-WHITE MOUNTAINS.
　　C. 1845-46. Wash drawing.
　　7⅛ x 9⅞ (18.1 x 25.1).
　　New Hampshire Historical Society (1983); *Historical New Hampshire* (Summer 1968), p. 33.

OLD MAN OF THE MOUNTAINS, FRANCONIA NOTCH, SEPT. 1, 1845; THE...
　　1845. Wash drawing.
　　New Hampshire Historical Society (1983).

WILLEY HOUSE, SEPTEMBER 8, 1845; THE...
　　1845. Wash drawing.
　　7⅝ x 10⅛ (19.4 x 25.7).
　　New Hampshire Historical Society (1983); *Historical New Hampshire* (Summer 1968), p. 34.

CARPENTER, ELLEN MARIA
C&H, F, G&W, S
Born Killingly, CT, Nov. 23, 1836
(or 1830/31). Died Boston, MA, c. 1909.
A landscape and portrait painter, Carpenter moved to Boston in 1858. She studied in Paris under Lefebreve and Fleury and at the Lowell Institute and taught painting in Boston for many years.
Information courtesy of Vose Galleries.

MOUNT CHOCORUA WITH AUTUMN FOLIAGE.
　　Vose Galleries.

MOUNT CHOCORUA, NH. S/L/R.
　　20 x 30 (50.8 x 76.2).
　　Sotheby PB catalog (Oct. 21, 1983), #79.

CARR, R. (?) P. (?) R.
Possibly **S. S. Carr** who was born in 1837 and died in 1908.

MOUNT WASHINGTON AND TUCKERMAN'S RAVINE FROM THE SACO RIVER. S/D/L/R.
　　1873.
　　Private collection (1974).

New Hampshire Scenery

CASILEAR, JOHN WILLIAM
A, B, Ce, C&H, DAB, E, F, G&W, K, Ka, N, R, S, T
Born New York, NY, June 25, 1811.
Died Saratoga, NY, Aug. 17, 1893.
Casilear was apprenticed as an engraver under Peter Maverick in 1826 and Asher Durand in 1831. After 1854 he did less and less engraving, completely dropping it by 1858 as he devoted more and more time to landscape painting. The Crayon of November 1855 (p. 330) noted that Casilear had done "a number of fine mountain studies...Mt. Washington taken from closer than others." In 1840 he went abroad with Durand, Kensett, and Rossiter to study. He became an associate of the NAD in 1835 and a member in 1851 and exhibited there from 1833 to 1893. He maintained a studio at West 10th Street (N.Y.C.) from 1859 to 1893 and was a friend of such important White Mountain painters as Benjamin Champney and Thomas Cole. He was a member of the Century Association from 1851 to 1893.

Bibliography:
Archives of American Art. Roll D177.
Pennsylvania State University Museum of Art catalog. *All That Is Glorious Around Us: Paintings from the Hudson River School* (1981), p. 52.
Sears, Clara Endicott. *Highlights Among the Hudson River Artists.* Boston: Houghton Mifflin, 1947, pp. 109-113.

A LANDSCAPE.
   Boston Public Library, Willietta Ball collection.
ANOCORUA [sic] PEAK, NH.
   Before 1871. Oil.
   NMAA Inventory; BIAP.
CASCADE, FRANCONIA MOUNTAINS.
   NAD, 1878, #568; Leonard Auction (Nov. 26-27, 1878), #28; MA Charitable (1878), #165.
CHOCORUA PEAK.
   C. 1859.
   Engraved by William Pate and Co., N.Y.C., for G. P. Putnam from a Casilear painting.
IN THE WHITE MOUNTAINS. S/L/R.
   1863.
   12 x 20 (30.5 x 50.8).
   Pre-1877; Frick Art Reference Library.
LANDSCAPE, WHITE MOUNTAINS.
   Before 1869. Oil.
   NMAA Inventory; BIAP.

MOUNTAIN WATERFALL, FRANCONIA, JULY 28, 1851.
   1851. Pencil.
   10⁹/₁₆ x 14¾ (26.8 x 37.5).
   Boston Museum of Fine Arts.
NEAR TAMWORTH, N.H. S/L/R.
   Oil.
   11¾ x 21 (29.9 x 53.3).
   Sotheby PB (June 23, 1983), #48. (Identical to David Johnson, 1863.)
NEW HAMPSHIRE LANDSCAPE.
   Oil on canvas.
   10 x 8 (25.4 x 20.3).
   Boston Athenaeum (1983); High Voltage Engineering Corp.
PRESIDENTIAL RANGE.
   North Conway Library Exhibition (1965); Frick Art Reference Library.
SCENE IN NEW HAMPSHIRE.
   NAD, 1877, #537.
TAMWORTH, NEW HAMPSHIRE, 1863. S/D/L/L.
   9½ x 15.
   Private collection.
TWILIGHT, SANDWICH MOUNTAINS, NH.
   NAD, 1881, #400.
VIEW OF TAMWORTH, NH.
   Aldine (April 1874), p. 88, #4 (sold for Artists' Fund).
VIEW OF LAKE WINNEPESAUKEE [sic], 1867.
   1867. Oil on canvas.
   19 x 27½ (48.3 x 69.9).
   Boston Athenaeum (1983); High Voltage Engineering Corp.
WHITE MOUNTAINS.
   Oil on canvas.
   12¾ x 8⅛ (32.4 x 20.7).
   Old Print Shop *Portfolio* 32:3 (1944), p. 70; NMAA Inventory.
WHITE MOUNTAINS VIEW.
   Before 1866. Oil.
   NMAA Inventory.

CASS, GEORGE NELSON
A, C, C&H, F, G&W, N, S
Born c. 1825.
Died Arlington Heights, MA, March 17, 1882.
Cass began his artistic career studying with George Inness. He exhibited at the AAU as early as 1849 and lived in Boston from 1831 until his death, but little else is known of this artist.

PROFILE LAKE (or PROFILE MOUNTAIN) AT FRANCONIA NOTCH. S/L/R.
C. 1870. Oil on board.
7¾ x 13½ (19.7 x 34.3).
Old Print Shop (1980 and 1978).

CHAMBERS, THOMAS
G&W
Born England, c. 1808. Died 1866.
Chambers came to America in 1832 and lived for a time in Albany and Boston before moving to New York City in 1858. This primitive artist probably used an engraving as the basis for his only known New Hampshire painting.
FLUMES, WHITE MOUNTAINS, NH; THE...
Oil on canvas.
24 x 18 (61 x 45.7).
Baridoff Gallery auction (Nov. 1980).

CHAMPNEY, BENJAMIN
A, C, Ce, DAB, F, G&W, R, S, T
Born New Ipswich, NH, Nov. 17, 1817.
Died Woburn, MA, Dec. 11, 1907.
Champney's name, more than any other in the field, is synonymous with the White Mountains paintings of the 19th century. He began his training as a lithographer under Pendleton in Boston. Most art historians consider him the catalyst of the White Mountain School of painters who came to North Conway and West Campton in the second half of the 19th century. His paintings, of which those listed below are only a sample, were often the basis for chromolithographs by Louis Prang of Boston. He exhibited regularly at the NAD, the Boston Athenaeum, and the PAFA and was a founder of the Boston Art Club. After his first trip to Europe in the 1840s, he painted a PANORAMA OF THE RHINE which was widely viewed. In 1853 he married, and bought a summer home and studio in North Conway. The following year, he purchased a home which he occupied for nearly 50 years.
Select Bibliography:
Information courtesy of Phyllis F. Greene.
Champney, Benjamin. *Sixty Years' Memories of Art and Artists.* Woburn, MA: Privately printed, 1899.
Dwight's Journal of Music 20 (Feb. 1862), p. 359.
Hennessy, William G., and Frederic Sharf. "Benjamin Champney and the American Barbizon School, 1850-1857." *Antiques* (Nov. 1963), pp. 566-569.

Frank S. Schwarz and Son catalog. *Philadelphia Collection 20* (Summer 1983).
Willey, Rev. Benjamin B. *Incidents in the White Mountains History*...Boston: Nathaniel Noyes, 1856.
A QUIET STREAM (Saco). S/D/L/L.
1863. Oil on board.
8¼ x 5½ (21 x 14).
Private collection (1983); Vose Galleries (1977); U.S. Sanitary Commission (1863).
A WHITE MOUNTAIN GORGE.
Boston Athenaeum (1861), #303.
ARTIST'S BROOK. S/L/L.
Oil.
Conway Library; private collection (1974).
ARTIST'S BROOK, CONWAY MEADOWS. S/D.
1881. Oil on canvas.
14 x 20 (35.6 x 50.8).
New-York Historical Society (1983).
ARTIST'S BROOK, CONWAY, NH.
Leonard Auction (Jan. 28, 1873), #15.
ARTIST'S BROOK, NORTH CONWAY. S/D/L/R.
1871. Chromolithograph.
Boston Public Library. From a painting by Champney.
ARTIST'S BROOK, NORTH CONWAY, NH.
Leonard Auction (Oct. 18, 1872), #25.
ARTIST [sic] BROOK, NORTH CONWAY, NH. S/D/L/L.
1878. Oil on canvas.
22 x 36¼ (55.9 x 92.1).
Frank S. Schwarz and Son catalog. *Philadelphia Collection 20* (Summer 1983), #18.
AUTUMN IN NEW HAMPSHIRE.
1881. Oil.
22 x 36 (55.9 x 91.4).
Richard Bourne, Inc., catalog (Aug. 18, 1972); Vose Galleries (sold to Sloan & Roman Gallery, Nov. 2, 1968).
AUTUMN IN THE WOODS, CONWAY, NH.
Leonard Auction (April 11, 1873), #17.
AUTUMN LANDSCAPE. S/D.
1881. Oil on canvas.
14 x 20 (35.6 x 50.8).
New-York Historical Society (1983).
AUTUMN PICNIC, NEW HAMPSHIRE.
Oil.
25 x 36 (66 x 91.4).
Ira Spanierman, Inc. (1969).
AUTUMN, OSSIPEE PLAIN AND LAKE.
Leonard Auction (May 23-24, 1871), #70.

View of Mount Washington from Conway Meadows
Harrison Bird Brown, 1866
Oil on canvas, 25" x 42 1/8" / Collection: Portland Museum of Art, Portland,
    Maine, gift of Mr. Louis L. Hills, Jr. in memory of Mrs. Louis L.
    Hills, Sr. and Mrs. Louis L. Hills, Jr., 1973 / Ref. page 21

BACK OF CHOCORUA, SPRING. S/L/L.
    15 x 10 (38.1 x 25.4).
    Strawbery Banke Museum, Gov. Goodwin
    House, Portsmouth, NH.

BANKS OF THE BEAR CAMP, WEST OSSIPEE,
NH.
    Leonard Auction (Jan. 28, 1873), #72.

BERLIN FALLS.
    Prang chromolithograph. From a painting by
    Champney.

BROOK AND FALL SCENE (Albany, NY, or
Intervale).
    12 x 20 (30.5 x 50.8).
    Private collection (1983).

CHICORUA [sic].
    8 x 5 (20.3 x 12.7).
    Kensett sale of his works after his death
    (1873), #217.

CHICORUA [sic].
    Pre-1877.

CHOCORUA.
    Boston Athenaeum (1859), #85.

CHOCORUA. S/L/R.
    Chromolithograph. From a painting by
    Champney.
    Shreve, Crump, & Low, Inc. (1982).

CHOCORUA, SOUTHERN APPROACH. Signed.
    1876.
    North Conway Library and Lion Gallery Ex-
    hibition (Aug. 27-Sept. 21, 1976).

CONWAY MEADOWS.
    1858.
    Antiques (Nov. 1963); NMAA Inventory.

CONWAY MEADOWS.
    Drawing.
    Conway Historical Society (1974).

CONWAY MEADOWS.
    1873. Oil.
    12¼ x 18½ (31.1 x 47).
    Robert Goldberg.

CONWAY MEADOWS.
    10 x 15 (25.4 x 38.1).
    Vose Galleries (sold Nov. 19, 1962).

CONWAY MEADOWS.
  Oil.
  25½ x 41½ (64.8 x 105.4).
  Vose Galleries (sold May 10, 1978).

CONWAY MEADOWS AND MOAT MOUNTAIN.
  Kennedy Galleries (1978).

CONWAY MEADOWS AND MOUNT WASHINGTON. S/D/L/R.
  1872. Oil.
  15 x 25 (38.1 x 63.5).
  Vose Galleries (sold May 14, 1971).

CONWAY MEADOWS AT MOUNT WASHINGTON. S/L/R.
  Oil on canvas.
  11¾ x 17½ (29.8 x 44.6).
  Nassau County Museum of Fine Arts catalog (1981), #55.

CONWAY MEADOWS, SUMMER AFTERNOON.
  Leonard Auction (May 22, 1863), #35.

CONWAY VALLEY.
  1857. Oil on canvas.
  8½ x 12 (21.6 x 30.5).
  Unlocated.

CONWAY VALLEY.
  1855-57. Oil.
  23¾ x 30¼ (60.3 x 76.8).
  NAD.

COUNTRY LANDSCAPE NEAR NORTH CONWAY, NEW HAMPSHIRE.
  Oil.
  20 x 16 (50.8 x 40.6).
  Raydon Gallery (1973).

CRYSTAL FALLS.
  1853. Lithograph.
  Appalachia (Dec. 1943), pp. 453-459. From a painting by Champney.

DIANA'S BATHS (AUTUMN).
  Lion Gallery (1976); North Conway Library Exhibition.

DIANA'S BATHS, CONWAY, NH. S/Center.
  1877. Oil on canvas.
  28¾ x 23¼ (73.1 x 60.4).
  Signal Co.

ECHO LAKE.
  Oil.
  Private collection (1983).

ECHO LAKE AND FRANCONIA NOTCH.
  1853. Chromolithograph.
  Appalachia (Dec. 1943), pp. 453-459. From a painting by Champney.

ELLIS RIVER NEAR JACKSON, NH.
  Oil.
  7½ x 9½ (19.1 x 24.1).
  Richard Bourne, Inc., catalog (Nov. 30, 1974).

ELLIS RIVER, PINKHAM NOTCH. S/D.
  1885. Oil.
  32⅛ x 47 (81.6 x 119.4).
  Vose Galleries (sold March 19, 1969).

FOUR SEASONS.
  Private collection (1983).

GATE OF THE NOTCH FROM NEAR CRAWFORD HOUSE.
  Chromolithograph.
  McClinton. From a painting by Champney.

GLEN ELLIS FALLS.
  Private collection (1983).

GLEN ELLIS FALLS, BELOW.
  1853. Chromolithograph.
  Appalachia (Dec. 1943), pp. 453-459. From a painting by Champney.

GLEN HOUSE FROM MOUNT WASHINGTON CARRIAGE ROAD.
  Chromolithograph.
  McClinton. From a painting by Champney.

HART'S LEDGE, NORTH CONWAY.
  Pre-1877; Leeds Gallery (Feb. 7, 1870).

HAYING IN CONWAY – LOOKING AT KEARSARGE. S/D/L/L.
  1871. Chromolithograph.
  14 x 20 (35.6 x 50.8).
  Nick's Antiques, Sandwich, NH. From a painting by Champney.

HAYING IN NEW HAMPSHIRE. S/D/L/L.
  1872. Oil.
  10 x 16 (25.4 x 40.6).
  Vose Galleries (sold Jan. 20, 1970).

HUMPHREY'S LEDGES, INTERVALE. S/L/R.
  Oil on canvas.
  8½ x 14½ (21.6 x 36.8).
  Baridoff Gallery auction (July 11, 1981).

INTERVALE.
  Woburn Public Library.

INTERVALE, 1852.
  1852.
  Appalachia (Dec. 1943), p. 456.

INTERVALES OF NORTH CONWAY.
  Leonard Auction (April 20-21, 1876), #102.

JACKSON, NH.
  1876. Oil.
  15¾ x 9¾ (40 x 24.8).
  NMAA Inventory.

JACKSON, NH.
1873. Oil.
12¼ x 18½ (31.1 x 47).
Richard Bourne, Inc., catalog (Aug. 6, 1974),
#126.

KEARSARGE.
1878.
North Conway Library Exhibition (1965).

KEARSARGE MOUNTAIN.
Oil.
Boston Art Club (May 1874), #92.

KEARSARGE. S/D/L.
1870. Oil.
9 x 15½ (22.9 x 39.4).
Private collection (1974).

KEARSARGE. S/D/L/R.
1870. Chromolithograph.
Shreve, Crump, & Low; Boston Public
Library.

LAFAYETTE MOUNTAIN.
Pre-1877; Massachusetts Academy of the
Fine Arts, Boston, 1st exhibition (1853),
Boston.

LAFAYETTE MOUNTAIN FROM FRANCONIA,
NH.
Pre-1877; New England Art Union (Boston
1852).

LAKE PONDICHERRY AND THE WHITE
MOUNTAINS.
Pre-1877; New England Art Union (Boston,
1852).

LANDSCAPE.
1870.
12 x 9 (30.5 x 22.9).
Unlocated.

LANDSCAPE, NEW ENGLAND (Conway
Meadows?).
Oil on canvas.
25 x 18 (63.5 x 45.7).
Kennedy Galleries (1978).

LANDSCAPE, SOURCE OF THE SACO.
Boston Athenaeum (1853), #162.

LANDSCAPE, VIEW IN NORTH CONWAY.
Leonard Auction (Oct. 18, 1872), #24.

MCMILLAN'S GROVE, NORTH CONWAY.
Leonard Auction (April 20-21, 1876), #15.

MILL BROOK, NORTH CONWAY.
Oil.
19 x 16 (48.3 x 40.6).
Private collection (1975).

MILL POND, KEARSARGE MOUNTAIN, NORTH
CONWAY.
Leonard Auction (April 20-21, 1976), #111.

MOAT MOUNTAIN FROM INTERVALE. S/L/L.
C. 1870. Oil.
15½ x 25¼ (39.4 x 64.2).
White Mountain National Bank, North Con-
way, NH; University Art Gallery exhibition,
University of New Hampshire (1980), #99.

MOAT MOUNTAIN RANGE.
North Conway Library Exhibition (1965).

MOTE [sic] MOUNTAIN AND CHOCORUA – A
VIEW FROM SUNSET HILL, NORTH CONWAY.
Leonard Auction (April 11, 1873), #11.

MOUNT ADAMS AND MADISON FROM
MOUNT WASHINGTON CARRIAGE ROAD.
1853. Chromolithograph.
Appalachia (Dec. 1943), pp. 453-459. From
a painting by Champney.

MOUNT CHOCORUA.
Chromolithograph.
Private collection.

MOUNT CHOCORUA.
19th century. Oil.
12⅜ x 8⁵/₁₆ (31.4 x 21.1).
Strawbery Banke Museum (1973).

MOUNT CHOCORUA.
Oil.
24 x 36 (61 x 91.4).
Vose Galleries (sold to H. C. Speed, dealer,
Oct. 4, 1956).

MOUNT CHOCORUA (Kearsarge). S/D.
1881. Oil.
30 x 25 (76.2 x 63.5).
Sotheby PB (June 5, 1980), PB 84 sale,
#766A, #163.

MOUNT CHOCORUA FROM CHOCORUA LAKE.
Chromolithograph.
15 x 24 (38.1 x 61).
Boston Public Library. From a painting by
Champney.

MOUNT CHOCORUA, NEW HAMPSHIRE.
1858. Oil.
12 x 18 (30.5 x 45.7).
Boston Museum of Fine Arts, Karolik collection (1969).

MOUNT CLINTON.
Chromolithograph.
Private collection (1974).

MOUNT JEFFERSON.
Pencil and wash.
Unlocated.

MOUNT JEFFERSON.
  1853. Chromolithograph.
  Appalachia (Dec. 1943), pp. 453-459. From
  a painting by Champney.
MOUNT KEARSARGE.
  1870. Prang chromolithograph.
  15 x 24 (38.1 x 61).
  Boston Public Library. From a painting by
  Champney.
MOUNT KEARSARGE.
  Oil on panel.
  5 x 8 (12.7 x 20.3).
  Private collection (1983).
MOUNT KEARSARGE, NORTH CONWAY.
  Boston Athenaeum (1859), #156.
MOUNT MOAT RANGE FROM LOCUST LANE.
S/L/L.
  1858. Oil on canvas.
  15¼ x 23¼ (38.8 x 59.1).
  Private collection (1980); University Art
  Gallery exhibition, University of New
  Hampshire (1980), #96.
MOUNT MONADNOCK, NH.
  1859. Oil.
  26 x 38 (66 x 96.5).
  Richard Bourne, Inc., catalog (Aug. 29,
  1970); NMAA Inventory.
MOUNT WASHINGTON.
  Boston Athenaeum (1859), #185.
MOUNT WASHINGTON.
  1853. Chromolithograph.
  Appalachia (Dec. 1943), pp. 453-459.
  From a painting by Champney.
MOUNT WASHINGTON.
  PAFA, 1863.
MOUNT WASHINGTON.
  Oil.
  15 x 25 (38.1 x 63.5).
  Vose Galleries (sold Nov. 5, 1963).
MOUNT WASHINGTON.
  Oil.
  Williams and Everett auction (Dec. 6, 1861).
MOUNT WASHINGTON AND MOORE POND
FROM CONWAY, NH (Moat Mountain and the
Saco).
  Oil on canvas.
  11½ x 19¾ (29.2 x 50.2).
  Private collection (1983); 3rd Art of North-
  ern New England Show (1973).
MOUNT WASHINGTON AND THE ELLIS RIVER.
  1890.
  Conway Library (1974).

MOUNT WASHINGTON FROM GOULD'S POND.
  NAD, 1859, #205.
MOUNT WASHINGTON FROM HIGHLAND
FARM ABOVE JACKSON, NH.
  1834. Oil.
  22 x 36 (55.9 x 91.4).
  Old Print Shop *Portfolio*, 17:5, p. 141.
MOUNT WASHINGTON FROM HIGHLAND
FARMS, CARTER NOTCH. S/D.
  1881.
  10 x 16 (25.4 x 41).
  Sotheby PB (June 5, 1980), PB 84 sale,
  #766A, #161.
MOUNT WASHINGTON FROM NORTH
CONWAY.
  Private collection (1983); PAFA, 1863, #195.
MOUNT WASHINGTON FROM SUNSET HILL.
  C. 1856-84. Oil.
  Conway Historical Society (1974).
MOUNT WASHINGTON, THE GLEN ROAD (or
THE MOUNTAIN). S/Reverse.
  Oil on panel.
  13 ⁹/₁₆ x 19⅝ (34.5 x 50).
  Signal Co.
MOUNT WASHINGTON FROM THE MEADOWS
IN NO [rth] CONWAY.
  54½ x 37½ (138.4 x 92.3).
  NAD, 1851, #60; AAU, 1852, #188.
MOUNT WASHINGTON FROM THE SACO
RIVER, NH.
  1865. Oil.
  14 x 12 (35.6 x 30.5).
  Private collection; Sotheby PB.
MOUNT WASHINGTON, NORTH CONWAY
MEADOWS. S/D/L/L.
  1870. Chromolithograph.
  Boston Public Library. From a painting by
  Champney.
MOUNTAIN STREAM, NH (Mount Washington).
  Appalachia (Dec. 1943), p. 457.
NEW HAMPSHIRE LAKE SCENERY – MOUNT
CHOCORUA IN DISTANCE.
  Boston Athenaeum (1856), #154.
NEW HAMPSHIRE LANDSCAPE.
  Oil.
  15¾ x 23⅝ (40 x 60).
  Hirschl and Adler Gallery (1968).
NEW HAMPSHIRE LANDSCAPE (EARLY FALL
SCENE).
  1864. Oil.
  7 x 10 (17.8 x 25.4).
  *Birmingham Collects: American Art Since
  1776.* Birmingham, AL, 1976.

New Hampshire Scenery

NORTH CONWAY.
  1855. Oil.
  10¾ x 19 (27.3 x 48.3).
  NAD.
NORTH CONWAY.
  Oil.
  12 x 20 (30.5 x 50.8).
  PAFA, 1863.
NORTH CONWAY IN JUNE.
  Leonard Auction (May 23-24, 1871), #9.
NORTH CONWAY MEADOWS.
  After 1870. Oil on canvas.
  18 x 25 (45.7 x 63.5).
  Baridoff Gallery auction (July 11, 1981).
NORTH CONWAY MEADOWS. S/L/R.
  Oil on canvas.
  25 x 30 (63.5 x 76.2).
  Skinner catalog (1977).
NORTH CONWAY, MOUNT WASHINGTON IN
THE DISTANCE.
  Leonard Auction (Dec. 29, 1864), #7.
NOTCH IN THE WHITE MOUNTAINS FROM
ABOVE THE NOTCH HOUSE.
  1839-40. Pencil.
  17 x 11¼ (43 x 28.5).
  Princeton sketchbook (1983).
NOTCH OF THE WHITE MOUNTAINS. S/L/L.
  Oil on canvas.
  21⅜ x 35¼ (54.3 x 89.5).
  Signal Co.
OLD MAN OF THE MOUNTAIN.
  Oil.
  14 x 20 (35.6 x 50.8).
  Private collection (1983).
ON ARTIST'S BROOK, NORTH CONWAY, NH.
  Boston Athenaeum (1859) #172.
ON THE BEAR CAMP RIVER.
  Leonard Auction (July 16, 1865), #66.
ON THE INTERVALE AT NORTH CONWAY.
  Boston Athenaeum (1857), #260.
ON THE MEADOWS, NORTH CONWAY.
  Boston Athenaeum (1858), #212.
ON THE SACO, NEW HAMPSHIRE, A STUDY
FROM NATURE.
  Leonard Auction (April 11, 1873), #70.
OSSIPEE LAKE.
  5⅜ x 9¾ (13.7 x 24.8).
  Robert Goldberg (1983).
OSSIPEE PLAIN AND LAKE, AUTUMN.
  Leonard Auction (May 23-24, 1871), #70.

OSSIPEE, NH.
  Oil.
  Boston Public Library (1884), #50.
PEAK OF CHOCORUA.
  PAFA, 1863, #291.
PICNIC ON ARTIST'S LEDGE, OVERLOOKING
CONWAY MEADOWS, NH. S/D/L/R.
  1874. Oil.
  30 x 48 (76.2 x 121.9).
  A private collector bought from Vose
  Galleries (Nov. 6, 1961).
PINE CREEK, HIGHLAND FARMS. S/Stretcher.
  14 x 20 (35.6 x 50.8).
  Sotheby PB, PB 84 sale (June 5, 1980).
PUDDING POND. S/L/R.
  Weygandt, *The Heart of New Hampshire.*
  New York: G. P. Putnam's Sons, 1944.
PUMPKIN TIME (Chocorua).
  1871. Chromolithograph.
  15 x 24 (38.1 x 61).
  Boston Public Library. From a painting by
  Champney.
RAMBLES, NORTH CONWAY, NH; THE...
  Oil.
  Boston Art Club (Jan. 17-Feb. 10, 1877),
  #115.
RATTLESNAKE LEDGE, NH.
  Leonard Auction (June 16, 1865), #66.
RIPLEY FALLS ON MOUNT WILLEY.
  History of Carroll County (New Hampshire,
  1889), p. 943.
SACO AND KEARSARGE.
  1890.
  New Hampshire Historical Society.
SACO AND MOAT MOUNTAIN.
  Chromolithograph.
  Private collection.
SACO RIVER ABOVE INTERVALE.
  1863. Oil.
  6⅛ x 9¼ (15.6 x 23.5).
  Private collection.
SACO RIVER AND MOAT MOUNTAINS [sic],
NORTH CONWAY.
  Leonard Auction (April 20-21, 1876), #117.
SACO RIVER AND MOTE [sic] MOUNTAIN,
NORTH CONWAY.
  Leonard Auction (April 20-21, 1876), #62.
SACO RIVER, NORTH CONWAY. S/D/L/R.
  1874. Oil on canvas.
  24 x 36 (61 x 91.4).
  New Hampshire Historical Society (1983).

SACO VALLEY.
    1855.
    New Hampshire Historical Society.
SACO; THE...
    1863. Oil on board.
    8¼ x 5½ (21 x 14).
    U.S. Sanitary Commission (1864).
SCENE IN NEW HAMPSHIRE.
    Oil.
    9½ x 15½ (24.1 x 39.4).
    Private collection (1973).
SCENE IN NORTH CONWAY, NH.
    1869.
    Society for the Preservation of New England
    Antiquities, Boston, MA.
SHADY NOOK, NORTH CONWAY.
    NAD, 1858, #92.
SKETCHBOOK.
    Conway Public Library.
SOUTH MOAT BRIDGE.
    North Conway Library Exhibition (1965).
STOP FOR A PICNIC. S/D/L/R.
    1876. Oil on canvas.
    12 x 18 (30.5 x 45.7).
    Baridoff Gallery auction (July 11, 1981).
STUDY ON KEARSARGE BROOK.
    Boston Athenaeum (1857), #326.
SUMMER – JULY IN CONWAY.
    Leonard Auction (July 16, 1865), #1.
SUMMER LANDSCAPE. S/L/R.
    Oil on board.
    5 x 8 (12.7 x 20.3).
    Skinner catalog (1977).
SUMMIT OF MOUNT LAFAYETTE, A SUMMER
HOUSE.
    Chromolithograph.
    McClinton. From a painting by Champney.
SWIMMERS AT SACO RIVER, NEAR NORTH
CONWAY.
    Oil.
    6 x 13½ (15.2 x 34.3).
    Raydon Gallery (1976).
THE MOUNTAIN, WASHINGTON FROM THE
GLEN ROAD. S/Reverse.
    Oil on canvas.
    14 x 20 (35.6 x 50.8).
    Skinner catalog (1977).
THOMPSON'S FALLS AND THE SACO VALLEY.
    1855.
    Allen Handy, Inc.; *Antiques* (Nov. 1963).

UNDER THE ELMS NEAR NORTH CONWAY, NH.
    Leonard Auction (April 11, 1873), #83.
VALLEY OF THE SACO.
    Boston Athenaeum (1858), #107.
VALLEY OF THE SACO, NEAR FRYEBURG, ME.;
THE...
    25½ x 35½ (64.8 x 90.2).
    NAD, 1851, #415; AAU, 1852, #198.
VIEW FROM CONWAY, 1876.
    1876.
    North Conway Library Exhibition (1965).
VIEW OF LA FAYETTE [sic] MOUNTAIN FROM
LITTLETON, AUTUMN EFFECT.
    Pre-1877; New England Art Union (Boston,
    1852).
VIEW OF THE WHITE MOUNTAINS.
    Oil on canvas.
    32 x 21 (81.3 x 53.3).
    New Hampshire Historical Society exhibition
    (July 4-Sept. 1, 1965).
VIEW IN THE WHITE MOUNTAINS. S/L/R
    Oil on canvas.
    10 x 14 (25.4 x 35.6).
VILLAGE PASTURE.
    1870. Chromolithograph.
    16 x 24 (40.6 x 61).
    Private collection.
WEST OSSIPEE, AUGUST 22, 1863.
    1863. Pencil.
    4½ x 7 (11.4 x 17.8).
    Private collection.
WHITE MOUNTAIN BROOK, NORTH CONWAY,
NH.
    Jordan Marsh Galleries (1896), #132.
WHITE MOUNTAIN GORGE; THE...
    Boston Athenaeum (1861), #303.
WHITE MOUNTAIN NOTCH, FROM FRANKEN-
STEIN CLIFF, LOOKING SOUTH.
    Oil.
    Boston Art Club (Jan. 15-Feb. 8, 1879), #161.
WHITE MOUNTAIN SCENE.
    Pre-1877; Metropolitan Fair to U.S. Sanitary
    Commission (NY, 1864).
WHITE MOUNTAINS (10 views).
    After 1875. Chromolithographs.
    Dartmouth and Boston Public Library. From
    paintings by Champney.
WHITE MOUNTAINS AND WALKER'S POND
FROM EATON, NH.
    Oil.
    Boston Art Club (Jan. 15-Feb. 8, 1879), #5.

New Hampshire Scenery

WHITE MOUNTAINS FROM NORTH CONWAY, WINTER SUNSET.
>Currier Gallery of Art catalog (1973), #2; Bierstadt Exhibition, New Bedford, 1858, #115; NAD, 1858, #461; Pre-1877.

WHITE MOUNTAINS IN WINTER FROM THE ARTIST'S STUDIO: THE... S/D.
>1863. Oil on board.
>5 x 7 (12.7 x 17.8).
>Christie's (Oct. 28, 1980), #57.

WHITE MOUNTAINS, NH.
>Private collection.

WHITE MOUNTAINS, NH.
>Oil.
>16 x 24 (40.6 x 61).
>Sotheby PB (1969).

WHITE MOUNTAINS, SUNSET: THE...
>Boston Athenaeum (1857), #318.

WHITE MOUNTAINS; THE... (MOUNT WASHINGTON). S/D/L/R.
>1856 or 1858. Oil on board.
>7¼ x 11¾ (18.4 x 29.8).
>Bartfield Gallery, N.Y.C., catalog 110, #7.

WHITE OAK, A NEW ENGLAND LANDSCAPE.
>1870.
>12 x 9 (30.5 x 22.9).
>NMAA Inventory.

WINTER IN THE WHITE MOUNTAINS, VIEW FROM NORTH CONWAY.
>Leonard Auction (Oct. 18, 1872), #40.

WOODLAND SCENE. S/L/L.
>New Hampshire Historical Society.

CHAMPNEY, EDWIN GRAVES

Born 1842. Died 1899.
Champney studied briefly with his uncle, Benjamin Champney, in North Conway in 1861. The elder Champney encouraged him to continue, but Edwin showed no inclination to pursue a career in art.
Information courtesy of Vose Galleries and Phyllis F. Greene.

WHITE MOUNTAINS FROM NORTH CONWAY.
>C. 1890. Oil.
>20 x 16 (50.8 x 40.6).
>Minute Man National Historic Park, Concord, MA; NMAA Inventory.

CHAPMAN

Possibly **John Gadsby Chapman.**
B, C&H, DAB, F, G&W, K, N, R, T
Born Alexandria, VA, Dec. 8, 1808.
Died Brooklyn, NY, Nov. 28, 1889.

A founder of the Apollo Gallery, Chapman was a prolific artist and was known for his etchings. Living in Italy until 1831, he was listed as a book illustrator in the New York City directory in 1834. He exhibited for many years at the Boston Athenaeum, the PAFA, the AAU, and the NAD. He was elected to the National Academy in 1836 and was a founder of the Century Association.

WHITE HILLS OF NEW HAMPSHIRE.
>Pre-1877; *Art Journal* Supplement (1857), p. 57; Cosmopolitan Art Association.

CHRISTIE, MRS. E. A.

Possibly **Mrs. Alexander E. Christie.**
A, R
Active 1867-68.
Research has discovered little about this artist except that she exhibited at the Boston Athenaeum in 1867 and the PAFA the following year.

MOUNT WASHINGTON.
>PAFA, 1868, #136.

CHURCH, FREDERIC EDWIN

B, C, Ce, C&H, DAB, F, G&W, Ka, N, R, S, T
Born Hartford, CT, May 4, 1826.
Died New York, NY, April 7, 1900.
In 1844, at the age of 18, Church became the only pupil Thomas Cole ever accepted. He was soon proficient enough to begin his long years of exhibiting. He became an associate member of the NAD in 1849 and a member the following year at which time he was also elected a member of the Century Association. Church traveled from the arctic to the tropics in search of material for his elegant paintings, for which he gathered copious sketches. His paintings were often of extremely large size, and they enthralled crowds with their realistic, technical virtuosity. Church's studio was in the 10th Street Studio Building (N.Y.C.) from 1858 to 1887. In 1876 he suffered his first attack of "inflammatory rheumatism," which led him to try to paint with his left hand. He was a founding trustee of the Metropolitan Museum in New York City and served with the institution from 1870 to 1887. By 1880 Church's painting activity declined markedly, and he turned his interest to the embellishment of his home, Olana, in Hudson, NY (now a museum to his memory).

Select Bibliography:
Archives of American Art. Roll DDU-1.

Avery, Myron H. "The Artist of Katahdin." *Appalachia* 25 (1944-45), pp. 147-154.
Huntington, David C. *The Landscapes of Frederic Edwin Church.* New York: George Braziller, 1966.
Linquist-Cock, Elizabeth. "Frederic Church's Stereographic Vision." *Art in America* 61:3 (1973), pp. 70-75.
National Collection of Fine Arts. *Frederic Edwin Church.* Washington, DC: Smithsonian Institution, 1966.
Pennsylvania State University Museum of Art catalog. *All That is Glorious Around Us: Paintings from the Hudson River School* (1981), p. 54.
Sears, Clara Endicott. *Highlights Among the Hudson River Artists.* Boston: Houghton Mifflin, 1947, pp. 98-108.
Stebbins, Theodore E., Jr. *Close Observation: Selected Oil Sketches By Frederic E. Church.* Washington, DC: Smithsonian Institution Press, 1978.
AUTUMN LANDSCAPE (or MOUNT WASHINGTON AND CONWAY MEADOWS) (formerly NEW HAMPSHIRE LANDSCAPE).
C. 1850.
Olana, Catskill, NY; Frick Art Reference Library Reprints #56705 and #56790.
AUTUMN LANDSCAPE, COWS AND STREAM.
C. 1850.
Private collection (1983); Olana, Catskill, NY; Frick Art Reference Library Reprint #56790.
INTERVALE AT NORTH CONWAY.
(formerly called A CATSKILL LANDSCAPE).
C. 1856. Oil on canvas.
13½ x 19¾ (34.3 x 50.2).
Private collection (1983); University Art Gallery exhibition, University of New Hampshire (1980), #46; Kennedy Galleries (1978).
LANDSCAPE WITH MOUNTAINS AND LAKE (Chocorua).
C. 1850.
Olana, Catskill, NY; Frick Art Reference Library Reprint #56753.

CLARK
Listed by Tichnor & Co. as painting in Jackson, NH, in 1850.

CLOUGH, D. A.
Nothing is presently known about this artist.

FRANCONIA NOTCH FROM WEST CAMPTON, NH.
Leonard Auction (Jan. 28, 1873), #61.

CLOUGH, GEORGE LAFAYETTE
Ce, G&W, N, S
Born Auburn, NY, Sept. 18, 1824.
Died Auburn, NY, Feb. 20, 1901.
At the age of 20, Clough studied under Charles Loring Elliott (1812-68) and began exhibiting at the NAD in 1848. In 1850 he traveled to Europe and, on his return in the 1860s, worked in Cleveland as a commercial artist, coloring and copying photographic portraits. He moved to New York City and was a frequent exhibitor at the Brooklyn Art Association and the Boston Art Club. He returned to his birthplace in 1896 where he became ill and never painted again.
Bibliography:
Kennedy, Terence J. "Art and Professional Artists of Cayuga Country." Auburn *Daily Advertiser*, March 14, 1878, republished by the Auburn Historical Society, Auburn, NY.
Witthoft, Brucia. "George L. Clough, Painter." *Antiques* (July 1982), pp. 130-137.
A NOTCH IN THE WHITE MOUNTAINS (probably Franconia).
Oil on board.
18 x 12 (45.7 x 30.5).
Kennedy *Quarterly* 5:4 (Aug. 1965), p. 274; NMAA Inventory.

COATES, EDMUND (or EDWIN or EDWARD) C.
C, Ce, G&W, K
Born England, 1816.
Died Brooklyn, NY, Aug. 12, 1871.
Coates's name appeared in the New York City directory in 1843 and in the Brooklyn directory from 1844 through 1871. A view of Niagara Falls is signed and dated 1845. Though generally listed as "artist" or "painter," in 1858-59 he was listed as "Coates and Company, Picture Frames." The subject matter for his paintings was largely drawn from the engravings in American Scenery, *after William H. Bartlett, though at least one large work is an allegorical subject. Coates was an accomplished professional artist of the Romantic School.*
Information courtesy of S. Morton Vose, Vose Galleries.
VIEW OF MEREDITH (formerly NEW HAMPSHIRE LANDSCAPE) (after Bartlett). S/D/L/L.
1863. Oil on canvas.

New Hampshire Scenery

Profile Lake (or Profile Mountain) at Franconia Notch
George Nelson Cass, 1870
Oil on board, 7³/₄" x 13¹/₂" / Collection: The Old Print Shop, Inc.,
    Kenneth M. Newman, New York City / Ref. page 26

23½ x 35½ (59.7 x 90.2).
Private collection.

COBB, CORNELIA DRAKE (MRS. LYMAN COBB, JR.)

C, Ce, N, K
Born probably Little Falls, NY, 1825.
Died Yonkers or New York, NY, Sept. 14, 1901.
Married at 20, Cornelia Drake Cobb moved to New York City with her husband. Her earliest-known work was executed the following year, 1845. In 1849 she exhibited at the AAU and in 1855 and 1872 at the NAD.

MOUNT LAFAYETTE.
    NAD, 1872, #176.

CODMAN, CHARLES

A, Ce, G&W
Born Portland, ME (Boston Athenaeum notes indicate Boston), 1800.
Died Portland, ME, Sept. 11, 1842.
A largely self-taught artist, Codman painted clockfaces for Simon Willard, the clockmaker, and military standards and signs in Portland,
ME. As early as 1819 he was mentioned with John S. Blunt in the Concord (NH) Patriot for October 4. He first exhibited at the Boston Athenaeum in 1828, and at the NAD in 1832 and 1838. His paintings have a gloomy, imaginative grandeur.

Bibliography:
Pennsylvania State University Museum of Art, catalog. *All That Is Glorious Around Us: Paintings of the Hudson River School* (1981), p. 56.
Sears, Clara Endicott. *Highlights Among the Hudson River Artists.* Boston: Houghton Mifflin, 1947, pp. 55-56.

FOOTBRIDGE IN THE WILDERNESS. S/L/R.
    1830. Oil on canvas.
    25½ x 38½ (64.8 x 97.8).
    Portland Museum of Art.

FRANCONIA NOTCH.
    Oil.
    21⅝ x 27¾ (54.9 x 70.5).
    Private collection (1960);
    NMAA Inventory.

Dictionary of Painters

LANDSCAPE. S/D/L/L.
>1828. Oil on canvas.
>30¼ x 40 (76.8 x 101.6).
>Portland Museum of Art.

VIEW OF THE NOTCH IN THE WHITE MOUNTAINS.
>Boston Athenaeum (1830), #21.

VIEW OF THE WHITE HILLS.
>Pre-1877; Maine Charitable Mechanic Association (Sept. 21-Oct. 6, 1838), Portland, ME (see Portland Museum of Art for information).

WILLEY SLIDE; THE . . .
>Conway Library.

CODMAN (or COLMAN), JOHN AMORY
C, G&W
Born 1824. Died 1886.
Codman was a portrait and marine painter who gave his address as Portland, ME, when he exhibited at the Apollo Association in 1839 at the tender age of 15. He was in Boston from 1849 to 1860 and exhibited at the AAU in 1849 and the Boston Athenaeum in 1856.

NEAR EAGLE CLIFF, FRANCONIA, NH.
>Pre-1877; Art Association exhibition, Mechanic's Hall, Montreal (Feb. 27, 1865).

NEW HAMPSHIRE LANDSCAPE WITH FIGURES.
>1849. Oil.
>34 x 42 (86.4 x 106.7).
>Parke-Bernet (1964).

SACO RIVER, NORTH CONWAY, NH.
>October 1847. Oil.
>12 x 15 (30.5 x 38.1).
>Parke-Bernet (1964).

VIEW OF MOUNT WASHINGTON FROM NORTH CONWAY.
>Pre-1877; New England Art Union (Boston, 1852).

WHITE MOUNTAIN SCENERY.
>Pre-1877; New England Art Union (Boston, 1852).

COFFIN, R. A.
Nothing is presently known about this artist.
NOTCH OF THE WHITE MOUNTAINS.
>Engraved by Gilbert.
>Before 1823. Woodcut.
>Same view as in 1823 *Gazeteer,* but this view most probably came first.

COLE, CHARLES OCTAVIUS
G&W, S
Born Newburyport, MA, July 1, 1814.
Died probably Portland, ME, 1858.
Mostly known as a portrait painter, Cole produced some landscapes. He worked in New Orleans, LA, from 1838 to 1841 and then settled in Portland, ME, where he remained at least until 1856. Though it is thought that he died in 1858, one of his paintings was exhibited at the Brooklyn Art Association in 1877, perhaps posthumously.

Bibliography:
Maine Library *Bulletin* 13 (July-Oct. 1927), p. 7, mentions him.

IMPERIAL KNOB AND GORGE, WHITE MOUNTAINS OF NH (or WHITE MOUNTAINS OF NEW HAMPSHIRE). S/D/Reverse.
>1853. Oil on canvas.
>44⅞ x 36⅛ (114 x 91.8).
>Adams, Davidson Gallery, Inc., *Antiques* (Sept. 1968); Brooklyn Museum (1976).

MOUNT CARTER.
>Pre-1877; Maine Charitable Mechanic Association, Portland, ME (Oct. 4, 1859); BIAP.

VIEW OF MOUNT MORIAH FROM STATION HOUSE AT GORHAM, NH. S/L/R.
>1850. Oil on canvas.
>22⅞ x 36⅝ (58.1 x 93).
>Portland Museum of Art (1977); NMAA Inventory.

COLE, ROBERT
Nothing is presently known of this artist.
MOUNT CARTER.
>Oil.
>Dartmouth National Bank (1974).

COLE, THOMAS
A, B, C, Ce, C&H, DAB, F, G&W, K, Ka, N, R, S, T
Born Bolton-le-Moors, England, Feb. 1, 1801.
Died Catskill, NY, Feb. 11, 1848.
Dubbed the founder of the Hudson River School, Cole was apprenticed to a calico designer and wood engraver in England before he came to the U.S. with his family in 1818. He helped to found the NAD in 1826. The rest of his life he spent much of his time sketching from nature in the Catskills, White Mountains, Adirondacks, and the coast of Maine. In 1827, at the behest of Daniel Wadsworth, Cole visited

the White Mountains for the first time. He visited the New Hampshire mountains again a year later with fellow artist Henry Cheever Pratt, only eight years after the first footpath was opened to Mount Washington. He returned to New Hampshire for the last time in 1839. In the winters, Cole returned to his New York City studio to paint romantic, amalgamative, grand, and enormous allegorical works such as the VOYAGE OF LIFE and the COURSE OF EMPIRE from the accumulated sketches of his summer excursions. Though he preferred allegorical subjects, he also painted many landscapes, often at the specific request of patrons. All his paintings are romantic in vein, for Cole felt it his duty to depict nature, especially American nature, as the "visible hand of God." From 1829 to 1832 Cole traveled abroad, but his unique genius was not affected by Old World contacts. His only pupil was his neighbor in Catskill, Frederic Church.

Select Bibliography:

Albany Institute of History and Art catalog. *The Works of Thomas Cole, 1801-1848.* Albany, NY, 1941.

Archives of American Art. Rolls D6, D39, D40, ALC1-ALC4, N582.

Campbell, Catherine H. "Two's Company: The Diaries of Thomas Cole and Henry Cheever Pratt on Their Walk Through Crawford Notch, 1828." *Historical New Hampshire* 33:4 (Winter 1978), pp. 109-133.

McNulty, J. Bard, ed. *Correspondence of Thomas Cole and Daniel Wadsworth,* Hartford, CT: Connecticut Historical Society, 1983.

Noble, Louis Legrand. *The Life and Works of Thomas Cole.* New York, 1853.

Parry, Ellwood C., III. "Gothic Elegies for an American Audience: Thomas Cole's Repackaging of Imported Ideas. "*American Art Journal* 7:2 (Nov. 1976), pp. 26-46.

Parry, Ellwood C., III. "Thomas Cole and the Problem of Figure Painting." *American Art Journal* 4:1 (Spring 1972), pp. 66-86.

Sears, Clara Endicott. *Highlights Among the Hudson River Artists.* Boston: Houghton Mifflin, 1947, pp. 57-97.

Wadsworth Atheneum catalog. *One Hundred Years Later.* Hartford, CT, 1948.

1839-44 SKETCHBOOK.
    Pencil.
    Princeton University Art Gallery (1983); *Record* of the Princeton Art Gallery 15:1 (1956), pp. 1-23.

A VIEW OF THE PASS CALLED THE NOTCH OF THE WHITE MOUNTAINS.
    NAD, 1840, #49.

ALTON BAY, WINNIPISSAGEE [sic].
    Pencil.
    11 3/16 x 16 15/16 (28.4 x 43).
    Princeton Art Museum (1979).

ANSIEDER'S BLOCKHAUS (NOTCH HOUSE).
    1828. Engraving.
    London: John Tallis and Co., 1830.

AUTUMN TWILIGHT, VIEW OF CORWAY PEAK (Chocorua). S/L/R.
    1834. Oil on wood panel.
    14 x 19½ (35.6 x 49.5).
    New-York Historical Society (1980); University Art Galleries catalog, University of New Hampshire (1980), #10; NAD, 1835, #37.

BRIDGE OF FEAR (NH PROVENANCE).
    Pencil on paper.
    7⅞ x 9⅜ (20 x 23.8).
    Boston Athenaeum.

CHOCORUA'S CURSE.
    1827-29.
    Boston Athenaeum (1830), #72; *The Token* (1830).

CORWAY PEAK, NH (Chocorua). S/D/L/Center.
    1844. Oil.
    18 x 24 (45.7 x 60.9).
    Randolph-Macon Women's College, Lynchburg, VA; *Crayon* (1858), p. 268.

FLUME IN THE WHITE MOUNTAINS.
    1827. Black ink and gray wash.
    14½ x 10½ (36.8 x 26.7).
    Detroit Institute of Fine Arts (1983).

FLUME IN THE WHITE MOUNTAINS.
    (another view).
    Detroit Institute of Fine Arts (1983).

HOME IN THE WOODS NEAR MOUNT CHOCORUA, NH. S/L/R.
    1847. Oil on canvas.
    44 x 66 (111.8 x 167.6).
    Reynolda House collection, Winston-Salem, NC (1970); Kennedy Galleries, 1969.

HUNTER'S RETURN; STUDY FOR THE . . . (Mount Chocorua in background).
    1845. Oil on paper.
    7⅞ x 10⅞ (20.0 x 27.6).
    Berry Hill Galleries catalog (1983), p. 8.

HUNTER'S RETURN; THE... (Mount Chocorua in background). S/D/L/C.
    1845. Oil on canvas on panel.
    40 x 60 (101.6 x 152.4).
    Adams-Davidson Gallery, Inc. (sold to Amon Carter Museum, 1983).

IN CENTRE HARBOR.
    1829.
    Wadsworth Atheneum.

LAKE IN NEW HAMPSHIRE.
    4.1 x 5.1 (includes frames).
    New-York Historical Society (April 1974), p. 95, fn. 10; exhibited in London (1831).

LAKE WINNIPESAUKEE, NH.
    C. 1827-28. Oil on canvas.
    24½ x 34½ (62.3 x 87.7).
    Albany Institute of History and Art (1980); University Art Gallery catalog, University of New Hampshire (1980), #12.

LANDSCAPE (UPPER SANDWICH RANGE).
    C. 1839. Oil on canvas.
    22⅝ x 18⅝ (57.5 x 47.3).
    Chicago Institute of Art.

LANDSCAPE, VIEW OF MOUNT WASHINGTON.
    Pre-1877; Western Art-Union, Masonic Hall, Cincinnati, OH (Nov. 8, 1847).

LAST OF THE MOHICANS (Chocorua); THE... S/D/Center.
    1827. Oil on canvas.
    28¼ x 40 1/16 (71.8 x 101.8).
    New-York Historical Society.

MOUNT CHOCORUA.
    C. 1827-28. Oil on canvas.
    23¼ x 32¼ (59.1 x 81.9).
    Whitney Downtown Gallery, N.Y.C. (1980); IBM Gallery of Arts and Sciences (1951).

MOUNTAIN FORD; THE...
    C. 1846. Pencil with chalk.
    6 13/16 x 9 13/16 (17.3 x 24.9).
    Corcoran Gallery (1979).

MOUNTAIN FORD; THE...
    1846. Oil.
    28¼ x 40 1/16 (71.8 x 101.8).
    Metropolitan Museum of Arts, Morris K. Jessup collection.

NEAR CONWAY, NH.
    C. 1828. Pen and black ink.
    7 x 10½ (17.8 x 26.7).
    Boston Museum of Fine Art, Karolik collection (1983).

NORTHWEST BAY, LAKE WINNEPESAUKEE [sic].
    1828? Oil.

18¾ x 26 (47.6 x 66).
    Wadsworth Atheneum (1974).

NOTCH OF THE WHITE MOUNTAINS; THE. S/D/L/L.
    1839. Oil on canvas.
    40 x 60½ (or 61½) (101.6 x 156).
    National Gallery of Art, Washington, DC (1976).

PEACE AT SUNSET (or EVENING IN THE WHITE MOUNTAINS). S/L/R.
    Oil on canvas.
    27⅛ x 32¼ (68.9 x 81.9).
    M. H. de Young Memorial Museum, San Francisco, CA (1959).

PIC-NIC THE...(Chocorua in background).
    1846. Oil.
    44⅞ x 71⅞ (121.6 x 182.6).
    Brooklyn Museum (1983).

SOLITARY LAKE IN NEW HAMPSHIRE.
    1830. Oil.
    Taconic State Park Commission (1969), Olana, Catskill, NY; *American Art Journal* 1:2 (1969), p. 51.

STORM NEAR MOUNT WASHINGTON.
    1828. Oil.
    19¾ x 26⅛ (50.2 x 66.4).
    Yale University Art Gallery (1983); Wadsworth Atheneum catalog (1976).

STUDY FOR THE MOUNTAIN FORD.
    C. 1846.
    6 13/16 x 9 13/16 (17.3 x 24.9).
    Corcoran Gallery catalog (July 21-Sept. 2, 1979).

SUMMER TWILIGHT, A RECOLLECTION OF A SCENE IN NEW HAMPSHIRE.
    NAD, 1835, #25.

THREE LANDSCAPE VIEWS ON THE WINNIPISOGE [sic] LAKE.
    AAU, 1828, #3.

VIEW FROM THE SUMMIT OF MOUNT WASHINGTON.
    NAD, 1828, #107.

VIEW IN NEW HAMPSHIRE.
    AAU, 1833, #173.

VIEW IN THE WHITE MOUNTAINS.
    1827. Pencil with pen and ink.
    14½ x 10½ (36.8 x 26.7).
    NAD, 1828, #2.

VIEW NEAR CONWAY.
    Engraving.
    44 x 66 (111.8 x 167.6).
    Boston Athenaeum catalog, plate XVI.

New Hampshire Scenery

VIEW NEAR CONWAY.
  1827-28. Engraving.
  Private collection; engraved from Hinton by
  Fenner Sears.

VIEW NEAR TAMWORTH, NEW HAMPSHIRE.
  1827. Pencil with pen and ink.
  14½ x 10½ (36.8 x 26.7).
  Boston Athenaeum catalog.

VIEW OF CORROWAY [sic] PEAK, NH.
  NAD, 1828, #48.

VIEW OF THE SLIDES THAT DESTROYED THE
WHILLEY [sic] FAMILY, WHITE MOUNTAINS.
  1830-35. Lithograph.
  Albany Institute of History and Art (1976);
  Imbert's lithograph.

VIEW OF THE WHITE MOUNTAINS IN NEW
HAMPSHIRE.
  9 x 13 (22.9 x 33).
  Wadsworth Atheneum, Hartford, CT;
  Pre-1877.

VIEW OF THE WHITE MOUNTAINS, NH (MOUNT
WASHINGTON).
  Spring 1827. Oil.
  25½ x 35 (64.8 x 88.9).
  Wadsworth Atheneum, (1974).

VIEW ON LAKE WINNIPISEOGEE [sic].
S/D/L/Center.
  1828.
  19¾ x 26⅛ (50.2 x 66.4).
  Wadsworth Atheneum; NAD, 1829, #54.

WHITE MOUNTAINS SKETCH.
  Boston Athenaeum catalog (no date), p. 41.

WHITE MOUNTAINS, MOUNT CHOCORUA.
  Oil on canvas.
  11¾ x 17¼ (29.8 x 43.8).
  Kennedy *Quarterly* 9:2 (1969), p. 87.

WHITEFACE MOUNTAIN, NEW HAMPSHIRE.
  Oil.
  24 x 28 (61 x 71.1).
  Private collection (1975); BIAP.

Attributed:
MOUNT WASHINGTON FROM THE UPPER
SACO INTERVALE.
  Oil on canvas.
  17 x 32 (43.2 x 81.3).
  NMAA Inventory.

COLEMAN, CHARLES CARYL

A, Ce, C&H, DAB, F, G&W, N, S
Born Buffalo, NY, April 25, 1840.
Died Capri, Italy, Dec. 4, 1928.
Coleman studied under William H. Beard and

*in 1864 exhibited at the Boston Athenaeum. He
was an associate of the NAD who spent most
of his life in Italy. He was a close friend of Elihu
Vedder and frequently sent paintings to the
NAD from 1864 to 1897.*

VIEW ON THE ANDROSCOGGIN.
  Boston Athenaeum (1864), #268.

COLMAN (or COLEMAN), SAMUEL, JR.

A, B, C, C&H, DAB, G&W, K, Ka, S, T
Born Portland, ME, March 4, 1832.
Died New York, NY, March 24, 1920.
*Though Samuel Colman's name is generally
spelled with an "e," the family spelled the name
"Colman" and the Aldine Press in its art column
(1868-79) referred to the artist as Colman. He
studied under Asher Durand and became an
associate of the NAD in 1854 and an academician 10 years later. In 1866 he helped found the
American Society of Painters in Water Colors
and was its first president. He became interested
in etching in 1867 and, in 1877, at the founding
of the New York Etching Club, exhibited a
number of landscape etchings. He spent the
summer of 1856 in Jackson, NH, sharing a
studio with his brother-in-law, Aaron Draper
Shattuck. The Crayon of that year noted: "Mr.
Colman had made wide advances on all his
previous studies. . . .He has a study of Mote [sic]
Mountain and the Ledges at North Conway,
with a wheat-field in the foreground." As early
as 1853, he exhibited at the NAD and shortly
thereafter at the Boston Athenaeum. He was
also a frequent exhibitor at the Brooklyn Art
Association. He visited Spain and Morocco and
painted scenes in a combination of pastel and
guache. He was a partner of Louis Comfort Tif-
fany in interior design and worked on Samuel
Clemens's house in Hartford, CT. For a time he
was a member of the Century Association but
resigned in 1884.*

Bibliography:
Archives of American Art. Roll 832.
Craven, Wayne. "Samuel Colman (1832-1920):
Rediscovered Painter of Far-Away Places."
American Art Journal 8:1 (May 1976), pp.
16-37.
Kennedy Galleries catalog. "The Romantic
Landscapes of Samuel Colman" (Sept.-Oct.
1983).

  ARTIST'S BROOK, NORTH CONWAY.
    Boston Athenaeum (1858), #227.

AUTUMN LANDSCAPE.
Oil on canvas.
14¾ x 23¾ (37.5 x 60.5).
Signal Co.

BIRCH TREES, NORTH CONWAY.
Drawing.
14½ x 10½ (36.8 x 26.7).
Baridoff Gallery catalog (Jan.-Feb. 1981), #88.

CHOCORUA.
Oil on canvas.
3 x 5½ (7.6 x 14).
Baridoff Gallery catalog (Jan.-Feb. 1981), #40.

CHOCORUA.
Oil on canvas.
16⅛ x 23 (41 x 58.4).
Baridoff Gallery catalog (Jan.-Feb. 1981), #23.

CHOCORUA POND AND MOUNTAIN.
Boston Athenaeum (1858), #331.

CONWAY ELMS.
NAD, 1858, #122; *Crayon* (1858), p. 147; U.S. Sanitary Commission (1864), #129.

CONWAY MEADOWS.
U.S. Sanitary Commission (1864), #91.

CONWAY VALLEY.
Brooklyn Art Association (1864), #140.

FRANCONIA MOUNTAINS, NH.
NAD, 1853, #173.

GREAT GULF IN THE WHITE MOUNTAINS; THE...
NAD, 1858, #581.

HARVEST SCENE (Mount Washington and Conway Meadows). S/L/R.
Oil on canvas.
10 x 17 (25.4 x 43.2).
Pennsylvania State University, Vessel collection.

HERMIT LAKE AND TUCKERMAN'S RAVINE, WHITE MOUNTAINS.
Boston Athenaeum (1855 or 1856), #199; Pre-1877.

MEADOWS AND WILDFLOWERS AT CONWAY.
1856. Oil.
16 x 14 (40.6 x 35.6).
Vassar College Art Gallery (1976); *American Art Journal* (May 1976), p. 18.

MOUNT WASHINGTON, CONWAY VALLEY.
Oil on canvas.
30 x 46 (76.2 x 116.8).

Richard Bourne, Inc., catalog (Aug. 14, 1979), #127.

NEAR CONWAY.
1866-67. Engraving.
Ladies' Repository.

ON THE ELLIS RIVER.
10 x 16½ (25.4 x 41.9).
Baridoff Gallery catalog (Jan.-Feb. 1981), #92.

ON THE SACO, WHITE MOUNTAINS.
NAD, 1878, #608.

ROCKS NEAR COMPTON [sic].
Oil.
9½ x 14 (24.1 x 35.6).
Baridoff Gallery catalog (Jan.-Feb. 1981), #86.

SUMMER LANDSCAPE (Conway Meadows and Moat Mountain). S/L/L.
Oil on canvas.
15 x 24 (38.1 x 61).
Pennsylvania State University, Vessel collection.

SUMMER ON THE SACO.
NAD, 1854, #75.

TWILIGHT, NEW HAMPSHIRE, RIVER SCENERY.
Brooklyn Art Association (1866), #117.

WHITE MOUNTAIN SCENERY.
Brooklyn Art Association (1866), #56.

WILLEY RAVINE.
U.S. Sanitary Commission (Feb. 1864), #11.

CONNER, JAMES L.
Ce, F(sup), G&W, N
Born Northfield, NH. Active 1849-69.
Little is known of Conner. He married in 1841 and is listed as a portrait painter in Lynn, MA, in 1849. When he exhibited at the NAD in 1858, he listed his address as Brooklyn, NY. He also exhibited there in 1869.

VIEW IN NEW HAMPSHIRE.
NAD, 1858, #218.

COOMBS, DELBERT DANA
A
Born Lisbon Falls, ME, July 26, 1850.
Died probably in Auburn, ME, after 1927.
Primarily self-taught, Coombs painted steadily for well over 50 years. Though known as a portraitist (many eminent Maine citizens sat for him), he also painted landscapes and cattle. He had a studio in Boston for several winters, but his major work was pursued in Maine, for he

New Hampshire Scenery

gave lessons in painting in Lisbon, ME, for 25 years.

Bibliography:
Maine Library *Bulletin* 13 (July-Oct. 1927), p. 7.

LANDSCAPE (Androscoggin).
Late 19th century.
17 x 11 (43.2 x 27.9).
Anderson Auction Galleries (April 27, 1905), #36.

NEW HAMPSHIRE MOUNTAINS (Mount Washington).
Oil on canvas.
14½ x 25½ (36.8 x 64.8).
Robert Goldberg (lost in 1979 fire).

COULSON, NELLIE MAGOON

Nothing is presently known about this artist.
SACO RIVER FROM INTERVALE.
1885.
Private collection; NMAA Inventory.

CRAIG, THOMAS BIGELOW (or BIEGELOW)

F, N, R, S
Born Philadelphia, PA, 1849.
Died New York, NY, 1924.
Craig was elected an associate member of the NAD and exhibited there from 1879 to 1900. He also exhibited at the PAFA and the Boston Art Club. He listed his residence as Philadelphia from 1879 to 1888, after which he moved to New York City for nine years, and then to the suburb of Rutherford, NJ.

WHITE MOUNTAIN LANDSCAPE.
1880. Oil.
30⅛ x 50⅜ (76.5 x 128.6).
Philadelphia Museum of Art (1975); NMAA Inventory.

CRAIG, WILLIAM C.

A, C&H, F, G&W, K, Ka, N, S
Born Dublin, Ireland, 1829.
Died Lake George, NY, by drowning, 1875.
Primarily a watercolorist, Craig came to the U.S. in 1863. He was one of the founding members of the American Society of Painters in Water Colors. The Art Journal for Oct. 1875 wrote: "Craig's early pictures were admirable specimens of the art, tender yet brilliant in tone, and possessed of that peculiar transparency of colouring which is so noticeable in the works of the English school. Of late, however, Mr. Craig painted almost exclusively for the auction-dealers, and his work appeared to lose quality as it increased in quantity" (quoted from Karolik). He exhibited at the NAD from 1864 to 1870.

MOUNT WASHINGTON.
American Society of Painters in Water Colors, 1867; Pre-1877.

O'SULLIVAN'S CASCADE, MOUNT WASHINGTON, NH.
1869. Watercolor.
27¾ x 20¾ (70.5 x 52.7).
Adam A. Weschler and Sons (1972); NMAA Inventory.

CRAWFORD, EMMA

Nothing is presently known about this artist.
VIEW OF MOUNT WASHINGTON, WHITE MOUNTAINS.
Pre-1877; Pittsburgh Art Association, (1859).

CRESSWELL, W.

Nothing is presently known about this artist.
GULF OF NEIGES, WHITE MOUNTAINS.
Pre-1877; Society of Canadian Artists, Montreal, 2nd exhibition (Feb. 7, 1870).

CROCKER, J. DENISON

F, G&W
Born Salem, CT, Nov. 25, 1823. Died 1907.
Crocker had some instruction from Charles Lanman but was otherwise self-taught. First a silversmith, he turned to portrait painting about 1840, later adding landscapes.

VIEW IN NEW HAMPSHIRE.
Private collection (1967); NMAA Inventory.

CROCKER, S. S.

The White Mountain Echo for Aug. 6, 1892, noted that Miss S. S. Crocker of Lakewood, NJ, was executing paintings of the Jefferson, NH, area.

CROCKER, V. B.

R
Active 1864.
There is no information on this artist at present.
MOUNT WASHINGTON. S/D/L/L.
1864. Oil on canvas.
30 x 50 (76.2 x 127).
Old Print Shop *Portfolio* 37:3 (1980), p. 71; *Antiques* (Nov. 1980).

CROPSEY, JASPER FRANCIS

A, B, Ce, DAB, F, C&H, G&W, K, Ka, N, R, S, T

Born New York, NY, 1823.

Died Hastings-on-Hudson, NY, June 22, 1900. *Cropsey received his early training as an architect and set up his own office in 1843. He began painting shortly thereafter and first exhibited at the NAD in 1844. A year later, he was elected an associate member and, in 1851, a full member. Cropsey's interest in architecture continued throughout his life and was a strong influence in his painting, most evident in his precise arrangement and outline of forms. But Cropsey was best known for his lavish use of color and, as a first-generation member of the Hudson River School, painted autumn landscapes that startled viewers with their boldness and brilliance. He traveled in Europe from 1847 to 1849, and lived in England from 1856 to 1863. Surviving sketchbooks indicate that Cropsey was in the White Mountains in the summer of 1852 and in 1856. He may have made another visit to the area in 1878. His sketches from nature done on these trips are often marked with color notes as well as the subject or location. Cropsey became interested in Luminism after the Civil War and also in watercolor painting, and founded the American Society of Painters in Water Colors in 1867. He exhibited at the NAD, the PAFA, the Boston Athenaeum, and at the Royal Academy in London. Failing health may have caused his later paintings to be overworked and consequently less popular.*

Select Bibliography:
American Art and Antiques (Nov. 1979), pp. 100-107.
Archives of American Art. Rolls 336-337.
Birmingham, Peter. *Jasper F. Cropsey, 1823-1900; A Retrospective View of America's Painter of Autumn.* College Park, MD: University of Maryland, 1968.
Cropsey, Jasper. *Paper Dealing with the White Mountains.* Washington, DC: Archives of American Art microfilm.
Maddow, Kenneth W. *An Unprejudiced Eye: The Drawings of Jasper F. Cropsey.* Hudson River Museum catalog (Dec. 22, 1979-Feb. 24, 1980).
Talbot, William S. *Jasper Cropsey, 1823-1900.* Washington, DC: National Collection of Fine Arts, Smithsonian Institution, 1970.

AFTERNOON IN AUTUMN, WHITE MOUNTAINS. S/D/L/R.
1856. Oil on canvas.
10 x 16¼ (25.4 x 41.3).
Private collection (1983); Kennedy Galleries (1977).

AMERICAN HARVESTING.
Engraving.
6½ x 10¼ (16.5 x 26).
Old Print Shop (1977). From a painting by Cropsey.

AUSABLE CHASM (ECHO LAKE, FRANCONIA). S/D/L/R.
1875. Oil on canvas.
14 x 24 (35.6 x 61).
Adams-Davidson Gallery, Inc. (1979); *Antiques* (July 1979).

AUTUMN IN AMERICA (Mount Washington).
Crayon (1860), p. 204.

BACKWOODS OF AMERICA. S/D.
1858. Oil on canvas.
42 x 70¼ (106.7 x 178.4).
Sotheby PB (April 23, 1981); *Antiques* (April 1981).

CHOCORUA MOUNTAIN.
Sept. 18, 1852. Pencil.
Hudson River Museum catalog (1979), #55.

CHOCORUA PEAK, 1855.
Oct. 8, 1855. Pencil on buff paper.
11½ x 18 (29.2 x 45.8).
Hudson River Museum catalog (1979), #68.

CONWAY, NEW HAMPSHIRE, SEPT. 13, 1857 [or SEPT. 28, 1858].
1857 or 1858. Drawing.
4¼ x 10½ (10.8 x 26.7).
Boston Museum of Fine Arts, Karolik collection.

EAGLE CLIFF.
54 x 37 (137.2 x 94).
AAU, 1852, #239.

EAGLE CLIFF, FRANCONIA NOTCH, 1852.
Sept. 13, 1852. Pencil on tan paper.
12⅜ x 18⅞ (31.5 x 48).
Hudson River Museum catalog (1979), #53.

EAGLE CLIFF, FRANCONIA NOTCH, NEW HAMPSHIRE. S/L/L.
1858. Oil on canvas.
24 x 39 (61 x 99.1).
North Carolina Museum of Art (1956); BIAP.

EAGLE CLIFF, NEW HAMPSHIRE.
1850. Oil on canvas.
23 x 40 (58.4 x 101.6).
St. Louis Art Museum (1976).

Mount Chocorua, New Hampshire
Benjamin Champney, 1858
Oil on canvas, 12" x 18" / Collection: Museum of Fine Arts, Boston, Bequest
    of Maxim Karolik, 1964 / Ref. page 29

EAGLE CLIFF, NEW HAMPSHIRE (AUTUMN SCENE). S/D.
    1851. Oil on canvas.
    37 x 53 (94 x 134.6).
    Boston Museum of Fine Arts, Karolik collection.

EARLY MORNING ON MOUNT WASHINGTON.
    Pre-1877; Chicago exhibition of fine arts (1859) (see Chicago Historical Society for information).

ELM TREE FROM NOTEBOOK IN THE WHITE MOUNTAINS.
    C. 1858.
    Hudson River Museum catalog (1979), #83.

FRANCONIA NOTCH, WHITE MOUNTAINS.
    1869. Pencil.
    9¾ x 8¾ (24.8 x 22.2).
    Bruce Museum catalog (undated).

INDIAN SUMMER MORNING IN THE WHITE MOUNTAINS. S/L/L.
    1857. Oil on canvas.

39¼ x 61¼ (99.7 x 155.6).
    Currier Gallery of Art (1980).

LANDSCAPE – NORTH CONWAY, NEW HAMPSHIRE.
    1856. Oil.
    10⅝ x 16½ (27 x 41.9).
    Private collection (1968); NMAA Inventory.

MOUNT CHOCORUA AND RAILROAD TRAIN, NEW HAMPSHIRE. S/L/R.
    1869. Oil on canvas.
    20 x 33 (50.8 x 83.8).
    Diplomatic Reception Rooms, State Department; Kennedy Galleries exhibition (1979).

MOUNT CHOCORUA, NEW HAMPSHIRE.
    1863. Oil on canvas.
    28½ x 35½ (72.4 x 90.2).
    Metropolitan Museum of Art; James Graham and Sons (1961).

MOUNT CHOCORUA, NEW HAMPSHIRE.
    1873. Oil on canvas.

Dictionary of Painters

20 x 35¼ (50.8 x 89.5).
Smithsonian Institution catalog (1970), #62.

MOUNT CHOCORUA, NEW HAMPSHIRE, AUTUMN. S/L/L.
C. 1872. Oil on canvas.
28½ x 35½ (72.4 x 90.2).
Metropolitan Museum of Art (1975); Smithsonian Institution catalog (1970), #60.

MOUNT JEFFERSON.
1868.
C&H.

MOUNT JEFFERSON, NEW HAMPSHIRE.
NAD, 1857, #79; exhibited at Paris in 1867 according to Dwight's *Journal of Music* 27 (Aug. 1867), p. 76.

MOUNT MONROE, WHITE MOUNTAINS.
1872 or 1873. Oil on canvas.
10½ x 9¼ (26.7 x 23.5).
Sotheby PB (1973), #590; (again in 1977).

MOUNT WASHINGTON.
Sept. 18, 1852. Pencil.
11⅝ x 17⅜ (29.5 x 44.1).
Corcoran Gallery (July 21-Sept. 2, 1979).

MOUNT WASHINGTON.
NAD, 1855, #35.

MOUNT WASHINGTON FROM CONWAY VALLEY.
Brooklyn Art Association (1884), #232.

MOUNT WASHINGTON FROM LAKE SEBAGO, MAINE.
1867. Oil.
10 x 18 (25.4 x 45.7).
PAFA, 1978.

MOUNT WASHINGTON FROM LAKE SEBAGO, MAINE. S/D/L/L.
1871. Oil.
16 x 30 (40.6 x 76.2).
Mint Museum of Art, Charlotte, NC (1972).

MOUNT WASHINGTON FROM SEBAGO LAKE, MAINE. S/D/L/R.
1867. Oil.
20 x 33 (50.8 x 83.8).
Sotheby PB (1978); *Antiques* (Nov. 1977).

MOUNT WASHINGTON, NEW HAMPSHIRE. S/D/L/L.
1870. Oil on canvas.
20 x 33⅛ (50.8 x 84.2).
Cleveland Museum (1970).

MOUNTAIN SCENE, AUTUMN, 1881 (Mount Washington?).
1881.
Smithsonian Institution catalog (1970), p. 40.

NEW HAMPSHIRE LANDSCAPE.
1862. Oil on canvas.
22½ x 18½ (57.2 x 47).
Coe Kerr Gallery (1976).

NEW HAMPSHIRE SCENERY.
16 x 12 (40.6 x 30.5).
AAU, 1849, #276.

NORTH CONWAY, NEW HAMPSHIRE.
1871. Oil.
10 x 14 (25.4 x 35.6).
Kennedy Galleries (1965).

OLD MAN OF THE MOUNTAINS.
Sept. 13, 1852. Pencil on buff paper.
11¼ x 17¾ (28.6 x 45.1).
Hudson River Museum catalog (1979), #54.

PASTORAL LANDSCAPE, NEW HAMPSHIRE.
1890. Watercolor.
10 x 17¼ (25.4 x 43.8).
Sotheby PB (1979).

PIONEER'S HOME, EAGLE CLIFF, WHITE MOUNTAINS.
1859. Oil on canvas.
19⅛ x 30 (48.6 x 76.2).
Hirschl and Adler Gallery; Charles Shoemaker, *American Art Review* (Sept.-Oct. 1975), p. 76.

PRESIDENTIAL RANGE, NEW HAMPSHIRE.
1872. Oil.
18 x 24 (45.7 x 61).
Smithsonian Institution catalog (1970), #59; private collection (1970).

PRESIDENTIAL RANGE, WHITE MOUNTAINS, NH.
Oil.
26 x 36 (66 x 91.4).
Schweitzer Gallery, N.Y.C. (April 1965).

SCENE IN THE WHITE MOUNTAINS.
NAD, 1860, #569.

SUNSET, EAGLE CLIFF, NEW HAMPSHIRE. S/L/R.
32½ x 44 (82.6 x 111.8).
Frick Art Reference Library notes.

SUNSET, EAGLE CLIFF, NEW HAMPSHIRE. S/L/R.
1851. Oil.
37 x 53 (94 x 134.6).
Boston Museum of Fine Arts, Karolik collection (1969); NAD, 1851.

SUNSET, EAGLE CLIFF, NEW HAMPSHIRE.
1867. Oil.

New Hampshire Scenery

8⅛ x 12⅛ (20.7 x 30.8).
Private collection (1970).

VIEW FROM MOUNT WILLARD.
  Sept. 1852.
  11 x 17 (27.9 x 43.2).
  Addison Gallery, Andover, MA.

WHITE MOUNTAIN LAKE SCENERY.
  1859. Lithograph.
  Cropsey, Jasper. *American Scenery* (London, 1859).

WHITE MOUNTAIN LANDSCAPE.
  1860. Oil.
  12¾ x 19½ (32.4 x 49.5).
  Private collection (1960); NMAA Inventory.

WHITE MOUNTAIN NOTCH. S/L/L.
  1852. Pencil on buff paper.
  9 ¹¹/₁₆ x 8¾ (24.6 x 22.2).
  Hudson River Museum catalog (1979), #56.

WHITE MOUNTAIN SCENERY (Mount Jefferson?).
  Watercolor.
  American Society of Painters in Water Colors (1869); Boston Art Club (1882), #180.

WHITE MOUNTAIN STUDIES, 1852. D/L/L.
  Sept. 18, 1852. Pencil on tan paper.
  12 x 9⅜ (30.5 x 23.9).
  Hudson River Museum catalog (1979).

WHITE MOUNTAIN, NEW HAMPSHIRE.
  Oil.
  20 x 12 (50.8 x 30.5).
  Coe Kerr Gallery (1977).

WHITE MOUNTAINS IN AUTUMN.
  Oil on canvas.
  21 x 35¼ (53.3 x 89.5).
  Georgia Museum of Art (1975).

WINTER LANDSCAPE, NORTH CONWAY, NEW HAMPSHIRE. S/D/L/R.
  1859. Oil on canvas.
  10¼ x 16½ (26 x 41.9).
  Private collection (1980); Whitney Downtown Gallery, N.Y.C. (June-July 1980).

WINTER, CHOCORUA PEAK, WHITE MOUNTAINS.
  NAD, 1857, #456.

WINTER (Conway Valley, New Hampshire). S/D/L/R.
  1859. Oil on canvas.
  9 ⁷/₁₆ x 15 ⁷/₁₆ (24 x 39.2).
  Private collecton; Hirschl and Adler Gallery (Oct.-Nov. 1969), #19D.

CUSTER, EDWARD L.
A, B, G&W, N, R, S
Born Basel, Switzerland, Jan. 24, 1837.
Died Boston, MA, Jan. 8, 1881.
Custer came to the U.S. with his family at about the age of 10, living first in Syracuse, NY, and later in Manchester, NH. There is no information on his training, but the Aldine for 1876-77 noted that he painted "a landscape studied in New Hampshire in early autumn, [which] is poetic in color and artistic in treatment." He exhibited as early as 1848 at the Boston Athenaeum, and later at the NAD and the PAFA.

A NEW HAMPSHIRE LANDSCAPE.
  1876.
  Aldine 7:1 (1876-77), p. 32.

DIXVILLE NOTCH. Signed.
  1864. Oil on canvas.
  11½ x 17½ (29.2 x 44.5).
  Balsams Hotel received from private collector who bought from Robert Goldberg.

D

DANA, J. F.

Probably **James Freeman Dana.**
A, DAB, G&W
Born Amherst, NH, Sept. 23, 1793.
Died New York, NY, April 14, 1827.
James Freeman Dana moved with his family to Exeter, NH, in 1804 and attended Phillips Exeter Academy. He graduated from Harvard in 1813 after studying chemistry, geology, and medicine, and received an M.D. degree in 1817. He moved to Hanover, NH, later that year to teach chemistry to medical students at Dartmouth. In 1818 he published Outlines of Mineralogy and Geology of Boston and Its Vicinity, *with his brother. Dana executed views of Dartmouth College and the White Mountains, paintings which were engraved by Abel Bowen.*

NEW HAMPSHIRE MOUNTAINS.
    Before 1823.
    Engraving.
    1823 *Gazeteer;* Stauffer, D. M., *American Engraving.* Vol. 5, p. 3.

DANFORTH, C. A.

No information is presently available on this artist.
WINNIPISEOGEE [sic] LAKE.
    MA Charitable (1874), #182.

DARLEY, FELIX OCTAVIUS CARR

A, C, C&H, DAB, F, G&W, Ka, N, T
Born Philadelphia, PA, June 23, 1822.
Died Claymont, DE, March 27, 1888.
Darley began as an apprentice in a mercantile house in Philadelphia but gradually worked his way into illustration. He became a prolific and popular illustrator and was made a member of the NAD by 1852, exhibiting there from 1845 through 1874. In 1859, after his marriage, he moved to Claymont, DE, where he drew for many books, magazines, bank note companies, and print producers. Though his work was mostly black and white, he also produced watercolors. He said of himself that he led an uneventful life and spent many of his summers hunting and fishing.

ANDROSCOGGIN RIVER.
    Watercolor.
    9⅜ x 14 (23.8 x 35.6).
    Delaware Art Museum (1975); NMAA Inventory.

DARLING, FRANK H.

There is presently no information on this artist.
AUTUMN (WHITE MOUNTAINS).
    Oil.
    Pre-1877; 8th Industrial Mechanics Institute of San Francisco, CA (Aug. 1879).

DARRAH, ANN SOPHIA TOWNE (MRS. ROBERT, K.)

A, C&H, G&W, R
Born Philadelphia, PA., Sept. 30, 1819.
Died Manchester, MA, Dec. 24, 1881.
A pupil of Paul Weber, Darrah exhibited at the Boston Athenaeum from 1855 to 1864 and the PAFA from 1856 to 1863. She was a competent artist whose long career included executing pastel portraits, landscapes, and marine views. In 1858 she took part in the Bierstadt Exhibition in New Bedford. In 1867 Darrah moved to Boston where she exhibited at the 1879 Contemporary Art Exhibit at the Boston Museum of Fine Arts. Sixty oils and 202 watercolors and charcoals were exhibited at a memorial exhibition of her work at the Museum of Fine Arts in Boston in 1882.

CRAWFORD NOTCH.
    1870. Oil on canvas.
    Private collection (1974).
MOUNT CHOCORUA.
    Boston Athenaeum (1856), #136.
MOUNT WASHINGTON.
    Boston Athenaeum (1858), #124.
WHITE MOUNTAINS; THE...
    Boston Athenaeum (1857), #323.

DAVIS, H. A.

There is no present information on this artist.
NEW HAMPSHIRE LANDSCAPE. S/L/R.
    Oil on canvas.
    22 x 36 (55.9 x 91.4).
    Baridoff Gallery auction (July 11, 1981).

DEFREES, T.

Active 1878-87.

Almost nothing is known of this White Mountain artist except that he/she was probably Belgian or French. Defrees's style of painting shows strong influence of the French Barbizon School. Instances of European artists coming to America to paint the landscape are significantly more rare than American painters in Europe, but the presence of Defrees in the White Mountains from around 1880 to at least 1887 indicates that the exchange occurred. He/she exhibited at the Boston Art Club in January 1878.

EARLY MORNING, MOUNT WASHINGTON.
  Oil.
  Boston Art Club (Jan. 16-Feb. 9, 1878), #153.

JACKSON ROAD TO BLACK MOUNTAIN
(Christmas Farm Inn).
  1880.
  Private collection (1974).

MIDSUMMER MORNING, MOAT MOUNTAIN FROM HILLSIDE PASTURE, JACKSON, NH. One of pair.
  1887. Oil.
  University Art Gallery catalog, University of New Hampshire (1980), p. 90.

MIDSUMMER MORNING, OLD TREES ON THE FIVE MILE ROAD, JACKSON, NH. S/L/R. One of pair.
  1887. Oil on canvas.
  14 x 24 (35.6 x 61).
  University Art Gallery catalog, University of New Hampshire (1980), #103.

MOUNTAIN HOMESTEAD, JACKSON, NEW HAMPSHIRE.
  1888.
  10 x 16 (25.4 x 40.6).
  Parke-Bernet (1945).

DE GRAILLY, VICTOR

G&W

Born Paris, France, Nov. 6, 1804.
Died France, 1889.

De Grailly learned his craft under the French artist, Jean Victor Bertin. At the Salon from 1830 to 1880, he regularly exhibited landscapes in the manner of, or as direct copies from, seventeenth-century Dutch masters. Copies by him of Van Ruisdael and Hobbema are known. However, De Grailly's most successful work seems to have been the execution of parlor-sized canvases after engravings of William Henry Bartlett's views of the eastern United States in American Scenery, *published in England in*

1838. Though there is no reason to think that De Grailly ever left his native country, such a number of the American views after Bartlett are in this country, often several representations of the same scene, that one wonders whether there was an outlet for his work in the United States.

Bibliography:
Banks, William Nathaniel. "The French Painter Victor De Grailly and the Production of Nineteenth-Century American Views." *Antiques* (July 1972), pp. 84-103.
Sears, Clara Endicott. *Highlights Among the Hudson River Artists.* Boston: Houghton Mifflin, 1947, pp. 1-2.

SILVER CASCADE.
  Haller Gallery.

SILVER CASCADE (after Doughty). S/L/R.
  Oil on canvas.
  25½ x 21 (64.8 x 53.3).
  Private collection (1983).

SILVER CASCADE (unsigned).
  C. 1845. Oil on canvas.
  24¾ x 20½ (62.2 x 52.1).
  Washburn Gallery (1975); Fruitlands Museum (1974).

SILVER CASCADE, WHITE MOUNTAINS (after Doughty). S/L/L.
  C. 1845. Oil.
  24¾ x 20½ (62.9 x 52.1).
  Fruitlands Museum (1974).

DE HAAS, WILLIAM FREDERICK

C&H, G&W, N, R, S

Born Rotterdam, Holland, 1830.
Died Fayal, Azores, July 16, 1880.

De Haas studied at the Hague before coming to the United States at the age of 24, where he made his home in New York City at the 10th Street Studio Building. Though mainly a marine painter like his brother, Mauritz De Haas, he also executed landscapes. He exhibited frequently at the NAD after 1865. He did many paintings of the Maine coast.

EARLY MORN, WHITE MOUNTAINS.
  Pre-1877; Utica (NY) Art Association exhibition (1871) (see Utica Public Library for information).

ON THE SACO, NEW HAMPSHIRE.
  NAD, 1867, #463.

DICKERMAN, A.

Nothing is presently known of this artist.

ECHO LAKE.
  MA Charitable (1881), #195.
SMOKE CLOUDS AFTER THE GREAT FIRE,
BAKER'S RIVER, NEW HAMPSHIRE.
  MA Charitable (1878), #437E.

DOGGETT, S.
Nothing is presently known of this artist.
NEW HAMPSHIRE SCENERY.
  Leonard Auction (March 23, 1865), #6.

DOLBEAR, AMOS EMERSON
Born Norwich, CT, Nov. 10, 1837.
Died after 1902.
Dolbear can be classified as an amateur artist because his main forte was in the field of science. He graduated from Ohio Wesleyan University and took a degree in mechanical engineering at the University of Michigan in 1867. He became a professor of physics and astronomy at Tufts College in 1874 and returned to Michigan for his advanced degree in 1883. Before becoming involved in science, Dolbear became interested in lithography, and, at 23 years of age, established a press for the practice of the art in Springfield, MA, with Bradley as printer.
Bibliography:
Allison, Hildreth M. "Some Painters of the Grand Monadnock." *Appalachia* 34 (1962-63), pp. 441-453.
MOUNT MONADNOCK. Signed.
  1860-64. Colored lithograph by Bradley, Springfield, MA.
  12⅝ x 15⅜ (32.1 x 39.1).
  Kennedy Galleries (1980);
  Peterborough Historical Society.

DOLPH, JOHN HENRY
B, C&H, F, G&W, N, R, T
Born Fort Ann, NY, April 18, 1835.
Died New York, NY, Sept. 28, 1903.
Although he was an exhibitor at the NAD as early as 1864, Dolph did not become an associate member until 1877 and a full member in 1898. Generally known as a painter of animals, he began as a portrait painter and also executed some landscapes.
Bibliography:
Historical New Hampshire (Summer 1965).
FRANCONIA MOUNTAIN.
  Oil on canvas.
  8 x 12 (20.3 x 30.5).

New Hampshire Historical Society exhibition (1965).

DOUGHTY, THOMAS
A, B, C, Ce, C&H, DAB, E, F, G&W, K, R, S, T
Born Philadelphia, PA, July 19, 1793.
Died New York, NY, July 24, 1856.
Doughty's first vocation was as a leather currier. It was not until 1820, at the age of almost 30, that he decided, "contrary to the wishes of my friends and family, to pursue painting as a profession." Encouraged by Thomas Sully, Doughty painted the scenery around Philadelphia and learned to master the effects of light and shade and the use of color. His first visit to New England was probably between 1820 and 1828. He was elected to membership at the NAD and exhibited there and at the PAFA and the Boston Athenaeum during the same period. From 1828 to 1838 he lived and worked in Boston, traveling in the summers to the White Mountains. Doughty, Alvan Fisher, and Chester Harding stayed at Thompson's Tavern in North Conway in those early years for two dollars a week. He journeyed to England in 1838-39 and again from 1845 to 1847. Doughty died in 1856 with his popularity as an artist waning. Though he was one of the first artists to visit the White Mountains, his painting was generally of a modest and unspectacular nature. James Thomas Flexner wrote of Doughty that his was "the first incomplete statement of the style of the Hudson River School."
Bibliography:
Doughty, Howard. *Life and Works of Thomas Doughty.* New-York Historical Society.
Fine Arts Source Materials Newsletter 1:1 (Jan. 1971). John Alan Walker, OP Art Books: Panorama City, CA, 91402.
Goodyear, Frank H., Jr. *Thomas Doughty, 1793-1856: An American Pioneer in Landscape Painting.* Philadelphia: Pennsylvania Academy of the Fine Arts, 1973.
A SUMMER SHOWER IN THE MOUNTAINS AT NEW HAMPSHIRE.
  1845. Oil.
  Fine Arts Source Material Newsletter (Jan. 1971), p. 19, #346.
AUTUMN, VIEW OF SWIFT RIVER, NEW HAMPSHIRE.
  Hardings Gallery (May 1834), #54.
ECHO LAKE (FRANCONIA).
  1836. Oil on canvas.

New Hampshire Scenery

20¾ x 28⅛ (52.7 x 71.4).
Georgia Museum of Art (1979).

FISHING DOWN ON THE FARM. Signed.
Oil on canvas.
28 x 36 (71.1 x 91.4).
Kennedy Galleries.

LANDSCAPE WITH FOOTBRIDGE AND FIGURES.
1835. Oil on canvas.
27 x 34 (68.6 x 86.4).
Private collection.

LANDSCAPE, MOUNT LAFAYETTE, NEW HAMPSHIRE.
Pre-1877; Albany Gallery of Fine Arts, 1st exhibition (1846).

LANDSCAPE, NEW HAMPSHIRE, SCENERY FROM RECOLLECTION.
AAU, 1838, #183.

NEW HAMPSHIRE LAKE. S/L/L.
C. 1828-30. Oil.
26 x 36 (66 x 91.4).
Boston Museum of Fine Arts, Karolik collection (1969).

NEW HAMPSHIRE LANDSCAPE.
C. 1840. Oil.
14½ x 18¾ (36.8 x 47.6).
Childs Gallery (1968).

NEW HAMPSHIRE SCENERY, NEAR MOUNT WASHINGTON – A SHOWERY DAY.
Before 1843. Oil.
Fine Arts Source Material Newsletter
(Jan. 1971), p. 17, #292.

RIVER SCENE WITH HUNTER AND FISHERMAN (Chocorua).
C. 1832.
28 x 36 (71.1 x 91.4).
Private collection (1950); Frick Art Reference Library notes.

SCENE IN NEW HAMPSHIRE.
1850.
30 x 21 (76.2 x 53.3).
AAU, 1850, #47; Fine Arts Source Material Newsletter (Jan. 1971), p. 18, #332.

SCENE ON SQUAM LAKE.
Oil.
31 x 21 (78.7 x 53.3).
Private collection (1971); NMAA Inventory;
AAU, 1840, #138.

SILVER CASCADE.
Before 1835.

SILVER CASCADE.
C. 1838.

SILVER CASCADE, NH FROM RECOLLECTION
(or LANDSCAPE, SILVER CASCADE).
Oil.
NMAA Inventory; private collection (1971);
AAU, 1841, #102.

SILVER CASCADE, WHITE MOUNTAINS, NEW HAMPSHIRE.
C. 1838. Oil.
25½ x 21 (64.8 x 53.3).
Private collection (1973); engraved for Willis, N.P. American Scenery.

SPORTSMAN BY A LAKE. S/D/L/R.
1835. Oil on canvas.
20 x 24¼ (50.8 x 61.6).
Private collection (1983); Vose Galleries.

SQUAM LAKE, NEW HAMPSHIRE.
Hardings Gallery (May 1834), #33.

SQUAM LAKE, NEW HAMPSHIRE, FROM RECOLLECTION.
Oil.
Fine Arts Source Material Newsletter
(Jan. 1971), p. 19, #337; AAU, 1841, #41.

STUDY OF WHITE MOUNTAINS SCENERY.
Hardings Gallery (1834), #37; Pre-1877.

TUCKERMAN'S RAVINE.
Oil on canvas.
19 x 27 (48.3 x 68.6).
Allen Memorial Art Museum (1980).

VIEW IN NEW HAMPSHIRE. S/L/L.
26 x 36 (66 x 91.4).
Boston Museum of Fine Arts, Karolik collection (1952); Currier Gallery exhibition (July 8-Aug. 17, 1952).

VIEW NEAR CONWAY, NEW HAMPSHIRE.
Oil.
Fine Arts Source Material Newsletter
(Jan. 1971), p. 21, #373; AAU, 1838, #91.

VIEW OF NEW HAMPSHIRE LAKE.
C. 1835. Oil.
11¾ x 17 (29.8 x 43.2).
Boston Museum of Fine Arts, Karolik collection (1969).

VIEW OF THE RIVER FROM THE WHITE MOUNTAINS.
Oil.
NMAA Inventory; Fine Arts Source Material Newsletter (Jan. 1971).

VIEW ON THE SACO.
Hardings Gallery (May 1834), #58.

VIEW OF THE WINNEPISCOGE [sic] LAKE.
Oil.
NMAA Inventory; AAU, 1838, #103.

Dictionary of Painters

VIEW TOWARD THE WHITE MOUNTAINS.
S/L/R.
   1832.
   14 x 18 (35.6 x 45.7).
   Frick Art Reference Library notes.
WINTER IN NEW HAMPSHIRE.
   Hardings Gallery (1834), #51.

DRYER, H. L. (MISS)

Nothing is presently known of this artist.
SUNSET IN THE WHITE MOUNTAINS.
   Pre-1877; Utica (NY) Art Association (1866).

DUGGAN, PETER PAUL

A, C, Ce, C&H, F, G&W, K, N, R, S, T
Born Ireland, c. 1810.
Died Paris, France, Oct. 15, 1861.
Duggan apparently came to the U.S. as a very
young child. He became an associate of the
NAD in 1850, a member in 1852, and a member
of the Century Association in 1849. He was a
frequent exhibitor at the AAU and the NAD un-
til ill health forced him to retire in 1856. The
Crayon *for that year noted, "P. P. Duggan,*
Esq., Professor of Drawing at the Free Academy
sailed for Europe in the Erricson, *on 13th*
September. Mr. Duggan visits Europe on ac-
count of his health." The artist was an ac-
complished medalist.
EAGLES [sic] CRAG, WHITE MOUNTAINS.
   NAD, 1851, #222.

DUNCANSON, ROBERT S.

A, Ba, C, G&W, S
Born New York State, 1821.
Died Detroit, MI, Dec. 21, 1872.
Duncanson was a black landscapist who grew
up in Canada. His adult life was spent in Cin-
cinnati and Detroit. He exhibited there and at
the AAU in 1850.
LANDSCAPE, NEW HAMPSHIRE.
   1862. Oil.
   20 x 16 (50.8 x 40.6).
   NMAA Inventory.

DUNNING, ROBERT SPEAR

Ba, C, Ce, F(sup), G&W, N, S
Born Brunswick, ME, 1829.
Died Westport Harbor, MA, Aug. 12, 1905.
Dunning was painting in oils by 1850 when he
exhibited at the AAU and the NAD. In 1870 he
founded the Fall River (MA) Evening Drawing
School. Though primarily a painter of still lifes,
Dunning made frequent visits to New Hamp-
shire to paint landscapes.
Bibliography:
Gerdts, William H., and Russell Burke.
American Still-Life Paintings (1971).
MOUNT CHOCORUA.
   1864. Oil.
   6½ x 10½ (16.5 x 26.7).
   NMAA Inventory.
STUDY FROM NATURE, WELCH MOUNTAIN.
S/Reverse.
   1864. Oil on canvas.
   6 x 10 (15.2 x 25.4).
   Private collection.
TROUTING AT CAMPTON, NEW HAMPSHIRE.
   1876. Oil.
   7¼ x 12 (18.4 x 30.5).
   Childs Gallery (Fall 1970).
WEST COMPTON [sic], NEW HAMPSHIRE.
S/D.
   1896.
   10 x 13 (25.4 x 33).
   Richard Bourne, Inc., catalog (1976), #108.

DURAND, ASHER BROWN

A, B, C, Ce, C&H, DAB, E, F, G&W, K, Ka,
N, R, S, T
Born Jefferson Village (now Maplewood), NJ,
Aug. 21, 1796.
Died Maplewood, NJ, Sept. 17, 1886.
Son of a watchmaker and silversmith, Durand
served a five-year apprenticeship to an engraver,
Peter Maverick, in Newark, NJ, after which he
became a partner in the business. His reputa-
tion as an engraver was firmly established with
the publication of his engraving after John
Trumbull's DECLARATION OF IN-
DEPENDENCE *in 1823. Between 1821 and 1831*
Durand helped found the New York Drawing
Association (1825), the NAD (1826), and the
Sketch Club (1827) and formed a partnership
with his brother Cyrus and Charles C. Wright,
which specialized in the production of bank
notes. In 1832 Durand dissolved his profitable
engraving business and entered into a short, suc-
cessful period as a portrait painter. A financial
panic in 1837 combined with encouragement
from Thomas Cole led him to try landscape
painting. He became the second president of the
NAD in 1845, a position he held until his
resignation in 1861, and in 1847 helped found
the Century Association. He visited the White
Mountains as early as 1839, and again from
1855 to 1857. The Crayon *for November 1856*

New Hampshire Scenery

View of Meredith
E. C. Coates, 1863
Oil on canvas / 23 ¹/₂" x 35 ¹/₂" / Private collection, photograph courtesy of
       Kennedy Galleries, New York / Ref. page 34

noted, "Mr. *Durand's* sketches of West Campton scenery, . . . *are both larger and of a*
character different from previous studies, being
almost wholly confined to mountain views." He
spent the rest of his life after 1857 painting in
New York City.

Select Bibliography:
Archives of American Art. Rolls N19-N21,
NY59/18, NY59/19, N25.
Craven, Wayne. "Asher B. Durand's Imaginary
Landscapes." *Antiques* (Nov. 1979), pp.
1120-1127.
Durand, John. *The Life and Times of Asher B.*
Durand. New York: Charles Scribner's Sons,
1894; reprint, NY: Da Capo Press, 1970.
Gussow, Alan. *A Sense of Place: The Artist and*
the American Land. San Francisco: Friends of
the Earth, 1973.
Montclair Art Museum catalog. *A. B. Durand,*
1796-1886. Montclair, NJ (Oct. 24-Nov. 28,
1971).

A GLIMPSE OF NEW HAMPSHIRE.
    1879. Oil.
    11½ x 16 (29.2 x 40.6).
    NMAA Inventory.
A PIONEER SETTLEMENT (Winnipesaukee?).
S/L/L.
    1853. Oil on canvas.
    48 x 72 (121.9 x 182.9).
    Boston Public Library, special clippings file.
CHOCORUA PEAK. S/L/R.
    1855. Pencil on paper.
    9 ¹⁵/₁₆ x 13⅞ (25.2 x 35.2).
    New-York Historical Society, Durand
    sketchbook.
CHOCORUA. S/L/R.
    1859. Oil on canvas.
    19 x 26¼ (48.3 x 66.7).
    Vose Galleries.

DREAM OF ARCADIA.
   1851. Engraving.
   6½ x 10¼ (16.5 x 26).
   Old Print Shop; AAU, 1851, #13.

EDGE OF THE FOREST.
   1871. Oil on canvas.
   78 x 64 (198.1 x 162.6).
   Corcoran Gallery.

FRANCONIA NOTCH.
   NAD, 1874, #264.

FRANCONIA, WHITE MOUNTAINS. S/L/L.
   C. 1857. Oil on canvas.
   20 x 30 (50.8 x 76.2).
   New-York Historical Society (1980).

IN NEW HAMPSHIRE.
   NAD, 1858, #585.

IN THE WHITE MOUNTAINS.
   Pre-1877; PAFA, 1864, to benefit U.S.
   Sanitary Commission.

IN THE WOODS, NORTH CONWAY.
   1855.
   Gussow, Alan. *A Sense of Place* (1973);
   Pre-1877.

LEDGES, NORTH CONWAY, NEW HAMPSHIRE.
   Before 1869. Oil.
   NMAA Inventory.

LONE TRAVELER (MOUNT WASHINGTON);
THE. . .
   Private collection.

MOUNT CHOCORUA.
   1855. Oil on canvas.
   41¼ x 60 (104.8 x 152.4).
   Rhode Island School of Design Museum of
   Art, Providence, RI.

MOUNT CHOCORUA, NEW HAMPSHIRE.
   Oil on canvas.
   27 x 39 (68.6 x 99.1).
   Joslyn Art Museum, Omaha, NE (1970).

MOUNT CHOCORUA, NEW HAMPSHIRE,
Aug. 22, 1855.
   1855. Pencil on paper.
   9 $^{15}/_{16}$ x 13⅞ (25.2 x 35.2).
   New-York Historical Society.

MOUNT CHOCORUA, WHITE MOUNTAINS, NH
(or CHOCORUA, WHITE MOUNTAIN SCENE).
S on frame.
   1855. Oil on millboard.
   10 x 14 (25.4 x 35.6).
   New-York Historical Society.

MOUNT KEARSARGE, NORTH CONWAY, NEW
HAMPSHIRE. S/L/R.
   Pencil on paper.
   9 x 11⅜ (22.9 x 28.9).
   New York Public Library, Prints Division;
   Whitney Downtown Gallery, N.Y.C. (June-
   July 1980).

MOUNT LAFAYETTE FROM FRANCONIA IRON-
WORKS, NEW HAMPSHIRE.
   1855. Pencil on paper.
   10 x 14 (25.4 x 35.6).
   New-York Historical Society.

MOUNT WASHINGTON FROM CONWAY
VALLEY. S/L/R.
   1855. Oil on canvas.
   16¾ x 23¾ (42.5 x 60.3).
   Private collection (1984); Childs Gallery
   (1983); NMAA Inventory.

MOUNT WASHINGTON FROM THORNE [sic]
HILL, NH, 1855.
   Sept. 25, 1855. Pencil on paper.
   9 $^{15}/_{16}$ x 13⅞ (25.2 x 35.2).
   New-York Historical Society.

MOUNT WASHINGTON, NEW HAMPSHIRE.
   Before 1869. Oil.
   NMAA Inventory.

NEW HAMPSHIRE LANDSCAPE.
   Oil on canvas.
   22 x 18 (55.9 x 45.7).
   Baridoff Gallery (1981); *Art and Antiques*
   (April 1981).

New Hampshire Scenery

NEW HAMPSHIRE SCENERY, FRANCONIA NOTCH.
 1857. Oil.
 35¼ x 54 (89.5 x 137.2).
 Hirschl and Adler Gallery (1972); NAD, 1858, #431.

NOTCH HOUSE, WHITE MOUNTAINS, NH, JULY 3, 1839.
 1839. Pencil on paper.
 10¼ x 14⅜ (26 x 36.5).
 New-York Historical Society.

ON THE PEMIGEWASSET.
 Brooklyn Art Association (1864), #17.

PASTORAL SCENE IN WEST CAMPTON, NH. S/L/R.
 C. 1855-57. Oil on canvas.
 20 x 30 (50.8 x 76.2).
 New-York Historical Society.

PEMIGEWASSET SCENERY.
 Brooklyn Art Association (1862), #171.

PLAIN AND MOUNTAIN, NORTH CONWAY, NEW HAMPSHIRE, 1855.
 Aug. 18, 1855. Pencil on paper.
 9 $^{15}/_{16}$ x 13⅞ (25.2 x 35.2).
 New-York Historical Society.

RIVER VALLEY AND DISTANT HILLS, CAMPTON, NH, 1855.
 Oct. 11, 1855. Pencil on paper.
 9 $^{15}/_{16}$ x 13⅞ (25.2 x 35.2).
 New-York Historical Society.

RIVER WITH HILLS, BEYOND WEST CAMPTON, NH, 1855.
 Oct. 12, 1855. Pencil on paper.
 9 $^{15}/_{16}$ x 13⅞ (25.2 x 35.2).
 New-York Historical Society.

SACO RIVER, NEW HAMPSHIRE.
 Aug. 25, 1855. Pencil on paper.
 9 $^{15}/_{16}$ x 13⅞ (25.2 x 35.2).
 New-York Historical Society.

SUNSET ON CHOCORUA.
 1876.
 Durand, John. *The Life and Times of Asher B. Durand*, p. 199.

VALLEY WITH MOUNTAIN RANGE BEYOND, NEW HAMPSHIRE.
 C. 1855. Pencil with white highlights.
 9 $^{15}/_{16}$ x 13⅞ (25.2 x 35.2).
 New-York Historical Society.

VIEW ACROSS A VALLEY TO DISTANT MOUNTAINS, MOUNT WASHINGTON, NH.
 C. 1855. Pencil on paper.
 10 x 14 $^{1}/_{16}$ (25.4 x 35.7).
 New-York Historical Society.

VIEW ACROSS THE VALLEY TO A DISTANT RANGE OF MOUNTAINS, NH.
 C. 1855. Pencil on paper.
 9 $^{15}/_{16}$ x 13⅞ (25.2 x 35.2).
 New-York Historical Society.

VIEW IN NEW HAMPSHIRE. S/L/L.
 C. 1855-57.
 16¾ x 24 (42.5 x 61).
 New-York Historical Society.

VIEW IN NEW HAMPSHIRE.
 C. 1855-57. Oil on canvas.
 20 x 30 (50.8 x 76.2).
 New-York Historical Society.

WELCH MOUNTAIN. S/D/L/L.
 1863. Oil on canvas.
 20½ x 30¼ (52.1 x 76.8).
 Nelson-Atkins Museum of Art, Kansas City, MO (1983).

WHITE MOUNTAINS SCENERY, FRANCONIA NOTCH.
 1857. Oil on canvas.
 48 x 72 (121.9 x 182.9).
 New-York Historical Society (1975).

WHITE MOUNTAINS, NEW HAMPSHIRE. S/L/L.
 1853. Oil on canvas.
 16¾ x 23¾ (42.5 x 60.3).
 Childs Gallery (1977).

WINNIPISEOGEE [sic] LAKE (after Cole).
 C. 1830. Engraving.
 Bliss, Elam. *American Landscape*.

E

EDDY, GABRIELLA F.

See White, Gabriella Eddy.

MOUNT MONADNOCK.
Watercolor.
Pre-1877; American Society of Painters in Watercolors (Feb. 26, 1876).

EDSON, ALLAN

There is presently no information on this artist.

MOUNT MADISON, WHITE MOUNTAINS.
Pre-1877; Ontario Society of Artists (June 1874), Toronto.

EDWARDS, THOMAS

A, F, G&W, Ka, S
Active 1825-65.
Edwards was a Boston lithographer with Pendelton in 1825 and was one of the first lithographers to draw on stone with a special type of lithographer's crayon. He exhibited at the Boston Athenaeum between 1827 and 1856, and at the Leonard Auction rooms (Boston) as late as 1865. He published an instruction book entitled Juvenile Drawing Book or Instructions in Landscape Drawing and Painting in Water-Colors, *in 1844.*

NEW HAMPSHIRE SCENERY.
Leonard Auction (May 22, 1863), #177.
VIEW AT CHOCORUA.
Leonard Auction (June 16, 1865), #5.

ELDRED, LEANDER D.

F, N, S
Born Fairhaven, MA, 1851. Died 1921.
Eldred studied under William Bradford and, after studying in Paris at the Académie Julien, he opened a studio in Boston in 1881. He was interested in etching and in light effects. He exhibited at the NAD in 1876.

Bibliography:
Robinson, Frank T. *Living New England Artists.* Boston: Samuel E. Casino, 1888, pp. 53-57.

MOUNT MADISON, VIEW FROM LEAD MINE BRIDGE.
1878. Oil on canvas.

12 x 20 (31 x 50.8).
Private collection (1984); Vose Galleries (1976).

NEW ENGLAND AT DUSK (Madison). S/D/L/L.
1878.
Pierce Galleries, Hingham, MA (1975).

SUMMER LANDSCAPE, WHITE MOUNTAINS, NEW HAMPSHIRE.
1877. Oil.
16 x 25½ (40.6 x 64.8).
Richard Bourne, Inc., catalog (Nov. 27, 1971).

WHITE MOUNTAIN SCENERY.
North Conway Library Exhibition (1965).

ELKINS, HENRY ARTHUR

F, S
Born Vershire, VT, 1847.
Died Georgetown, CO, 1844.
Elkins was self-taught. He moved to Chicago in 1856.

VIEW OF MOUNT WASHINGTON FROM OAK HILL.
Pre-1877; Chicago Industrial Exposition (1875).

ENNEKING, JOHN JOSEPH

B, C&H, DAB, F, Ka, S
Born Minster, OH, Oct. 4, 1841.
Died Hyde Park, MA, Nov. 16 (or 17), 1916.
When Enneking was orphaned at the age of 16 he left his father's farm to live with an aunt. His first art lessons, taken at Mount St. Mary's College in Cincinnati, were interrupted when he enlisted in the Union Army during the Civil War. Severely wounded in action and discharged from service, Enneking eventually made his way to Boston to continue art lessons. For a time he studied industrial drawing and lithography, but dropped it when his eyes weakened. Tinsmithing proved more profitable, and while he flourished at this occupation he married and built a large home in Hyde Park, MA. He became a partner in a wholesale establishment that soon after failed, and again Enneking returned to art. His efforts finally met success, and by the time he sailed for Europe in 1872,

his career as an artist had been assured. His later style became more and more impressionistic, losing much of the grandeur of his earlier European teachers. He won medals in Boston, St. Louis, and at the Pan-American Expositions of 1901 and 1915, in Buffalo and San Francisco, respectively.

Bibliography:
"Exhibition and Sale of Paintings by John J. Enneking," catalog. Vose Galleries (Oct. 20-Dec. 20, 1975), Boston, MA.
Pierce, Patricia Jobe, and Rolf Kristiansen. *John Joseph Enneking: American Impressionist Painter.* Abington, MA: Fougere Printing, 1972.
Robinson, Frank T. *Living New England Artists.* Boston: Samuel E. Cassino, 1888, pp. 59-65.

A SUMMER AFTERNOON ON THE ANDROS-COGGIN.
   Williams and Everett Auction, Boston (1878).

CHICOURA [sic] LAKE AND MOUNTAIN. S/D/L/R.
   1898. Oil on canvas.

22¼ x 30 (56.5 x 76.2).
Richard Bourne, Inc. (sold Nov. 25, 1983).

MOUNT CHOCORUA.
   Oil.
   18 x 24 (45.7 x 61).
   Private collection (1974); NMAA Inventory.

MOUNT CHOCORUA.
   1894. Oil.
   20 x 24 (50.8 x 61).
   Private collection (1974); NMAA Inventory.

MOUNT WASHINGTON FROM BETHLEHEM.
   MA Charitable (1874), #96; Pre-1877.

MOUNT WASHINGTON FROM GREENE'S HILL IN JACKSON, NEW HAMPSHIRE.
   Private collection (1982).

OLD MAN OF THE MOUNTAIN. S/L/L.
   Oil on academy board.
   9⅛ x 12⅛ (23.2 x 30.8).
   University Art Galleries, University of New Hampshire (1980), #105.

WHITE MOUNTAINS FROM BETHLEHEM.
   Leonard Auction (May 24, 1871), #114.

F

FAIRMAN, COLONEL JAMES
G&W, N, R, S
Born Glasgow, Scotland, 1826.
Died New York, NY, March 12, 1904.
Fairman came to the U.S. in 1832 and studied at the NAD in 1842. After serving as a colonel in the Civil War, he opened a studio in New York City. In 1871 he went to Europe where he spent the next 10 years. He exhibited at the NAD and the PAFA.

BRIDLE PATH, MOUNT WASHINGTON.
   Pre-1877.

MOUNT CHICOURA [sic], NEW HAMPSHIRE.
   NAD, 1865, #550.

MOUNTS MADISON AND JEFFERSON, AND ANDROSCOGGIN RIVER, NEAR GORHAM, NH.
   NAD, 1867, #191.

VALLEY OF THE ANDROSCOGGIN AND BETHEL, MAINE (DISTANT VIEW OF THE WHITE MOUNTAINS).
   NAD, 1866, #380; PAFA, 1867, #215.

WHITE MOUNTAINS.
   Pre-1877; Young Men's Association, Troy, NY (1878-79).

YOUTH OF CHICOURA [sic]; THE . . .
   PAFA, 1869, #22.

FARR, ELLEN B.
Born 1840. Died 1907.
Nothing else is presently known of this artist.

FLUME, NEW HAMPSHIRE.
   Oil.
   19½ x 11½ (49.5 x 29.2).
   Private collection (1976); NMAA Inventory.

FARRER (or FARRAR), THOMAS CHARLES
C, C&H, F, G&W, N, R, S
Born London, England, 1838.
Died probably England, 1891.
A student of John Ruskin, Farrer came to the U.S. about 1860 and became involved in the American pre-Raphaelite movement. He was a friend of John Henry Hill and W. J. Stillman and

did illustrations for The New Path. *He exhibited at the NAD in 1860 and every year thereafter until his return to England in 1872. He also exhibited at the Brooklyn Art Association and the PAFA.*

Bibliography:
Boston Public Library, special clippings file.
Dickason, David Howard. *The Daring Young Men: Story of the American Pre-Raphaelites.* Indiana University Press, 1953.
Ferber, Linda. "Ripe for Revival, Forgotten American Artists." *Artnews* (Dec. 1980), p. 71.

EVENING IN NEW HAMPSHIRE.
 NAD, 1865, #9; *New Path* (1865), p. 95.

EVENING ON MOUNT WASHINGTON.
 Brooklyn Art Association (1865), #93.

MOUNT WASHINGTON AND ADAMS.
 Brooklyn Art Association (1864), #57.

MOUNT WASHINGTON UNDER THREE FEET OF SNOW.
 Brooklyn Art Association (1864), #56: NAD, 1865, #361; *New Path* (1865), p. 95.

MOUNT WASHINGTON, NORTH CONWAY.
 Brooklyn Art Association (1868), #43.

FENN, HARRY

B, E, F, K, Ka, N, S
Born Richmond, Surrey, England, Sept., 14, 1845.
Died Montclair, NJ, April 21, 1911.
Fenn began his career as a wood engraver but quickly switched to pencil drawings. He came to the U.S. in 1864 and stayed for six years, then traveled to Italy to study. In 1870 he came back to the U.S. to gather material to be used for illustrations in Picturesque America *(edited by William Cullen Bryant), a book which was published in 1872. About 1874 he built an unusual home on Orange Mountain, NJ, and kept a studio in New York City from 1881 on. Later in life, Fenn concentrated on watercolor paintings, and he helped to found the Society of American Painters in Water Colors. He exhibited at the NAD in 1864 and at various times at the Brooklyn Art Association between 1864 and 1885.*

CANNON MOUNTAIN CLIFF – WHITE MOUNTAINS.
 Engraving.
 Bryant, William Cullen, ed. *Picturesque America.* Vol. 1 (1872).

CLIFFS ABOVE DISMAL POOL.
 Engraving.
 Bryant. *Picturesque America.* Vol. 1 (1872), p. 170.

COLUMN ROCK, DIXVILLE NOTCH.
 Engraving.
 Bryant. *Picturesque America.* Vol. 1 (1872), p. 172.

CRAWFORD NOTCH, NEW HAMPSHIRE.
 Signed.
 C. 1870. Watercolor.
 10 x 18 (25.4 x 45.7).
 Anderson Auction Galleries, sale 919, #46.

CRYSTAL CASCADE.
 Engraving.
 Bryant. *Picturesque America.* Vol. 1 (1872), p. 162.

DESCENT FROM MOUNT WASHINGTON; THE . . .
 Steel engraving.
 Bryant. *Picturesque America.* Vol. 1 (1872), p. 158.

ELEPHANTS HEAD, CRAWFORD NOTCH.
 Engraving.
 Bryant. *Picturesque America.* Vol. 1 (1872), p. 153.

EMERALD POOL, PEABODY-RIVER GLEN.
 Engraving.
 Bryant. *Picturesque America.* Vol. 1 (1872), p. 166.

FLUME; THE . . .
 Engraving.
 Bryant. *Picturesque America.* Vol. 1 (1872), p. 169.

GATE OF THE NOTCH; THE . . .
 Engraving.
 Bryant. *Picturesque America.* Vol 1 (1872), p. 156.

MOUNT WASHINGTON FROM THE CONWAY ROAD.
 Wood engraving.
 Bryant. *Picturesque America.* Vol. 1 (1872), p. 152.

MOUNT WASHINGTON FROM TOP OF THOMPSON'S FALLS, PINKHAM PASS.
 Wood engraving.
 Bryant. *Picturesque America.* Vol. 1 (1872), p. 164.

MOUNT WASHINGTON ROAD; THE . . .
 Engraving.
 Bryant. *Picturesque America.* Vol. 1 (1872), before p. 151; *Appalachia* (Spring 1981).

PROFILE MOUNTAIN.
Engraving.
Bryant. *Picturesque America.* Vol. 1 (1872), p. 168.

TUCKERMAN'S RAVINE FROM HERMIT'S LAKE.
Engraving.
Bryant. *Picturesque America.* Vol. 1 (1872), p. 160.

WHITE MOUNTAINS FROM CONWAY MEADOWS; THE . . .
Engraving.
Bryant. *Picturesque America.* Vol. 1 (1872), p. 150.

WILLEY SLIDE; THE . . .
Engraving.
Bryant. *Picturesque America.* Vol. 1 (1872), p. 155.

FENNIMORE (or FENIMORE), T.J.
R
Active 1861-69.
There is presently no information on this artist.

HART'S LEDGE, ECHO LAKE, NEAR NORTH CONWAY, NEW HAMPSHIRE.
1867.
12 x 22 (30.5 x 55.9).
Old Print Shop *Portfolio* 25:9, p. 213.

MOUNT CHOCORUA.
Pre-1877; Philadelphia Sketch Club held at PAFA, Dec. 1865.

MOUNT WASHINGTON.
1869.
PAFA.

SACO RIVER.
1867.
PAFA.

SUNRISE ON THE SACO.
1866.
PAFA.

FERGUSON, HENRY A. (or N.)
F, N, R, S
Born 1842. Died 1911 (1917 according to Naylor).
Ferguson began exhibiting at the Brooklyn Art Association in 1864 and continued to do so until 1891, exhibiting at the NAD during the same period. In 1884 he is listed in the New York City directory. He was a member of the Century Association from 1879 until his death in 1911.

A VIEW IN NORTH CONWAY.
Brooklyn Art Association (1864), #53.

FRANCONIA NOTCH, EAGLE CLIFF.
C. 1870. Oil.
17½ x 13 (44.5 x 33).
NMAA Inventory.

FRANCONIA VALLEY AND MOUNT LAFAYETTE.
NAD, 1884, #204.

GOODRICH FALLS, NEW HAMPSHIRE.
Oil on canvas.
9 x 5¾ (22.9 x 14.6).
Kennedy Galleries (Nov. 1977).

IN FRANCONIA.
Brooklyn Art Association (1869), #61; (1870), #68.

MOUNT LAFAYETTE.
Brooklyn Art Association (1883), #98.

SCENE ON THE ELLIS RIVER, WHITE MOUNTAINS IN THE DISTANCE.
Pre-1877; Utica (NY) art exhibition, Utica Mechanics Association (1865).

TUCKERMAN'S RAVINE AND MOUNT WASHINGTON. S/D.
1869.
Gallery 44.

VIEW OF THE VILLAGE AND GLIMPSES OF THE VALLEY OF CONWAY.
Pre-1877; Utica (NY) art exhibition, Utica Mechanics Association (1865).

VIEW ON THE SACO AND MOUNT WASHINGTON.
Pre-1877; Utica (NY) art exhibition, Utica Mechanics Association (1864).

WHITE MOUNTAINS.
Pre-1877; U.S. Sanitary Commission (1864), #73.

FISHER, ALVAN
A, Ba, C, Ce, DAB, F, G&W, K, Ka, R, T
Born Needham, MA, Aug. 9, 1792.
Died Dedham, MA, Feb. 14 (or 13), 1863.
Fisher was a Boston painter who studied decorative painting on furniture with John Ritto Penniman early in his career. He aspired to paint pictures, however, and worked hard to shake off that "mechanical, ornamental touch." By 1816 Fisher was producing scenes of stables and barnyards that were novel at that time and showed his skill in painting animals and the effects of light. He had enough portrait commissions as well to enable him to make an adequate living and to become well established in the Boston artistic community. The PAFA first exhibited Fisher's work in 1817, and later his work

was shown at the NAD, where he was elected an honorary member in 1827, and at the Boston Athenaeum. Throughout his career, Fisher traveled extensively along the east coast of the U.S., and in 1825 he visited Europe briefly, taking numerous sketches and notes. Fisher was in the White Mountains with Thomas Doughty and other Boston artists prior to 1856. Working in a romantic tradition of the early Hudson River School, Fisher's landscape compositions were sometimes imaginary scenes and often featured animal as well as human forms.

Bibliography:

Sears, Clara Endicott. *Highlights Among the Hudson River Artists.* Boston: Houghton Mifflin, 1941, pp. 26-31.
Vose, Robert C., Jr. "Alvan Fisher, 1792-1863, American Pioneer in Landscape and Genre." Connecticut Historical Society *Bulletin* 27:4 (Oct. 1962), pp. 97-129.

A SUNNY SPOT, PASS OF THE MOUNTAINS.
Leonard Auction (May 15, 1857), #35.

BOWL OF THE WHITE MOUNTAINS; THE . . .
Hardings Gallery (May 1834), #138.

CHOCORUA PEAK, POND AND ADJACENT SCENERY AS SEEN TOWARDS EVENING.
Childs Gallery; Leonard Auction (May 15, 1857), #37; Bierstadt Exhibition, New Bedford, 1858, #16.

CROSSING THE SACO RIVER, CONWAY, NEW HAMPSHIRE.
Oil on canvas.
27½ x 39¾ (69.9 x 101).
University Art Gallery catalog, University of New Hampshire (1980), #106; Connecticut Historical Society exhibition (1963).

FISHING IN NEW HAMPSHIRE.
1852. Oil.
27 x 22 (68.6 x 55.9).
Vose Galleries (1962).

GATE OF THE NOTCH OF THE WHITE MOUNTAINS WITH THE SOURCE OF THE SACO RIVER.
Hardings Gallery (May 1934), #453.

GENERAL VIEW OF MOUNT WASHINGTON RANGE FROM THE NORTHERN PART OF THE TOWN OF NORTH CONWAY, NH.
Leonard Auction (May 15, 1857), #59.

INDIANS CROSSING A FROZEN LAKE. S/L/L.
1845. Oil on canvas.
24 x 30 (61 x 76.2).
University Art Gallery catalog, University of New Hampshire (1980), #87.

LANDSCAPE COMPOSITION FROM SCENERY IN THE VICINITY OF THE WHITE MOUNTAINS.
Boston Athenaeum (1837), #41; Apollo Association, N.Y.C. (March 1841), #92.

LANDSCAPE, PRESIDENTIAL RANGE.
Private collection.

MONADNOC [sic] MOUNTAIN FROM DUBLIN, NEW HAMPSHIRE – PAINTED DIRECTLY FROM NATURE.
Leonard Auction (May 15, 1857), #13.

MOUNT CHOCORUA.
1855.
Private collection; Wellesley College exhibition (1973).

MOUNT CHOCORUA, FROM SANDWICH NH, A VIEW FROM THE ROAD LEADING TO YOUNG MOUNTAIN.
Leonard Auction (May 15, 1857), #49.

MOUNT JEFFERSON ON THE ROUTE FROM GORHAM TO THE GLEN HOUSE, NH.
Leonard Auction (May 15, 1857), #11.

MOUNT LAFAYETTE AND FRANCONIA NOTCH, VIEW FROM THE WEST OF FRANCONIA VILLAGE.
Leonard Auction (May 15, 1857), #9.

MOUNT WASHINGTON IN AUTUMN, AS SEEN FROM PINKHAM NOTCH, ELLIS RIVER IN FOREGROUND.
Leonard Auction (May 15, 1857), #63.

NEW HAMPSHIRE LANDSCAPE, FRANCONIA NOTCH.
1834.
Unlocated.

NEW HAMPSHIRE SCENERY.
Leonard Auction (Dec. 29, 1864), #95; (March 23, 1865), #12.

NOTCH; THE . . .S/D/L/L.
1834.
30⅜ x 42½ (77.2 x 108).
Fruitlands Museum (1975).

NOTCH: THE . . .
1834.

PULPIT ROCK (CRAWFORD NOTCH, NEW HAMPSHIRE). S/D/L/L.
1862. Oil on canvas.
30 x 25 (76.2 x 63.5).
Albany Institute of History and Art (1974).

SANDWICH, NEW HAMPSHIRE, SCENE ON THORNTON ROAD.
Boston Athenaeum, (1856), #127; Leonard Auction (May 15, 1857), #7.

New Hampshire Scenery

Eagle Cliff, New Hampshire
Jasper Francis Cropsey, 1851
Oil on canvas, 37" x 53" / Collection: Museum of Fine Arts, Boston, gift of
    Mrs. Maxim Karolik for the Karolik Collection of American Paintings,
    1815-1865 / Ref. page 43

SCENE OF THE SACO RIVER AT THE NOTCH OF THE WHITE MOUNTAINS.
    Boston Athenaeum (1836), #74.

SCENE ON THE ROADSIDE BETWEEN NORTH CONWAY AND ALBANY, NEW HAMPSHIRE.
    Leonard Auction (May 15, 1857), #23.

SCENE ON THE SACO RIVER AT THE NOTCH OF THE WHITE MOUNTAINS.
    Boston Athenaeum (1836), #74.

SKETCHBOOKS.
    Boston Museum of Fine Arts.

SOUL OF THE WHITE MOUNTAINS.
    Pre-1877.

STUDY FROM MY SKETCHES IN NEW HAMPSHIRE.
    Hardings Gallery (May 1834), #124.

SUGAR LOAF MOUNTAIN.
    1821. Oil on canvas.

25½ x 33 (64.8 x 83.8).
    Boston Museum of Fine Arts, Karolik collection (1983).

VIEW IN LOWER BARTLETT, NH, OF THE INTER-VALE, LEDGES, AND MOTE [sic] MOUNTAIN.
    Leonard Auction (May 15, 1857), #39.

VIEW IN NORTH CONWAY FROM THE WEST SIDE OF THE SACO RIVER (Kearsarge).
    Leonard Auction (May 15, 1857), #36.

VIEW IN NORTH CONWAY, NEW HAMPSHIRE.
    Leonard Auction (May 15, 1857), #31; (May 22, 1863), #179.

VIEW NEAR THE GATE OF THE NOTCH OF THE WHITE MOUNTAINS.
    Boston Athenaeum (1846), #134.

VIEW ON THE BEAR-CAMP RIVER, SANDWICH, NH.
    Leonard Auction (May 15, 1857), #12.

Dictionary of Painters

WHITE MOUNTAINS; THE . . . S/L/L.
  19¼ x 23 (48.9 x 58.9).
  Fruitlands Museum.

FISHER, D. A. (or D. H.)

Nothing is known of Fisher's work or training.
ANDROSCOGGIN RIVER NEAR BETHEL, MAINE.
  1895. Watercolor.
  9½ x 14½ (24.1 x 36.8).
  Private collection (1975);
  NMAA Inventory.
CARTER NOTCH. S/D.
  1894. Oil on artboard.
  9 x 12 (22.9 x 30.5).
  Private collection (1893).
VIEW OF PEABODY STREAM, NEAR GORHAM,
NH, WHITE MOUNTAINS. S/D/L/L.
  1889. Oil on canvas.
  25 x 35 (63.5 x 88.9).
  Richard Bourne, Inc., catalog (May 20,
  1981).

FITCH, JOHN LEE

A, Ce, C&H, F, G&W, N, S
Born Hartford, CT, June 25, 1836.
Died Yonkers, NY, March 5, 1895.
*Fitch studied in Hartford before leaving for
Europe in 1855, where he painted in Munich and
Milan, Italy, for three years. Returning to the
U.S., he opened a studio in Hartford, CT, where
he remained until 1866 at which time he
removed permanently to New York City. He
began exhibiting at the NAD in 1860 and was
elected an associate of the NAD in 1870. He also
exhibited at the Brooklyn Art Association from
1868 to 1884. From 1872 to 1892 he kept a studio
in the 10th Street Studio Building (N.Y.C.) and
joined the Century Association in 1867. He
painted in the White Mountains with Winslow
Homer and Homer D. Martin. He is one of the
artists depicted in Homer's ARTISTS
SKETCHING IN THE WHITE MOUNTAINS.*
BROOK IN NEW HAMPSHIRE.
  NAD, 1872, #200.
MOUNT WASHINGTON.
  Oil on canvas.
  11¾ x 17⅝ (29.8 x 44.8).
  Wadsworth Atheneum, Hartford, CT (1976).
ROAD SCENE IN NEW HAMPSHIRE.
  NAD, 1875, #392.

FLUTHY, F.

*Perhaps the same artist as Luthy. Possibly
French. Nothing is known of this artist at
present.*
WHITE MOUNTAINS.
  Pre-1877; Leeds Gallery (Feb. 7, 1870).

FOSTER, SAMUEL BIRKET

A, G&W
Active 1833-60.
*This portrait painter exhibited at Chester Har-
ding's Exhibition Hall in Boston in 1834 and
also at the Boston Athenaeum in 1842 and 1846.
He was apparently a merchant by trade. He
lived in Concord, NH, in 1860.*
MOUNT WASHINGTON.
  North Conway Library Exhibition (1965).

FRANKENSTEIN, GEORGE LEO

G&W
Probably born in Germany, June 26, 1825.
Probably died Ohio, Sept. 15, 1911.
*George was a brother of Godfrey Nicholas
Frankenstein and painted in the White Moun-
tains in August 1887.*
FROM THE SUMMIT OF MOUNT WASHINGTON.
  Aug. 1887.
  Gallery 44; picture on the concert program
  for Fabyan's Hotel.

FRANKENSTEIN, GODFREY NICHOLAS

Ba, C, Ce, F(sup), G&W, R
Born Darmstadt, Germany, Sept. 20, 1820.
Died Springfield, OH, Feb. 24, 1873.
*After a year's study with a sign painter in Cin-
cinnati, Frankenstein, a precocious artist,
opened his own shop in 1833 and worked as a
sign painter for the next six years. He then
turned to portraiture and by the age of 21
became the first president of the Cincinnati
Academy of Fine Arts. His first trip to the White
Mountains in 1847 and a trip to Niagara Falls
in 1844 sparked his interest in landscape. He did
over 100 paintings of the latter for a panorama
which he exhibited in 1853. He was the only artist to brave sketching there in winter. He exhibited at the AAU in 1849, the NAD from 1847
to 1854, and produced two illustrations for
William Oakes's White Mountain Scenery after
his first visit to the White Mountains. He
traveled in Europe from 1867 to 1869.*
Bibliography:
Coyle, William. *The Frankenstein Family in*

New Hampshire Scenery

Springfield. Clark County Historical Society pamphlet. Springfield, OH, 1967.
Morey, Florence. "The Cliff's Frankenstein." *Appalachia* (June 1948).
DISMAL POOL.
  Private collection.
LAKE BEMIS, WHITE MOUNTAINS.
  24 x 18 (61 x 45.7).
  AAU, 1849, #333.
LAKE SCENERY, NEW HAMPSHIRE.
  24 x 18 (61 x 45.7).
  AAU, 1849, #338.
MOUNT WASHINGTON OVER TUCKERMAN'S RAVINE.
  1848. Oil.
  16 x 12 (40.6 x 30.5).
  Oakes, William. *White Mountain Scenery.* (1848), plate 16.
  Private collection (1978); NMAA Inventory.
NOTCH FROM MOUNT CRAWFORD.
  5⅛ x 7½ (13.1 x 19.1).
  Oakes, William. *White Mountain Scenery* (1848), plate 14.
SACO RIVER.
  1847. Oil on paper.
  8 x 11 (20.3 x 27.9).
  New Hampshire Historical Society.
SCENE IN THE WHITE MOUNTAINS (Kearsarge and the Saco).
  Oil on composition board.
  7 x 11 (17.8 x 27.9).
  New Hampshire Historical Society.
WHITE MOUNTAIN SCENERY (2).
  Pre-1877; Western Art Union Distribution, 1850.
WHITE MOUNTAINS AND THE SACO RIVER.
  Oil on board.
  10¼ x 13¾ (26 x 34.9).
  Kennedy Galleries (1976).
WHITE MOUNTAINS IN OCTOBER.
  24 x 18 (61 x 45.7).
  AAU, 1849, #346.

FRASER, CHARLES
A, Ba, C&H, DAB, F, G&W, R, S, T
Born Charleston, SC, May (or Aug.) 20, 1782.
Died Charleston, SC, Oct. 5, 1860.
Primarily a miniaturist, Fraser studied and practiced law until 1818 when he took up painting. In 1825 he was made an honorary member of the American Academy of Fine Arts and exhibited there in 1831, 1833, and 1834 and at the AAU in 1849. He was a popular and respected artist who numbered Thomas Sully and Washington Allston among his friends.
GAP IN THE WHITE MOUNTAINS (2).
  Pre-1877.
LANDSCAPE, NOTCH IN THE WHITE MOUNTAINS.
  Pre-1877; Charleston, SC (March 1857), The "Fraser" Gallery.
LANDSCAPE, VIEW OF MOUNT WASHINGTON.
  Pre-1877; Charleston, SC (March 1857), The "Fraser" Gallery.
MOUNTAIN SCENERY IN NEW HAMPSHIRE.
  Pre-1877; Charleston, SC (March 1857), The "Fraser" Gallery.
MOUNTAIN SCENERY IN NEW HAMPSHIRE – ANOTHER VIEW.
  Pre-1877; Charleston, SC (March 1857), The "Fraser" Gallery.

FRASER, J. (perhaps JOHN A.)
B, S
Born London, England, 1839.
Died New York, NY, 1898.
Primarily a watercolorist, Fraser is nearly anonymous as various sources may be referring to different artists.
MOUNT WASHINGTON.
  Pre-1877; Art Association of Montreal, 4th exhibition (1867).
STORM ON MOUNT JEFFERSON.
  Pre-1877; Art Association of Montreal, 4th exhibition (1867).

FREELAND (or FRIEDLAND or FRIELAND), ANNA C.
G&W
Born 1837. Died 1911.
Anna Freeland worked for the most part from her studio in Jackson, NH. For many years she ran the summer Boston Art School, concentrating on the watercolor classes.
Information courtesy of Phyllis F. Greene.
CIDER MAKING IN TAMWORTH.
  Private collection.
CIDER MILL, TAMWORTH.
  1891.
  North Conway Library Exhibition (1965).
GIANT STEPS.
  Watercolor.
  Lion Gallery (Aug. 1976).

FREEMAN, BRADFORD

A, G&W
Born Duxbury, MA, Feb. 12, 1821.
Died possibly 1874.
Nothing else is presently known of this artist.
LAKE WINNIPESEOGEE [sic].
    Boston Athenaeum (1858), #73.

FRERICHS, WILLIAM CHARLES ANTHONY

Ce, F, G&W, S
Born Belgium, c. 1829.
Died Tottenville, Staten Island, NY, March 16,
1905.
*Frerichs was educated in Belgium and came to
the U.S. about 1852, at which time he exhibited
at the NAD. He taught art in Greensboro, SC,
until 1863 and later moved to Newark, NJ,
where he operated an art school.*
Bibliography:
*William C. A. Frerichs, 1829-1905: A Retrospec-
tive Exhibition.* North Carolina Museum of Art
(Sept. 15-Oct. 20, 1975).
MOUNT WASHINGTON, CONWAY VALLEY,
NEW HAMPSHIRE.
    C. 1865. Oil on canvas.
    20 x 40 (50.8 x 101.6).
    North Carolina Museum of Art (1974).
PANORAMIC LANDSCAPE (Mount Washington
from Sunset Hill). S/L/L.
    Oil on canvas.
    24 x 48 (71.1 x 121.9).
    Baridoff Gallery sale (July 5, 1980), #99.

FROST, FRANCIS SHEDD

A
Born 1825.
Died Cambridge (or Arlington), MA, Dec. 26,
1902.
*Frost studied under Jasper Cropsey in 1850 and
began exhibiting at the Boston Athenaeum in
1854. In 1858 he showed a painting at Bierstadt's
New Bedford exhibition and accompanied
Bierstadt on his first trip west in 1859. Apparent-
ly his friend, Bierstadt, absconded with Frost's
wife. From 1864 to 1866 Frost had a studio in
Boston and lived in Cambridge, then briefly
took up photography before opening a shop for
artist's materials in Boston from 1869 to 1874.*
Bibliography:
Information courtesy of the Dedham Historical
Society, Dedham, MA, and Valdemar F.
Jacobsen Antiques, Cold Spring Harbor, Long
Island, NY 11724.

Talbot, William S. *Jasper Cropsey 1823-1900.*
Washington, DC National Collection of Fine
Arts, Smithsonian Institution, 1970, p. 71.
AUTUMN SCENERY, NORTH CONWAY.
    Boston Athenaeum (1856), #18.
CHOCORUA. S/D/L/Center.
    1858. Oil on canvas.
    15⅜ x 23⅜ (39.1 x 59.4).
    Private collection (1976).
CONWAY LAKE AND MOUNTAINS.
    1863.
    Private collection.
ECHO LAKE.
    Leonard Auction (May 22, 1863), #58.
MOUNT CHOCORUA, TAMWORTH.
    1861.
    Leonard Auction.
NEW HAMPSHIRE LANDSCAPE.
    1857. Oil.
    12 x 18 (30.5 x 45.7).
    Private collection; Dwight Art Museum
    exhibition.
SANBORNTON RIVER.
    Boston Athenaeum (1864), #251.
SCENE AT NORTH CONWAY.
    Boston Athenaeum (1856), #125.
VALLEY OF THE PEMIGEWASSET.
    Boston Athenaeum (1858), #140.
VIEW IN TUCKERMAN'S RAVINE, WHITE
MOUNTAINS.
    Boston Athenaeum (1854), #226.
VIEW OF THE ANDROSCOGGIN.
    Boston Athenaeum (1858), #235.
WHITE MOUNTAINS FROM LAKE UMBAGOG.
    Bierstadt Exhibition, New Bedford, 1858,
    #35; Pre-1877.

FROST, GEORGE ALBERT

F(sup), S
Born Boston, MA, Dec. 13, 1827.
Died Cambridge, MA, Nov. 13, 1907.
*At age 11 Frost left school and went to work
on a farm, where he had no opportunity to
follow his artistic inclinations. At the outbreak
of the Civil War he enlisted and served for more
than two years. During these years he must have
practiced his art for, by his mid-30's, he joined
Colonel Pope's division of the Western Union
surveying party to British Columbia for which
he produced sketches. In 1866 he was assigned
to Asia for the same purpose. He studied in Germany from 1874 to 1876 and for the next ten*

New Hampshire Scenery

years had a studio in North Cambridge, MA. In 1885 he accompanied George Kennan to Siberia to record the life of Russian exiles. For a good many years, Frost had a summer home in Brownfield, ME, near the Conway area of New Hampshire and painted many scenes along the Saco.

Bibliography:
Boston *Globe*, obituary, Nov. 13, 1907, p. 2.

MOUNT SURPRISE.
    North Conway Library Exhibition (1965).

FUESCHEL, HERMAN TRAUGOTT LOUIS

A, C, Ce, F, G&W, K, N, R
Born Braunschweig, Germany, Aug. 8, 1833.
Died New York, NY, Sept. 30, 1915.
Fueschel studied in Munich and Düsseldorf before coming to the U.S. in 1858. He began exhibiting in 1860 at the Boston Athenaeum and the AAU. The Crayon for February of that year noted: "Mr. Fueschel has completed a sunny mountain scene, suggested by a view from the

top of Mt. Kearsarge" (p. 57). He continued exhibiting frequently at the NAD from 1861 to 1900 and also at the Brooklyn Art Association. In 1882 he took a studio at the 10th Street Studio Building (N.Y.C.) which he occupied until his death.

ON THE SACO, MOUNT WASHINGTON IN THE DISTANCE.
    Boston Athenaeum (1860), #242.

ON THE SACO, NORTH CONWAY.
    NAD, 1879, #227.

ON THE TOP OF MOUNT KIARSARGE [sic], NORTH CONWAY.
    Boston Athenaeum (1860), #243; AAU, 1860, #1.

REMINISCENCE OF CONWAY, WHITE MOUNTAINS.
    NAD, 1890, #181.

VIEW OF MOUNT WASHINGTON AT SUNSET, NORTH CONWAY, NEW HAMPSHIRE.
    NAD, 1861, #470.

WHITE MOUNTAINS.
    NAD, 1862, #450.

G

GALLISON, HENRY HAMMOND

F, N, S
Born Boston, MA, May 20, 1850.
Died Boston, MA, Oct. 12, 1910.
Gallison studied in Boston and in Paris with Bonnefoy. He received prizes in Turin, Italy, Paris, and the St. Louis expositions for his landscapes. He exhibited at the Boston Art Club in 1881 and 1883, the Massachusetts Charitable Mechanic Association in 1881, and the NAD in 1895.

CARTER'S NOTCH FROM JACKSON, NEW HAMPSHIRE.
    Oil.
    Boston Art Club (1883), #25.

CHOCORUA. (Untitled). S/L/L.
    Oil on canvas.
    33¾ x 45½ (85.7 x 115.6).
    Holderness (NH) Free Library.

JACKSON, NEW HAMPSHIRE, WOOD INTERIOR.
    MA Charitable (1881), #326.

WINTER, RUMNEY, NEW HAMPSHIRE.
    Boston Art Club (1881), #98.

GARIGLE, WILLIAM

Nothing is presently known about this artist.
FRANCONIA MOUNTAINS. S/D/L/L.
    1858. Oil on panel.
    13⅛ x 18½ (33.4 x 47).
    Signal Co.

GARNIER, HIPPOLYTE LOUIS

Born 1802. Died 1855.
This artist was probably French and possibly connected with Victor De Grailly, who copied William Bartlett's engravings in profusion. The three known paintings are of Bartlett scenes, two of which were exhibited at the Leonard Auction Rooms in 1865.

Bibliography:
Banks, William Nathaniel. "The French Painter Victor De Grailly, and the Production of Nineteenth-Century American Views." *Antiques* (July 1974), pp. 84-103.
MOUNT JEFFERSON FROM MOUNT WASHINGTON (after Bartlett).
C. 1845. Oil.
21⅛ x 18¹/₁₆ (53.7 x 45.9).
New Hampshire Historical Society (1974).
SILVER CASCADE, WHITE MOUNTAINS.
Leonard Auction (March 23, 1865), #73.

GAULEY, ROBERT DAVID
F
Born Canaveigh County, Monaghan, Ireland, 1875. Died. 1943.
He studied with Denman W. Ross in Cambridge, MA. It is not known when he came to the U.S.
LANDSCAPE, INTERVALE, NEW HAMPSHIRE.
1894. Oil.
18 x 24 (45.7 x 61).
Parke-Bernet (1964); NMAA Inventory.

GAY, MICHAEL
Active 1877.
Nothing is presently known of this competent artist.
MOUNT LAFAYETTE, FRANCONIA, NH. S/L/R.
1877. Oil on canvas.
8 x 14½ (20.3 x 36.8).
Kennedy Galleries (1977).

GAY, MIRIAM
Active 1878-79.
There is no information available on this artist at present.
MOUNT LAFAYETTE.
Oil.
Boston Art Club (April 17-May 4, 1878).
MOUNT LAFAYETTE, FRANCONIA, NEW HAMPSHIRE.
Oil.
Boston Art Club (Jan. 15-Feb. 8, 1879), #144.
VIEW NEAR PLYMOUTH, NEW HAMPSHIRE.
Oil.
Boston Art Club (Jan. 16-Feb. 9, 1878), #79.
VIEW, FRANCONIA, NEW HAMPSHIRE.
Oil.
Boston Art Club (Jan. 16-Feb. 9, 1878), #81.

GAY, WINKWORTH ALLAN
A, Ce, C&H, DAB, F, G&W, N, R, S, T
Born Hingham, MA, Aug. 18, 1821.
Died Hingham, MA, Feb. 23, 1910.
Gay first studied painting with Robert Weir at West Point and, in 1847, with Constant Troyon in Paris. He returned from Europe in 1850 and established a studio in Boston, where he stayed for most of the remainder of his life. Benjamin Champney had been Gay's traveling companion in Europe, and the two friends visited North Conway together in 1853. While Champney later made that village his New Hampshire home and painted many views of the surrounding scenery, Gay became more closely associated with the Franconia Notch area. He often stayed at the Stag and Hounds Inn in Campton Village with other artists such as Asher Durand, Samuel Gerry, Samuel Griggs, and George Loring Brown. Gay exhibited at the Boston Athenaeum and in New York City and Philadelphia, showing European and New England landscapes and coastal scenes. Typical of his style, which showed the strong influence of his early training in the French and English landscape traditions, were broad, panoramic compositions painted with careful attention to detail and topographical accuracy. Henry Tuckerman wrote in his Book of the Artists *in 1861 that the expressions of "truth, beauty and grandeur" in Gay's paintings were comparable to the writings of Hawthorne, Thoreau, Emerson, and Dana.*
Bibliography:
Craven, Wayne. "Boston Painter of the White Mountains, Paris, the Nile and Mount Fujiyama." *Antiques* (Nov. 1981), pp. 1222-1232.
A SCENE IN THE WHITE MOUNTAINS.
Crayon (Feb. 1860).
AT NORTH CONWAY, MOUNT WASHINGTON.
Oil on board.
8⅛ x 12 (20.6 x 31).
Art Fund Gallery, Washington, DC (1982).
CENTRE HARBOR BAY, FROM SUNRISE HILL. S/L/L.
Oil on canvas.
14 x 20 (35.6 x 50.8).
Vose Galleries.
CONWAY MEADOWS (looking south?).
25 x 32 (63.5 x 81.3).
Private collection.
EAGLE CLIFF ON ECHO LAKE, FRANCONIA.
Boston Athenaeum (1858), #168.
ECHO LAKE, FRANCONIA.
Boston Athenaeum (1857), #217.

FRANCONIA MOUNTAINS, FROM WEST CAMPTON, NEW HAMPSHIRE.
    Boston Athenaeum (1857), #216; NAD, 1859, #615.

FRANCONIA NOTCH, WHITE MOUNTAINS.
    1857. Oil on canvas.
    29¼ x 44 (74.3 x 111.8).
    Yale University Art Gallery (1980).

FROM WEST CAMPTON, NEW HAMPSHIRE.
    NAD, 1859, #61.

LEDGES; THE . . .
    Boston Athenaeum (1858), #135.

MOAT MOUNTAIN.
    Boston Athenaeum (1858), #134.

MOUNT MADISON.
    Crayon (July 1858), p. 206.

MOUNT WASHINGTON. S/D/L/R.
    1861.
    18 x 36 (45.7 x 91.4).
    Boston Museum of Fine Arts; Boston Athenaeum (1862), #283.

PRESIDENTIAL RANGE IN EARLY AUTUMN.
    Oil.
    12 x 18¼ (30.5 x 46.4).
    Boston Museum of Fine Arts (1983).

ROADSIDE, SHELBURNE, NEW HAMPSHIRE.
    NAD, 1860, #309.

SANDWICH RANGE MOUNTAINS FROM WEST CAMPTON.
    Boston Athenaeum (1857), #241; Bierstadt Exhibition, New Bedford, 1858, #91.

SANDWICH WOODS.
    Boston Athenaeum (1864), #296.

VIEW FROM THE FLUME HOUSE.
    Boston Athenaeum (1857), #242; Bierstadt Exhibition, New Bedford, 1858, #92.

WELCH MOUNTAIN FROM WEST CAMPTON, NEW HAMPSHIRE. S/D/Reverse.
    1856. Oil on cardboard.
    8⅛ x 12⅛ (20.6 x 30.8).
    Brooklyn Museum (1983).

WELCH MOUNTAIN FROM WEST CAMPTON, NEW HAMPSHIRE.
    1858. Oil on canvas.
    20⅛ x 30⅛ (51.1 x 76.5).
    Brooklyn Museum (1976); *Crayon* (July 1858), p. 206; Boston Athenaeum (1858), #136.

WHITE MOUNTAINS FROM NORTH CONWAY; THE . . .
    Oil.
    Leonard Auction (Dec. 6, 1861).

GERLACH, ANTHONY
R
Active 1860-85.
Gerlach worked in Philadelphia, but there is presently no further information on him.

LAKE WINNIPESEOGEE [sic].
    PAFA, 1866, #756.

VIEW ON LONG POND (now LAKE KANASATKA). S/D/L/L.
    1865. Oil on canvas. New Hampshire Historical Society. PAFA, 1866, #558.

GERRY, SAMUEL LANCASTER
A, B, C, Ce, C&H, F, G&W, N, R, S, T
Born Boston, MA, May 10, 1813.
Died Roxbury, MA, April 1891.
Like many of his contemporaries, Gerry had no formal training but was a sign and decorative painter in 1835 and 1836. He made the ritualistic trip abroad to study paintings of the masters for the following three years before opening a studio in Boston in 1840. For a while Gerry, an accomplished artist, conducted art classes at the Tremont Street Studio Building. He supported the Boston Art Club from its inception in 1854 and was one of its first presidents. Throughout his career, Gerry painted genre, portraits, and animals, as well as landscapes. He was a familiar figure in the lake district and White Mountains regions of New Hampshire. The Crayon *of October 1856 noted that "Gerry [was] at West Campton from August on at the 'Stag and Hounds.' " He exhibited at the Boston Athenaeum, the Boston Art Club, the NAD, the AAU, and the PAFA.*

Select Bibliography:
Gerry, Samuel Lancaster. "Reminiscences of the Boston Art Club, and Notes on Art." MS, c. 1885, Boston Athenaeum.
Pennsylvania State University Museum of Art catalog, *All That Is Glorious Around Us: Paintings from the Hudson River School* (1981), p. 72.

A STUDY FROM NATURE, WEST CAMPTON, NEW HAMPSHIRE.
    Boston Athenaeum (1857), #37.

A SUMMER NOOK IN CONWAY.
    Oil.
    Boston Art Club (Jan. 12-Feb. 2, 1876), #74.

A TROUT-NOOK IN THE ELLIS RIVER, IN THE GLEN, NH.
Oil.
Leonard Auction (May 2, 1862), #31.

A TROUT BROOK IN THE GRANITE STATE.
Oil.
Leonard Auction (May 2, 1862), #2.

ANDROSCOGGIN FROM LEAD-MINE BRIDGE, SHELBURNE; THE . . .
Oil.
Leonard Auction (May 2, 1862), #72.

ARTIST'S BROOK, NORTH CONWAY, NEW HAMPSHIRE.
C. 1857. Oil on canvas.
26⅜ x 40⅜ (67 x 102.7).
Monclair (NJ) Art Museum exhibition (1971), #74.

AT WEST CAMPTON, NEW HAMPSHIRE.
Oil.
Boston Art Club (1886), #93.

BANKS OF THE WINNEPESAUKEE [sic].
Leonard Auction (Jan. 28, 1873), #20.

BEACH HILL, NEW HAMPSHIRE.
20 x 36 (50.8 x 91.4).
Vose Galleries.

BRIDGE AND STREAM AT THORNTON, A TRIBUTARY OF THE PEMIGEWASSET.
Oil.
Leonard Auction (May 2, 1862), #29.

BRINGING IN THE HAY.
Oil.
16 x 24 (40.6 x 61).
New Hampshire Historical Society; Vose Galleries (sold Dec. 18, 1956).

CATTLE SCENE, SHELBURNE, NH.
Oil.
Leonard Auction (May 2, 1862), #32.

CENTRE HARBOR, NEW HAMPSHIRE.
AAU, 1848, #150.

DELLS, LITTLETON, NEW HAMPSHIRE.
C. 1879. Oil.
12 x 18½ (31 x 47).
Private collection.

EARLY MORNING IN WINTER, ON THE WINNIPISEOGEE [sic].
NAD, 1859, #711.

ECHO LAKE AND EAGLE CLIFF.
C. 1875. Charcoal on paper.
13⅝ x 21 (34.6 x 53.3).
New Hampshire Historical Society.

ECHO LAKE WITH EAGLE CLIFF. S/L/R.
Oil on canvas.
14 x 20 (35.6 x 50.8).
New Hampshire Historical Society exhibition (1965).

ECHO LAKE, FRANCONIA NOTCH. S/L/R.
14 x 20 (35.6 x 50.8).
New Hampshire Historical Society.

FLUME; THE . . . S/L/L.
Oil on canvas.
31⅝ x 20 (80.4 x 50.8).
New Hampshire Historical Society (1980), #108; Boston Art Club (1882), #129.

FOSTER BROOK – A PLEASANT RESORT OF ARTISTS AT CONWAY.
Oil.
Leonard Auction (May 2, 1862), #12.

FRANCONIA MOUNTAINS NEAR THORNTON, NEW HAMPSHIRE.
1857. Oil.
20 x 30 (50.8 x 76.2).
Old Print Shop *Portfolio* 28:3, p. 70.

GLEN ELLIS RIVER AND PINKHAM NOTCH.
C. 1855. Oil on canvas.
18½ x 25½ (47 x 64.8). Oval.
Private collection (1982).

GRASSY POOL WITH COWS AND AN ARTIST SKETCHING, NH. S/D/L/L.
1857. Oil on canvas.
14 x 20 (35.6 x 50.8).
Private collection; *Antiques* (July 1964), p. 66.

HARVEST TIME, RED HILL, SQUAM LAKE, NH. S/L/R.
C. 1857. Oil on canvas.
14 x 20 (35.6 x 50.8).
Private collection; University Art Gallery catalog, University of New Hampshire (1980), #107.

HAYING SCENE, A GROVE IN CONWAY.
Oil.
Leonard Auction (May 2, 1862), #28.

HUNTER AND DOGS IN THE WHITE MOUNTAINS.
Oil.
18 x 30 (45.7 x 76.2).
NMAA Inventory.

IN THE FRANCONIA NOTCH.
Boston Art Club (1880), #126.

IN THE WOODS, BARTLETT, NEW HAMPSHIRE.
1855. Oil.
22 x 27¼ (55.9 x 69.2).
Sotheby PB (1979).

New Hampshire Scenery

New Hampshire Lake
Thomas Doughty, c. 1828-1830
Oil on canvas, 26" x 36" / Collection: Museum of Fine Arts, Boston, bequest
     of Maxim Karolik, 1964 / Ref. page 49

INDIAN SUMMER (Squam or Winnipesaukee).
    Oil on canvas.
    26 x 40 (66 x 101.6).
    Kennedy Galleries (Oct. 1969).
INTERVALE MEADOWS WITH COWS (looking
south). Signed.
    26½ x 37 (67.3 x 74).
    Private collection (1983).
LAKE IN THE WHITE MOUNTAINS (Echo Lake).
    Oil on canvas.
    36 x 54 (91.4 x 137.2).
    Kennedy *Quarterly* 5:4 (Aug. 1965).
LAKE WINNEPESAUKEE [sic].
    1848. Oil.
    30 x 25 (76.2 x 63.5).
    Private collection.
LAKE WINNEPESAUKEE [sic]. Signed.
    C. 1850. Oil.
    14 x 20 (35.6 x 50.8).

Vose Galleries (sold Nov. 29, 1976 to Gallerie
de Tours).
LAKE WINNIPESAUKEE, NEW HAMPSHIRE.
S/L/L.
    C. 1850. Oil.
    14 x 24 (35.6 x 61).
    Old Print Shop *Portfolio* 32:1 (1972),
    p. 23.
LANDSCAPE WITH COWS AND PLOUGHMAN
(North Conway Meadows and Kearsarge).
    1852. Oil on canvas.
    40⅛ x 52⅛ (101.9 x 132.4).
    High Museum.
LANDSCAPE, SCENERY ON THE BEAR CAMP
RIVER.
    40 x 28 (101.6 x 71.1).
    AAU, 1850, #186.

Dictionary of Painters

MEADOW BROOK, IN THE GROVE, CONWAY.
Oil.
Leonard Auction (May 2, 1862), #23.

MOUNT CHOCORUA. S/D/L/R.
1849. Oil on canvas.
24 x 36 (61 x 91.4).
Pennsylvania State University, Vessel collection; Vose Galleries (sold Sept. 2, 1977).

MOUNT ISRAEL FROM RED HILL (or NORTH CONWAY AREA). Signed.
1856. Oil.
36 x 40 (91.4 x 101.6).
Private collection (1983).

MOUNT WASHINGTON FROM THE GLEN.
Leonard Auction (May 2, 1862), #63.

MOUNT WASHINGTON FROM THORN HILL, THE GRANDEST VIEW OF THE MONARCH.
Oil.
Leonard Auction (May 2, 1862), #49.

MOUNT WASHINGTON VIEWED FROM JACKSON, NEW HAMPSHIRE.
Oil.
20½ x 30½ (52.1 x 77.5).
Richard Bourne, Inc., catalog (Aug. 29, 1970).

NEW HAMPSHIRE LANDSCAPE.
Oil.
13⅛ x 20 (33.4 x 50.8).
Richard Bourne, Inc., catalog (Oct. 22, 1976).

NEW HAMPSHIRE LANDSCAPE.
Oil.
16½ x 22 (41.9 x 55.9).
Private collection (1980); NMAA Inventory.

NEW HAMPSHIRE LANDSCAPE (probably Campton). S/L/Center.
1853. Oil on canvas.
14 x 20 (35.6 x 50.8).
James R. Bakker, Littleton, MA, dealer (1975); Antiques (July 1975).

NORTHERN SLOPES OF MOUNT LAFAYETTE; THE . . .
Oil on canvas.
14 x 20 (35.6 x 50.8).
Private collection; NAD, 1859, #719.

OLD MAN OF THE MOUNTAINS. Signed.
C. 1871.
20 x 14 (50.8 x 35.6).
Private collection (1983).

OLD MAN. S/R.
Crayon on paper.

17½ x 11 (44.5 x 27.9).
Private collection.

ON CONWAY INTERVALE, MOUNTAINS AND MEADOW.
Oil.
Leonard Auction (May 2, 1862), #52.

ON CONWAY MEADOWS, BROOK VISTA.
Oil.
Leonard Auction (May 2, 1862), #60.

ON THE INTERVALE, NORTH CONWAY.
Boston Art Club (1885), #201.

ON THE ISRAEL RIVER, JEFFERSON, NH.
Leonard Auction (Jan. 28, 1873), #51.

PEMIGEWASSET RIVER, THORNTON, NEW HAMPSHIRE. S/D/L/R.
1857. Oil on canvas.
19¼ x 29 (48.9 x 73.7).
Boston Public Library, Brockton catalog.

RED HILL FROM LAKE KANASATKA. S/L/L.
Oil on board.
6¾ x 10 (17.1 x 25.4).
Private collection (1983); Baridoff Gallery (Nov. 1979), #75.

RED MOUNTAIN IN DISTANCE, VIEW FROM CENTER HARBOR, NH. (or VIEW NEAR RED MOUNTAIN). S/D.
1847. Oil on canvas.
22 x 30 (55.9 x 76.2).
Vose Galleries.

RUSTIC BRIDGE, SHELBURNE, NH.
Oil.
Leonard Auction (May 2, 1862), #15.

SACO WITH MOUNTAINS. (Untitled). Signed.
20½ x 12½ (52.1 x 31.8).
Private collection (1983).

SCENE IN THE WOODS, BARTLETT, NH.
Leonard Auction (May 22, 1863), #176.

SCENE ON THE GLEN ELLIS RIVER, WHITE HILLS, JACKSON, NH.
1856. Oil.
20½ x 30½ (52.1 x 77.5).
Kennedy Quarterly 10:4 (1971).

SNOW LINE, MOUNT WASHINGTON; THE . . .
1855. Oil on canvas.
26 x 36 (66 x 91.4).
North Carolina Museum of Art (1956).

SQUAM LAKE FROM RED HILL. S/L/L.
Oil on canvas.
13⅛ x 20 (33.3 x 50.8).
Private collection (1976); Vose Galleries (1976).

SQUAM LAKE FROM SHEPHERD'S HILL.
Leonard Auction (May 22, 1863), #10.

SQUAM LAKE, SUNSET. S/L/R.
C. 1850. Oil.
22 x 30 (55.9 x 76.2).
Vose Galleries (sold March 6, 1962, to a private collector).

STARR KING VIEW, WEST CAMPTON, NEW HAMPSHIRE.
Oil.
Boston Art Club (Jan. 17-Feb. 10, 1877), #95.

SURVEYING SCENE, LAKE WINNIPESAUKEE.
North Conway Library Exhibition (1965).

VALLEY OF THE ANDROSCOGGIN, MOUNTS MADISON AND WASHINGTON IN THE DISTANCE; THE . . .
Oil.
Leonard Auction (May 2, 1862), #56.

VALLEY OF THE PEMIGEWASSET.
1858. Oil.
36 x 67 (91.4 x 170.2).
University of Michigan Museum of Art (1975); Boston Athenaeum (1858), #356; NAD, 1858, #412.

VIEW AT CAMPTON.
Leonard Auction (June 16, 1865), #26.

VIEW AT NORTH CONWAY.
Leonard Auction (Jan. 28, 1873), #66.

VIEW IN CONWAY, MOAT MOUNTAIN IN DISTANCE.
Oil.
Leonard Auction (May 2, 1862), #66.

VIEW IN NEW HAMPSHIRE.
AAU, 1850, #86.

VIEW IN THE NEW HAMPSHIRE MOUNTAINS. S/L/R.
C. 1875. Charcoal on gray paper.
13⅝ x 21 (34.6 x 53.3).
Childs Gallery (1973).

VIEW OF SQUAM LAKE (or VIEW FROM CENTER HARBOR WITH RED MOUNTAIN).
Oil.
30 x 22 (76.2 x 55.9).
Vose Galleries (sold Oct. 4, 1963); AAU, 1850, #166.

VIEW ON PEMIGEWASSET AT THORNTON, NEW HAMPSHIRE.
1857. Oil.
20 x 30 (50.8 x 76.2).
Boston Athenaeum (1857), #269; NMAA Inventory.

VIEW ON THE SACO RIVER, NEW HAMPSHIRE.
AAU, 1848, #147.

WELCH MOUNTAIN, A VIEW AT CAMPTON ON THE PEMIGEWASSET.
Oil.
Leonard Auction (May 2, 1862), #7.

WHITE HILLS, JACKSON, SCENE ON THE GLEN ELLIS RIVER.
1836. Oil on canvas.
20½ x 30½ (52.1 x 77.5).
Kennedy *Quarterly* 10:4 (1971), p. 182.

WHITE MOUNTAIN SCENERY.
26 x 18 (66 x 45.7).
AAU, 1849, #124.

WHITE MOUNTAIN VIEW.
Wood Library, Bradford, VT.

WHITE MOUNTAINS.
U.S. Sanitary Commission (1864), #19.

WHITE MOUNTAINS FROM SHELBURNE, NH, VALLEY OF THE ANDROSCOGGIN.
Oil.
Leonard Auction (May 2, 1862), #36.

WHITE MOUNTAINS, NEW HAMPSHIRE.
C. 1859. Oil on canvas.
14 x 20 (35.6 x 50.8).
Frick Art Reference Library.

WHITEFACE IN THE WHITE MOUNTAINS. S/D/L/R.
1849. Oil on canvas.
24½ x 29½ (62.2 x 74.9).
Private collection (1984); Old Print Shop (July 1972).

WILLOW ROAD, NORTH SANDWICH, NH.
Oil on canvas.
12 x 20 (30.5 x 50.8).
Sotheby PB (Oct. 21, 1983), #81.

WINNIPESAUKEE FROM DANE'S HILL, CENTRE HARBOR.
Unlocated.

GETTY, FRANCIS
Born 1861. Died 1944.
There is no further information on this artist.
NEW HAMPSHIRE SCENERY (2).
North Conway Library Exhibition (1965).

GIBSON, WILLIAM HAMILTON
B, F, N, S
Born Sandy Hook, CT, 1850. Died 1896.
Gibson was an illustrator and watercolorist known for his botanical drawings. He frequently exhibited at the Brooklyn Art Association

from 1873 to 1891, and at the NAD in 1881. His work as illustrator in The Heart of the White Mountains by Samuel Adams Drake was much admired. He was made a member of the Century Association in 1890.

Bibliography:
Drake, Samuel Adams. *The Heart of the White Mountains: Their Legend and Scenery.* New York: Harper and Brothers, 1882.

CARTER NOTCH; THE...
    Drake, Samuel Adams. *Heart of the White Mountains,* p. 134.

CASCADES, MOUNT WEBSTER.
    Drake. *Heart of the White Mountains,* p. 85.

ELEPHANT'S HEAD, WINTER.
    Drake. *Heart of the White Mountains,* p. 88.

FALL OF THE BOWLDER [sic]. (Flume).
    Harper's Weekly (July 14, 1883), cover.

KEARSARGE IN WINTER.
    Lithograph.
    5½ x 5½ (14 x 14).
    New Hampshire Historical Society, Robert Hoskin, printer.

MOUNT LAFAYETTE FROM BETHLEHEM.
    Drake, *Heart of the White Mountains,* p. 280.

MOUNT WASHINGTON FROM FABYAN'S.
    Drake. *Heart of the White Mountains,* p. 301.

MOUNT WASHINGTON FROM THE SACO.
    Drake. *Heart of the White Mountains,* p. 40.

NORTHERN PEAKS FROM JEFFERSON; THE...
    Drake. *Heart of the White Mountains,* p. 292.

TRAVELLERS IN A STORM, MOUNT WASHINGTON.
    Drake. *Heart of the White Mountains,* frontispiece.

WELCH MOUNTAIN FROM MAD RIVER.
    Drake. *Heart of the White Mountains,* p. 217.

WINNIPISEOGEE [sic] FROM RED HILL.
    Drake. *Heart of the White Mountains,* p. 15.

GIFFORD, ROBERT SWAIN

A, B, C&H, DAB, E, F, G&W, N, R, S, T
Born Naushon Island, MA, Dec. 23, 1840.
Died New York, NY, Jan. 15, 1905.

Gifford studied under Albert Van Beest in New Bedford, MA, in 1864. He became interested in the medium of watercolor the following year and was one of the founders of the American Society of Painters in Water Colors. After 1865 he traveled widely in this country, Europe, and Africa. He began exhibiting at the NAD in 1863; became an associate in 1870 and a full member in 1878. He was a frequent exhibitor at the Brooklyn Art Association. A member of numerous societies, he belonged to the Society of American Artists, the New York Etching Club, and the British Society of Painter-Etchers. He was elected to the Century Association in 1868.

Bibliography:
Archives of American Art. Rolls 594-595.
Hall, Elton W. "R. Swain Gifford." *American Art Review* 1:4 (May-June 1974), pp. 51-67.
Koehler, S. R. *Robert Swain Gifford.* Boston, 1880.

NORTH CONWAY, BIRCHES. S/D.
    July 28, 1872.
    Lion Gallery (1976); North Conway Library Exhibition (1965).

WOODLAND SCENE, NORTH CONWAY.
    1872.
    North Conway Library Exhibition (1965).

GIFFORD, SANFORD ROBINSON

A, B, C, DAB, F, G&W, K, Ka, N, R, S, T
Born Greenfield, NY, July 10, 1823.
Died New York, NY, Aug. 29, 1880.

One of the few artists of the 19th century to attend college, Gifford studied from 1842 to 1844 at Brown University. He left Providence, RI, for New York City to pursue a career in art in 1845. A sketching trip to the Catskills and the Berkshires in the following year focused Gifford's interest on landscape painting. He became an associate member of the NAD in 1850 and a full member in 1854, contributing regularly to exhibitions there after 1847. Gifford was in the White Mountains with Samuel Colman, Benjamin Champney, and Richard W. Hubbard as early as 1853-54 and again, following his service in the war, in 1865 and 1866. He made several trips to Europe, one from 1855 to 1857, another in 1859, and again from 1868 to 1870. A growing interest in western scenery led to his exploration of the Rocky Mountains in 1870 with fellow artists Worthington Whittredge and John F. Kensett and prompted Gifford to make a second trip west in 1874. He exhibited frequently at the Brooklyn Art Association and kept a studio at the 10th Street Studio Building (N.Y.C.) from 1858 until his death. He was elected to the Century Association in 1859.

Bibliography:

Archives of American Art. Rolls D21, D254, 672, 688.
Cikovsky, Nikolai, Jr. "Introduction." *Sanford Robinson Gifford, 1823-1880.* Austin, TX: University of Texas Art Museum, 1970.
Memorial Catalogue of the Paintings of Sanford Robinson Gifford, N.A. New York: Metropolitan Museum of Art, 1881; reprinted Olana Gallery, 1974.
Weiss, Ila. "Sanford R. Gifford in Europe, a Sketchbook of 1868." *American Art Journal* 9:2 (Nov. 1977), pp. 81-103.

A HOME IN THE WILDERNESS.
 1866.
 30½ x 54¼ (77.5 x 137.8).
 Cleveland Museum.

A SKETCH IN THE WHITE MOUNTAINS.
 9 x 15 (22.9 x 38.1).
 Metropolitan Museum of Art exhibition (1881), #146.

A SKETCH OF ECHO LAKE IN THE FRANCONIA MOUNTAINS, NH.
 12 x 10 (30.5 x 25.4).
 Metropolitan Museum of Art exhibition (1881), #148.

A SKETCH OF MOTE [sic] MOUNTAIN.
 Before 1863.
 Metropolitan Museum of Art exhibition (1881), #334.

A SKETCH OF MOUNT CHICORUA [sic].
 Before 1863.
 Metropolitan Museum of Art exhibition (1881), #339.

A SKETCH OF MOUNT WASHINGTON.
 1859.
 8 x 14 (20.3 x 35.6).
 Metropolitan Museum of Art exhibition (1881), #144.

A SKETCH OF MOUNT WASHINGTON FROM THE SACO RIVER.
 Before 1858.
 Metropolitan Museum of Art exhibition (1881), #141.

A SKETCH OF WHITE MOUNTAIN SCENERY.
 6 x 10 (15.2 x 25.4).
 Metropolitan Museum of Art exhibition (1881), #145.

AUTUMN EVENING IN THE WHITE MOUNTAINS.
 NAD, 1859, #601.

AUTUMN IN THE WHITE MOUNTAINS.
 3½ x 7 (8.9 x 17.8).
 Metropolitan Museum of Art exhibition (1881), #267.

CHOCORUA.
 Before 1870. Oil.
 NMAA Inventory.

CHOCORUA PEAK.
 NAD, 1855, #94.

CONWAY VALLEY (WITH MOUNT WASHINGTON).
 NAD, 1855, #22.

CONWAY VALLEY FROM CATHEDRAL LEDGE.
 Amherst College.

CONWAY VALLEY, NEW HAMPSHIRE.
 Before 1867. Oil.
 NMAA Inventory.

CONWAY, NEW HAMPSHIRE.
 12 x 18 (30.5 x 45.7).
 Metropolitan Museum Art exhibition (1881), #58.

EARLY OCTOBER IN THE WHITE MOUNTAINS.
 1861.
 12 x 24 (30.5 x 61).
 Metropolitan Museum of Art exhibition (1881); Pre-1877; Art Gallery of the Mississippi Valley Sanitary Fair, St. Louis (1864).

EARLY SEPTEMBER IN THE WHITE MOUNTAINS.
 Pre-1877; 1st exhibition of the Western Academy of Art, St. Louis.

ECHO LAKE, WHITE MOUNTAINS.
 17 x 21 (43.2 x 53.3).
 NAD, 1851, #150; Metropolitan Museum of Art exhibition (1881), #43.

INDIAN SUMMER IN THE WHITE MOUNTAINS.
 Before 1862.
 16 x 30 (40.6 x 76.2).
 Metropolitan Museum of Art exhibition (1881), #268.

LAKE SINAPEE [sic].
 Before 1861.
 12 x 22 (30.5 x 55.9).
 Metropolitan Museum of Art exhibition (1881), #231.

LAKE WINNIPISEOGEE [sic].
10½ x 20 (26.7 x 50.8).
Metropolitan Museum of Art exhibition (1881), #149.

LAKE WINNIPISEOGEE [sic].
1858.
13½ x 25 (34.3 x 63.5).
Metropolitan Museum of Art exhibition (1881), #150.

LAKE WINNIPISEOGEE [sic].
Before 1858.
Metropolitan Museum of Art exhibition (1881), #151.

LAKE WINNIPISEOGEE [sic] FROM RED HILL.
Boston Athenaeum (1858), #330; Bierstadt Exhibition, New Bedford, 1858, #118.

LANDSCAPE, WHITE MOUNTAINS.
Mid-19th century. Oil.
12 x 9 (30.5 x 22.9).
Littleton Community Center.

MOAT MOUNTAIN FROM ECHO LAKE.
1863.
12 x 20 (30.5 x 50.8).
Metropolitan Museum of Art exhibition (1881), #289.

MOTE [sic] MOUNTAIN, NEW HAMPSHIRE.
1868.
20 x 36 (50.8 x 91.4).
Metropolitan Museum of Art exhibition (1881), #456.

MOUNT CHICORUA [sic], NEW HAMPSHIRE.
Before 1863.
18 x 30 (15.7 x 76.2).
Metropolitan Museum of Art exhibition (1881), #290.

MOUNT CHOCORUA. S/Center.
9½ x 16½ (24.1 x 41.9).
Private collection.

MOUNT HAYES. S/L/L.
C. 1860-70. Oil on canvas.
30½ x 54 (76.2 x 137.2).
Vose Galleries (Fall 1976).

MOUNT WASHINGTON.
7½ x 12½ (19.1 x 31.8).
Metropolitan Museum of Art exhibition (1881), #143.

MOUNT WASHINGTON.
1871. Oil.
9 x 14½ (22.9 x 36.8).
New Britain Museum of American Art (1975).

MOUNT WASHINGTON FROM THE SACO RIVER.
1858 or 1854-55. Oil on canvas.
10½ x 20 (26.7 x 50.8).
Private collection (1984); Kennedy Galleries (1978); Metropolitan Museum of Art exhibition (1881), #142.

MOUNT WASHINGTON FROM THE SACO RIVER. S/D.
C. 1854. Oil on canvas.
12 x 20 (30.5 x 50.8).
Private collection.

MOUNTAIN VALLEY (CONWAY MEADOWS FROM CATHEDRAL LEDGE).
C. 1854. Oil on canvas.
14 x 20 (35.6 x 50.8).
Amherst College.

SKETCHBOOK.
1854.
Albany Institute of History and Art — 1854 sketchbook.

SUMMER AFTERNOON (Chocorua).
1853. Oil on canvas.
29 x 41 (73.7 x 104.1). Oval.
Newark Museum; University of Texas Art Museum exhibition.

SUNSET AT WHITE MOUNTAINS (Mount Washington).
Boston Athenaeum (1869), #343.
(Engraved by Wellstood for the *Ladies' Repository.*)

TROUT FISHNG MOOSE-HILLOCK BROOK. (Moosilaukee).
Leonard Auction (March 23, 1865), #22.

WHITE MOUNTAINS.
Before 1870. Oil.
NMAA Inventory.

WHITE MOUNTAIN NOTCH.
Sept. 18, 1854. Pencil.

WHITE MOUNTAINS SCENERY.
1859.
6 x 11½ (15.2 x 29.2).
Metropolitan Museum of Art exhibition (1881), #175.

WHITE MOUNTAINS; THE...
Before 1871.
9 x 14 (22.9 x 35.6).
Metropolitan Museum of Art exhibition (1881), #574.

Attributed:
Pair: MOUNT CHICHOURA [sic], NEW HAMPSHIRE, and INTERVALE, NEW HAMPSHIRE. Oil.

New Hampshire Scenery

12 x 18 (30.5 x 45.7).
Sporting Gallery (1969); *Antiques* (Sept. 1969).

GIGNOUX, MARIE-FRANÇOIS REGIS
A, Ce, C&H, F, G&W, K, N, R, S, T
Born Lyons, France, June 16, 1814.
Died Paris, Aug. 14, 1882.
Gignoux studied in Paris under Paul Delaroche. At the age of 24 he came to the U.S. and settled in the Brooklyn, NY, area. In 1842 he exhibited at the NAD, became an associate member in 1844, and was elected a full member in 1851. He was the first president of the Brooklyn Art Association, which he helped found, and exhibited there for many years. In 1858 he joined fellow artists in the 10th Street Studio Building (N.Y.C.). From 1857 to 1876 he was a member of the Century Association. He kept ties with the French world, for in 1867 he exhibited MOUNT WASHINGTON in Paris. He returned to France in 1869 and remained there the rest of his life.
Bibliography:
Feber, Linda. "Ripe for Revival—Forgotten American Artists." *Artnews* (Dec. 1980), pp. 69-71.
Sears, Clara Endicott. *Highlights Among the Hudson River Artists.* Boston: Houghton Mifflin, 1947, pp. 179-180.
AUTUMN LANDSCAPE (Echo Lake?).
   Oil on canvas.
   28 x 45 (71.1 x 114.3).
   Private collection (1982); NMAA Inventory.
MOUNTAIN LANDSCAPE.
   21 x 17 (53.4 x 43.2).
   Sotheby PB catalog (April 1976).
MOUNT WASHINGTON.
   C&H; Fielding.
NEW HAMPSHIRE MOUNTAIN VIEW.
   48 x 84 (121.9 x 213.4).
   Private collection; NMAA; *Antiques* (Nov. 1960).
NEW HAMPSHIRE SCENERY.
   Brooklyn Art Association (1863), #120.
WINTER IN NEW HAMPSHIRE.
   NAD, 1858, #441; Boston Athenaeum (1858), #61.

GILES, HORACE P.
G&W
Born 1806. Died 189?.
Primarily a crayon portraitist, Giles was listed

in the Boston directory from 1872 to 1893 as a fresco painter, scenic and photographic background painter, and artist.
LAFAYETTE FROM FRANCONIA.
   North Conway Library Exhibition (1965).

GOODWIN, ARTHUR CLIFTON
F, N, S
Born Portsmouth, NH, 1866. Died 1929.
Goodwin was a painter and illustrator, but nothing else is presently known of him.
NEW HAMPSHIRE LAKE.
   Pastel.
   19 x 24 (48.3 x 61).
   NMAA Inventory.
NEW HAMPSHIRE LAKE.
   Pastel.
   17½ x 23½ (44.5 x 59.7).
   Richard Bourne, Inc., catalog (Aug. 6, 1974).

GRANBERY, VIRGINIA
G&W, N, R
Born probably Norfolk, VA, Aug. 7, 1831.
Died New York, NY, Dec. 17, 1921.
Granbery gave her address as New York City when she exhibited at the NAD from 1861 to 1890. She taught at the Packer Institute in Brooklyn for 11 years and at various times exhibited at the PAFA, the Leonard Auction Rooms in Boston, and the Massachusetts Charitable Mechanic Association. More of her paintings of fruit were lithographed by Prang than those of any other artist.
HILLSIDE PASTURE, JACKSON, NEW HAMPSHIRE.
   MA Charitable (1881), #204.

GREAVES, HARRY E.
Born 1854. Died 1919.
A painter, illustrator, and watercolorist, Greaves lived in Concord, NH, from 1892 to 1896. Several of his works are listed in the BIAP and NMAA Inventory lists.
Information courtesy of the New Hampshire Historical Society and Howard R. Chase.
VIEW OF WINNEPESAUKEE [sic] FROM ABOVE THE WEIRS.
   Late 19th century. Watercolor.
   Private collection.

GREENE, N. (MRS.)

A, G&W
Active 1842.
Nothing else is presently known of this artist.
THE GREAT CARBUNCLE OF THE WHITE MOUNTAINS.
   Boston Athenaeum (1842), #77.

GREGORY, A. M.

Active 1886 - c. 1890.
About 1890, Gregory was an assistant in the painting department of the Academy of Art which was situated in Boston at 460 Washington Street while William H. Titcombe (or Titcomb) was the Academy's principal.
WINTER SUNSET, WALKER'S POND, CONWAY, NH. S/D/L/R.
   1886. Oil on canvas.
   11¼ x 19¾ (28.6 x 50.2).
   University Art Gallery catalog, University of New Hampshire (1980), #111.

GRIGGS, SAMUEL W.

A, F(sup), G&W
Born perhaps Roxbury, MA, Dec. 1827.
Died Boston, MA, May 16, 1898.
Griggs was listed as an architect in the Boston City directory from 1848 to 1852 and as an artist from 1854 until his death. The competency of his work strongly suggests that he had professional training. His earliest currently datable painting of a White Mountain scene is 1858. That year he exhibited three paintings, one of which was a White Mountain view, in an exhibition coordinated by Albert Bierstadt and held in New Bedford, MA. He also exhibited at the Boston Athenaeum from 1855 to 1863 and at the Boston Art Club at various times. At the time of his death he was living at 63 Studio Building in Boston.
AN OCTOBER DAY, SANDWICH, NEW HAMPSHIRE.
   Leonard Auction (Feb. 17, 1876), #56.
CONWAY MEADOWS.
   Crawford House Auction (July 1976); Leonard Auction (May 22, 1863), #34.
DINAH'S [Diana's] BATHS IN NORTH CONWAY.
   Private collection (1983).

FARM IN NEW HAMPSHIRE.
   1867.
   12 x 18½ (30.5 x 47).
   Parke-Bernet (1946).
GLIMPSE OF LAKE WINNIPISEOGEE [sic] FROM SANDWICH, NH.
   Leonard Auction (June 5, 1874), #69.
HAYING TIME IN NEW ENGLAND (Whiteface?). S/D/L/R.
   1876. Oil on canvas.
   15¼ x 25⅜ (38.7 x 64.5).
   Private collection (1983); University Art Gallery catalog, University of New Hampshire (1980), #112.
KEARSARGE FROM THE SACO. Signed.
   Oil on canvas.
   16 x 26 (40.6 x 66).
   Private collection (1983).
LAKE WINNIPISEOGEE [sic].
   Leonard Auction (May 22, 1863).
LAKE WINNIPISEOGEE [sic], FROM CENTER HARBOR.
   Leonard Auction (June 5, 1874), #33.
Signed Griggs or Greggs, S. W.
LANDSCAPE, WHITE MOUNTAINS.
   Mid-19th century. Oil.
   18 x 33 (45.7 x 83.8).
   Colonel Town Community House, Lancaster, NH (1979).
Signed Griggs or Greggs, S. W.
LANDSCAPE, WHITE MOUNTAINS.
   Mid-19th century. Oil.
   12 x 19 (30.5 x 48.3).
   Littleton Community Center (1979).
MOAT MOUNTAIN AND WASHINGTON – SACO RIVER.
   Private collection (1974).
MORNING ON SWIFT RIVER, SANDWICH, NEW HAMPSHIRE.
   Leonard Auction (Feb. 17, 1876), #79.
MORNING, NEAR SANDWICH, NH.
   Leonard Auction (May 23, 1871), #59.
MOUNT LAFAYETTE FROM ORE HILL. S/D.
   1879.
   22 x 36 (55.9 x 91.4).
   Richard Bourne, Inc., catalog (1976), #46.
MOUNT LAFAYETTE FROM ORE HILL. S/D/L/L.
   1870. Oil on canvas.
   21½ x 27 (54.6 x 68.6).
   Richard Bourne, Inc., catalog (Aug. 6, 1974), #17.

New Hampshire Scenery

Mount Washington from the Saco River
Sanford Gifford, c. 1854
Oil on canvas, 12" x 20" / Private collection, photograph courtesy of
  Hirschl & Adler Galleries, Inc., New York / Ref. page 72

NEW ENGLAND SUMMER LANDSCAPE (Mount Washington).
  Richard Bourne, Inc., catalog (Aug. 6, 1974), #35.
ON THE ARTIST'S BROOK, WEST CAMPTON, NEW HAMPSHIRE.
  Boston Art Club (1883), #110.
ON THE ROAD FROM LANCASTER TO JEFFERSON, NEW HAMPSHIRE.
  Boston Art Club (1898), #251.
OSSIPEE VALLEY, SANDWICH, NH.
  Leonard Auction (Feb. 17, 1876), #32.
RED HILL, SQUAM LAKE, NH.
  North Conway Library Exhibition (1965).
SANDWICH, NEW HAMPSHIRE.
  North Conway Library Exhibition (1965).
VALLEY OF THE PEMIGEWASSET, THORNTON, NH.
  Leonard Auction (Feb. 17, 1876), #25.
VIEW ON THE PEMIGEWASSET.
  Bierstadt Exhibition, New Bedford, 1858, #77; Leonard Auction (March 23, 1865), #25.

WHITE MOUNTAINS FROM SILVER LAKE.
  North Conway Library Exhibition (1965).
WILLEY BROOK, NORTH CONWAY, NEW HAMPSHIRE. S/D/L/R.
  1861. Oil on canvas.
  13½ x 19½ (34.3 x 49.5).
  Boston Public Library, Brockton catalog; NMAA Inventory.

GRITTEN, HENRY
A, C, Ce, G&W
Born England. Active 1835-53.
From 1835 to 1849 Gritten exhibited landscapes in London. Moving to the U.S. and New York City about 1849, he exhibited at the AAU in 1850 and 1851.

KEARSARGE MOUNTAIN.
  NAD, 1850, #88.
RECOLLECTION OF NEW HAMPSHIRE SCENERY.
  NAD, 1851, #314.

Dictionary of Painters

GRUNEWALD (GREENWALD), GUSTAVUS
C, Ce, C&H, F, G&W, R, S
Born Gnadau, Germany, Dec. 10, 1805.
Died Gnadenburg, Germany, Aug. 1, 1878.
Grunewald came to the U.S. at the age of 26 and taught art in Bethlehem, PA, from 1836 to *1866 while supplementing his income with lithography. He exhibited during this time at the NAD and the PAFA. Returning to Germany in 1868, he died there 10 years later.*
THE NOTCH.
PAFA, 1857.

H

HALLETT, HENDRICKS A.
F, S
Born Charlestown, MA, 1847.
Died Boston, MA, 1921.
Primarily a marine and historical painter, Hallett studied in Antwerp and Paris. He was a member of the Boston Society of Water Color Painters and exhibited at the Massachusetts Charitable Mechanic Association in 1892.
MOUNT MONADNOCK, NEW HAMPSHIRE.
　　Oil.
　　20 x 24 (50.8 x 61).
　　Private collection (1976); NMAA Inventory.

HALSALL, WILLIAM FORMBY (or FORMSBY)
A, C&H, F
Born Kirkdale, England, Nov. 1841.
Died Provincetown, MA, March 21, 1919.
Halsall, primarily known for his marine paintings, came by his love of the ocean early in life, for he went to sea at the age of 12 and was a sailor for the next seven years. In 1860, he moved to Boston and turned to art, trying fresco painting with William E. Norton, who was also his teacher. After serving for two years in the Navy during the Civil War, he returned to Boston and took up fresco painting again in 1863. He studied at the Lowell Institute for eight years, and, during this time, he began to do marine paintings, while sharing a studio with Norton. There is no evidence that Halsall ever visited the White Mountains, but many stereographic views attest to the accuracy of his painting.
Bibliography:
Archives of American Art. Roll 1406.

SUMMIT OF MOUNT WASHINGTON IN WINTER. S/D/L/R.
　　1889 or 1887. Oil on canvas.
　　19 x 27 (48.3 x 68.6).
　　Littleton Public Library (1983); University Art Gallery catalog, University of New Hampshire (1980), #113.

HAMMER, JOHN J.
N
Born Germany, 1838 or 1842. Died 1906.
Hammer exhibited at the NAD from 1870 to 1900. His address was generally New York City, but he was in Pittsburgh in 1889.
MOUNT WASHINGTON.
　　Before 1887. Oil on canvas.
　　7⅛ x 11 $^{11}/_{16}$ (18.1 x 29.7).
　　Allen Memorial Art Museum catalog (1967), Oberlin College, Oberlin, OH (1967), p. 318; BIAP.

HAMMOND, GEORGE F.
There is presently no information on this artist.
MOUNT ADAMS AND MADISON FROM SHELBURNE.
　　MA Charitable (1881), #364.
SHELBURNE MEADOWS.
　　Watercolor.
　　MA Charitable (1881), #412.
WHITE MOUNTAINS FROM GLEN HOUSE.
　　Watercolor.
　　MA Charitable (1881), #402.

HAPPEL, CARL
A, N
Born Heidelberg, Germany, 1819. Died 1914.
Happel is purported to be the first painter from Heidelberg to visit the U.S. He lived in this country from 1860 to 1867 and exhibited at the Brooklyn Art Association in 1863, 1865, and

New Hampshire Scenery

1867 and at the NAD in 1865. He kept a studio in New York City and, in 1864, visited the White Mountains.

Bibliography:
University of Maryland, European Division, catalog. *A Heidelberg Painter Visits America* (June 21-Aug. 21, 1976).

FLUME (several versions).
    Before 1864. Watercolor.
    University of Maryland, European Division, exhibition (June 21-Aug. 21, 1965).

WHITE MOUNTAINS, NEW HAMPSHIRE.
    1864.
    University of Maryland, European Division, exhibition (June 21-Aug. 21, 1965), #41.

HART, JAMES MCDOUGALL (or MCDONALD)

A, B, Ce, C&H, DAB, F, G&W, K, Ka, N, S, T
Born Kilmarnock, Scotland, May 10, 1828.
Died Brooklyn, NY, Oct. 24, 1901.
Younger brother of William Hart, James moved with his family to Albany, NY, in 1831. There he was apprenticed to a sign painter and developed an interest in art. In 1851 he went to Düsseldorf, Germany, to study, and remained for three years. He returned to Albany and opened a studio but in 1857 moved to New York City. He became an associate member of the NAD in 1858, a full member in 1859, and served as vice-president for a time. Hart exhibited there from 1853 to 1900 and also exhibited at the Brooklyn Art Association, the Boston Athenaeum, the AAU, and the PAFA. Sinclair Hamilton noted that James and his brother "painted in a language intelligible for the artistically illiterate."

HAYING TIME, NEW HAMPSHIRE.
    Brooklyn Art Association (1869), #77.

LANDSCAPE (A RANGE OF MOUNTAINS). S/L/L.
    July 16, 1867.
    14½ x 31 (36.8 x 78.7).
    Old Print Shop (1948).

OAKS NEAR LITTLETON, NEW HAMPSHIRE; THE...
    MA Charitable (1878), #161 (won medal for the painting, Boston, 1874).

PRESIDENTIAL RANGE, WHITE MOUNTAINS, NH. S/D/L/L.
    Sept. 11, 1867. Oil on canvas.
    14½ x 24 (36.8 x 61).
    Private collection.

SACO RIVER.
    1872.
    Private collection (1983).

STUDY NEAR LANCASTER, NEW HAMPSHIRE. S/D/L/R.
    Sept. 20, 1867. Pencil on paper.
    11 5/16 x 14⅞ (28.7 x 37.8).
    Hirschl and Adler Gallery.

WHITE MOUNTAINS.
    Pre-1877; Derby Athenaeum, NY (1868).

HART, WILLIAM M.

A, B, Ce, C&H, DAB, F, G&W, Ka, N, S, T
Born Paisley, Scotland, March 31, 1823.
Died Mount Vernon, NY, June 17, 1894.
Brought to this country by his parents as a youngster, Hart began his career as a coach and ornamental painter in Troy, NY. For several years he traveled throughout Michigan as an itinerant painter doing portraits, before going to Europe to study. From 1852 on he kept a studio in New York City, working out of the 10th Street Studio Building from 1859 to 1870. He became an associate member of the NAD in 1855 and a full member in 1858. From the dates of his White Mountain views, he must have traveled in the area many times between 1859 and 1870. CHOCORUA PEAK was engraved by the Boston engraver William Wellstood in 1861, giving Hart's work a wide audience. He exhibited at the Boston Athenaeum and at the NAD throughout his active life as an artist. Albany, NY, was an important art center in the mid-19th century, and Hart's work was exhibited at the studio of Erastus Dow Palmer in that city in 1864 as a benefit for the U.S. Sanitary Commission.

Bibliography:
Sears, Clara Endicott. *Highlights Among the Hudson River Artists.* Boston: Houghton Mifflin, 1947, pp. 209-210.

A SCENE NEAR GORHAM.
    NAD, 1863, #357.

A VIEW FROM MOUNT HAYES, NEAR GORHAM, NEW HAMPSHIRE.
    NAD, 1866, #216.

AN AUTUMN SCENE ON THE PEABODY RIVER, NEW HAMPSHIRE.
    Brooklyn Art Association (1863), #74; Pre-1877.

AUTUMN DAY ON MOOSE BROOK, NEW HAMPSHIRE.
    NAD, 1865, #367.

AUTUMN IN THE WHITE MOUNTAINS.
Pre-1877; Fine Arts Department of the Cleveland (OH) Sanitary Fair (Feb. 22, 1864) (see Western Reserve Historical Society for information).

AUTUMN VIEW OF MOUNT CHOCORUA.
Pre-1877; Chicago Industrial Exposition (1875).

BROOK SCENE AT CONWAY, NH.
Boston Athenaeum (1856), #131.

CHOCORUA MOUNTAIN, NEW HAMPSHIRE.
Oil on canvas.
34 x 49½ (86.4 x 125.7).
University of Southern California, Fisher collection.

CHOCORUA MOUNTAIN, NEW HAMPSHIRE.
Oil.
32 x 48 (81.3 x 121.9).
University of Southern California (1973); NMAA Inventory.

CONWAY   VALLEY   AND   MOUNT WASHINGTON. S/L/R.
1850-60. Oil on canvas.
10 x 16 (25.4 x 40.6).
Vose Galleries (1983); private collection (1983); Hirschl and Adler Gallery (Oct.-Nov. 1969).

FIRST SNOW, THE WHITE MOUNTAINS.
Pre-1877; 3rd annual exhibition at Young Men's Association in the Athenaeum, Troy, NY, 1860.

GORHAM, NEW HAMPSHIRE.
Brooklyn Art Association (1868), #178.

LANDSCAPE WITH STREAM AND CATTLE.
Pencil and wash.
Boston Museum of Fine Arts, Karolik collection.

LOWER BERLIN FALLS.
1861.
12¼ x 18¾ (31.1 x 47.6).
Vassar College Art Gallery (1970).

MOONLIGHT ON MOUNT CARTER, GORHAM. S/D/L/Center.
1859. Pencil and white wash.
12¼ x 18⅞ (31.1 x 47.9).
Vassar College Art Gallery (1980); University Art Gallery catalog, University of New Hampshire (1980), #7.

MORNING ON THE MOOSE RIVER.
NAD, 1863, #367.

MOUNT CHOCORUA.
Boston Athenaeum (1864), #314; Pre-1877;

Art Gallery of the Inter-State Industrial Exposition of Chicago (1876).

MOUNT MADISON.
Watercolor.
U.S. Sanitary Commission (1864), #42; C&H; Centennial exhibition (1876); Pre-1877.

MOUNT WASHINGTON FROM NORTH CONWAY.
Boston Athenaeum (1859), #317.

ON THE ANDROSCOGGIN.
Boston Athenaeum (1862), #313.

PIONEER IN LANDSCAPE.
1847. Oil.
25 x 33½ (63.5 x 85.1).
Unlocated.

PRESIDENTIAL MOUNTAINS, NEW HAMPSHIRE. S/L/L.
7½ x 14 (19.1 x 35.6).
Liros Gallery, Alexandria, VA (1980); Antiques (Nov. 1980).

SACO AND WASHINGTON. S/L/R.
Wash and pencil.
8⅝ x 11⅝ (21.9 x 29.5).
Boston Museum of Fine Arts, Karolik collection.

SACO AT NORTH CONWAY AND MOUNT KEARSARGE.
Before 1869. Oil on canvas.
10 x 15 (25.4 x 38.1).
Vassar College Art Gallery (1972); Florence Lewison Gallery (Dec. 1974), #7.

SCENE ON THE WHITE MOUNTAINS.
Pre-1877; Art Association exhibition at Mechanic's Hall, Montreal (Feb. 27, 1865).

VALLEY OF CONWAY.
U.S. Sanitary Commission (1864), #62.

VIEW FROM ANDROSCOGGIN.
1859.
12¼ x 18⅞ (31.1 x 47.9).
Vassar College Art Gallery (1970).

VIEW OF GORHAM.
Brooklyn Art Association (1870), #231.

WHITE MOUNTAIN RANGE FROM JEFFERSON HILL.
1859. Pencil and white wash.
12¼ x 18⅞ (31.1 x 47.9).
Vassar College Art Gallery (1970); Florence Lewison Gallery (Dec. 1974), #19.

WHITE MOUNTAIN SCENE.
Pre-1877; Art Association of Montreal (Feb. 11, 1864).

New Hampshire Scenery

WHITE MOUNTAINS.
    Before 1870. Oil.
    NMAA Inventory.
WHITE MOUNTAINS FROM SHELBURNE; THE . . .
    1859. Pencil and white wash.
    12¼ x 18⅞ (31.1 x 47.9).
    Vassar College Art Gallery (1972); Florence
    Lewison Gallery (Dec. 1974), #16.
WHITE MOUNTAINS NEAR CONWAY.
    Pre-1877; Chicago exhibition of the fine arts
    (May 9, 1859).

HASELTINE (or HAZELTINE), ELIZABETH STANLEY (MRS. JOHN)

G&W, Ka, R
Born Philadelphia, PA, April 22, 1811.
Died Boston, MA, June 29, 1882.
*Haseltine, considered an amateur due to the
demands of her family, painted in the 1860s and
exhibited at the PAFA.*
STUDY NEAR COTTAGE ROCK, KEARSARGE
MOUNTAIN.
    PAFA, 1868, #216.

HAVELL, ROBERT, JR.

Ce, DAB, E, F, G&W, K, Ka, N, R, S
Born Reading, Berkshire, England, Nov. 25,
1793.
Died Tarrytown, NY, Nov. 11, 1878.
*Havell is best known for engraving nearly all
the plates, executed in England between 1827
and 1838, for John James Audubon's* Birds of
America. *He came to the U.S. in 1839 and
devoted himself to landscape painting and
sometimes published his work as aquatints. He
exhibited at the AAU and the NAD from 1840
to 1866.*
Bibliography:
Stauffer, D. M. *American Engravings upon
Copper and Steel* (1907).
VIEW OF LAKE WINIPISEOGEE [sic].
    AAU, 1849, #92.
WINNEPISSEGEE [sic] LAKE NEAR CENTRE
HARBOR.
    Pencil.
    Boston Museum of Fine Arts, Karolik col-
    lection (1983).

HAY, DEWITT CLINTON

F, G&W, K, S
Born Caldwell, Lake George, NY, about 1819.
Died Tarrytown, NY, July 22, 1877.
A bank note engraver, Hay moved to New York

*City about 1850. He was one of the founders
of the Society of American Painters in Water
Colors and did many charming small water-
colors on his travels through the world. He
never exhibited his work publicly.*
CONWAY (Swift River?).
    Watercolor.
    2¾ x 4⅝ (7 x 11.7).
    Private collection (1984); Dufty (1973).
KEARSARGE MOUNTAIN, NH.
    1863. Watercolor.
    3⅜ x 7 (8.6 x 17.8).
    Private collection (1984); Dufty (1973).
WHITE MOUNTAINS (A NOTCH).
    Watercolor.
    3⅝ x 6¾ (9.2 x 17.1).
    Private collection (1984); Dufty (1973).

HEADE, MARTIN JOHNSON

A, C, Ka, R, T
Born Lumberville, PA, Aug. 11, 1819.
Died St. Augustine, FL, Sept. 4, 1904.
*Heade was first educated in art by Thomas
Hicks and later studied in Italy, France, and
England. A prolific painter, perhaps best known
for the delicate depictions of the hummingbirds
and orchids he gathered on his trips to South
America, Heade exhibited widely at Boston, the
PAFA and the NAD. The Bucks County In-
telligencer for August 9, 1864, noted, "Heade
has executed a number of sketches of the White
Mountain regions, and of the wild ravines near
Conway." He kept a studio in the 10th Street
Studio Building (N.Y.C.) from 1859 to 1861 and
again, after the Civil War, from 1866 to 1879.*
Bibliography:
Stebbins, Theodore E., Jr. *Life and Works of
Martin Johnson Heade.* New Haven: Yale
University Press, 1975.
Attributed:
WHITE MOUNTAINS LANDSCAPE (Kearsarge).
S/D/L/L.
    1871. Oil on paper on canvas.
    9 x 15¼ (22.9 x 38.7).
    Pennsylvania State University, Vessel collec-
    tion (1975); Sotheby PB (1971), #11.

HEINE, WILLIAM (or WILHELM) PETER BERNARD

A, Ce, G&W, K, R
Born Dresden, Germany, Jan. 30, 1827.
Died near Dresden, Germany, Oct. 5, 1885.
Heine came to the U.S. in 1849 and remained

in this country for 10 years, during which time he exhibited at the NAD.

MOUNT WASHINGTON, NORTH CONWAY.
   NAD, 1858, #422; 1859, #509.

HEKKING, J. ANTONIO
Ce, G&W, N, R
Born Germany. Active 1859-75.
Hekking came to the U.S in 1859 and exhibited from that year through 1875 at the NAD while living in upstate New York and later in Connecticut. He may have returned to Europe after 1875.

WARD HOMESTEAD (MOUNT WASHINGTON); THE... S/L/R.
   C. 1860. Oil on canvas.
   26 x 40 (66 x 101.6).
   Old Print Shop (Oct. 1972), #39.

WHITE MOUNTAIN LANDSCAPE. S/L/R.
   Oil on canvas.
   10 x 14 (25.4 x 35.6).
   Skinner catalog (1977).

HERRICK, HENRY W.
F(sup), G&W, N, S
Born Hopkinton, NH, Aug. 23, 1824.
Died Manchester, NH, 1906.
At the early age of nine years Herrick was seriously studying art. In his teens he took up wood engraving on his own and worked for firms in Concord and Manchester. In 1844 he went to New York City and studied for a time at the NAD. He continued engraving, his best-known work being copies of the paintings of Felix O. C. Darley, but also did watercolors. From 1852 to 1858 he taught at the New York School of Design for Women. He did engravings for various firms, including the American Bank Company. In 1865 Herrick returned to Manchester, NH, where he founded the Manchester Art Association.

Bibliography:
Manchester Historic Association catalog. *The World of Henry W. Herrick, An Exhibition of His Watercolors.* Manchester, NH (no date).

BEECHER'S CASCADE, WHITE MOUNTAINS.
   Watercolor.
   Boston Art Club (1891), #188.

FLUME AT FRANCONIA, NEW HAMPSHIRE.
   Manchester (NH) Historic Association exhibition (1969).

OLD MAN OF THE MOUNTAINS.
   Private collection (1969).

HERZOG, HERMAN
N, R, S
Born Germany, 1831. Died 1932.
Herzog was trained as a painter in Düsseldorf, Germany, and left for the U.S. in the late 1860s or early 1870s. He sketched in Valleyhouse, NH, in 1871 and exhibited at the Brooklyn Art Association in 1869 and 1872 and at the NAD in 1882.

Bibliography:
Lewis, Donald S., Jr. "Herman Herzog (1831-1932): German Landscapist in America." *American Art Review* 3:4 (July-Aug. 1976), pp. 52-67.

BEECHER'S FALLS, WHITE MOUNTAINS.
   Pre-1877; PAFA exhibition, 1876.

ELEPHANT'S HEAD, CRAWFORD HOUSE.
   Before 1885.

NOTCH NEAR CRAWFORD HOUSE, NEW HAMPSHIRE.
   Watercolor.
   8½ x 11½ (21.6 x 29.2).
   Chapellier Gallery catalog (1974), #11.

SKETCHBOOKS.
   Undated. Before 1885. Pen, ink, and wash.
   9 x 11¾ (22.9 x 29.8).
   Ausleu Gallery, Norfolk, VA.

HIDLEY, JOSEPH HENRY
G&W
Born North Greenbush, NY, March 22, 1830.
Died Poestenskill, NY, Sept. 28, 1872.
A naive artist best known for his townscapes, Hidley also did religious views and copies of landscapes. He executed a painting of the Conway area, but it is not known if he ever ventured as far as New Hampshire from the circumscribed area of Troy and Poestenskill, NY.

Bibliography:
Lipman, Jean, and Tom Armstrong. *American Folk Painters of Three Centuries.* Brunswick (NY) Historical Society, 1978, pp. 78-103.

CONWAY INTERVALE (Moat Mountain and Ledges).
   24 x 48 (61 x 121.9).
   Esther Bloch, The Art Searcher (1982).

MOUNT WASHINGTON FROM THE VALLEY OF CONWAY (after Kensett).
   After 1851.
   Unlocated.

New Hampshire Scenery

HIGGINS, GEORGE F.

A, F(sup), G&W

Active 1859-84.

Higgins lived near the White Mountains during his active years, claiming East Somerville, MA, as his residence in 1873 and Melrose, MA, in 1876. He exhibited at the Boston Athenaeum in 1859, 1861, and 1862, at the Leonard Auction Rooms in Boston during that same period, and at the Boston Art Club in 1883.

KEARSARGE BROOK, NORTH CONWAY.
    10 x 14 (25.4 x 35.6).
    Vose Galleries (1972).

LAKE WINNIPESEOGEE [sic].
    Leonard Auction (May 23, 1871), #16.

LANDSCAPE, SCENE IN NEW HAMPSHIRE.
    Leonard Auction (June 16, 1865), #71.

ON THE ANDROSCOGGIN.
    Boston Athenaeum (1861), #320; (1862), #306.

RATTLESNAKE ISLAND, WINNEPISEOGEE [sic].
    Leonard Auction (May 24, 1871), #112.

RUSTIC BRIDGE, WASHINGTON, NEW HAMPSHIRE.
    Boston Art Club (1883), #17.

SQUAM LAKE, NEAR CENTER HARBOR.
    Leonard Auction (May 22, 1863), #50.

VIEW AT LITTLETON, NH.
    Leonard Auction (Feb. 4, 1875), #32.

VIEW AT NORTH CONWAY.
    Leonard Auction (May 22, 1863), #3.

VIEW AT NORTH CONWAY.
    Leonard Auction (May 22, 1863), #72; (Feb. 4, 1875), #11.

VIEW AT WOLFBOROUGH, NH.
    Leonard Auction (Feb. 4, 1875), #40.

WHITE MOUNTAINS; THE...
    16 x 23 (40.6 x 58.4).
    Vose Galleries (sold Aug. 21, 1934, at Richard Bourne, Inc., auction).

WINNEPISEOGEE [sic].
    Leonard Auction (May 24, 1871), #91.

HILL, EDWARD

Born Wolverhampton, England, Dec. 9, 1843. Died Hood River, OR, 1923.

Less well known than his brother, the artist Thomas, Edward Hill was a landscape painter, primarily of New Hampshire scenery. He grew up in Taunton and Salem, MA, and began work as a decorative painter at the Heywood-Wakefield Company in Gardner, MA, where his brother also worked. In 1864 he married and moved to Nashua, NH. Ten years later he bought land farther north in Lancaster, NH, and probably built a home there. He traveled to North Carolina in 1879 and made several trips to England and Italy between 1880 and 1895. His surviving paintings of the White Mountains date from the late 1870s through the 1890s. In 1895 he probably moved back to Nashua where he was listed in the city directory for that year. Hill painted at the Glen House in Pinkham Notch with John Paul Selinger and at the Flume House, where he is said to have had his own studio. His friendship with the photographer Benjamin West Kilburn of Littleton (see Section IV) may hold further clues to his history. About 1879 Hill had a studio in Littleton, and many of his paintings bear a close relationship to Kilburn's stereographic views produced in the latter's factory between 1867 and 1909. Late in his life, Hill visited Colorado, and he died in Oregon in 1923.

Bibliography:

Information courtesy of Charles and Gloria Vogel.

Bell, Irving. "They Painted Hills." *Historical New Hampshire* (Feb. 1946), pp. 11-21.

Giffin, Daniel. "Five New Paintings by Thomas and Edward Hill." *Historical New Hampshire* (Spring 1967).

BROOK; THE...
    Watercolor.
    Boston Art Club watercolor show (April 1886), #115.

CARRIAGE ROAD ON MOUNT WASHINGTON, NH. S/D/L/R.
    1887. Oil on canvas.
    30 x 50 (76.2 x 127).
    Littleton Public Library (1983).

CARRIAGE ROAD, MOUNT WASHINGTON, NH.
    1892. Oil.
    24 x 36 (61 x 91.4).
    Littleton Community Center (1983).

COMING STORM, ECHO LAKE; THE... S/L/R.
    C. 1877. Oil on canvas.
    12⅛ x 20⅛ (30.8 x 51.1).
    New Hampshire Historical Society (1983).

CRAWFORD NOTCH FROM MOUNT WILLARD.
    Oil on canvas.
    12 x 20 (30.5 x 50.8).
    New Hampshire Historical Society (1983).

DARRAH'S POND, LITCHFIELD, N.H.
  1895. Oil on canvas.
  25⅞ x 42 (65.7 x 106.7).

DEEP WOODS – LITTLEFIELD RAVINE, JACKSON, NH. S/D/L/L.
  One of pair (see GOODRICH FALLS).
  1881. Oil on canvas.
  20 x 14 (50.8 x 35.6).
  Private collection (1984); Old Print Shop (March 1980).

DEEP WOODS AND FISHERMAN.
  1878. Oil on canvas.
  18 x 14 (45.7 x 35.6).
  New Hampshire Historical Society (1983).

EAGLE CLIFF AND EAGLE PASS.
  Oil on board.
  New Hampshire Historical Society.

EAGLE CLIFF AND ECHO LAKE. S/D/L/L.
  1881. Oil on canvas.
  43 x 37 (109.2 x 94).
  Littleton Public Library (1983).

EAGLE CLIFF FROM PROFILE LAKE. S/D.
  1897. Oil on canvas.
  29½ x 21½ (74.9 x 54.6).
  Private collection (1983).

EAGLE CLIFF, ECHO LAKE.
  1878.
  Dartmouth College Art Galleries – lent to Dartmouth National Bank.

ECHO LAKE AND EAGLE CLIFF.
  Oil on canvas.
  18 x 14 (45.7 x 35.6).
  New Hampshire Historical Society exhibition (1965).

ECHO LAKE AND PROFILE HOUSE.
  1887. Oil on canvas.
  38 x 62 (96.5 x 157.5).
  New Hampshire Historical Society (1983).

ENTHRONED ABOVE THE CLOUDS (OLD MAN OF THE MOUNTAIN, FRANCONIA NOTCH).
  April 5, 1880. Oil on canvas.
  24 x 20 (61 x 50.8).
  Littleton Public Library (1983).

FRANCONIA NOTCH AND EAGLE PASS.
  Oil on board.
  New Hampshire Historical Society.

FRANCONIA NOTCH FROM ARTIST'S LEDGE.
  1877.
  Littleton Public Library.

FRANCONIA NOTCH FROM BALD MOUNTAIN. S/D.
  1877. Oil on canvas.

14 x 24 (35.6 x 61).
  Littleton Public Library (1983).

FRANCONIA NOTCH, THE WHITE MOUNTAINS, ECHO LAKE AND PROFILE HOUSE.
  1887. Oil on canvas.
  35¾ x 59¾ (90.8 x 151.8).
  Richard Bourne, Inc., catalog (Oct. 1976); New Hampshire Historical Society exhibition (1965).

FRANCONIA RANGE, SUNSET FROM GALE RIVER. S/D.
  1892. Oil on canvas.
  20 x 30 (50.8 x 76.2).
  Private collection (1983).

GOODRICH FALLS. S/D/L/R.
  One of pair (see DEEP WOODS).
  1881. Oil on canvas.
  20 x 14 (50.8 x 35.6).
  Private collection (1984); Old Print Shop (March 1980).

HAYING BELOW MOUNT WASHINGTON.
  Oil.
  27 x 44 (68.6 x 111.7).
  Littleton Community Center (1983).

LAFAYETTE AND PROFILE HOUSE.
  1892. Oil.
  Crawford House Auction (July 1976); New Hampshire Historical Society.

LAKE AND MOUNTAINS (Echo Lake).
  1877.
  20 x 14 (35.6 x 50.8).
  New Hampshire Historical Society; Historical New Hampshire (Spring 1967).

LAKE OF THE CLOUDS, MOUNT LAFAYETTE.
  Oil.
  Boston Art Club (1882), #25.

LANCASTER MEADOWS. S/D/L/L.
  1879. Oil on canvas.
  14 x 24 (35.6 x 61).
  Littleton Public Library (1983).

LOGGING IN WINTER (or LUMBERING CAMP IN WINTER). S/D/L/L.
  1882. Oil on canvas.
  20 x 30 (50.8 x 76.2).
  New Hampshire Historical Society (1983); University Art Gallery catalog, University of New Hampshire (1980), #32.

LOOKING DOWN CRAWFORD NOTCH.
  C. 1880. Oil on canvas.
  7 x 12 (17.8 x 30.5).
  Private collection (1984); Kennedy Galleries (1975).

New Hampshire Scenery

Presidential Range, White Mountains
James Hart, 1867
Oil on canvas, 14 1/2" x 24" / Private collection, photograph courtesy of
     M. Knoedler & Co., Inc., New York / Ref. page 77

MOUNT WASHINGTON FROM NORTH CON-
WAY AND THE SACO.
   1896. Oil.
   Private collection.

MOUNT WASHINGTON FROM PINKHAM
NOTCH. S/D/L/L.
   1892. Oil.
   Unlocated.

MOUNTAINS AT SUNSET (Franconia Notch).
S/D/L/R.
   1888. Oil on canvas.
   28 x 48¼ (71.1 x 122.6).
   New Hampshire Historical Society (1983).

OLD MAN OF THE MOUNTAINS.
   Late 19th century. Oil.
   20 x 12 (50.8 x 30.5).
   Private collection; NMAA Inventory.

OLD MAN OF THE MOUNTAINS. S/D/L/R.
   1876.
   17½ x 14 (44.5 x 35.6).
   Private collection (1983).

OLD MAN OF THE MOUNTAINS.
   1879 or 1874. Oil on canvas.

16 x 12 (40.6 x 30.5).
New Hampshire Historical Society (1983).

ON THE AMMONUSAC [sic] RIVER.
   1882. Oil.
   10 x 7 (25.4 x 17.8).
   Private collection (1975).

ON THE PEMIGEWASSET RIVER. S/D/L/L.
   1896. Oil on canvas.
   30 x 22 (76.2 x 55.9).
   Adam A. Weschler and Sons., Washington,
   DC (Dec. 1978), #1007.

PRESIDENTIAL RANGE (from Littleton?). S/L/L.
   1886. Oil on canvas.
   30 x 50 (76.2 x 127).
   Gift of the W. N. Banks Foundation to the
   New Hampshire Historical Society (1981);
   Craig and Tarleton, Raleigh, NC (1980);
   Richard Bourne, Inc., catalog (Oct. 1976).

PRESIDENTIAL RANGE FROM MAPLEWOOD.
   White Mountain Echo (July 16, 1892), p. 8.
   Hung in the Maplewood Hotel, Bethlehem,
   NH.

Dictionary of Painters

PROFILE LAKE AT FRANCONIA, NEW HAMP-
SHIRE. S/L/R.
> 1876. Oil on canvas.
> 18 x 14 (45.7 x 35.6).
> Private collection (1984); Old Print Shop
> (1978); New Hampshire Historical Society
> (1965).

RAVINE BROOK, WHITE HILLS.
> Oil on canvas.
> 14 x 20 (35.6 x 50.8).
> New Hampshire Historical Society;
> *Historical New Hampshire* (Spring 1967).

SUGAR SCENE.
> Oil.
> 24 x 44 (61 x 111.8).
> Littleton Community Center (1983).

SUMMIT OF MOUNT WASHINGTON IN
WINTER.
> 1889. Oil.
> 19 x 27 (48.3 x 68.6).
> Littleton Public Library (1983).

VIEW FROM MOUNT WILLARD. S/L/L.
> C. 1877. Oil on canvas.
> 12 x 20 (30.5 x 50.8).
> New Hampshire Historical Society (1983);
> University Art Gallery catalog, University of
> New Hampshire (1980), #114.

WATERFALL, CRAWFORD NOTCH. S/D/L/R.
> 1887. Oil on canvas.
> 30 x 20 (76.2 x 50.8).
> Littleton Public Library (1983).

WHITE MOUNTAINS.
> 1886. Oil on canvas.
> 22 x 30 (55.9 x 76.2).
> Butler Institute of American Art,
> Youngstown, OH.

WHITE MOUNTAINS LANDSCAPE, EAGLE CLIFF,
ECHO LAKE. S/L/R.
> Oil on canvas.
> 14 x 22 (35.6 x 55.9).
> Baridoff Gallery sale (July 1980), #100.

WOODLAND SCENE IN THE NOTCH.
> 1878. Oil on canvas.
> 17½ x 13½ (44.6 x 34.3).
> New Hampshire Historical Society exhibition
> (1965).

HILL, JOHN HENRY
Ba, Ce, E, F, G&W, K, Ka, N, R, S
Born West Nyack, NY, April 1839.
Died West Nyack, NY, Dec. 18, 1922.
Hill was known for his etchings, watercolors,
and aquatints. He studied under his father, John
William Hill, and in England. Hill was elected
an associate member of the NAD in 1859 where
he exhibited from 1858 to 1891. He also showed
at the Brooklyn Art Association. He was involv-
ed with the American Pre-Raphaelite Movement
and their magazine, The New Path.

Bibliography:
Dickason, David Howard. *Daring Young Men.*
Indiana University Press, 1953.
Koke, Richard J. "John Hill, Master of Aqua-
tint." New-York Historical Society *Quarterly*
(1959).

IMP AND CARTER MOUNTAINS.
> NAD, 1858, #132.

LAKE WINNIPESAUKEE, NEW HAMPSHIRE.
> 1868. Watercolor on paper.
> 10 x 15 (25.4 x 38.1).
> Dartmouth College Art Galleries (1974).

MOONLIGHT ON ANDROSCOGGIN.
> Private collection.
> Dickason. *Daring Young Men,* pp. 266-267.

MOUNT JEFFERSON.
> NAD, 1858, #531.

MOUNT WASHINGTON.
> Before 1867. Watercolor.
> NMAA Inventory; BIAP.

MOUNT WASHINGTON.
> NAD, 1860, #117; 1861, #182.

MOUNT WASHINGTON AND MADISON.
> Brooklyn Art Association (1867), #19.

MOUNT WASHINGTON FROM CONWAY.
> Brooklyn Art Association (1875), #59.

MOUNT WASHINGTON FROM GORHAM, NEW
HAMPSHIRE.
> NAD, 1858, #292.

PEABODY RIVER NEAR GORHAM.
> Washburn Gallery catalog (June 1973).

TWILIGHT ON THE WHITE MOUNTAINS.
> 1895. Watercolor.
> 17¾ x 23¼ (45.1 x 59.1).
> New Hampshire Historical Society exhibition
> (1965).

WHITE MOUNTAINS.
> Brooklyn Art Association (1866), #120.

WHITE MOUNTAINS.
> Watercolor.
> Brooklyn Art Association (1879), #307.

WHITE MOUNTAINS FROM GORHAM.
> Brooklyn Art Association (1872), #80.

WHITE MOUNTAINS FROM GORHAM; THE. . .
> NAD, 1864, #135.

New Hampshire Scenery

WHITE MOUNTAINS FROM SHELBURNE.
NAD, 1860, #66.

HILL, JOHN WILLIAM

A, Ce, E, F, G&W, K, Ka, N, R, S
Born London, England, Jan. 13, 1812.
Died West Nyack, NY, Sept. 24, 1879.
John William was the son of John Hill, the British landscape engraver and aquatintist, and father of John Henry Hill. He immigrated with the family to this country in 1816. He was apprenticed to his father in 1822. By the age of 21 he was elected an associate of the NAD and became interested in the American Pre-Raphaelite Movement and The New Path. A versatile artist, he worked in lithography, aquatint, and watercolor. He exhibited at the NAD from 1829 until his death and also at the Brooklyn Art Association. He traveled to the White Mountains in 1852 and again in 1857.

ANDROSCOGGIN NEAR SHELBURNE, 1857.
Signed J. W. Hill (probably John William).
1857. Watercolor.
8¾ x 14½ (22.2 x 36.8).
Museum of Fine Arts, Springfield, MA (1972); NMAA Inventory.

CRYSTAL CASCADE, WHITE MOUNTAINS.
Watercolor.
Pre-1877; NAD, watercolor show (1873).

MOUNT WASHINGTON FROM SHELBURNE, NEW HAMPSHIRE.
Metropolitan Museum of Art.

PEABODY AT THE GLEN, NEW HAMPSHIRE.
Washburn Gallery catalog (June 1973).

ROAD TO THE GLEN, WHITE MOUNTAINS SCENERY.
Pre-1877; Utica (NY) art exhibition at Utica Mechanics Hall (1864).

VALLEY OF ANDROSCOGGIN AT BIRBANKS FERRY, NEW HAMPSHIRE.
1859.
9 x 13¼ (22.9 x 33.7).
University of Nebraska Art Gallery (1975).

VIEW IN NEW HAMPSHIRE.
1859. Oil.
25½ x 36 (64.8 x 91.4).
Parke-Bernet (1939).

HILL, THOMAS

A, B, C&H, DAB, F, G&W, K, S, T
Born Birmingham, England, Sept. 11, 1829.
Died Raymond, CA, June 30, 1908, by suicide.
The Hill family brought Thomas and his brother, Edward, to Taunton, MA, from England in 1840. Both brothers worked as furniture decorators for the Heywood-Wakefield Company in Gardner, MA, for a time. Thomas enrolled in the PAFA in 1853 under the tutelage of Rothermel and, at the age of 24, won first prize in the Maryland Institute in Baltimore. He settled in Cambridge, MA, in 1855, but ill health forced him to move to San Francisco in 1861. With improved health, he traveled to Paris in 1866 and settled in Boston upon his return in 1867. He exhibited at the Boston Athenaeum, the Childs Gallery, the Boston Art Club, and the Leonard Auction Rooms. He became a friend of Champney, Casilear, and Gifford and as early as 1862 was a guest at the Conway House. Although ill health forced him to return to California in the 1870s, he traveled with his daughter to New Hampshire and stayed at the Kearsarge House in 1886 where he entertained Champney. He was known for his enormous paintings of grand landscape views such as the oil of Crawford Notch, which measures 6 by 10 feet.

Bibliography:
Archives of American Art. Roll NDA, Cal. I.
Catalogue of the David Hewes Collection of Valuable and Historical Paintings by the Late Thomas Hill, the Great American Artist. San Francisco Museum of Fine Arts (Nov. 27-Dec. 9, 1916).
Giffin, Daniel. "Five New Paintings by Thomas and Edward Hill." *Historical New Hampshire* (Spring 1967).
Majorie, Dakin Arkelian. *Thomas Hill: The Grand View,* Oakland Museum Art Department, 1980.
Sears, Clara Endicott. *Highlights Among the Hudson River Artists.* Boston: Houghton Mifflin, 1947, pp. 205-208.

ARTIST'S BROOK.
Boston Athenaeum (1873), #159.

CANNON MOUNTAIN AND FRANCONIA NOTCH.
Oil on board.
17⅞ x 12 (45.4 x 30.5).
New Hampshire Historical Society (1983).

CLIFFS AND BOULDERS.
Oil on board.
12¾ x 18 (32.4 x 45.7).
New Hampshire Historical Society; *Historical New Hampshire* (Spring 1967).

CRAWFORD NOTCH.
1872. Oil on canvas.
72 x 124 (182.9 x 315).
New Hampshire Historical Society (1984).

ECHO LAKE, FRANCONIA NOTCH. S/L/L.
Oil on canvas.
14 x 18 (35.6 x 45.7).
Baridoff Gallery (1979).

FLUME, FRANCONIA NOTCH, WHITE MOUN-
TAINS; THE . . . S/L/R.
Oil on canvas.
30 x 21 (76.2 x 53.3).
Oakland Museum exhibition (1980).

FRANCONIA NOTCH.
Oakland Museum catalog (1980), p. 30.

GOODRICH FALLS.
1868.
Oakland Museum exhibition (1980), p. 18.

HEADWATERS OF SACO; THE . . .
Oakland Museum exhibition (1980), p. 24.

IN THE WOODS, NEW TRAIL, MOUNT
LAFAYETTE.
Leonard Auction (Jan. 28, 1873), #86.

MOUNT WASHINGTON (study).
Oil.
Boston Art Club (March 1873), #109.

MOUNT WASHINGTON – SNOW.
Private collection.

NEW HAMPSHIRE LAKE SCENE. S/D/L/R.
1869. Oil.
18 x 30 (45.7 x 76.2).
John H. Garzoli Gallery, San Francisco, CA
(1980).

NEW HAMPSHIRE MOUNTAIN SCENE
(Chocorua).
Oil on canvas.
20 x 30 (50.8 x 76.2).
Bowdoin College Museum of Art (1972).

OLD MAN OF THE MOUNTAINS.
18 x 12¾ (45.7 x 32.4).
New Hampshire Historical Society.

PEMIGEWASSET VALLEY, NEW HAMPSHIRE.
S/L/R.
Oil on canvas.
27 x 35½ (68.6 x 90.2).
John Howell, Books, San Francisco, CA.

PROFILE LAKE, NEW HAMPSHIRE. S/D/L/R.
1869. Oil.
18 x 30 (45.7 x 76.2).
Oakland Museum exhibition (1980); John H.
Garzoli Gallery, San Francisco, CA.

PROFILE LAKE, NEW HAMPSHIRE. S/L/R.
C. 1868. Oil on paper on panel.
12¾ x 18¼ (32.4 x 46.4).
John H. Garzoli Gallery, San Francisco, CA
(1981); *Antiques* (May 1981).

STAG HOLLOW FROM NEAR WAMBUK [sic].
Leonard Auction (Jan. 28, 1873), #3.

VIEW OF FRANCONIA NOTCH.
Oil on board.
18 x 12¾ (45.7 x 31.8).
New Hampshire Historical Society;
Historical New Hampshire (Spring 1967).

VIEW ON SACO RIVER.
Leonard Auction (May 24, 1871), #125.

VIEW TO ELEPHANT [sic] HEAD FROM
CRAWFORD HOUSE. S/D/L/L.
1869.
12⅝ x 18 (32.1 x 45.7).
New Hampshire Historical Society (1980).

WE GO A' FISHING.
Oil on canvas.
29 x 19 (73.7 x 48.3).
New Hampshire Historical Society.

WHITE MOUNTAIN NOTCH, NEW HAMPSHIRE.
1865. Oil.
11 x 15 (27.9 x 38.1).
Maxwell Gallery, San Francisco, CA (1975);
Pre-1877 (2).

WHITE MOUNTAINS.
Oil.
12½ x 18 (31.8 x 45.7).
Private collection (1978).

WHITE MOUNTAINS, FRANCONIA NOTCH.
Oil on board.
18¼ x 12¾ (46.4 x 32.4).
New Hampshire Historical Society (1983);
Oakland Museum exhibition (1980), p. 30;
Historical New Hampshire (Spring 1967).

WINTER IN NEW HAMPSHIRE.
Oakland Museum (1980), p. 26.

HILLIARD (or HILLARD), WILLIAM HENRY
C&H, F, G&W, N, S
Born Auburn, NY, 1836.
Died Washington, DC, April 1905.
*Hilliard studied in New York City and also
abroad under Lambinet. For a while he kept a
studio in New York City, but by 1878 settled
in Boston where he became known for his New
England landscapes. He exhibited at the NAD
from 1876 to 1888 and also at the Brooklyn Art
Association.*

New Hampshire Scenery

Bibliography:
McGrath, Robert L. "The White Mountains in the Brown Decades." Dartmouth College Library *Bulletin* (Nov. 1978), pp. 15-20.

ARTISTS [sic] BROOK, NORTH CONWAY, NEW HAMPSHIRE.
Brooklyn Art Association (1876), #176.

CAMPTON MEADOWS.
C&H.

CRAWFORD NOTCH, WHITE MOUNTAINS.
1884. Oil on canvas.
30 x 50 (76.2 x 127).
Reading Public Museum and Art Gallery (1953); BIAP.

FRANCONIA MOUNTAINS, NEW HAMPSHIRE.
1876. Oil on canvas.
15 x 27 (38.1 x 68.6).
NMAA Inventory; BIAP.

FRANCONIA NOTCH AND BROOK. (Untitled).
S/L/L.
Oil on canvas.
16 x 12 (40.6 x 30.5).
Littleton Community Center.

GATES OF THE NOTCH.
NAD, 1877, #371; Boston Art Club (Jan. 16-Feb. 9, 1878), #151.

KEARSARGE AND THORN MOUNTAINS, INTERVALE, NEW HAMPSHIRE.
June 14, 1895. Oil.
27 x 33 (68.6 x 83.8).
Private collection (1975); NMAA Inventory.

MIRROR LAKE, WHITEFIELD, NEW HAMPSHIRE.
MA Charitable (1878), #320; NAD, 1878, #590.

ON THE ROAD TO THE NOTCH (Franconia).
July 14, 1877. Charcoal on gray paper.
7⅞ x 5⅞ (20 x 15).
Dartmouth College, Baker Library (1983).

PROFILE LAKE.
Late 19th century. Oil.
14 x 10 (35.6 x 25.4).
Littleton Community Center (1979).

HILLYER, HENRY LIVINGSTON
C, Ce, F(sup), G&W, N
Born 1840. Died 1886.
Hillyer lived in Jersey City when he exhibited at the NAD from 1859 until 1868. He also exhibited frequently at the Brookyn Art Association until 1877 when he gave up painting for commercial enterprise.

A SPUR, MOUNT WASHINGTON.
Brooklyn Art Association (1875), #75.

EARLY AUTUMN ON THE SACO.
NAD, 1861, #464.

MOUNT WASHINGTON.
Oil on canvas.
4½ x 8¾ (11.4 x 22.2).
Washington County Museum of Art (1973).

SACO RIVER.
Watercolor.
5½ x 10 5/16 (14 x 26.2).
Washington County Museum of Art (1973).

STUDY FROM NATURE NEAR THORNTON, NEW HAMPSHIRE.
NAD, 1867, #166.

SUMMER AFTERNOON AT LOWER BARTLETT, NEW HAMPSHIRE.
NAD, 1861, #465.

WHITE MOUNTAIN NOTCH.
NAD, 1861, #137.

HINKLEY, THOMAS HEWES
A, B, C, Ce, C&H, F, G&W, R
Born Milton, MA, Nov. 4, 1813.
Died Milton, MA, Feb. 15, 1896.
Hinkley was apprenticed in 1829 to a Philadelphia businessman but managed to take art lessons during his business training. In 1833 he returned to Milton, MA, and opened a studio as a sign and ornamental artist. By 1840 he owned a studio in Quincy, MA, and had enlarged his repertoire to include portraits, genre, and landscape, but his forte and later reputation lay with paintings of animals. He exhibited at the Boston Athenaeum and the NAD in 1846. In 1851 he went to England, studied under Landseer, and exhibited at the Royal Academy. He returned to the U.S. and settled in the Boston area with a short trip to California in 1870. He exhibited at the Brooklyn Art Association in 1865 and 1870.

Bibliography:
Milton (MA) Historical Society, the account books of Thomas Hewes Hinkley.

STAG AT BAY, MOUNT CHOCORUA IN WINTER.
1851. Oil on canvas.
40½ x 54¼ (102.9 x 137.8).
Hirschl and Adler Gallery; Boston Museum of Fine Arts contemporary exhibition (April 1879), #459.

VIEW OF MOUNT MONADNOCK.
  1858. Oil.
  35 x 52 (91.4 x 132.1).
  Old Print Shop *Portfolio* 1:8, p. 16.

HITCHINGS, HENRY

A, C, F(sup), G&W
Born Boston, MA, 1824.
Died probably Boston, MA, Jan. 17, 1902.
*Hitchings's forte lay in watercolor landscapes.
He exhibited at the AAU in 1849 and at the
Boston Athenaeum in 1856. From 1861 to 1869
he served as a professor of drawing at the U.S.
Naval Academy. He was a clerk in the art goods
store of Francis Shedd Frost in 1869 and the
following year began a career as one of the most
successful art teachers in the Boston area public
school system and the Boston Latin School.*

Bibliography:
Dedham Historical Society, Dedham, MA
02026.

SWIFT RIVER, CONWAY, NEW HAMPSHIRE.
S/D.
  1848. Lithograph.
  Old Print Shop (1975); Tappan and Bradford, Lithographers, Boston.

WHITE MOUNTAINS FROM GORHAM ROAD.
  1861.
  North Conway Library Exhibition (1965).

WOOD INTERIOR, JACKSON, NEW HAMP-
SHIRE.
  Watercolor.
  Boston Art Club (1883), #114.

HODGDON, SYLVESTER PHELPS

A, F(sup), G&W, N
Born Salem, MA, Dec. 25, 1830.
Died Dorchester, MA, Aug. 20, 1906.
*Hodgdon first studied with Benjamin Champ-
ney in Boston and later under Samuel Rouse in
New York City. In the early 1850s he worked
as a lithographer for the firm of L. H. Bradford
in Boston, during which time he executed views
of the Flume and the Old Man of the Mountains.
For 30 years he kept a studio in the Tremont
Street Studio Building in Boston. Though
known primarily for his landscapes, Hodgdon
also taught life classes in both the Boston
Museum of Fine Arts School and the Boston Art
Club, of which he was a charter member. He
exhibited at the Boston Athenaeum from 1855
to 1873 and also at the NAD and the Brooklyn*

*Art Association. During the 1870s, he worked
in the then popular medium of etching. His later
work lost the tight linearity of his early
paintings.*

Bibliography:
Archives of American Art. Roll 104, Frames
680-806.

CRAWFORD NOTCH.
  Private collection (1965).

ECHO LAKE, MORNING.
  Leonard Auction (April 20-21, 1876), #99.

ECHO LAKE, FRANCONIA.
  Private collection (1980); Boston Athenaeum
  (1858), #243; Bierstadt Exhibition, New Bedford, 1858, #83.

ECHO LAKE, FRANCONIA, NEW HAMPSHIRE.
  Leonard Auction (Jan. 28, 1873), #46.

ECHO LAKE, FRANCONIA, NEW HAMPSHIRE.
  1886. Oil.
  22 x 36 (55.9 x 91.4).
  Malden (MA) Public Library (1978); NMAA
  Inventory.

ECHO LAKE, NEW HAMPSHIRE.
  Leonard Auction (June 16, 1865), #58.

FLUME; THE. . .
  1856. Lithograph.
  16 x 12 (40.6 x 30.5).
  Private collection (1983); F. F. Oakley,
  printers, Boston.

FLUME; THE. . .
  1856. Lithograph.
  19¾ x 15¾ (50.2 x 40).
  New Hampshire Historical Society exhibition
  (1965); lithograph by F. F. Oakley.

FRANCONIA   NOTCH   FROM   NORTH
WOODSTOCK.
  Unlocated.

JACKSON AND MOUNT WASHINGTON FROM
THE CONFLUENCE OF THE ELLIS AND WILDCAT
RIVERS. Signed.
  1867. Oil.
  26 x 46 (66 x 116.8).
  Private collection.

LADY ON HORSEBACK, TUCKERMAN'S
RAVINE. S/L/L.
  Withington Auction (Jan. 8, 1977).

MOUNT WASHINGTON FROM JACKSON
ROAD.
  Leonard Auction (April 20-21, 1876), #49.

MOUNT WASHINGTON FROM THE SOUTH.
  Denver Art Museum.

MOUNT WASHINGTON FROM THORN HILL.
  Leonard Auction (April 20-21, 1876), #116.
MOUNT WASHINGTON FROM WILDCAT AND
ELLIS RIVER.
  1867.
  North Conway Library Exhibition (1965).
OLD MAN OF THE MOUNTAINS.
  1858. Lithograph.
  Starr King special edition, New Hampshire
  Historical Society.
ON THE SACO (or RIVER IN SPRING).
  1863. Oil on board.
  Private collection (1984); Vose Galleries
  (1977); U.S. Sanitary Commission (1864).
ON THE SACO, MOUNT WASHINGTON.
  Leonard Auction (April 20-21, 1876), #33.
ON THE SACO, WHITE MOUNTAIN NOTCH.
S/D/L/R.
  1850 or 1880. Oil on board.
  10½ x 8½ (26.7 x 21.6).
  Private collection (1983).
SUNSET AFTER A SHOWER, WHITE MOUN-
TAINS.
  Boston Athenaeum (1863), #347; (1863) (2),
  #245.
WHITE MOUNTAINS.
  Pre-1877; Leeds Gallery (Feb. 7, 1870).
WHITE MOUNTAINS FROM SHELBURNE.
  Pre-1877; Leeds Gallery (Feb. 7, 1870).
WHITE MOUNTAINS IN SEPTEMBER, NORTH
CONWAY, NH. S/D/L/R.
  1853. Oil on canvas.
  20 x 30 (50.8 x 76.2).
  University of Michigan Museum of Art
  (1980).

HOIT (or HOYT), ALBERT GALLATIN

A, C, F, G&W, S
Born Sandwich, NH, Dec. 13, 1809.
Died Jamaica Plain or West Roxbury, MA, Dec.
18, 1856.
*Hoit seems to have been a self-taught artist,
although he did receive a college education at
Dartmouth. For 10 years he traveled in Maine
and the Maritimes, finally settling in Boston in
1839 and traveling twice to Europe. He was con-
sidered a fine and popular enough artist for The
Crayon to print an obituary, and for the Boston
Athenaeum to exhibit his work posthumously.
He died suddenly, leaving his wife with three
young children.*
Bibliography:
Heard, Patricia L. "Albert Gallatin Hoit, Sand-

wich Artist." *Antiques* (Nov. 1972), pp. 862-867.
CHOCORUA.
  C. 1835. Oil on wood panel.
  12 x 18 (30.5 x 45.7).
  Private collection (1983).
MOUNT CHOCORUA FROM SANDWICH, NEW
HAMPSHIRE.
  Boston Athenaeum (1857), #242.
MOUNT CONWAY, NEW HAMPSHIRE BY
TWILIGHT.
  Pre-1877; Leeds Gallery (Feb. 7, 1870).
MOUNT WASHINGTON.
  Boston Athenaeum (1857), #31.
MOUNT WASHINGTON FROM BARTLETT.
  Boston Athenaeum (1857), #283.
NORTH CONWAY.
  Aug. 30, 1852. Pen and ink.
  Boston Museum of Fine Arts.
PLUMMER MILL, NORTH SANDWICH. S/D.
  1826.
  Fruitlands Museum, Harvard, MA.

HOLMES, GEORGE W.

Ce, F(sup), G&W, R
Born Ireland, c. 1812. Died after 1868.
*Little is known of this artist, who exhibited at
the PAFA from 1840 to 1868 and at the NAD
in 1845. He apparently made a trip to the White
Mountains about 1847/48.*
MOUNT WASHINGTON.
  PAFA, 1848.
THE NOTCH.
  PAFA, 1848.
WHITE MOUNTAINS.
  PAFA, 1848.

HOLMES, HENRY

G&W
Born New York, NY, about 1832.
Died after 1878.
*Nothing is known of this engraver except that
he also executed oil paintings and visited the
Plymouth area of New Hampshire at some time
prior to 1878 when he exhibited a New Hamp-
shire landscape at the Boston Art Club.*
BAKER'S RIVER, RUMNEY, NEW HAMPSHIRE.
  Oil.
  Boston Art Club (April 17-May 3, 1878),
  #71.

HOMER, WINSLOW
A, B, Ce, C&H, DAB, E, F, G&W, K, Ka, N, S
Born Boston, MA, Feb. 24, 1836.
Died Prout's Neck, ME, Sept. 29, 1910.
At the age of 19, Homer was apprenticed to J. H. Bufford's lithographic firm in Boston. Although the superior quality of his work earned him more and more responsibility, he found the work stifling and tedious, and upon attaining his majority he left the shop to become a freelance illustrator. In 1859 Homer moved to New York City, where he studied briefly at the NAD, took a few painting lessons with Frederic Rondel, and set up a studio at the 10th Street Studio Building. For the next 17 years, his major source of income came from drawings for illustrated weekly magazines, such as Harper's Weekly, Frank Leslie's Illustrated Weekly Newspaper, *and* Appleton's Journal. *He devoted increasing attention to painting, however, and in 1865 was elected a member of the NAD and was further distinguished by the exhibition of his PRISONERS AT THE FRONT in the Paris Exposition of 1866. Homer went to Paris that year, but little is known of his activities during the 10 months he spent abroad. Domestic travel for the next 15 years included trips to the White Mountains the summers of 1868 and 1869, the Adirondacks, and Gloucester, MA, in 1873. It is significant that, when Homer returned to Europe in 1881, he did not go back to Paris, which was bursting with American art students at the ateliers, but chose, instead, the small fishing community of Tynemouth, on the cold gray northeast coast of England. Following his return home in 1882, Homer moved from his New York studio to the rugged coast of Prout's Neck, ME. For the remainder of his life this was his home, though he continued seasonal travels to Quebec and the Adirondacks in the summer months, and to Florida, Bermuda, and Nassau in the Bahamas in the winter. He exhibited almost annually at the Brooklyn Art Association, and the NAD, where he was elected an academician in 1865, and was a member of the Century Association from 1865 until his death.*

Select Bibliography:
Gardner, Albert Ten Eyck. *Winslow Homer.* New York, 1961.
Goodrich, Lloyd. *Winslow Homer.* New York: The Macmillan Company for the Whitney Museum of American Art, 1944.

Heller, Nancy, and Julia Williams. "Winslow Homer: The Great American Coast." *American Artist* (Jan. 1976), pp. 34-40.

ARTIST IN THE COUNTRY; THE...
1869. Engraving.
Appalachia (June 1968); *Appleton's Journal* 1:12 (June 19, 1869), p. 353.

ARTISTS SKETCHING IN THE WHITE MOUNTAINS.
1868. Oil.
9½ x 15½ (24.1 x 39.4).
Private collection (1966); Bowdoin College Museum of Art exhibition (1966).

BRIDLE PATH, WHITE MOUNTAINS; THE... S/D/L/L.
1869. Oil on canvas.
24⅛ x 38 (61.3 x 96.5).
Sterling and Francine Clark Art Institute, Williamstown, MA (1972).

COOLEST SPOT IN NEW ENGLAND, SUMMIT OF MOUNT WASHINGTON; THE...
1870. Engraving.
Harper's Bazar (July 23, 1870), p. 473.

END OF THE BRIDLE PATH, MOUNT WASHINGTON.
Pre-1877; Cincinnati Industrial Exposition (1873).

IN THE MOUNTAINS.
1869. Engraving.
Appalachia (June 1966).

MOUNT WASHINGTON. S/D/L/R.
1869. Oil on canvas.
16 x 24⅛ (40.6 x 61.3).
Chicago Institute of Art (1981); BIAP; Kennedy *Quarterly* (April 1960).

STUDY FOR ARTISTS SKETCHING IN THE WHITE MOUNTAINS.
C. 1868-69. Pencil.
5¾ x 8 5/16 (14.7 x 21.1).
Ithaca (NY) College Museum of Art catalog (1971), #20.

STUDY FOR BRIDLE PATH, WHITE MOUNTAINS.
Aug. 24, 1868. Pencil.
6¾ x 9 9/16 (17.1 x 24.3).
Ithaca (NY) College Museum of Art catalog (April-May 1971), #19.

STUDY FOR COOLEST SPOT IN NEW ENGLAND, SUMMIT OF MOUNT WASHINGTON.
C. 1870. Crayon on paper.
7¾ x 13⅞ (19.7 x 35.3).
Ithaca (NY) College Museum of Art catalog (1971), #21.

New Hampshire Scenery

SUMMIT OF MOUNT WASHINGTON.
   1869. Engraving.
   Appalachia (June 1966); *Harper's Weekly*
   (July 10, 1869).

WHITE MOUNTAIN WAGON.
   Appalachia (June 1968), pp. 94, seq.

HOOPER, EDWARD
F, G&W, S
Born London, England, May 24, 1829.
Died Brooklyn, NY, Dec. 13, 1870.
*A wood engraver and watercolorist, Hooper
received his training in England and came to the
U.S. about 1850. Though his main source of income was work as a commercial artist and
printer, he was a fine watercolorist and one of
the founders of the American Society of Painters
in Watercolors.*

CRYSTAL FALLS, WHITE MOUNTAINS.
   Pre-1877; 2nd Annual Collection of the
   American Society of Painters in Watercolors,
   1869.

HOPE, JAMES
C, Ce, F, G&W, N, R, S, T
Born Drygrange, Roxboroughshire, Scotland,
Nov. 29, 1818 or 1819.
Died Watkins Glen, NY, 1892.
*Hope was always something of a mystic. After
being brought to Canada in his childhood, he
was apprenticed to a wagon maker in Fairhaven,
VT, where he attended Castleton Seminary (and
later taught). He began painting in 1843 and was
elected an associate of the NAD in 1871. He ex-
hibited there from 1854 to 1882 and at the
Brooklyn Art Association from 1862 to 1876.*

LANDSCAPE AT CONWAY, NEW HAMPSHIRE.
   1851. Oil.
   18 x 24 (45.7 x 61).
   Old Print Shop *Portfolio* 11:4, p. 87.

WHITE MOUNTAINS.
   Private collection (1967); BIAP.

WHITE MOUNTAINS. S/D/L/R.
   1851. Oil on canvas.
   18¼ x 24 (46.4 x 61).
   Sotheby PB (Nov. 21, 1980), #27.

HOPKIN, ROBERT
F, G&W, S
Born Glasgow, Scotland, Jan. 3, 1832.
Died Detroit, MI, March 21, 1909.
*It is not known when Hopkin came to the U.S.,
but he settled in Detroit. He seems to have made
a trip to the White Mountains in the late 1870s.*

IN THE WHITE MOUNTAINS.
   1878. Oil on canvas.
   27 x 34 (68.6 x 86.4).
   Detroit Institute of Fine Arts (1979).

MOUNT CHOCORUA, NEW HAMPSHIRE, FROM
WALKER'S POND.
   1880. Oil.
   34⅜ x 58½ (87.3 x 148.3).
   University of Michigan Museum of Art
   (1975).

HOTCHKISS, THOMAS HIRAM
C, Ce, G&W, K, N, R, T
Born near Hudson, NY, c. 1834.
Died Taormina, Italy, Aug. 19, 1869.
*Hotchkiss first exhibited at the NAD in 1857 and
was elected an associate member in 1860. He
was a friend of Asher B. Durand and John Rollin
Tilton. His first documented trip to the White
Mountains was recorded in the December 1856
Crayon. "Mr. Hotchkiss has . . . a number of rich
foreground material of the Saco River." He
visited the White Mountains again in 1857 and
1858. His career was cut short by his death from
tuberculosis at about age 35.*

MEADOWS OF NORTH CONWAY, NEW
HAMPSHIRE.
   NAD, 1857, #428.

MOUNT WASHINGTON. S/D/L/Center.
   1857. Oil on canvas.
   20⅛ x 30 (51.2 x 76.2).
   New-York Historical Society (1975).

MOUNTAIN STREAM, WHITE MOUNTAINS (or
BROOK IN THE WHITE MOUNTAINS). S/D/L/L.
   1858. Oil on canvas on cardboard.
   10 x 7⅛ (25.4 x 18.1).
   New-York Historical Society.

STUDY FROM NATURE, NORTH CONWAY.
   NAD, 1857, #168.

SUMMER, CONWAY VALLEY.
   NAD, 1858, #407.

HOWE, E. R.
Nothing is presently known of this artist.
ON THE ROAD TO THE NOTCH.
   MA Charitable (1878), #410.

HOWS (or HOWES), JOHN AUGUSTUS
C&H, G&W, N, S
Born New York, NY, 1832.
Died New York, NY, Sept. 27, 1874.
Hows did not settle on a career in art until after

graduating from Columbia University (at the age of 20), and after some years' study of ministry and the law. He was elected an associate member of the NAD in 1862.

STARR KING'S RAVINE, WHITE MOUNTAINS.
NAD, 1864, #243.

HOYT, E. C. (MRS.)

F(sup), G&W, R
Active 1858-68.
Hoyt apparently spent her career years as an artist in the vicinity of Philadelphia, where she exhibited from 1858 to 1868.

WHITE MOUNTAINS.
PAFA, 1862-63.

HUBBARD, RICHARD WILLIAM

A, B, C, Ce, DAB, F, G&W, N, R, S, T
Born Middletown, CT, Oct. 15, 1817 (or 1816).
Died Brooklyn, NY, Dec. 21, 1888.
After a year at Yale in 1837, Hubbard quit to study art under Daniel Huntington and Samuel Morse and followed that, in 1840-41, with further study abroad. He became an associate member of the NAD in 1852 and a full member in 1859. He exhibited there and at the Brooklyn Art Association frequently. In 1854 he was at Conway Center, NH, sketching with Champney, Miss Bangs, and Ordway, a scene recorded by Sanford Gifford in his sketchbook. The Crayon for December 1856 noted that "Mr. Hubbard has . . . made a study of the 'Stepping-Stones,' a favorite Conway subject which Daniel Huntington also recorded." Hubbard kept a studio in the 10th Street Studio Building (N.Y.C.) for 30 years. He was elected to the Century Association in 1865 and served as president of the Brooklyn Art Association for several years.

ARTISTS BROOK, NORTH CONWAY.
NAD, 1861, #242.

BOY FISHING (Mount Washington and the Saco).
Signed.
1863.
16 x 30 (40.6 x 76.2).
Sotheby PB (April 1976).

CHOCORUA.
Pre-1877; 3rd annual exhibition at Young Men's Association in the Athenaeum, Troy, NY (1860).

GLIMPSE OF THE VALLEY OF THE SACO.
NAD, 1881, #386.

HIGH PEAK, NORTH CONWAY, NEW HAMPSHIRE.
NAD, 1856, #57.

MOUNT LAFAYETTE FROM NEWBURY, VT.
NAD, 1866, #347.

NEW HAMPSHIRE SCENERY (Chocorua?).
Engraving.
Ladies' Repository.

PATH TO THE MEADOWS, NORTH CONWAY.
NAD, 1861, #504.

POOL IN THE WOODS, NORTH CONWAY.
NAD, 1861, #510.

STUDY OF THE STEPPING STONES.
Crayon (Dec. 1856), p. 375.

HUDSON, JOHN BRADLEY

A, F(sup), G&W
Born Portland, ME, 1832.
Died Weston, MA, 1903.
Hudson studied under Charles Octavius Cole about 1850. Like many 19th-century artists, he was an ornamental painter, decorating signs, coaches, fire buckets, and fireplace boards, as well as a landscapist. He wrote "Journey to the White Mts" in 1859, a diary which he illustrated profusely. His work was exhibited at the Boston Athenaeum in 1868. He resided and worked in Portland until the 1890s before removing to Massachusetts.

Bibliography:
Boston Museum of Fine Arts. John Bradley Hudson, journal.
"John Bradley Hudson." Antiques (Jan. 1968).

1859 JOURNAL AND SKETCHBOOK.
Boston Museum of Fine Arts.

SUNRISE IN THE WHITE MOUNTAINS.
Boston Athenaeum (1868), #227.

VIEW OF THE WHITE MOUNTAINS (or PANORAMA LANDSCAPE OF NEW HAMPSHIRE).
26 x 46 (66 x 116.8).
Victor Spark, dealer, 1000 Park Ave., New York, NY; Lowe Art Museum (1975).

HUNT, WILLIAM MORRIS

A, Ba, DAB, G&W, Ka, T
Born Brattleboro, VT, March 31, 1824.
Died Isle of Shoals, NH, Sept. 8, 1879, by drowning.
Hunt left for Europe before graduating from Harvard. He studied painting in Düsseldorf, Germany, and with Thomas Couture in Paris. While in Paris he met and became friends with

New Hampshire Scenery

Crawford Notch
Thomas Hill, 1872
Oil on canvas, 72" x 124" / Collection: New Hampshire
    Historical Society / Ref. page 86

Jean François Millet, an artist whose work greatly influenced Hunt. He came back to the U.S. in 1856 and, after some further travel, settled in Boston in 1862. He stayed at the Conway House in Conway, NH, in 1862, before September. No New Hampshire views by Hunt are presently known, but it is likely that he painted some. He was unhappy in his later years, and many have speculated that his "accidental" death was actually suicide.
Bibliography:
Knowlton, Helen M. *Art Life of William Morris Hunt* (1899).
Knowlton, Helen M. *Talks on Art by W. M. Hunt* (1879).

HUNTING, CHARLES

Active 1880s.
There is presently no other information on this artist.
ECHO LAKE.
    C. 1880.
    North Conway Library Exhibition (1965).

KEARSARGE AND THE SACO RIVER.
    C. 1880.
    North Conway Library Exhibition (1965).

HUNTINGTON, DANIEL

A, B, C, Ce, C&H, DAB, F, G&W, K, Ka, N, R, S, T
Born New York, NY, Oct. 14, 1816.
Died New York, NY, April 18, 1906.
After graduating from college, Huntington studied under Samuel Morse, who was then president of the NAD. Huntington is probably best known for his portraits, though his landscapes elicited comment in The Crayon *of May 1858: "M. Huntington was born a landscape painter, and it is to be regretted that the pictures he paints in the high department of Art are not more frequent. . . . His landscapes seem to be more the pastime of leisure hours than of steady laborious purpose. . . . [He possesses] a recognition of the spirit and principles of light . . . as may be seen in the MILL POND AT CHOCORUA,"a painting exhibited at the NAD in the same year. Huntington was a member of*

Dictionary of Painters

the NAD from 1839 to his death in 1906, president from 1862 to 1870, and president again from 1877 to 1891. He also exhibited at the PAFA from 1842 to 1868. He joined the Century Association in 1847 and was its president from 1879 to 1895. He was also vice-president of the Metropolitan Museum of Art for 33 years. He often went abroad during his long career, traveling and sketching in Italy, England, and Spain. He seems to have particularly enjoyed painting Chocorua while visiting the White Mountains, making sketches there as early as 1854. A view he executed in 1860 was engraved by John Filmore. A friend of Champney and the convivial group who congregated every summer in North Conway to paint and "talk shop," Huntington was often in the White Mountains and produced many sketches of the area. He shared a studio at Jackson, NH, maintained by Samuel Colman, with many associates, among them George L. Brown, Frank Shapleigh, Asher Durand, and Aaron D. Shattuck.

Bibliography:
Ithaca College Museum of Art. *Daniel Huntington.* Ithaca, NY, 1971.

A STUDY OF MAPLES IN AUTUMN COLOR.
    Crayon (Dec. 1856), p. 375.

A STUDY OF STEPPING STONES ON KIARSARGE [sic] BROOK.
    Crayon (Dec. 1856), p. 375.

AN AUTUMN VIEW OF KUHN MOUNTAINS.
    Crayon (Dec. 1856), p. 375.

CHICORUA [sic] POND AND MOUNTAIN (or CHOCORUA FROM CARA'S POND).
    Sept. 28, 1854. Pencil on paper.
    10⅛ x 14 (25.7 x 35.5).

Cooper-Hewitt Museum (1980); University Art Gallery catalog, University of New Hampshire (1980), #56; Ithaca (NY) College Museum of Art catalog (March-April 1971), #37.

CHOCORUA FROM HILL TO RIGHT OF ALBANY ROAD.
    Sept. 12, 1854. Pencil with white crayon.
    11⅝ x 15¾ (29.6 x 40).
    Ithaca (NY) College Museum of Art catalog (March-April 1971), #36.

CHOCORUA PEAK IN NEW HAMPSHIRE. S/L/R on rock.
    1860. Oil on panel.
    13¼ x 16½ (33.7 x 41.9).
    New-York Historical Society (1975).

DISTANT VIEW OF WHITE MOUNTAINS.
    NAD, 1858, #501.

MILL POND AT CHOCORUA.
    NAD, 1858, #61; *Crayon* (1858), p. 147.

SACO LOOKING NORTHWEST (JEFFERSON IN THE DISTANCE).
    Drawing.
    Private collection (1974).

STUDY OF FIGURES FOR CHOCORUA.
    Pencil and white chalk.
    16 x 11¾ (40.6 x 29.9).
    Ithaca (NY) College Museum of Art catalog (March-April 1971), #41.

SWIFT RIVER.
    Sept. 21, 1854. Pencil and white chalk.
    11 ⁷/₁₆ x 16 ¹³/₁₆ (29.1 x 42.7).
    Corcoran Gallery (July-Sept. 1979).

WHITE MOUNTAIN SCENERY.
    Pre-1877; Chicago Academy of Design, Opera House (1868).

New Hampshire Scenery

I

INNESS, GEORGE

A, B, Ba, C, Ce, C&H, DAB, F, G&W, K, Ka, N, R, S, T

Born Newburgh, NY, May 1, 1825.
Died, while traveling, Bridge-of-Allan, Scotland, Aug. 3, 1894.

Inness began his career in 1841 as an apprentice in a map engraver's firm in New York City, where he worked for one year. The only formal training he received came from Regis Gignoux. Following that, Inness opened his own studio in 1845, the same year he first exhibited at the AAU. He exhibited at the NAD in 1844 and continued to do so for the rest of his life. He also exhibited frequently at the Brooklyn Art Association. He was elected a member of the Century Association in 1853 and resigned in 1890. Inness seems to have had an inner restlessness, for he moved frequently and made numerous trips to England, Italy, and France, where he was exposed to the Barbizon School. The last 16 years of his life included trips to Mexico City, Cuba, Florida, the Yosemite Valley, and Europe. Inness was fond of New Hampshire and kept a studio on the second floor of the North Conway Academy for several years before 1876. Following Inness's exposure to the Barbizon School, his compositions lost the tight linearity of his early work. Of his painting and of an artist's obligations, Inness said, "A work of art does not appeal to the intellect. It does not appeal to the moral sense. Its aim is not to instruct, not to edify, but to awaken an emotion." Such a philosophy is a direct contradiction of the aims of earlier landscapists such as Thomas Cole and Alvan Fisher, and of the topographical clarity of David Johnson and Asher Durand.

Select Bibliography:
Inness, George, Jr. *Life, Art and Letters of George Inness* (1917).
Ireland, Leroy. *George Inness*, catalog. Austin: University of Texas, 1965.
Trumble, A. *George Inness, N.A. A Memorial of the Student, the Artist and the Man.* New York, 1895.

A QUIET SPOT IN NEW ENGLAND.
C. 1882. Oil.
12 x 9¼ (30.5 x 23.5).
University of Texas Art Museum Art Gallery (1965); NMAA Inventory.

APPROACHING STORM (overpainted MOUNT WASHINGTON). S/D/L/L.
1893. Oil on canvas.
60 x 120 (152.4 x 304.8).
St. Louis Art Museum (sold 1946).

ARTIST'S BROOK, NORTH CONWAY.
1875. Oil.
16 x 24 (40.6 x 61).
Private collection (1965).

CONWAY MEADOWS (or SUMMER SQUALL ON MOAT MOUNTAIN).
1876. Oil.
38 x 63½ (96.5 x 161.3).
Mount Holyoke College (1965).

CONWAY VALLEY.
1875. Oil.
20 x 30 (50.8 x 76.2).
University of Texas Art Museum catalog (1965), #722.

CONWAY VALLEY (or LATE SUMMER AFTERNOON).
1882. Oil.
12 x 18 (30.5 x 45.7).
University of Texas Art Museum catalog (1965), p. 257; NMAA Inventory.

FORD OF THE SACO (MOTE [sic] MOUNTAIN IN BACKGROUND); THE . . .
Aldine 8:9 (Sept. 1876), p. 272.

IN THE WHITE MOUNTAINS.
30 x 20 (76.2 x 50.8).
Private collection (1965).

IN THE WHITE MOUNTAINS.
30 x 20 (76.2 x 50.8).
Private collection (1965).

IN THE WHITE MOUNTAINS. S/L/L.
1859. Oil on canvas.
10¼ x 18 (26 x 45.7).
William A. Farnsworth Library and Art Museum, Rockland, ME (1975).

KEARSARGE VILLAGE. S/D/L/R.
  1875. Oil on canvas.
  16 x 24 (40.6 x 61).
  Boston Museum of Fine Arts (1965); University of Texas Art Museum catalog (1965), #751.

LANDSCAPE – A NEW ENGLAND VALLEY. S/L/R.
  C. 1875. Oil on paper on board.
  9 ¹/₁₆ x 13⅞ (23 x 35.2).
  Worcester Art Museum (1973).

LANDSCAPE, NORTH CONWAY (2). S/L/R.
  C. 1875. Oil on academy board.
  8¾ x 14 (22.2 x 35.6).
  Kende Gallery (1965); University of Texas Art Museum catalog (1965), #742, #743.

LEDGE, MORTE [Moat] MOUNT, NORTH CONWAY.
  Oil.
  Boston Art Club (Jan. 12-Feb. 2, 1876), #134.

MOUNT WASHINGTON.
  1875. Oil.
  14¾ x 18¾ (37.5 x 47.6).
  Private collection; University of Texas Art Museum catalog (1965), #717.

MOUNT WASHINGTON. S/L/R.
  1875. Oil on canvas.
  20 x 30 (50.8 x 76.2).
  Coe Kerr Gallery (1977); University of Texas Art Museum catalog (1965), #716.

MOUNT WASHINGTON FROM NORTH CONWAY.
  1875. Oil.
  12 x 17¼ (30.5 x 43.8).
  University of Texas Art Museum catalog (1965), #178.

MOUNT WASHINGTON, NEW HAMPSHIRE.
  C. 1877. Oil.
  30 x 45 (76.2 x 114.3).
  Babcock Gallery (1965).

MOUNT WASHINGTON, NORTH CONWAY, NEW HAMPSHIRE. S/D/L/R.
  1875. Oil on canvas.
  20 x 30 (50.8 x 76.2).
  Sotheby PB (April 25, 1980); Davis and Long Co. (1980); *Antiques* (May 1974).

NEAR NORTH CONWAY.
  1878. Oil.
  16 x 24 (40.6 x 61).
  University of Texas Art Museum catalog (1965).

NORTH CONWAY.
  1875. Oil.
  9½ x 14 (24.1 x 35.6).
  Madison Art Center, Madison, WI (1976).

NORTH CONWAY. S/L/R.
  1875-77. Oil on canvas.
  10 x 15 (25.4 x 38.1).
  Canton Art Institute (1965); University of Texas Art Museum catalog (1965), #748.

NORTH CONWAY (Mount Washington). S/L/R.
  1875. Oil.
  12 x 18 (30.5 x 45.7).
  David B. Findlay Galleries, N.Y.C.; University of Texas Art Gallery catalog (1965), #714; Grant Art Auction Gallery, Chicago, IL.

NORTH CONWAY, NEW HAMPSHIRE (Mount Washington). S/L/R.
  C. 1870. Oil on panel.
  12¼ x 18⅜ (31.1 x 46.7).
  University of California at Los Angeles Art Gallery.

NORTH CONWAY, NEW HAMPSHIRE. Signed.
  C. 1870. Oil on panel.
  11¼ x 17 (28.6 x 43.2).
  University of California at Los Angeles Art Gallery (1966); Long Beach Museum of Art catalog (Nov. 1966), #29.

NORTH CONWAY, NEW HAMPSHIRE, THE WHITE MOUNTAINS.
  1875. Oil.
  21½ x 28 (54.6 x 71.1).
  Montrose Gallery, Bethesda, MD; *Antiques* (Feb. 1977).

NORTH CONWAY, WHITE HORSE LEDGE. S/L/R.
  C. 1875. Oil.
  12 x 18 (30.5 x 45.7).
  University of Texas Art Gallery catalog (1965), #735.

NORTH CONWAY, WHITE MOUNTAINS.
  1875. Oil.
  12¾ x 18¾ (32.4 x 47.6).
  University of Texas Art Gallery catalog (1965), #746.

NORTH CONWAY, WHITE MOUNTAINS.
  12 x 17 (30.5 x 43.2).
  Parke-Bernet (1945).

NORTH CONWAY, WHITE MOUNTAINS.
  C. 1875. Oil.
  17½ x 22 (44.5 x 55.9).
  Vose Galleries (1965); University of Texas Art Gallery catalog (1965), #723.

New Hampshire Scenery

NORTH CONWAY, WHITE MOUNTAINS, NEW HAMPSHIRE. S/L/L.
    1875. Oil.
    11¾ x 17½ (29.8 x 44.5).
    University of Texas Art Gallery catalog (1965), #747.

OLD TIME SKETCHING GROUND, NORTH CONWAY.
    C. 1879. Oil.
    NAD, 1879, #360; NMAA Inventory.

RIGOUR OF THE GAME, KEARSARGE HALL, NH (or CROQUET, CONWAY, NH). S/L/L.
    C. 1875. Oil.
    20 x 30 (50.8 x 76.2).
    Private collection (1965); University of Texas Art Gallery catalog (1965), #749.

SACO FORD, CONWAY MEADOWS.
    1872. Oil.
    38½ x 63¼ (97.8 x 160.7).
    Mount Holyoke College (1974).

SACO RIVER VALLEY (or IN THE WHITE MOUNTAINS or WHITE MOUNTAIN VALLEY). S/L/R.
    1875-78. Oil on canvas.
    20 x 30 (50.8 x 76.2).
    Private collection; University of Texas Art Gallery catalog (1965), #741.

SACO VALLEY, NORTH CONWAY. S/L/R.
    1875. Oil on academy board.
    9½ x 13¾ (24.1 x 34.9).
    Madison Art Center; University of Texas Art Gallery catalog (1965), #715.

SCENE FROM CONWAY, NEW HAMPSHIRE.
    1885. Oil.
    20⅞ x 14⅞ (53 x 37.8).
    Private collection (1972).

STORM ON MOUNT WASHINGTON.
    C. 1875. Oil on canvas.
    20 x 30 (50.8 x 76.2).
    University of Texas Art Museum catalog (1965), #715.

SUMMER AFTERNOON IN NORTH CONWAY.
    University of Texas Art Gallery catalog (1965); NMAA Inventory.

TROUT STREAM, NORTH CONWAY. S/L/L.
    1875. Oil on academy board.
    17 x 13¼ (43.2 x 33.7).
    Parke-Bernet (1939).

VIEW NEAR MOUNT WASHINGTON.
    University of Texas Art Gallery catalog (1965); NMAA Inventory.

WHITE MOUNTAIN VALLEY.
    20 x 30 (50.8 x 76.2).

University of Texas Art Gallery catalog (1965).

WHITE MOUNTAINS.
    Oil.
    8 x 12½ (20.3 x 31.8).
    Reading Public Museum and Art Gallery (1953).

WHITE MOUNTAINS (or HILLS AND VALLEY).
    1858-62.
    10 x 16 (25.4 x 40.6).
    Private collection; NMAA Inventory.

WHITE MOUNTAINS, NORTH CONWAY, NEW HAMPSHIRE. S/L/L.
    1875. Oil on canvas on board.
    13½ x 18¾ (34.3 x 47.6).
    Private collection (1965); University of Texas Art Gallery catalog (1965), #713.

WHITE MOUNTAINS; THE . . .
    1875. Oil.
    21½ x 28 (54.6 x 71.1).
    Montrose Gallery, Bethesda, MD; *American Art Review* (July 1977).

WIND CLOUDS (or NORTH CONWAY).
    1864-68.
    9¼ x 14 (23.5 x 35.6).
    John Levy Gallery, N.Y.C. (1965).

Attributed:
SUNSET IN THE WHITE MOUNTAINS.
    Oil.
    29¾ x 47⅞ (75.6 x 121.6).
    Pioneer Museum and Haggin Gallery, Stockton, CA.

INSLEY, ALBERT BABB
N
Born 1842. Died 1937.
Insley seems to have spent the major part of his adult life in and around New York City. He exhibited at the NAD from 1862 to 1898 and moved to a studio in the 10th Street Studio Building in 1874, where he remained for many years.

INTERVALE, NEW HAMPSHIRE.
    1881. Oil.
    12 x 18 (30.5 x 45.7).
    Delaware Art Museum (1975).

MOUNT WASHINGTON FROM THE CONWAY INTERVAL [sic].
    NAD, 1876, #209.

ON THE SACO RIVER, NEW HAMPSHIRE.
NAD, 1882, #447.

WHITE MOUNTAIN MEADOWS.
Oil.
12¼ x 18¼ (31 x 46.4).
Christie's (May 22, 1980).

J

JACKSON, CHARLES THOMAS
DAB, G&W
Born Plymouth, MA, June 21, 1805.
Died Somerville, MA, Aug. 28, 1880.
Jackson graduated from Harvard Medical School in 1829 and continued his studies at the Sorbonne in Paris, but he soon found himself more interested in geology. He returned to Boston and practiced medicine for a short time, but by 1836 he turned his attention fully to chemistry and geology. He spent three years as Maine's state geologist (1837-39) and followed it with a similar stint in Rhode Island. Jackson was made New Hampshire's state geologist in 1841 and served in that position through 1844. He produced a group of drawings in his book on the geology of New Hampshire in 1844. Controversy seems to have stalked Jackson throughout his medical and scientific careers, and he suffered a breakdown in 1873.

Bibliography:
Allison, Hildreth M. "The Painters of the Grand Monadnock." *Appalachia* 34 (1962-63), pp. 441-448.
Jackson, Charles T., M.D. *Final Report of the Geology and Mineralogy of the State of New Hampshire.* Concord, NH: Carroll and Baker, State Printers, 1844.
See Jackson's *Final Report* for pictures of New Hampshire's geology.

MONADNOCK MOUNTAIN FROM JAFFREY.
1844. Lithograph.
9 x 11⅛ (22.9 x 28.3).
Peterborough (NH) Historical Society in Jackson's *Final Report*.

JENKINS, A. R. (MISS)
There is presently no information on this artist.
WHITE MOUNTAIN SCENERY.
Pre-1877; 1st exhibition of Associated Artists of Cincinnati (1866-67) (see Cincinnati Historical Society for information).

JOHNSON, DAVID
A, B, C, Ce, C&H, F, G&W, N, R, S
Born New York, NY, May 10, 1827.
Died Walden, NY, Jan. 30, 1908.
Johnson's only specific training as an artist was a year's study, in 1850, under Jasper Cropsey. The following year he was in New Hampshire making sketches for a large, extremely detailed and crisp view of Mount Washington from the village of North Conway (now in the Boston Museum of Fine Arts). He often returned to New Hampshire in ensuing years to paint works which he exhibited at the Brooklyn Art Association, the PAFA, and the NAD, to which he was elected a member in 1861. Benjamin Champney, in his 1900 autobiography, prophetically stated of his friend Johnson: "the solid and unpretending in art must patiently wait its time." It has taken almost a century for such solid and unpretending landscapes as Johnson's and others of his era again to be appreciated.

Bibliography:
Baur, John I. H. " '. . . the exact brushwork of Mr. David Johnson,' An American Landscape Painter, 1827-1908." *American Art Journal* 12:4 (Autumn 1980), pp. 32-65.

A STUDY AT TAMWORTH, NEW HAMPSHIRE.
S/D/L/L.
1863. Oil on canvas.
14 x 17 (35.6 x 43.2).
Sotheby PB (Jan. 29, 1981); NAD, 1865, #523.

A STUDY FOR CONWAY, NEW HAMPSHIRE.
Sept. 29, 1851. Pencil.
7 ¹¹/₁₆ x 12 ¹¹/₁₆ (19.5 x 32.2).
Corcoran Gallery (July-Sept. 1979).

A STUDY OF BIRCH, VIEW IN LANCASTER, NH.
S/D/L/R.
1867. Oil.
16 x 25¾ (40.6 x 65.4).
Kenneth Lux Gallery (Nov. 15-Dec. 10, 1977).

A STUDY, MOUNT CHOCORUA. S/D/L/L.
  1851.
  Pennsylvania State University, Vessel collection.

CHOCORUA PEAK. S/D/L/R.
  1856. Oil on canvas.
  19⅛ x 24¼ (48.6 x 61.6).
  Private collection; Hirschl and Adler Gallery (1979).

CONNECTICUT RIVER, SOUTH LANCASTER, NH.
  1875. Oil.
  12⅛ x 20⅛ (30.8 x 51.1).
  Fine Arts Museum of San Francisco; M. H. de Young Memorial Museum.

CONWAY.
  Drawing.
  James Graham and Sons (1979).

CONWAY VALLEY, NEW HAMPSHIRE. Signed.
  1859. Oil on panel.
  5⅛ x 8¼ (13 x 21).
  Private collection (1979).

EAGLE CLIFF.
  Drawing.
  University of Vermont, Robert Hull Fleming Museum.

EAGLE CLIFF, FRANCONIA NOTCH, NEW HAMPSHIRE. S/D/Reverse.
  1869. Oil on wood panel.
  31 x 25 (78.7 x 63.5).
  Private collection; Chapellier Gallery (1974); *American Art Review* (1974); NAD, 1869, #298.

ECHO LAKE, FRANCONIA NOTCH, NEW HAMP-SHIRE. S/D.
  1867. Oil on canvas.
  28¼ x 44 (71.8 x 111.8).
  Schweitzer Gallery (1979).

ECHO LAKE, WHITE MOUNTAINS.
  Pre-1877; Utica (NY) Art Association exhibition (1868) (see Utica Public Library for information).

FRANCONIA MOUNTAINS.
  1867.
  16 x 27 (40.6 x 68.6).
  Parke-Bernet (1949 and 1950); NMAA Inventory.

FRANCONIA MOUNTAINS.
  Oil.
  15 x 26 (38.1 x 66).
  Wadsworth Atheneum, Hartford, CT (1974); NMAA Inventory.

LAFAYETTE FROM THE LOWER AMMONOO-SUC.
  1874-75. Oil on canvas.
  30 x 50 (76.2 x 127).
  Private collection (1979).

LAKE WINNEPESAUKEE [sic]. S/D.
  1867.
  28 x 43 (71.1 x 109.2).
  Private collection (1981).

LANCASTER, NEW HAMPSHIRE.
  Drawing.
  James Graham and Sons (1979).

LANCASTER, NEW HAMPSHIRE, 1867 (or STUDY AT LANCASTER, NH). S/D/L/R.
  1867. Oil.
  15 x 25 (38.1 x 63.5).
  Thomas Colville; *Antiques* (Jan. 1978), p. 138.

MOAT MOUNTAIN, NEW HAMPSHIRE. S/D/L/L.
  1851. Oil on canvas.
  16 x 23 (40.6 x 58.4).
  Pennsylvania State University, Vessel collection.

MOUNT CHACOROA [sic].
  6 x 10 (15.2 x 25.4).
  Adams-Davidson Gallery (Oct. 9, 1980).

MOUNT CHOCORUA, NEW HAMPSHIRE. S/D/L/L.
  1851. Oil on canvas.
  16 x 23 (40.6 x 58.4).
  Pennsylvania State University, Vessel collection.

MOUNT LAFAYETTE.
  Oil.
  17 x 14 (43.2 x 35.6).
  Guild Hall, East Hampton, NY (1979).

MOUNT LAFAYETTE FROM FRANCONIA, NEW HAMPSHIRE.
  1874. Oil on canvas.
  30 x 50 (76.2 x 127).
  Private collection (1980).

MOUNT LAFAYETTE FROM MILL POND, FRAN-CONIA. S/D/L/R.
  1871. Oil on canvas.
  15 x 26 (38.1 x 66).
  Private collection.

MOUNT LAFAYETTE, NEW HAMPSHIRE.
  1871.
  10¼ x 17½ (26 x 44.5).
  Parke-Bernet (1943).

MOUNT WASHINGTON.
    1853.
    North Conway Library Exhibition (1965).

NEAR LITTLETON, NH.
    NAD, 1867, #302.

NEAR SQUAM LAKE, NEW HAMPSHIRE.
S/D/L/Center.
    1856. Oil on canvas.
    18 $^{15}/_{16}$ x 28 (48.1 x 71.1).
    Metropolitan Museum of Art (1955); NAD,
    1856, #150.

NORTH CONWAY (Mount Washington). S/D/L/R.
    1852. Oil.
    16 x 23 (40.6 x 58.4).
    Boston Museum of Fine Arts, Karolik col-
    lection (1969).

OCTOBER IN NEW HAMPSHIRE.
    Brooklyn Art Association (1863), #73.

OLD MAN IN THE MOUNTAIN (IN FRANCONIA
NOTCH).
    1876. Oil on canvas.
    60 x 48 (152.4 x 121.9).
    State of New Hampshire, Concord (1983);
    Pre-1877; C&H (see Standard Source
    Reference List).

PRESIDENTIAL RANGE, NEW HAMPSHIRE.
    Oil on canvas.
    13 x 23 (33 x 58.4).
    Robert Schoelkopf Gallery (1982); Baridoff
    Gallery (Nov. 1982), #44.

SCENE IN NEW HAMPSHIRE.
    NAD, 1865, #385.

SKETCHBOOK.
    Probably 1851.
    Kennedy Galleries (1979).

STARR KING MOUNTAIN, LANCASTER, NH.
    1869. Oil on canvas.
    12 x 20 (30.5 x 50.8).
    Private collection (1972); NMAA Inventory.

STONY GAP, NEW HAMPSHIRE.
    Oil.
    22 x 30 (55.9 x 76.2).
    Parke-Bernet (1954); NMAA Inventory.

STUDY OF FRANCONIA MOUNTAINS FROM
WEST COMPTON [sic]. S/L/R.
    C. 1860-65. Oil on canvas.
    14½ x 26 (36.8 x 66).
    Wadsworth Atheneum, Hartford, CT (1980);
    University Art Gallery catalog, University of
    New Hampshire (1980), #8.

TAMWORTH SCENERY (Chocorua and Lake).
    Engraving.

4⅛ x 6⅜ (10.5 x 15.6).
Ladies' Repository, engraved by William
Wellstood, Boston, MA.

TAMWORTH, NEW HAMPSHIRE, 1863. S/L/L.
    1863. Oil on canvas.
    9½ x 15 (24.1 x 38.1).
    Private collection (1984); Kennedy Galleries
    (1977).

VIEW AT JACKSON, NEW HAMPSHIRE.
    1852. Oil.
    17 x 23 (43.2 x 58.4).
    Bernard Danenberg Gallery, N.Y.C.; *An-
    tiques* (April 1971); NAD, 1852, #65.

VIEW OF LANCASTER, NEW HAMPSHIRE.
    1869. Oil.
    14½ x 22½ (36.8 x 57.2).
    Private collection (1972).

VIEW ON THE ANDROSCOGGIN RIVER, MAINE
(possibly NH). S/D.
    1869-70. Oil on canvas.
    28 x 44 (71.1 x 111.8).
    Museum of Fine Arts, Houston, TX,
    Thyssen-Bornemisza collection (1983).

WEST CAMPTON, NEW HAMPSHIRE.
    Drawing.
    James Graham and Sons (1979).

WEST COMPTON [sic], NEW HAMPSHIRE.
    1867. Oil.
    14 x 20 (35.5 x 50.8).
    Sotheby PB (1979); NMAA Inventory.

WHITE MOUNTAINS FROM NORTH CONWAY,
NEW HAMPSHIRE.
    NAD, 1852, #59.

YOUNG ELMS AT WEST COMPTON [sic], NH.
    Oil.
    14 x 22 (35.6 x 55.9).
    NMAA Inventory.

JOHNSTON, DAVID CLAYPOOLE

C, F, G&W, R, S
Born Philadelphia, PA, March 1798.
Died Dorchester, MA, Nov. 8, 1865.
*Primarily an illustrator, lithographer, and
watercolorist, Johnson's work was of a satirical
nature. In 1861 he exhibited VIEW NEAR
BOSTON, NH, at the Boston Athenaeum.*

Bibliography:
Tatham, David. *A Note About David
Claypoole Johnson.* Syracuse University
Library, 1970.

WHITE MOUNTAIN PEDESTRIANS.
    C. 1855.
    Houghton Library, Harvard University
    (1984).

New Hampshire Scenery

K

KEITH, WILLIAM

Ba, DAB, F, G&W, Ka, N
Born Old Meldrum, Aberdeenshire, Scotland,
Nov. 21, 1839.
Died Berkeley, CA, April 13, 1911.
*Keith emigrated to America as a boy and began
his career as a engraver for* Harper's *in New
York. In 1859 he moved to California and took
up landscape painting. At the age of 30 he went
to Düsseldorf, Germany, to study and was a
pupil of Achenbach and Carl Marr. Two years
later he returned to California where he became
a friend of John Muir, the naturalist. He made
two more European trips and spent several years
in New Orleans before finally settling in California where he was an influential artist. In 1890
Keith met, and was influenced by, George Inness, who had traveled west, and the two
became close friends. He apparently made at
least one journey to New Hampshire, probably
around 1880. In 1872 he opened a studio in
Boston for a short time with Wilhelm Hahn. He
also resided in Maine in 1870 in the home of his
first wife.*

AUTUMN, COLORED TREES, NEW HAMPSHIRE.
Oil.
10 x 16½ (25.4 x 41.9).
St. Mary's College, Moraga, CA (1975).

CONWAY MEADOWS.
1881. Oil.
30½ x 49⅞ (77.5 x 126.7).
William Rockhill Nelson Gallery of Art,
Kansas City, MO (1973).

KENSETT, JOHN FREDERICK

A, C, Ce, C&H, DAB, F, G&W, K, Ka, R, S, T
Born Cheshire, CT, March 22, 1816.
Died New York, NY, Dec. 14, 1872.
*Kensett first received instruction in the art of
engraving from his father and later from his uncle, Alfred Daggett, who was a bank note
engraver. At the age of 24, Kensett sailed for
England with Asher B. Durand, John W.
Casilear (both landscape painters who also
began as engravers), and Thomas P. Rossiter
(a portrait painter). While abroad for seven
years, Kensett traveled widely through France,
Germany, Italy, and Switzerland, painting from
nature. In 1845 he gained recognition from the
Royal Academy and the British Institution in
London, where some of his paintings were exhibited. During the 45 years after his return to
America, before his sudden death of a heart attack, Kensett enjoyed a productive and successful artistic career. His active membership in
many art organizations and his philanthropic
contributions to young, struggling artists earned
him great esteem. He served on the council of
the NAD and was a founder of the Metropolitan
Museum of Art and the Artist's Fund Society
of New York. In 1859 President Buchanan appointed Kensett a member of the first Federal
Art Commission. In 1850 he traveled with Benjamin Champney, whom he had first met in
Paris, to the White Mountains. During his
lifetime, Kensett's paintings commanded handsome prices. Sketches of Mount Washington
and Franconia Notch sold for $50 and $60 in
1851, and* MOUNT CHOCORUA, *when com-
missioned by the Century Association in New
York City, where it still hangs, brought him
$5,000 in 1866.*

Select Bibliography:
American Federation of Arts. *John Frederick
Kensett.* New York, 1968. "The Collection of
over Five hundred paintings and studies by the
late John F. Kensett...Auction at Association
Hall...." Reprinted by Olana Gallery (1977).
Skimore College catalog. *John Frederick
Kensett.* Saratoga Springs, NY, 1967.

A GLIMPSE OF MOUNT WASHINGTON.
Brooklyn Art Association (1873), #178.

ARTIST'S BROOK, NORTH CONWAY, NEW
HAMPSHIRE.
18¾ x 15½ (47.6 x 39.4).
Olana Gallery catalog (1977), #514;
Pre-1877.

CASCADE IN THE WHITE MOUNTAINS.
8½ x 9¼ (21.6 x 23.5).
Olana Gallery catalog (1977), #144;
Pre-1877.

CHICORUA [sic] FROM FRIBURG [sic], MAINE.
12 x 14 (30.5 x 35.6).
Olana Gallery catalog (1977), #101;
Pre-1877.

CHICORUA [sic] FROM NEAR FRIBURGH [sic], ME.
  Pre-1877; executor's sale of the late J. F. Kensett (see New York Public Library for information).

CHICOURA [sic] MOUNTAIN, NEW HAMPSHIRE (study for a picture in the Century Association).
  19¾ x 13⅞ (50.2 x 35.2).
  Olana Gallery catalog (1977), #77; Pre-1877.

CHICORUA [sic], NEW HAMPSHIRE.
  19½ x 29½ (49.5 x 74.9).
  Olana Gallery catalog (1977), #633; Pre-1877.

CHICORUA [sic], NEW HAMPSHIRE AT SUNSET.
  10¾ x 17¾ (27.3 x 45.1).
  Olana Gallery catalog (1977), #565; Pre-1877.

CHICORUA [sic], WHITE MOUNTAINS.
  12 x 14 (30.5 x 35.6).
  Olana Gallery catalog (1977), #103; Pre-1877.

CHOCORUA FROM CONWAY MEADOW.
  12 x 18 (30.5 x 45.7).
  Alexander Gallery (1978).

CHOCORUA, NEW HAMPSHIRE.
  1864. Oil on canvas.
  14 x 20 (35.6 x 50.8).
  Yale University Art Gallery.

CHOCORUA, NEW HAMPSHIRE, WHITE MOUNTAINS (or WHITE MOUNTAIN SCENERY).
  1864. Oil.
  48 x 84 (121.9 x 213.4).
  Century Association (1977); NMAA Inventory.

CLIFFS AT NORTH CONWAY.
  21¾ x 15½ (55.2 x 39.4).
  Olana Gallery catalog (1977), #13.

CLIFFS, NEW HAMPSHIRE; THE...
  18¾ x 15¾ (47.6 x 40).
  Olana Gallery catalog (1977), #47.

COMING STORM, CHICORUA [sic], NEW HAMPSHIRE; THE...
  17¾ x 11⅝ (45.1 x 29.5).
  Olana Gallery catalog (1977), #324; Pre-1877.

COMING STORM, CHICORUA [sic], NH; THE...
  10 x 18 (25.4 x 45.7).
  Olana Gallery catalog (1977), #205; Pre-1877.

CONWAY BLUFFS.
  20 x 24 (50.8 x 61).
  Olana Gallery catalog (1977), #186; Pre-1877.

CONWAY VALLEY.
  1851.
  32¾ x 48 (83.2 x 121.9).
  John Howat, American Federation of Art catalog, formerly published by *Artnews*.

CONWAY VALLEY.
  1854. Oil.
  James Graham and Sons (1961); *Antiques* (Feb. 1961).

CONWAY VALLEY. S/D.
  1854.
  38 x 49 (96.5 x 124.5).
  Worcester Art Museum.

CONWAY VALLEY, NEW HAMPSHIRE. S/D.
  1854. Oil on canvas.
  32¾ x 48 (83.2 x 121.9).
  Worcester Art Museum (1980); Whitney Downtown Gallery, N.Y.C. (June-July 1980).

CONWAY VALLEY, NH.
  Oil.
  11 x 16¾ (27.9 x 42.5).
  Parke-Bernet (1941); NMAA Inventory.

CONWAY VALLEY, NH (or RANGE OF CATSKILLS).
  1859. Oil.
  10½ x 16¾ (26.7 x 42.5).
  NMAA Inventory.

EAGLE CLIFF FROM DEVIL'S PASS.
  18 x 25 (45.7 x 63.5).
  Unlocated.

EAGLE CLIFF FROM LAKE PEMIGEWASSET, FRANCONIA NOTCH.
  NAD, 1853, #321.

EARLY AUTUMN IN THE FRANCONIA MOUNTAINS.
  NAD, 1852, #140.

EASTERN MOUNTAIN LAKE (probably Mount Washington and the Saco). S/D/L/L.
  1869. Oil on canvas.
  12½ x 23 (31.8 x 58.4).
  Baridoff Gallery auction (Nov. 7, 1981), #76.

FLUME, FRANCONIA MOUNTAINS; THE...
  8 x 12 (20.3 x 30.5).
  Olana Gallery catalog (1977), #410.

FLUME, FRANCONIA MOUNTAINS; THE...
  Olana Gallery catalog (1977), #666.

New Hampshire Scenery

White Mountains in September, North Conway, N. H.
Sylvester Phelps Hodgdon, 1853
Oil on canvas, 20" x 30" / Collection: The University of Michigan Museum
of Art, bequest of Henry C. Lewis / Ref. page 89

FLUME, FRANCONIA NOTCH – A STUDY;
THE . . .
NAD, 1852, #64.

FLUME, FRANCONIA NOTCH, NEW HAMP-
SHIRE; THE . . . S/L/L.
C. 1850. Oil on canvas.
40¼ x 34 (102.2 x 86.4).
James Maroney, Inc., N.Y.C. (1979); An-
tiques (Feb. 1979); Whitney Downtown
Gallery, N.Y.C. (1980).

FLUME, NEW HAMPSHIRE; THE . . .
18 x 10 (45.7 x 25.4).
Olana Gallery catalog (1977); #108.

FLUME, NEW HAMPSHIRE; THE . . .
10 x 18 (25.4 x 45.7).
Olana Gallery catalog (1977), #629.

FOOT OF THE CLIFFS, NORTH CONWAY, NEW
HAMPSHIRE.
23¾ x 15¾ (60.3 x 40).
Olana Gallery catalog (1977), #481;
Pre-1877.

FRANCONIA MOUNTAINS.
NAD, 1854, #360; 1856, #125.

FRANCONIA NOTCH. S/D/L/L.
1871. Oil on board.
12 x 10 (30.5 x 25.4).
Sotheby PB (Oct. 17, 1980), #106.

GLEN ELLIS FALLS, NEW HAMPSHIRE.
19 x 16⅛ (48.2 x 40.8).
Christie's (1980); NMAA Inventory.

GLIMPSE OF THE WHITE HILLS.
NAD, 1859, #285.

HINT FROM THE WHITE HILLS.
12½ x 14 (31.7 x 35.6).
AAU, 1852, #205.

IN THE WHITE MOUNTAINS.
17¾ x 13⅝ (40.1 x 34.6).
Olana Gallery catalog (1977), #80.

Dictionary of Painters

IN THE WHITE MOUNTAINS.
 1871. Oil.
 14 x 20 (35.6 x 50.8).
 Reading Public Museum and Art Gallery
 (1953); NMAA Inventory.

LAKE WINNIPESEOGEE [sic].
 10 x 6 (25.4 x 15.2).
 Olana Gallery catalog (1977), #676.

LANDSCAPE — WHITE MOUNTAINS.
 Pre-1877; Clinton Hall Art Gallery and Book
 Sale Room (May 22, 1868), N.Y.C.

MOAT MOUNTAIN.
 11 x 16½ (27.9 x 41.9).
 Sotheby PB (April 1976).

MOONRISE, ECHO LAKE.
 12⅓ x 16 (31.3 x 40.6).
 Olana Gallery catalog (1977), #70.

MORNING IN THE WHITE MOUNTAINS.
 NAD, 1863, #123.

MOUNT CHICORUA [sic].
 8 x 13 (20.3 x 33).
 Olana Gallery catalog (1977), #28.

MOUNT CHOCORUA.
 1857.
 Private collection (1983); Webster Inc., Fine
 Art, Chevy Chase, MD; Adam Weschler and
 Sons (1976).

MOUNT CHOCORUA. S/D/L/L.
 1857. Oil on canvas.
 14½ x 24 (36.8 x 61).
 Pennsylvania State University, Vessel
 collection.

MOUNT CHOCORUA, NEW HAMPSHIRE. S/D.
 1856. Oil.
 18 x 27¼ (45.7 x 69.2).
 Sotheby PB (April 19, 1972), #59; NMAA
 Inventory.

MOUNT CHOCURA [sic], NEW HAMPSHIRE.
 1873. Oil.
 11⅛ x 16⅛ (28.3 x 41).
 Oakland Museum (1974); NMAA Inventory.

MOUNT JEFFERSON.
 4⅛ x 8 (10.5 x 20.3).
 Olana Gallery catalog (1977), #498;
 Pre-1877.

MOUNT LAFAYETTE.
 19¾ x 11¾ (50.2 x 29.8).
 Olana Gallery catalog (1977), #403.

MOUNT LAFAYETTE. S/D.
 Oct. 22, 1850. Pencil.
 9⅞ x 13¾ (25.1 x 34.9).
 Babcock Gallery (1980); Whitney
 Downtown Gallery, N.Y.C. (June-July
 1980).

MOUNT WASHINGTON.
 Oil on canvas.
 36 x 56 (91.4 x 142.2).
 Private collection (1970); BIAP.

MOUNT WASHINGTON.
 20 x 33⅛ (50.8 x 84.1).
 Cleveland Museum.

MOUNT WASHINGTON. S/D/L/R.
 1851. Oil on canvas.
 11⅜ x 20 (28.9 x 50.8).
 Corcoran Gallery (1980); University Art
 Gallery catalog, University of New Hampshire (1980), #115.

MOUNT WASHINGTON AND CONWAY VAL-
LEY. S/L/L.
 1867. Oil on canvas.
 24⅛ x 36⅜ (61.3 x 92.4).
 Wadsworth Atheneum, Hartford, CT (1976).

MOUNT WASHINGTON AND JEFFERSON, NEW
HAMPSHIRE.
 17¾ x 21¾ (45.1 x 55.2).
 Olana Gallery catalog (1977), #608;
 Pre-1877.

MOUNT WASHINGTON FROM THE CONWAY
VALLEY.
 Oil on canvas.
 24 x 60 (61 x 152.4).
 Wadsworth Atheneum, Hartford, CT (1974);
 NMAA Inventory.

MOUNT WASHINGTON FROM THE VALLEY OF
CONWAY.
 40½ x 60½ (102.9 x 153.7).
 AAU, 1852, #353.

MOUNT WASHINGTON FROM THE VALLEY OF
CONWAY. S/D/L.
 1851. Oil on canvas.
 14 x 20 (35.6 x 50.8).
 Esther Bloch, The Art Searcher (1980);
 NMAA Inventory.

MOUNT WASHINGTON, NEW HAMPSHIRE, IN
OCTOBER.
 15 x 23½ (38.1 x 59.7).
 Olana Gallery catalog (1977), #642;
 Pre-1877.

MOUNTAIN LANDSCAPE (Mount Washington).
 Pencil and wash.
 Corcoran Gallery.

New Hampshire Scenery

MOUNTAINS IN NEW HAMPSHIRE.
17¼ x 11¼ (43.8 x 28.6).
Olana Gallery catalog (1977), #402.

MOUNTAINS IN NEW HAMPSHIRE.
Oil on paper.
10¼ x 14⅛ (26 x 35.9).
Smithsonian Institution, National Collection
of Fine Arts (1976); NMAA Inventory.

NEAR NORTH CONWAY.
19¾ x 13¾ (50.2 x 34.9).
Olana Gallery catalog (1977), #24.

NORTH CONWAY (CLIFFS AND ROCKS).
22 x 16 (55.9 x 40.6).
Old Print Shop (1948).

NORTH CONWAY, NEW HAMPSHIRE.
Olana Gallery catalog (1977), #663.

OCTOBER DAY IN THE WHITE MOUNTAINS
(Chocorua). S/D/L/R.
1854. Oil on canvas.
31⅜ x 48⅜ (79.7 x 122.9).
Cleveland Museum (1973); Skidmore College
exhibition (1967), #6.

ON THE ARTIST'S BROOK, NORTH CONWAY.
10 x 14 (25.4 x 35.6).
Olana Gallery catalog (1977), #124.

PINE WOODS, CONWAY, NEW HAMPSHIRE.
13⅜ x 15½ (34 x 39.4).
Olana Gallery catalog (1977), #164.

PRESIDENTIAL RANGE.
North Conway Library Exhibition (1965).

RAVINE IN THE WHITE MOUNTAINS.
Brooklyn Art Association (1872), #68.

REMINISCENCES OF THE WHITE MOUNTAINS.
NAD, 1852, #417.

ROCKS IN THE WHITE MOUNTAINS.
23¾ x 17¾ (60.3 x 45.1).
Olana Gallery catalog (1977), #104;
Pre-1877.

ROCKS, CONWAY, NEW HAMPSHIRE.
9¾ x 7¾ (24.8 x 19.7).
Olana Gallery catalog (1977), #504.

SACO, WHITEFACE IN THE DISTANCE.
Pre-1877; executor's sale (March 24-29, 1872)
(see New York Public Library for
information).

SCENE IN CONWAY, NEW HAMPSHIRE.
C. 1850-55.
12 x 18½ (30.5 x 47).
Sotheby PB (1978); NMAA Inventory.

SCENE IN THE WHITE MOUNTAINS.
Pre-1877; Yale School of the Fine Arts exhibition, 1867.

SKETCH AT NORTH CONWAY.
Oil on academy board.
12⅛ x 18⅜ (30.8 x 46.7).
Old Print Shop Portfolio 4:6 (1945), p. 127,
#3; NMAA Inventory.

SKETCH OF CHOCORUA.
12 x 18 (30.5 x 45.7).
Alexander Gallery (1978).

SKETCH OF MOUNT WASHINGTON. S/D/L/R.
1851. Oil on canvas.
11 x 20 (27.9 x 50.8).
Corcoran Gallery.

SKETCH NEAR CONWAY – WATERFALL.
14 x 12 (35.6 x 30.5).
AAU, 1852, #305.

STUDY AT CONWAY, NEW HAMPSHIRE.
15¾ x 11¾ (40 x 29.8).
Olana Gallery catalog (1977), #591.

STUDY OF MOUNT WASHINGTON.
19½ x 29½ (49.5 x 74.9).
Olana Gallery catalog (1977), #641;
Pre-1877.

STUDY OF ROCKS AT CONWAY, NEW HAMP-
SHIRE.
23¼ x 15⅞ (59.1 x 40.3).
Olana Gallery catalog (1977), #635.

STUDYING IN THE WOODS, NORTH CONWAY,
NH.
17¾ x 11⅝ (45.1 x 29.5).
Olana Gallery catalog (1977), #342.

SUNRISE IN THE WHITE MOUNTAINS.
Private collection (1972); NMAA Inventory.

VIEW OF THE WHITE MOUNTAINS.
C. 1850. Oil on canvas.
4 x 6 (10.2 x 15.2).
Anglo-American Art Museum, Louisiana
State University, Baton Rouge, LA (1979);
NMAA Inventory.

WATERFALL (possibly New Hampshire). S/L/R.
19 x 16 (48.3 x 40.6).
Rosenberger Gallery, Centerport, NY (1979).

WHITE MOUNTAIN NOTCH.
Aug. 5, 1851. Pencil with white highlights.
10⅝ x 14⅞ (27 x 37.8).
Princeton University Art Gallery (1983);
University Art Gallery catalog, University of
New Hampshire (1980), #41.

WHITE MOUNTAIN SCENERY. S/D/L/L.
1859. Oil on canvas.
45 x 36 (114.3 x 91.4).
New-York Historical Society (1975).

Dictionary of Painters

WHITE MOUNTAINS.
    14 x 24 (55.9 x 61).
    Old Print Shop (1948).
WHITE MOUNTAINS.
    Pre-1877. Massachusetts Academy of the Fine Arts, Boston (1853).
WHITE MOUNTAINS, MOUNT WASHINGTON; THE... S/D.
    1869. Oil on canvas.
    40 x 60 (101.6 x 152.4).
    Wellesley College (1980); University Art Gallery catalog, University of New Hampshire (1980), #116.
WHITE MOUNTAINS; THE...
    Oil.
    11 x 16½ (27.9 x 41.9).
    Sotheby PB (1972); NMAA Inventory.

KEY, JOHN ROSS
A, B, C&H, F, G&W, N, R, S, T
Born Hagerstown, MD, July 16, 1832.
Died Baltimore, MD, March 24, 1920.
Though practically self-taught, Key did have some training in Munich and Paris. He was an accurate draftsman who also produced charcoal drawings of great beauty. He lived in Boston for many years and exhibited nearly 100 paintings at the Boston Athenaeum, the Boston Art Club, and Leonard Auction Rooms. He was a friend of Whistler, Inness, and Frank Duveneck.
CHERRY MOUNTAIN.
    Oil on canvas.
    17¾ x 39½ (40.1 x 100.3).
    Kennedy Galleries (1980).
CHERRY MOUNTAIN FROM JEFFERSON, NH.
    Pre-1877; Industrial Exposition, Chicago (1874) (see University of Chicago for information).
CHERRY MOUNTAIN, WHITE MOUNTAINS. S/D/L/L.
    1873. Oil on canvas.
    12 x 26 (30.5 x 66).
    Kennedy Galleries (1980).

CLOUDY MORNING, MOUNT LAFAYETTE.
    Oil.
    Boston Art Club (Jan. 16-Feb. 9, 1878), #71; C&H (see Standard Source Reference List); NAD, 1878, #667.
IN THE WHITE MOUNTAINS (Mount Washington). S/L/R.
    1872. Oil on canvas.
    12 x 20 (30.5 x 50.8).
    Richard Bourne, Inc. (Oct. 22, 1976).
MOONLIGHT, CHERRY MOUNTAIN, NEW HAMPSHIRE.
    Leonard Auction (Jan. 28, 1873), #14.
MORNING STROLL, LAKE WINNIPISEOGEE [sic].
    Oil.
    Boston Art Club (Jan. 17-Feb. 10, 1877), #57.
MOUNT WASHINGTON.
    Oil on canvas.
    12 x 26 (30.5 x 66).
    Kennedy Galleries (1980).
MOUNT WASHINGTON. S/D.
    1873.
    Kennedy Galleries (Nov. 1978).
MOUNT WASHINGTON TOPPED WITH FIRST SNOW IN SEPTEMBER FROM...NORTH CONWAY.
    Private collection (1983).
PINKHAM NOTCH, NEW HAMPSHIRE. Signed.
    Oil.
    14 x 26 (35.6 x 66).
    Private collection (1975).
PRESIDENTIAL RANGE FROM JEFFERSON.
    Burned in one of the first of three Glen House fires.

KITTELL, NICHOLAS BIDDLE
C, G&W
Born 1822. Died New York, NY, June 25, 1894.
Kittell first exhibited at the NAD in 1847, giving his address as Norwich, NY. From 1861 to 1891, he lived in New York City and exhibited portraits during the time at the NAD. Groce and Wallace listed him as a landscapist as well as a portraitist. He visited Benjamin Champney in the White Mountains frequently from 1878 to 1887, often signing Champney's guest book, and is believed to have been a student or friend of the well-known artist. No New Hampshire landscapes by Kittell have yet come to light.
Information courtesy of Phyllis F. Greene.

New Hampshire Scenery

KNAPP, CHARLES W., SR.
Ce, F, G&W, N
Born Philadelphia, PA, 1823.
Died Philadelphia, PA, May 15, 1900.
Knapp first exhibited at the NAD in 1859, at which time he listed his address as New York City, but does not seem to have sent pictures for exhibition there after 1861. He exhibited two New Hampshire views at the Massachusetts Charitable Mechanic Association in 1878.

AUTUMN SCENERY (New Hampshire?). S/L/L.
C. 1860. Oil on canvas.
20 x 36 (50.8 x 91.4).
Old Print Shop *Portfolio* 39:2 (1979), p. 47.

ELLSWORTH BROOK, WEST CAMPTON, NEW HAMPSHIRE. S/L/R.
C. 1860. Oil on canvas.
24 x 32 (61 x 81.3).
Old Print Shop *Portfolio* 39:2 (1979), p. 47.

ENTRANCE TO FRANCONIA NOTCH.
1855.
Private collection (1974).

MOUNT CHOCORUA, SILVER LAKE, NEW HAMPSHIRE.
1863. Oil.
Dartmouth College Art Galleries (1974).

MOUNT WASHINGTON FROM NORTH CONWAY, NH.
1881. Oil.
20 x 36 (50.8 x 91.4).
Henry B. Holt, dealer, Essex Falls, NJ; *Antiques* (July 1983).

ON THE PEABODY RIVER, MOUNT WASHINGTON. S/L/L.
Oil on canvas.
20 x 36 (50.8 x 91.4).
Richard Bourne, Inc. (Aug. 14, 1979), #26.

SACO AND KEARSARGE.
Vose Galleries (1979); Withington Auction (Jan. 8, 1977).

SCENE ON THE SACO RIVER.
Pre-1877; *Cosmopolitan Art Journal* 3:5 (Dec. 1859).

VIEW ON THE ANDROSCOGGIN.
MA Charitable (1878), #402.

WHITE MOUNTAINS FROM BERLIN.
MA Charitable (1878), #21.

WHITE MOUNTAINS FROM THE ANDROSCOGGIN VALLEY.
Pre-1877; Louisville (KY) Industrial Exposition (1875).

KNOWLTON, CHARLES
All that is known about this painter is that he was a design painter for Abbot Downing of Concord, N.H.

MOUNTAIN LANDSCAPE.
Oil.
Oval, 6½ x 10¼ (15.9 x 26.1).
New Hampshire Historical Society.

KNOWLTON, HELEN MARY
B, C&H, Co, F, G&W, N, S
Born Littleton, MA, Aug. 16, 1832. Died 1918.
Knowlton, a fine exponent of charcoal sketches and oil portraits, studied under William Morris Hunt. She became a close associate of the artist and later taught in his classes. Knowlton and Hunt were influential in guiding Boston collectors to buy works by the Barbizon School. In 1879 she wrote Talks on Art by W. M. Hunt *and, in 1899,* The Art Life of William Morris Hunt. *She opened her own studio in Boston in 1867 and exhibited at the NAD and the Boston Art Club. The Boston* Transcript *for September 21, 1875, noted that she "spent the summer with several of her students at the Glen House, White Mountains. She contemplates building a studio there next summer." There is no evidence that she carried out her proposal. Much of her work was destroyed by fire in 1878.*

WOODS NEAR GLEN, NEW HAMPSHIRE.
Oil.
Boston Art Club (Jan. 12-Feb. 2, 1876), #57.

WOODS NEAR GLEN, NEW HAMPSHIRE.
Oil.
Boston Art Club (Jan. 12-Feb 2, 1876), #61.

KURTZ (or KUNTZ), HENRY
A, G&W
Born Massachusetts, c. 1822.
Kurtz, probably self-trained, was an engraver who also painted portraits and landscapes. He was active in Boston from 1844 to the 1860s.

ECHO LAKE, WHITE MOUNTAINS.
MA Charitable (1874), #216; Pre-1877.

L

LANMAN, CHARLES

A, C, Ce, DAB, F, G&W, K, Ka, N, S
Born Monroe, MI, June 14, 1819.
Died Georgetown, DC, March 4, 1895.

Lanman was a writer, illustrator, and painter. After a preliminary education at Plymouth Academy in Norwich, MA, he moved to New York City and worked for the East India mercantile house. During this period (1836-45), he studied under Asher B. Durand and in 1843 was elected an associate of the NAD, where he exhibited frequently. He acted as Daniel Webster's personal secretary in 1850 and was later author of the Memorials of Daniel Webster. *By 1859 he moved permanently to Georgetown, in Washington, DC, from which he apparently traveled widely. There he ambitiously undertook the execution of 350 titles of American scenery to be sold in portfolios of 10 pictures in oil (18 x 22), subjects to be chosen by the subscriber, at a price of $250. The subjects included Florida, Minnesota, and Canada. He met Albert Bierstadt at the Glen House in Pinkham Notch, NH, about 1869. Of his art, the* American Art Review *in 1883 noted: "they call for kindly attention for the freshness and fine feeling they display, and the truth of local color."*

Bibliography:
Archives of American Art. Roll #551.
Lanman, Charles. *Letters from a Landscape Painter.* Boston: James Monroe and Co., 1844.

A DOUBLE WATERFALL, NEW HAMPSHIRE, A TROUT BROOK.
    Oil on canvas.
    10 x 4 (25.4 x 10.2).
    Merwin Gallery (Feb. 18-19, 1915), #97.

A LOVELY LAKE.
    Before 1870. Oil.
    18 x 22 (55.9 x 45.7).
    Archives of American Art. Roll 551, Frames 447-448.

A MOUNTAIN STREAM.
    Before 1870. Oil.
    18 x 22 (55.9 x 45.7).
    Archives of American Art. Roll 551, Frames 447-448.

A ROCKY STREAM.
    NAD, 1859, #140.

A TROUT STREAM, WHITE MOUNTAINS. S/L/L.
    1884. Oil on board.
    Boston Public Library, special clippings file.

CONWAY VALLEY.
    Before 1870. Oil.
    18 x 22 (55.9 x 45.7).
    Archives of American Art. Roll 551, Frames 447-448.

FALL OF GLEN ELLIS.
    Before 1870. Oil.
    18 x 22 (55.9 x 45.7).
    Archives of American Art. Roll 551, Frames 447-448.

IN THE DIXVILLE NOTCH.
    Before 1870. Oil.
    18 x 22 (55.9 x 45.7).
    Archives of American Art. Roll 551, Frames 447-448.

IN THE WOODS, NEW HAMPSHIRE.
    Oil on canvas.
    10 x 4 (25.4 x 10.2).
    Merwin Gallery (Feb. 18-19, 1915), #100.

LAKE WINNEPESOG [sic].
    Before 1870. Oil.
    18 x 22 (55.9 x 45.7).
    Archives of American Art. Roll 551, Frames 447-448.

MOUNT COCOURA [sic].
    Before 1870. Oil.
    18 x 22 (55.9 x 45.7).
    Archives of American Art. Roll 551, Frames 447-448.

MOUNT LAFAYETTE.
    Before 1870. Oil.
    18 x 22 (55.9 x 45.7).
    Archives of American Art. Roll 551, Frames 447-448.

MOUNT WASHINGTON.
    Before 1870. Oil.
    18 x 22 (55.9 x 45.7).
    Archives of American Art. Roll 551, Frames 447-448.

NEW HAMPSHIRE FOREST SCENE.
    Before 1870. Oil.

22 x 18 (55.9 x 45.7).
Archives of American Art. Roll 551, Frames
447-448; Merwin Gallery (Feb. 1915), #190.
NEW HAMPSHIRE TROUTING.
Before 1870. Oil.
15 x 16 (38.1 x 40.6).
Archives of American Art. Roll 551, Frames
447-448.
NOTCH IN THE WHITE MOUNTAINS.
Before 1870. Oil.
18 x 22 (55.9 x 45.7).
Archives of American Art. Roll 551, Frames
447-448.
ON THE AMMANUSUC [sic].
Before 1870. Oil.
18 x 22 (55.9 x 45.7).
Archives of American Art. Roll 551, Frames
447-448; Merwin Gallery (Feb. 1915), #151.
ON THE ANDROSCOGGIN.
Before 1870.
Archives of American Art. Roll 551, Frames
447-448.
ON THE PEABODY.
Before 1870. Oil.
18 x 22 (55.9 x 45.7).
Archives of American Art. Roll 551, Frames
447-448.
ON THE PEMIGEWASSET.
Before 1870. Oil.
18 x 22 (55.9 x 45.7).
Archives of American Art. Roll 551, Frames
447-448.
ON THE SACO.
Before 1870. Oil.
18 x 22 (55.9 x 45.7).
Archives of American Art. Roll 551, Frames
447-448.
PASTURE IN THE WOODS, NEW HAMPSHIRE.
Oil on canvas.
10 x 4 (25.4 x 10.2).
Merwin Gallery (Feb. 18-19, 1915), #94.
PINE WOODS IN NEW HAMPSHIRE.
Private collection (1978).
SCENE IN THE WHITE MOUNTAINS.
Before 1870. Oil.
20 x 30 (50.8 x 76.2).
Archives of American Art. Roll 551, Frames
447-448; Merwin Gallery (1915), #193.
STREAM, WHITE MOUNTAINS.
Pre-1877; Washington, DC, art exhibition
(1859).

TROUTING IN NEW HAMPSHIRE.
Oil.
18 x 16 (45.7 x 40.6).
Sotheby PB (1979).
TUCKERMAN'S RAVINE.
Before 1870. Oil.
18 x 22 (55.9 x 45.7).
Archives of American Art. Roll 551, Frames
447-448.
VIEW NEAR GLEN HOUSE.
Before 1870. Oil.
18 x 22 (55.9 x 45.7).
Archives of American Art. Roll 551, Frames
447-448.
WINTER BRIDGE ON THE PEABODY.
Before 1870. Oil.
18 x 22 (55.9 x 45.7).
Archives of American Art. Roll 551, Frames
447-448.

LANSIL, WALTER F.

B, C&H, F, N, S
Born Bangor, ME, 1846. Died after 1892.
Studied under J. P. Hardy and also worked with Sylvester Rosa and Koehler. His particular interest was oil paintings of marine subjects, but he also produced pencil sketches. He exhibited at the NAD from 1878 to 1892 and at the Boston Art Club in 1877.
CAMP CHOCORUA.
Pencil on colored paper.
Vose Galleries (1982).
CAMP CHOCORUA, SWIFT RIVER, INTERVALE.
Pencil on colored paper.
Private collection (1983); Vose Galleries
(1982).
MOUNT KEARSARGE AND MOUNT CHOCOR-UA.
Pencil on colored paper.
Vose Galleries (1982).

LARSON, HAROLD MAGNUS

Born Stockholm, Sweden, 1865.
Died New York, NY, 1952.
Larson moved to Brooklyn as a young adult and began work as a short-order cook, an occupation he begrudgingly followed for most of the rest of his life, being forced by financial circumstances to curtail his painting to holidays and free time. He often spent his vacations with his sister and brother-in-law on their farm in

Ossipee, NH. Shortly after 1900 Larson travel-ed to Paris and was much influenced by the French impressionists. His work was very poin-tillist in style.

Information courtesy of Vose Galleries.

NEW HAMPSHIRE TWILIGHT, OSSIPEE.
>   32 x 26 (81.3 x 66).
>   Richard Bourne, Inc. (1976), #47.

LAW, RALPH

Nothing is presently known of this artist.

MOUNT CHOCORUA.
>   Oil on canvas.
>   13½ x 24½ (34.3 x 62.2).
>   Childs Gallery (March 1969); BIAP.

LAWRIE (or LAURIE), ALEXANDER

A, C, Ce, C&H, DAB, F, G&W, N, R, S, T
Born New York, NY, Feb. 25, 1828.
Died Lafayette, IN, Feb. 15, 1917.
Lawrie trained as an engraver and also studied at the NAD. He moved to Philadelphia in 1852 and exhibited at the PAFA from 1852 to 1854. In 1855 he continued his art studies in Düsseldorf, Paris, and Florence, returning to the U.S. in 1858. After service in the Civil War, Lawrie reentered the art world, exhibiting in 1866 at the Boston Athenaeum, and for many years thereafter at the NAD and the Brooklyn Art Association. He was elected a member of the Century Association in 1867 and kept a studio in the 10th Street Studio Building (N.Y.C.) for one year in 1895.

Bibliography:
Gerdts, William H. "Revealed Masters: 19th Century American Art." Exhibition organized by the American Federation of Fine Arts, N.Y.C. (undated).

LANDSCAPE, WHITE MOUNTAINS, NEW HAMPSHIRE.
>   Oil.
>   10 x 12 (25.4 x 30.5).
>   Private collection (1975); NMAA Inventory.

LEGANGER, NICOLAY TYSLAND

N
Born 1832. Died 1894 or after 1896.
*Little is known of Leganger except that he was active in both New York City and Boston. He exhibited at the NAD in 1891, when he gave his address as Newton Center, MA, and at the Brooklyn Art Association between 1871 and 1882. His work was represented at an impor-*tant sale of paintings at Noyes and Blakeslee in Boston, December 1880. There is a discrepan-cy in his date of death, generally given as 1894, for a painting of his is dated on the back as having been executed in 1896.

Bibliography:
Robinson, F. T. *Living New England Artists* (Boston, 1888).

AFTERNOON AT TAMWORTH, NEW HAMPSHIRE.
>   1894.
>   Private collection (1974).

ON THE MEADOWS, TAMWORTH, NEW HAMPSHIRE.
>   NAD, 1891, #47.

SUMMER AFTERNOON, SOUTH TAMWORTH, NEW HAMPSHIRE. S/L/L.
>   1896. Oil on canvas.
>   30 x 28 (76.2 x 71.1).
>   Richard Bourne, Inc. (Aug. 14, 1979), #69.

LEIGHTON, NICHOLAS WINFIELD SCOTT

F, N, S
Born Auburn, ME, Aug. 1849.
Died Waverly, MA, Jan. 18, 1898.
Mainly a painter of animals, Leighton studied under Harrison Bird Brown. He opened a studio in Boston in 1874 and exhibited at the NAD in 1883, 1886, and 1887.

Bibliography:
Bain, Sherwood. "Nicholas Winfield Scott Leighton." *Antiques* (March 1979), pp. 544-551.

MOUNT MONADNOCK.
>   Oil.
>   6 x 10 (15.2 x 25.4).
>   Private collection (1975); NMAA Inventory.

LEWIN, JAMES MORGAN

A, F(sup), G&W
Born Swansea, MA, 1836.
Died Milton, MA, Sept. 1877.
Employed as an engraver of jewelry and a painter of photographs early in his adult life, Lewin later turned his talents to landscape paint-ings. In 1858 he taught in Providence, RI, at the Charles Field Street Family and Day School. For the next two years he exhibited at the Boston Athenaeum. The Crayon for October 1859 noted that "Jas. M. Lewin, a landscape painter of great popularity here, is spending the sum-mer at Conway, NH, taking sketches of the White Mountains." He exhibited at the Boston Art Club in 1875.

New Hampshire Scenery

CONWAY .MEADOWS WITH MOAT MOUN-
TAINS [sic] AND CATHEDRAL LEDGE.
   1859-60.
   17 x 31¼ (43.2 x 79.4).
   Vose Galleries (1979).

ON THE MOOSILAUK [sic].
   Oil.
   Boston Art Club (April 1875), #53.

LEWIS, EDMUND DARCH
A, Ce, DAB, F, G&W, K, Ka, R, S, T
Born Philadelphia, PA, Oct. 17, 1835.
Died Philadelphia, PA, Aug. 12, 1910.
*Lewis was a man of substantial means who
studied under Paul Weber from 1850 to 1855.
He exhibited at the PAFA for many years where
his work was widely esteemed. He also sent
paintings to the Boston Athenaeum and in 1860
to the NAD. His early work is considered
technically better because he later greatly increased his output, even doing two to three canvases a day at times. His "mass-produced" work
made him a handsome profit, and he became
known as a collector of antiques, furniture, and
art. He seems to have visited the White Mountains frequently, for dated paintings of the area
range form 1858 to 1875.*

CANOEING ON THE LAKE, WHITE MOUNTAINS
(Echo Lake, Conway). S/D/L/L.
   1865. Oil on canvas.
   15 x 25 (38.1 x 63.5).
   Private collection (1984); Kennedy Galleries
   (1981).

CHOCORUA MOUNTAIN.
   Watercolor.
   PAFA, 1858, #414.

CONWAY VALLEY, NEW HAMPSHIRE. S/L/L.
   1870. Oil on canvas.
   15½ x 26½ (39.4 x 67.3).
   Richard Bourne, Inc. (Aug. 14, 1979), #73.

DISTANT VIEW OF MOUNT WASHINGTON.
   PAFA, 1859, #334.

EARLY AUTUMN IN WHITE MOUNTAINS.
   Pre-1877; U.S. Sanitary Commission (1864),
   Philadelphia.

ECHO LAKE, FRANCONIA.
   Boston Athenaeum (1859), #214.

EMERALD POOL, WHITE MOUNTAINS.
   Pre-1877; Union League Club of Philadelphia
   (Dec. 8-10, 1870).

EVENING AT NORTH CONWAY.
   PAFA, 1858, #323.

EVENING ON LAKE WINNIPESEOGEE [sic].
   PAFA, 1862, #26.

INTERVALE, NEW HAMPSHIRE.
   1863. Oil.
   31 x 49 (78.7 x 124.5).
   Old Print Shop *Portfolio* 26:9, p. 213.

INTERVALE, NORTH CONWAY, MOUNT
WASHINGTON.
   PAFA, 1859, #477.

LAKE IN THE CLOUDS; THE. . .
   Boston Athenaeum (1869), #239.

LAKE WINNIPISEOGEE [sic].
   PAFA, 1858, #390.

LAKE WINNIPISEOGEE [sic].
   PAFA, 1865, #717; 1866, #659.

LANDSCAPE, MOUNT WASHINGTON, WHITE
MOUNTAINS.
   Pre-1877; private collection (1870).

MOAT MOUNTAIN.
   North Conway Library Exhibition (1965).

MOUNT WASHINGTON.
   Watercolor.
   PAFA, 1858, #408; Boston Athenaeum
   (1858), #322 and #336.

MOUNT WASHINGTON IN THE VALLEY OF
CONWAY. S/L/L.
   1870. Oil on canvas.
   15½ x 26½ (39.4 x 67.3).
   Private collection (1983).

MT. KEARSARGE, NORTH CONWAY, NEW
HAMPSHIRE.
   Pre-1877; Louisville (KY) Industrial Exposition (1877); Utica (NY) Art Association
   (1871).

SCENE IN WHITE MOUNTAINS.
   PAFA, 1862, #819.

VALLEY OF THE AMONOOSUCK [sic] (or VALE
OF THE AMONOOSUCK [sic]). S/D/L/R.
   1875. Oil on canvas.
   60½ x 96¼ (153.6 x 243.9).
   Sotheby PB (Nov. 21, 1980), #83; Boston
   Athenaeum (1868), #301.

VALLEY OF THE PEMIGEWASSET. S/D.
   1863. Oil on canvas.
   30½ x 50 (77.5 x 127).
   Berry Hill Galleries (Oct. 1970); BIAP.

VIEW IN NORTH CONWAY.
   Bierstadt Exhibition, New Bedford, 1858, #8.

VIEW IN THE WHITE MOUNTAINS.
   PAFA, 1859, #164; Pre-1877; Bierstadt Exhibition, New Bedford, 1858.

VIEW NEAR THE WHITE MOUNTAINS.
   Pre-1877; Washington (DC) Art Association,
   1857 (see Columbia Historical Society for
   information).

WHITE MOUNTAINS SCENERY (2).
   Pre-1877; Buffalo Fine Arts Academy (1872
   and 1873).

LINDSAY, THOMAS C.

F(sup), G&W
*Lindsay was active in Cincinnati from 1860
through 1864. Nothing else is presently known
about him.*

RECOLLECTIONS OF THE WHITE MOUNTAINS.
S/D.
   1864.
   24 x 28 (61 x 71.1).
   Private collection; Vose Galleries.

LINSLEY (or LINSLY), WILFORD

N, S
Born probably 1840s. Died 1898.
*A landscapist who worked mainly in oils,
Linsley lived in New York City and exhibited
at the NAD from 1868 to 1883. He kept a studio
in the 10th Street Studio Building (N.Y.C.) from
1882 to 1898.*

A GRAY DAY, SHELBURNE, NEW HAMPSHIRE.
   NAD, 1873, #312.

MOUNT MORIAH FROM THE ANDROSCOGGIN
RIVER.
   Pre-1877; Louisville (KY) Industrial Exposi-
   tion (1877).

STUDY OF A BRIDGE, SHELBURNE, NEW
HAMPSHIRE.
   NAD, 1868, #533.

STUDY, MOUNT WINTHROP, SHELBURNE, NEW
HAMPSHIRE.
   NAD, 1871, #331.

LIVINGSTON, MONTGOMERY

C, Ce, F(sup), G&W, R
Born Clermont, NY, Aug. 31, 1816.
Died after 1860.
*Livingston may have received his art education
in Switzerland, for the first pictures he exhibited
at the NAD were views of that country. He
became an associate of the NAD in 1843 and
an honorary professional member in 1848, at
which time he lived in upper New York State.*

VIEW IN THE WHITE MOUNTAINS.
   NAD, 1851, #394.

VIEW IN WHITE MOUNTAINS.
   NAD, 1851, #402.

WILLIE [sic] HOUSE, WHITE MOUNTAINS.
   NAD, 1848, #80.

LONGWORTH, H. M. (or L. M.)

Active 1867.
Possibly **Montreville Longworth**, who was born
in New York City in 1813.

NEW HAMPSHIRE LANDSCAPE.
   1867. Oil.
   19½ x 32 (49.5 x 81.3).
   Groton School, Groton, MA (1975).

LOOMIS, OTIS (or OSBERT) BURR

Ce, F(sup), G&W, N
Born Windsor, CT, July 30, 1813.
Died after 1873.
*Any artistic training Loomis may have had
probably came from Yale where he graduated
in 1835. He immediately set out as a portraitist
in New York City after leaving New Haven and
later moved to Charleston, SC. His landscapes
include not only the White Mountains but also
a panorama of Cuba. By 1864 he was back in
New York City.*

MOUNT WASHINGTON FROM ISRAEL RIVER.
   NAD, 1864, #6.

MOUNT WASHINGTON FROM THE HILL BACK
OF GLEN HOUSE.
   NAD, 1858, #69.

MOUNT WASHINGTON, JEFFERSON, ADAMS,
AND MADISON FROM SURPRISE MOUNTAIN.
   NAD, 1865, #266.

VIEW IN THE WHITE MOUNTAINS.
   NAD, 1864, #303.

LOVERIDGE, CLINTON

G&W, N
Active 1857-99.
*Loveridge worked in Albany, NY, from 1857
to 1860 and exhibited periodically at the NAD
from 1867 to 1899.*

KEARSARGE AND THE SACO.
   Oil on panel.
   9⅛ x 15 (23.2 x 38.1).
   Private collection.

New Hampshire Scenery

Mount Washington
Winslow Homer, 1869
Oil on canvas, 16" x 24 1/8" / Collection: The Art Institute of Chicago,
    gift of Mrs. Chauncey McCormick and Mrs. Richard E.
    Danielson / Ref. page 90

WHITE MOUNTAINS ON THE SACO.
    Oil on panel.
    9⅛ x 15 (23.2 x 38.1).
    Private collection (1983).

LOWELL, ABNER

Active 1874.
Nothing is known of this artist except that he
worked in Portland, ME, in 1874.
MOUNT WASHINGTON AND OTHER SUMMITS
IN THE WHITE MOUNTAINS RANGE
FROM. . .PORTLAND.
    1874. Sketch.
    Goodspeed's Gallery (Aug. 1980).

LOWELL, LEMUEL L.
S
Active before 1877. Died Watertown, NY, 1914.
Nothing else is presently known of this artist.

CHICORUA [sic] PEAK, WHITE MOUNTAINS.
    Pre-1877; Utica (NY) exhibition (1867).

LUTHY (or LUETHY or FLUTHY), L.
(JOHANNES?)
A
Born Switzerland? 1803. Died 1863.
This elusive artist exhibited a pen drawing at
the Boston Athenaeum in 1856. His name has
been interpreted in various ways. One other oil
painting was exhibited in 1854. (See Fluthy, F.).
WHITE MOUNTAINS (Mount Washington from
Sunset Hill, North Conway). S/L/R.
    Probably 1854. Oil on canvas.
    26 x 36⅛ (66 x 91.8).
    University of Michigan Museum of Art
    (1975).

Dictionary of Painters

M

MACKIE (or MACKEY), ANNIE E.

A

Mackie was a pupil of Benjamin Champney.
Information courtesy of Phyllis F. Greene.

ARTIST'S BROOK.
  Oil on canvas.
  13¼ x 23 (33.7 x 58.4).
  Private collection.

MAGUIRE, MARTHA A.

Nothing is presently known about this artist.

VIEW OF THE WHITE MOUNTAINS.
  Pre-1877; Fair of Hartford (CT) County
  Agricultural Society (Oct. 1852).

MAINE, WILLIAM S. B.

Nothing is presently known of this artist.

AUTUMN, LITTLETON, NEW HAMPSHIRE.
  Oil.
  Boston Art Club (1884), #157.

MANSFIELD, JOHN W.

N

Active 1877-80.
*The only thing that is known of Mansfield is
that he exhibited at the NAD from 1877 to 1880.*

CASCADE IN FRANCONIA MOUNTAINS, NEW
HAMPSHIRE.
  NAD, 1880, #581.

MARTIN, H. E. (MRS.)

Active 1884.
*There is presently no other information on this
artist.*

MOUNT MONADNOCK.
  1884. Oil on canvas.
  18 x 23¾ (45.7 x 60.3).
  Private collection.

MARTIN, HOMER DODGE

B, Ba, C, C&H, DAB, F, G&W, K, Ka, N, R,
S, T
Born Albany, NY, Oct. 28, 1836.
Died St. Paul, MN, Feb. 12, 1897.

*After trying several trades unsuccessfully, Mar-
tin's family family finally allowed him to study
painting, with the encouragement of Erastus
Dow Palmer about 1856. He moved to New
York City in 1862 shortly after his marriage and
exhibited at the Exhibition of Paintings and
Sculpture at the Studio of Erastus Dow Palmer,
February 1864, for the Benefit of the U.S.
Sanitary Commission. In the 1860s and 1870s
he traveled often to the White Mountains and
other parts of New England, making sketches
and improving his art. In 1865 he opened his
studio at the 10th Street Studio Building
(N.Y.C.), which he kept until 1882. He was
forced by circumstances to try illustrations and
worked for* Scribner's Magazine *and* Century *for
a short time. He exhibited at the NAD and the
Brooklyn Art Association from 1861 to 1894.
His art did not gain recognition until years after
his death, and he died deeply in debt and, for
the most part, unrecognized.*

Bibliography:
Coffin, C. H. *American Masters of Painting*
(1902).
Mather, Frank Jewett, Jr. *Homer Martin: Poet
in Landscape* (1912).

A WHITE MOUNTAINS BROOK.
  1870. Engraving.
  Aldine #11, (Nov. 1873), p. 219.

AUTUMN LANDSCAPE, NEW HAMPSHIRE.
  1868. Oil.
  14 x 12½ (35.6 x 31.8).
  Private collection (1976).

BROOK SCENE IN WHITE MOUNTAINS.
  Brooklyn Art Association (1877), #310;
  Pre-1877.

CRYSTAL CASCADES.
  Vassar College Art Gallery.

IN THE WHITE MOUNTAINS.
  U.S. Sanitary Commission (Feb. 1864), #87;
  Pre-1877.

LAKE AND MOUNTAIN (probably New
Hampshire).
  July 12, 1861. Pencil.
  8 ⁵/₁₆ x 11¾ (21.1 x 29.8).
  Boston Museum of Fine Arts, Karolik col-
  lection (1983).

New Hampshire Scenery

MORNING – VALLEY NEAR GORHAM.
Brooklyn Art Association (1864), #28.

MORNING ON THE ANDROSCOGGIN.
Brooklyn Art Association (1865), #111.

WHERE TROUT ABIDE (Eagle Cliff, Franconia, New Hampshire).
Oil.
20⅛ x 14 (51.1 x 35.6).
Los Angeles County Museum (1973).

WHITE MOUNTAIN VIEW.
Brooklyn Art Association (1863), #63.

WHITE MOUNTAINS, MOUNT MADISON AND MOUNT ADAMS; THE...S/L/L/Center.
Oil on canvas.
30 ¹/₁₆ x 50¼ (76.4 x 127.6).
Metropolitan Museum of Art (1975).

WHITE MOUNTAINS; THE...
NAD, 1864, #286.

MARTIN, THOMAS MOWER (or MOURER)
N, S
Born London, England, 1838. Died after 1885.
Little is known of Martin except that he exhibited at the Boston Art Club in 1881 and at the NAD in 1885, at which time he lived in New York City.

BERLIN FALLS.
Watercolor.
Boston Art Club (1881), #94.

MATTHEWS, FERDINAND SCHUYLER
F, N
Born 1854. Died 1938.
Matthews worked for Prang in Boston and produced three paintings which were the basis for a series of monochromes in the firm. He exhibited at the NAD in 1877.

CRYSTAL HILLS; THE...
Prang chromolithograph.
McClinton, p. 117.

FRANCONIA NOTCH FROM WOODSTOCK, NEW HAMPSHIRE.
Oct. 11, 1881. Watercolor.
7⅞ x 10¾? (197.8 x 27.3).
Dartmouth College Art Galleries (1983).

PEMIGEWASSET VALLEY; THE...
Prang chromolithograph.
McClinton, p. 117.

SACO VALLEY; THE...
Prang chromolithograph.
McClinton, p. 117.

MAXWELL, CARRIE E.
A
Active 1889.
Maxwell was a pupil of Harrison Bird Brown, and in 1885 she lived at 59 Hampshire Street in Portland, ME.

Information courtesy of Vose Galleries and Phyllis F. Greene.

RAMBLE ON ARTIST'S BROOK; THE...
1889. Oil on canvas.
14 x 18 (35.6 x 45.7).
Private collection.

MC CHESNEY, CLARA TAGGART
N
Born Brownsville, CA, 1861. Died 1928.
McChesney was a pupil of Virgil Williams in San Francisco and Courtois and others in Paris. Primarily a figure painter, she was a member of the National Art Club, the Barnard Club, and the American Society of Painters in Water Colors. She was the winner of many medals and prizes both in this country and in Paris. McChesney exhibited at the NAD during the 1890s and lived in New York City while active.

Bibliography:
Clement, Clara Erskine. *Women in the Fine Arts.* Boston: Houghton Mifflin, 1904.
Rubinstein, Charlotte Steifer. *American Women Artists.* Boston: G. K. Hall, 1982.

DIXVILLE NOTCH.
37 x 26 (94 x 66).
BIAP; *Antiques* (Jan. 1974).

MC CONNELL, GEORGE
Born 1852. Died 1929.
Nothing further is presently known of this artist.

Information courtesy of Vose Galleries.

MOUNT WASHINGTON AND THE SACO.
Lion Gallery (1976).

MC ENTEE, JERVIS
A, B, Ce, C&H, DAB, E, F, G&W, K, N, R, S, T
Born Rondout, NY, July 14, 1828 or 1829.
Died Kingston, NY, Feb. 3, 1891, or Rondout, NY, Jan. 27, 1891.
McEntee, like many other artists of the period, began his training as an engraver, and later switched to painting. He finally settled on an artistic career at age 31 when he opened a studio

in the 10th Street Studio Building (N.Y.C.) and began to study with Frederic Church. In 1861 he was elected a member of the NAD, where he had exhibited since 1850. He also exhibited frequently at the Brooklyn Art Association. In 1862 he was elected to the Century Association. He was a friend of many of his White Mountain School contemporaries, including Sanford Gifford, with whom he made a trip to Europe in 1859.

Bibliography:
Archives of American Art. Roll D180.

EAGLE CLIFF, FRANCONIA, NEW HAMPSHIRE.
S/D/L/L.
    1866. Oil on canvas.
    16 x 28 (40.6 x 71.1).
    Pennsylvania State University, Vessel collection; Alexander Gallery.

INDIAN SUMMER (possibly New Hampshire).
    1881/82. Oil on canvas.
    39⅞ x 68 (101.3 x 172.7).
    Detroit Institute of Fine Arts (1983).

SUMMIT OF MOUNT LAFAYETTE.
    Pre-1877; Utica (NY) exhibition (1867).

MC ILVAINE, WILLIAM, JR.

Ce, G&W, K, Ka, N, R
Born Philadelphia, PA, June 5, 1813.
Died Brooklyn, NY, June 16, 1867.
William McIlvaine, primarily a watercolorist, received a master of arts degree from the University of Pennsylvania in 1835 and then traveled and studied in Europe for the next five years. Upon his return, he spent a number of years in his father's business but managed to exhibit several paintings at the PAFA. About 1850 he decided to devote his life to painting, and traveled widely gathering ideas and exhibiting at the NAD and the Brooklyn Art Association.

ECHO POND, NEW HAMPSHIRE.
    NAD, 1858, #304.

MOUNT WASHINGTON NEAR FABYAN'S, NEW HAMPSHIRE.
    PAFA, 1854, #265.

SILVER CASCADE, WHITE MOUNTAINS, NEW HAMPSHIRE.
    PAFA, 1855, #289.

MC LEOD (or MACLEOD), WILLIAM

Ce, G&W, K
Born Alexandria, VA, 1811.
Died Washington, DC, 1892.

McLeod was an artist and an illustrator in Washington, DC. He moved to New York City from 1848 to 1856, at which time he did a series of illustrations for Harper's Monthly on Franconia Notch (1852). In 1874 he became the first curator of the Corcoran Gallery.

Bibliography:
McLeod, William. "The Summer Tourist—Scenery of the Franconia Mountains, NH." Harper's New Monthly Magazine 5 (June-Nov. 1852), 4-11.

BASIN; THE...
    1852. Illustration.
    Harper's Monthly 5 (1852), pp. 4-11.

EAGLE CLIFF.
    1852. Illustration.
    Harper's Monthly 5 (1852), pp. 4-11.

EASTERN FRONT OF PROFILE MOUNTAIN.
    1852. Illustration.
    Harper's Monthly 5 (1852), pp. 4-11.

FLUME; THE...
    1852. Illustration.
    Harper's Monthly 5 (1852), pp. 4-11.

FRANCONIA NOTCH.
    1852. Illustration.
    Harper's Monthly 5 (1852), pp. 4-11.

MORNING IN THE FRANCONIA NOTCH.
    Pre-1877; Washington (DC) Art Association Gallery (1859) (see Columbia Historical Society).

OLD MAN OF THE MOUNTAIN; THE...
    1852. Illustration.
    Harper's Monthly 5 (1852), pp. 4-11.

PROFILE MOUNTAIN.
    1852. Illustration.
    Harper's Monthly 5 (1852), pp. 4-11.

VIEW OF MOUNT LAFAYETTE FROM FRANCONIA VALLEY.
    NAD, 1852, #330. Private collection, 1983.

VIEW ON THE PEMIGEWASSET.
    1852. Illustration.
    Harper's Monthly 5 (1852), pp. 4-11.

MEADE, J.

Active 1860s.
Nothing is presently known of this artist.

INTERVALE FROM NORTH CONWAY.
    C. 1860. Oil on canvas.
    24 x 40 (61 x 101.6).
    Northeast Merchants Bank, Boston, MA (28 State Street).

New Hampshire Scenery

MEEKER, JOSEPH RUSLING
B, Ce, F, G&W, Ka, N, S
Born Newark, NJ, April 21, 1827.
Died after 1880.
Meeker studied at the NAD for a year or so when he was 18. He moved to Buffalo, NY, where he stayed for several years and then to Louisville, KY. During the Civil War he served with the Confederate forces. He exhibited at the AAU in 1852 and at the NAD in 1868.
VIEW OF THE WHITE MOUNTAINS. S/D/L/L.
    1880. Oil on canvas.
    20 x 36 (50.8 x 91.4).
    Wigmore Fine Arts (Jan. 1982).

MELROSE, ANDREW W.
F(sup), G&W, K, N
Born Selkirk, Scotland, March 9, 1836.
Died West New York, NJ, Feb. 23, 1901.
Melrose was a self-taught artist who became very proficient at landscape. Many of his paintings and sketches were used as chromolithographs and as illustrations for books. He exhibited at the NAD from 1867 to 1883 and at the Brooklyn Art Association.
CRAWFORD NOTCH, NEW HAMPSHIRE. S/L/L.
    Oil on canvas.
    15 x 20½ (38.1 x 52.1).
    Richard Bourne, Inc. (Oct. 22, 1976).
NEW HAMPSHIRE LANDSCAPE.
    Oil.
    23 x 19½ (58.4 x 49.5).
    Parke-Bernet (1968).

MERRILL, GEORGE N.
Died 1898. Drowned during the Spanish-American War.
The August 15, 1885, White Mountain Echo reported that Merrill kept an art studio in Jackson, NH, and again discussed the studio on July 16, 1892. He worked in pastels and oils and painted with Asher Durand, Samuel Colman, Aaron Shattuck, George Inness, and his special friend, Albert Fitch Bellows. He also was associated with the Selingers when they took over Frank Shapleigh's studio at the Crawford House, and with Daniel Huntington.
Information courtesy of Phyllis F. Greene.
CHOCORUA AND THE SANDWICH RANGE.
    Pastel.
    Private collection.
WHITE MOUNTAIN SCENERY.
    Leonard Auction (March 23, 1865), #38.

METCALF, WILLARD LEROY
Ba, F, S
Born Lowell, MA, 1858.
Died New York, NY, 1925.
Metcalf was a pupil of George Loring Brown while in the U.S. and Boulanger and Lefebvre while abroad. He won many prizes for his work.
BLACK MOUNTAIN FROM CAMPTON VILLAGE.
    Sept. 1875. Oil on canvas.
    10¾ x 18½ (27.3 x 47).
    BIAP.
MAD RIVER BELOW THE DAM, CAMPTON, NH. S/D/R.
    Sept. 1875. Oil on canvas.
    9⅛ x 14¼ (23.2 x 36.2).
    Berry Hill Galleries (1983).

MIGNOT, LOUIS REMY
B, C, Ce, C&H, DAB, F, G&W, K, N, R, S, T
Born Charleston, SC, 1831.
Died Brighton, England, Sept. 22, 1870.
Mignot studied drawing in his hometown and moved to Holland at the age of 20 to continue his studies for the following four years. Shortly after his return to the U.S., he opened a studio in the 10th Street Studio Building (N.Y.C.), which he kept from 1858 to 1863. In 1858 he was elected to the Century Association, and the following year he became an associate member of the NAD and in 1860 a full member. Shortly after the outbreak of the Civil War he moved permanently to England.
SUNSET ON THE WHITE MOUNTAINS.
    Pre-1877; Fine Arts Department of Cleveland (OH) Sanitary Fair (Feb. 22, 1864).
WHITE MOUNTAIN SCENERY.
    Pre-1877; Schaus Gallery, 749 Broadway, N.Y.C. (1862).
WHITE MOUNTAINS.
    Pre-1877; Art Gallery of the Mississippi Valley Sanitary Fair, St. Louis (1864).
WINTER SCENE, NEW HAMPSHIRE.
    30 x 53 (101.6 x 134.6).
    Crayon (April 1859).

MILES, JOHN C.
Born St. Johns, New Brunswick, 1831 or 1832.
Died St. Johns, New Brunswick, 1911.
Miles began his studies in 1866 at the Lowell Institute in Boston and continued later with Benjamin Champney. He was a member of the Boston Art Club for 11 years and kept a studio in Boston. He returned to St. Johns in 1877.

Bibliography:
Information courtesy of Vose Galleries.
New Brunswick Museum Memo. Vol. 2, #3 (Sept. 1970).
MONADNOCK MOUNTAIN FROM JAFFREY.
  Oil.
  Boston Art Club (Jan. 17-Feb. 10, 1877), #59.
MONADNOCK MOUNTAIN IN A STORM.
  Oil.
  Boston Art Club (Jan. 17-Feb. 10, 1877), #126.
MOUNT LAFAYETTE FROM SUGAR HILL, NH.
  Boston Art Club (1899), #120.
PEMIGEWASSET RIVER – NORTH WOOD-STOCK.
  Boston Art Club (1899), #179.

MILLARD, H. T.

Possibly Hannah Millard, who exhibited at the NAD in 1862, 1864, and 1865.
FLEECY CLOUDS, MOUNT WASHINGTON, U.S. OBSERVATORY.
  Watercolor.
  Pre-1877; 5th annual exhibition of the American Society of Painters in Water Colors.

MILLER, F.

Active 1867.
There is presently no information on this artist.
MOUNT WASHINGTON.
  Leonard Auction (Nov. 7, 1867), #7.

MONTAGUE, FANNIE S.

Active 1898.
Nothing else is presently known about this artist.
MOUNT WASHINGTON – A SKETCH AT SUNSET.
  Boston Art Club (1898), #379.

MONTALANT, JULIUS O.

A, G&W, R
Active 1851-64.
Montalant was apparently a peripatetic artist, for during his decade of exhibition in the U.S., he listed his addresses as Philadelphia; Rome, Italy; and Europe. He was a friend of the sculptor, E. S. Bartholomew, and painted in southern Italy for several years, returning to the U.S. and New York City in mid-1859. The

Crayon mentioned him twice, in July 1858 (p. 211) and June 1859 (p. 184).
MOUNT WASHINGTON.
  PAFA, 1855.
VIEW FROM MOUNT KEARSARGE.
  PAFA, 1855.

MOORE, CHARLES HERBERT

Ba, Ce, DAB, F, G&W, K, Ka, N, S
Born New York, NY, April 10, 1840.
Died Hartfield, Hampshire, England, Feb. 15, 1930.
Moore's long life included painting landscapes, teaching fine arts and art principles at Harvard, and writing on the subject of art and art history. He was fascinated by the looming bulk of Mount Washington and studied it from every angle during the summers of 1869 and 1870. His style was the meticulous rendering of the English Pre-Raphaelite School, extolled by John Ruskin, and also embraced by William Trost Richards at about the same time. Both Richards and Moore produced exquisite watercolors of New Hampshire scenes. Though Moore painted professionally from 1858 to 1871, at which time he turned to teaching, his method was perforce slow and laborious, and his oeuvre is consequently small.

Bibliography:
Mather, Frank Jewett, Jr. *Charles Herbert Moore, Landscape Painter.* Princeton, NJ: Princeton University Press, 1957.
MOUNT KEARSARGE.
  C. 1869-70. Oil on canvas.
  11⅞ x 17 (30.2 x 43.2).
  Princeton University Art Gallery (1983).
MOUNT WASHINGTON.
  C. 1870. Watercolor over panel.
  11 15/16 x 18 (30.3 x 45.7).
  Princeton University Art Gallery (1983).
MOUNT WASHINGTON (Moat Mountain).
  C. 1870. Watercolor on paper.
  16 x 22 (40.6 x 55.9).
  Princeton University Art Gallery (1980); University Art Gallery catalog, University of New Hampshire (1980), #117.
NORTH CONWAY, NEW HAMPSHIRE. S/D/L/L.
  1872. Watercolor.
  5⅞ x 8 15/16 (14.9 x 22.7).
  Boston Museum of Fine Arts, Karolik collection.
WHITE MOUNTAIN – AUTUMN.
  NAD, 1870, #405.

New Hampshire Scenery

WHITE MOUNTAINS (Mount Washington).
   C. 1870. Pen and ink and wash.
   15 $^{15}/_{16}$ x 22¼ (40.5 x 56.5).
   Fogg Museum, Harvard University.

WHITE MOUNTAINS COUNTRY (Mount Washington).
   C. 1870. Graphite.
   15⅛ x 24⅛ (38.4 x 61.3).
   Fogg Museum, Harvard University.

MORAN, EDWARD

Ce, DAB, F, G&W, K, S, T
Born Bolton, Lancashire, England, Aug. 19, 1829.
Died New York, NY, June 9, 1901.
Moran's career began as a weaver in England. The family emigrated to Maryland in 1844, and Moran continued as a weaver, cabinetmaker, and house painter before studying art under Paul Weber and James Hamilton. He is best known for his marine paintings. He opened a studio in Philadelphia in 1857 and exhibited at the NAD. Moran worked in lithography as well as oils. In 1862 he traveled to England to study at the Royal Academy in London. He studied briefly in England before the Civil War and made an extended stay in Paris in the late 1870s. Returning to the U.S. in 1880, he took up permanent residence in New York City.

Bibliography:
Duty, Michael. "Thomas Moran's Watercolors of the American West." *Antiques* (Jan. 1981), pp. 212-215.
Fern, Thomas S. *The Drawings and Watercolors of Thomas Moran (1837-1926).* University of Notre Dame Art Gallery catalog (April 4-May 30, 1976).

HALF WAY UP MOUNT WASHINGTON. S/L/L.
   1868. Oil on canvas.
   30 x 50 (76.2 x 127).
   Ira Spanierman, Inc. (1979); Weschler catalog (Oct. 1972), Lot #885.

MORAN, EDWARD PERCY

C&H, F, K, N, S, T
Born Philadelphia, PA, July 29, 1862.
Died East Hampton, L.I., NY, March 25, 1935.
Moran studied under his father, Edward Moran, and also at the PAFA and the NAD. He had further training in London and Paris and kept studios in New York and Long Island after returning to the U.S. He exhibited frequently at the NAD and the Brooklyn Art Association from 1861 to 1899.

MONADNOCK.
   Watercolor.
   15⅝ x 11⅝ (39.7 x 29.5).
   BIAP.

MORAN, THOMAS

B, Ba, C&H, DAB, F, G&W, K, Ka, N, T
Born Bolton, Lancashire, England, Jan. 12, 1837.
Died Santa Barbara, CA, Aug. 26, 1926.
Moran, the younger brother of Edward Moran, came to Maryland in 1844 with his family. He studied and painted with his brother and accompanied him to England before the Civil War where he came under the influence of William Turner. He painted many large western canvases. He exhibited at the NAD from 1866 to 1900, as well as at the Brooklyn Art Association from 1862 to 1885. Like his brother, Thomas practiced lithography in addition to oil painting. He was elected to the Century Association in 1882. Though only one New Hampshire work has come to light thus far, Winthrop Packard (see bibliography) wrote that Moran visited the White Mountains region with Kensett, the Hills, Bierstadt, and Frederic Church. John Moran, brother of Edward and Thomas, was a stereographer from 1859 through the 1870s and took, among others, White Mountains views.

Bibliography:
Archives of American Art. Rolls NTM1-NTM5, N730.
Darrah, William Culp. *The World of the Stereograph.* Gettysburg, PA, 1977.
Jackson, W. H. "Famous American Mountain Paintings: With Moran in the Yellowstone." *Appalachia* 21 (1936-1937), pp. 149-158.
Packard, Winthrop. *Historical New Hampshire* (Feb. 1946), p. 11.
Wilkins, Thurman. *Thomas Moran* (1966).

WHITE MOUNTAINS – MOUNT WASHINGTON FROM ONE OF THE MANY PASSES (Carter Notch?).
   1874. Chromolithograph.
   Aldine chromolithograph for 1874.

MORRISON, WILLIAM (or WELLMAN)

A, G&W
Died 1857.
Morrison exhibited at the Boston Athenaeum in 1846, 1847, and 1856.

CONWAY VALLEY.
   1853. Oil.
   20¾ x 26¾ (52.7 x 67.9).
   Childs Gallery (March 1969).

LANDSCAPE WITH FERRYBOAT ON LAKE WINNIPESAUKEE.
   22 x 27 (55.9 x 68.6).
   Dartmouth College Art Galleries (1974).

MORVILLER (or MORVEILLER or MOR-VILIER), JOSEPH

A, F(sup), G&W, N, R
Active 1850 to 1867-68.
Morviller's first known painting is dated 1850 and, according to Prang's Chromo *of Sept. 1868, SUNLIGHT IN WINTER, a chromo, was "one of his last pictures that he finished before his untimely death." He exhibited at the NAD in 1865, when he gave his address as Boston, and at the PAFA and the Boston Athenaeum between 1855 and 1864. The* Chromo *for April 1868 noted: "the late Mr. Morveiller of Malden [painted a] NEW ENGLAND WINTER LAND-SCAPE .... Morveiller made a specialty of winter scenes and was admitted to be the best painter of snow in America." Prang produced several chromolithographs of his works.*

NEW ENGLAND VILLAGE, SNOW-SCENE.
   NAD, 1865, #251.

NEW ENGLAND WINTER LANDSCAPE.
   1868. Chromolithograph.
   Prang (April 1868), p. 7.

ON THE AMMONOOSUC.
   Oil.
   Boston Art Club (Jan. 12-Feb. 2, 1876), #126.

MUSSEY, JOSEPH OSGOOD

C, G&W
Born New Hampshire, c. 1818. Died 1856.
Mussey moved with his family to Cincinnati in 1848, and in 1850 the family owned real estate valued at $25,000. He exhibited at the AAU in 1848.
Information courtesy of Vose Galleries.

NOTCH IN THE WHITE MOUNTAINS.
   Pre-1877; Records of Western Art-Union, Cincinnati, OH, 1849.

N

NEWCOMB (or NEWCOMBE), GEORGE W.

A, Ce, F, G&W, R, S
Born England, Sept. 22, 1799.
Died New York, NY, Feb. 10, 1845.
Newcomb was in New York City by 1829 and became an associate of the NAD in 1832. He exhibited at the Boston Athenaeum, the Artists' Fund Society in Philadelphia, and the NAD. The major portion of his oeuvre was portraits and miniatures.

AUTUMN AT DIANA'S BATH, NORTH CONWAY.
   MA Charitable (1874), #203.

NEWLAND, F. E. (MISS)

Nothing is presently known of this artist.

WHITE MOUNTAINS (after William Hart).
   Pre-1877; Utica (NY) Art Association, at Utica Mechanics Association (1867).

NICHOLS, EDWARD WEST

A, Ce, F, G&W, N, R, S, T
Born Orford, NH, April 28, 1819/20.
Died Peekskill, NY, Sept. 18, 1871.
Though Nichols began his career as a lawyer, he turned to art as a profession by 1848, studying in New York City with Jasper Cropsey, and continuing his education in Europe in 1853. In 1858 he opened a studio in the 10th Street Studio Building (N.Y.C) which he kept until 1862. He began exhibiting at the NAD in 1862, where he became an associate member the following year,

New Hampshire Scenery

and later also exhibited at the Boston Athenaeum. *He was a popular figure, and* The Crayon *in March 1858 noted that "Nichols is painting a view of Mount Washington: the view selected is different from any of those hitherto painted on a similar scale." In March of the following year* The Crayon *reported that "Nichols is engaged upon a view on the north side of the White Mountains; it presents a wilder, grander aspect of White Mountain scenery than is usually portrayed by our pictorial investigators in that region."*

AUTUMN SCENE, WHITE MOUNTAINS.
  S
  1854. Oil on canvas.
  32 x 52 (81.3 x 132.1).

JEFFERSON MOUNT, WHITE MOUNTAINS.
  Pre-1877; Utica (NY) Art Association, at Utica Mechanics Association (1865).

MOUNT OSCEOLA.
  Brooklyn Art Association (1867), #27; NAD, 1867, #526.

MOUNT WASHINGTON FROM THORN HILL.
  NAD, 1858, #134.

MOUNTS JEFFERSON AND ADAMS, FROM THE GLEN.
  Boston Athenaeum (1859), #205; NAD, 1860, #165.

QUINCY STATION, NEAR RUMNEY, NH.
  1866. Oil on canvas.
  15 x 25 (38.1 x 63.5).
  Kennedy *Quarterly* 10:4, p. 181.

VIEW IN TAMWORTH, NEW HAMPSHIRE.
  Boston Athenaeum (1859), #81.

VIEW OF MOUNT WASHINGTON.
  Crayon (1858), p. 147.

WHITE MOUNTAINS FROM LUNENBERG.
  Brooklyn Art Association (1868), #197.

WHITE MOUNTAINS FROM MOUNT CARTER.
  NAD, 1861, #148.

WHITE MOUNTAINS IN OCTOBER – FROM LANENBURG [sic], VT.
  NAD, 1870, #175.

NILES, GEORGE E.

Born 1837. Died 1898.
Niles was a lithographer as well as a painter. He kept a studio at Jackson, NH, where he exhibited the work of many artists.

Information courtesy of Phyllis F. Greene.

CAMPTON, ARTIST'S BROOK.
  Leonard Auction (June 5, 1874), #37.

LAFAYETTE FROM SUNSET HILL.
  C. 1860.
  Vose Galleries (1972); Franconia Bicentennial Art Show (July 1972).

MOUNT LAFAYETTE. S/L/R.
  1870. Oil on canvas.
  6½ x 5 (16.5 x 12.7).
  Private collection (1983).

NORTH CONWAY, INDIAN SUMMER.
  Leonard Auction (June 5, 1874), #45.

NUTTING, BENJAMIN F.

A, G&W, S
Born New Hampshire between 1801 and 1813.
Died Watertown, MA, Dec. 21, 1887.
Nutting was apprenticed at Pendleton's lithographic business in Boston with Nathaniel Currier from about 1828 to 1833. He was a frequent exhibitor at the Boston Athenaeum between 1831 and 1865.

Bibliography:
Folson, George. *History of Saco and Biddeford* (Saco, 1830); carries an illustration of his work.

AT THORNTON, NEW HAMPSHIRE.
  Watercolor.
  Boston Art Club (1881), #204.

BLACK MOUNTAIN FLUME.
  Watercolor.
  Boston Art Club (1882), #115.

WHITE MOUNTAINS FROM BETHLEHEM.
  Boston Athenaeum (1864), #320.

WHITE MOUNTAINS FROM JEFFERSON HILL.
  Boston Athenaeum (1863), #184.

O

OAKES, A. T. (MRS.)
Co
Active 1852-56.
Nothing else is presently known of this landscapist.
WHITE MOUNTAIN LANDSCAPE. S/L/R.
    1852. Oil on canvas.
    14 x 20⅛ (35.6 x 51.1).
    Richard Bourne, Inc., catalog (Aug. 14, 1979), #99.

OCHTMAN, LEONARD
F, N, S
Born Zonnenmaire, Holland, 1854.
Died 1934.
Ochtman, a self-taught landscapist in oils and watercolors, grew up in Albany, NY. He began exhibiting at the NAD in 1882 and continued to do so until 1900. He also exhibited in Philadelphia, Brooklyn, and Boston, winning medals in all these cities.
NORTH CONWAY INTERVALE TOWARDS ATTITASH.
    Private collection (1983).

OGILVIE, CLINTON
A, C&H, F, G&W, N, R, S, T
Born New York, NY, 1838.
Died New York, NY, Nov. 29, 1900.
Ogilvie studied under James Hart and began exhibiting at 22 years of age at the Boston Athenaeum. He studied abroad for four years, returned to the U.S., and was elected an associate member of the NAD. He exhibited at the NAD from 1861 to 1900 and at the Brooklyn Art Association from 1863 to 1886. He was elected to the Century Association in 1887 and remained a member the rest of his life.
MOUNT WASHINGTON FROM JACKSON.
    1880. Oil on board.
    8½ x 11½ (21.6 x 29.2).
    Private collection (1982).
NEAR JACKSON, WHITE MOUNTAINS. S/D/L/L.
    1885. Oil on canvas.
    16¼ x 26¼ (41.3 x 66.7).
    Metropolitan Museum of Art (1975).

WIDLCAT RIVER, NEW HAMPSHIRE.
    NAD, 1889, #237.

ORDWAY, ALFRED T.
A, C&H, F, G&W, N, S, T
Born Roxbury, MA, March 9, 1821.
Died Boston, MA, Nov. 17, 1897.
Ordway studied portraiture under G. P. A. Healy and in 1845 opened a studio in Tremont Row, Boston. Being of an executive turn of mind, he founded the Boston Art Club in 1854, the Paint and Clay Club of Boston, and also served as director of exhibitions at the Boston Athenaeum from 1856 to 1863. In September 1854 he was at Conway Center with Miss Bangs, Champney, Hubbard, and Sanford Gifford, trying his hand at landscape. He exhibited frequently at the NAD and the Brooklyn Art Association from 1868 until his death.
Bibliography:
Archives of American Art. Roll 1406.
The Lowell Book (Boston, 1899).
A PATH IN WATERVILLE, NEW HAMPSHIRE.
    Oil.
    Boston Art Club (Jan. 15-Feb. 8, 1879), #165.
ARTIST'S BROOK, NORTH CONWAY.
    Oil.
    30 x 49½ (76.2 x 125.7).
    Richard Bourne, Inc., catalog (July 25, 1972).
IN SHELBURNE, NEW HAMPSHIRE.
    Boston Athenaeum (1861), #171.
KEARSAGE [sic].
    Boston Athenaeum (1862), #284.
MOUNT CHOCORUA AND LAKE.
    Leonard Auction (May 23, 1871), #99.
MOUNT CHOCORUA, NEW HAMPSHIRE.
    NMAA Inventory.
MOUNT WASHINGTON.
    NAD, 1891, #266.
SACO AND VALLEY.
    Leonard Auction (May 23, 1871), #27.
UNDER THE PINES (NORTH CONWAY).
    Oil.
    Boston Art Club (March 1873), #53.
VIEW ON THE SACO.
    Leonard Auction (Jan. 28, 1873), #11.

New Hampshire Scenery

White Mountains
Charles Herbert Moore, c. 1870
Pen and black ink and wash on white paper, 15 15/16" x 22 1/4" / Collection:
the Fogg Art Museum, Harvard University, gift of
Miss Margaret Norton / Ref. page 119

OSGOOD, CHARLES
A, F, G&W, S
Born Salem, MA, Feb. 24, 1809.
Died Salem, MA, Dec. 26, 1890.
It is not known under whom Osgood received his training, but he made his living as a portraitist until 1863. It can be conjectured that the advent of the daguerreotype and the photograph created serious inroads on the business of the average portraitist and caused Osgood and others to try a hand at landscapes. Interestingly, Osgood never included figures in his very distinctive landscapes. The Essex Institute catalog wrote that Osgood "did not achieve any great warmth of color in these paintings."
Bibliography:
Charles Osgood. Essex Institute catalog, special loan exhibition (Nov. 1978-Jan. 1979). Essex Institute, Salem, MA.

MOUNT CHOCORUA.
Oil on canvas.
7½ x 11¾ (19.1 x 29.8).
Private collection (1975); BIAP.
Attributed:
MOUNT WASHINGTON FROM CARTER NOTCH
(or VIEW OF MOUNT WASHINGTON).
Oil on canvas.
36 x 55 (91.4 x 139.7).
Private collection (1984); Vose Galleries (1972).

OTTER, THOMAS PROUDLEY
A, Ce, F, G&W, R
Born Montgomery Square, PA, 1832.
Died Doylestown, PA, March 3, 1890.
Otter entered the engraving firm of David Scattergood in 1849 and was taught by James Hamilton and Paul Weber in the art of painting.

Dictionary of Painters

He continued taking lessons at the PAFA while teaching art in local schools. He exhibited at the Boston Athenaeum in 1859 and the 1860s, at the NAD in 1860, and at the PAFA from 1855 to 1867. He shared a studio with his teacher, James Hamilton, in 1859. He apparently became an accomplished photographer and used his photographs as an aid to his paintings. In 1876 his illustrations were used in the History of Bucks County (PA).

Bibliography:
"Thomas P. Otter." *Antiques* (Nov. 1978), pp. 1028-1035.

MOUNT WASHINGTON.
  Oil.
  Doylestown (PA) *Democrat* (Oct. 10, 1876).

OWEN (or OWENS), GEORGE
A, Ce, G&W, N, R
Active 1858-77.
Little is known of this artist, who exhibited frequently at the NAD from 1863 to 1877 and in Boston and Philadelphia between 1858 and 1877. The majority of his paintings were New England landscapes, although only one New Hampshire painting is presently known. He lived in Providence, RI, Boston, and New York City.

MOUNT CHOCORUA.
  Oil.
  Pre-1877; Rhode Island Society for the Encouragement of Domestic Industry (Sept. 3, 1867).

P

PAGE, WILLIAM
A, B, Ba, C, Ce, C&H, F, G&W, N, R, S, T
Born Albany, NY, Jan. 23, 1811.
Died Tottenville, Long Island, NY, Sept. 30, 1885.
Page spent the early years of his training in New York City under the tutelage of Samuel F. B. Morse and James Herring. His interest lay mostly in portraiture and figure painting. He began exhibiting at the NAD at the tender age of 16 and was always intimately involved with that organization. He became an associate member in 1832, a full member in 1837, and served as president from 1871 to 1873. For a short time, from 1850 to 1857 he was a member of the Century Association. Page resided in Italy from 1849 to 1860 where he was an influential member of the American colony in Rome. In 1861 he returned to the U.S. and took a room in the 10th Street Studio Building (N.Y.C.), which he kept until 1880. He was a Swedenborgian (of the Church of the New Jerusalem) and a mystic who believed in spirit writing. He was particularly interested in the effects of color, which he felt should be a pulsing, living force in a work of art.

Bibliography:
Taylor, Joshua C. *William Page, The American Titian* (Chicago, 1957).

VIEW OF THE WHITE MOUNTAINS.
  Before 1867. Oil on canvas.
  BIAP. Unlocated.

PALMER, FRANCES FLORA BOND (or FANNY)
A, Ba, C, Ce, DAB, E, F, G&W, K, Ka, N
Born Leicester, England, July 24, 1812.
Died Brooklyn, NY, Aug. 20, 1876.
It is not generally known that Palmer was an accomplished artist in her own right, for her work is associated with the lithographers, Currier and Ives, for whom she worked. They respected her ability at producing landscapes, and hers is one of the very few names the lithographers allowed to appear on their plates. After a failed attempt to open her own lithographic business, soon after her immigration to the U.S. in 1843, she joined the firm in 1849 and helped perfect a lithographic crayon. She was known, in her search for verisimilitude, to make on-the-spot sketches which she later transferred to stone. She exhibited at the NAD in 1844 and the Brooklyn Art Association in 1869. Her original oeuvre might have been greater had she not had to support an indolent husband and a large family.

New Hampshire Scenery

Bibliography:
Antiques. Vol. 7, pp. 10-14.
Peters, Harry T. *Currier and Ives, Printmakers* (1931).
MOUNT WASHINGTON AND THE WHITE MOUNTAINS FROM THE VALLEY OF CONWAY.
  1860. Sketch.
  Peters, Harry T. *Currier and Ives, Printmakers* (1931), plate 71; Currier and Ives calendar (Aug. 1963).
WINNEPISEOGEE [sic], CENTRE HARBOR.
  1850.
  Antiques. Vol. 7, pp. 10-14.

PARKER, JOHN ADAMS, JR.
Ce, C&H, F, G&W, N, S
Born New York, NY, Nov. 29, 1829, or Nov. 27, 1827.
Died c. 1905.
It is not known where Parker trained as a landscapist. He seems to have confined his work to views of the Adirondacks, the Catskills, and the White Mountains. He first exhibited at the NAD in 1858 and was elected an associate member in 1864. He often gave his address as Brooklyn and exhibited at the Brooklyn Art Association from 1863 to 1879.
AMONG THE WHITE MOUNTAINS.
  Brooklyn Art Association (1873), #265.
AUTUMN ON THE SACO.
  Brooklyn Art Association (1879), #9.
CHICORUA [sic] PEAK.
  Pre-1877; Utica (NY) Art Association exhibition (1866).
CHO-COR-UA [sic] PEAK.
  Brooklyn Art Association (1863), #85; Pre-1877.
CONWAY'S [sic] MEADOW.
  Brooklyn Art Association (1873), #263.
EAGLE CLIFF AT SUNSET.
  Brooklyn Art Association (1874), #250.
EAGLE CLIFF, FRANCONIA.
  NAD, 1858, #587.
EAGLE CLIFF, WHITE MOUNTAINS.
  Brooklyn Art Association (1864), #91; NAD, 1864, #218; Pre-1877.
ECHO LAKE.
  Brooklyn Art Association (1873), #264.
MORNING MISTS – FROM CHICORUA [sic].
  NAD, 1868, #239.

MOUNT CHOCORUA. S/L/L.
  Oil on canvas.
  24¼ x 20 (61.6 x 50.8).
  Baridoff Gallery (April 4, 1981), #71.
MOUNT JEFFERSON FROM PEABODY RIVER.
  Brooklyn Art Association (1868), #132.
NEAR LACONIA, NEW HAMPSHIRE.
  Boston Art Association (1865), #161.
OLD MAN OF THE MOUNTAIN, WHITE MOUNTAINS, NEW HAMPSHIRE.
  Pre-1877; Maryland State Fair, Baltimore (April 1864) (see Maryland Historical Society for information).
ON ECHO LAKE.
  Brooklyn Art Association (1872), #41.
ON THE ANDROSCOGGIN.
  Brooklyn Art Association (1863), #203.
ON THE PEABODY RIVER, FOOT OF MOUNT JEFFERSON, WHITE MOUNTAINS.
  NAD, 1859, #746.
PULPIT ROCK, WHITE MOUNTAIN NOTCH.
  NAD, 1859, #75.
SCENE IN THE WHITE MOUNTAINS.
  Pre-1877; Great North-Western Fair at Chicago, IL (June 1865).
SILVER CASCADE, CRAWFORD NOTCH, WHITE MOUNTAINS.
  NAD, 1858, #11.
SPRING SHOWER, WHITE MOUNTAINS.
  Pre-1877; Utica (NY) Art Association (1868) (see Utica Public Library for information).
SUNSET, WHITE MOUNTAINS.
  Boston Art Association (1864), #24.
WHITE MOUNTAINS FROM BENNETT'S POND.
  Brooklyn Art Association (1879), #69.
WHITE MOUNTAINS NEAR SHELBURNE.
  Brooklyn Art Association (1863), #200.
WHITE MOUNTAINS SCENERY.
  Boston Art Association (1865), #160.
WHITE MOUNTAINS, AUTUMN.
  Brooklyn Art Association (1863), #199.

PARKHURST, DANIEL S.
G&W
Active 1852-59.
Parkhurst was an engraver in Providence, RI, who also painted in oils.

FRANCONIA MOUNTAINS FROM CRAWFORD NOTCH. Signed.
>1860 or 1840. Oil on canvas.
>14½ x 22½ (36.8 x 57.1).
>Private collection (1965).

PARMALEE, ELMER EUGENE
Ce, F(sup), G&W
Born Middletown, VT, June 12, 1839.
Died Brandon, VT, Oct. 31, 1861.
Parmalee studied painting in New York City and begun exhibiting at the NAD in 1857. The following year he became a painting instructor at the Grammar School of New York University. A talented artist, he had barely begun his career before he died at the age of 22.
MOUNT WASHINGTON.
>NAD, 1858, #78; *Crayon* (1858), p. 175.

PASKELL, WILLIAM F.
Born Kensington, England, Oct. 5, 1866.
Died Dorchester, MA, Feb. 23, 1951.
Paskell came to Boston at the age of six. He studied under H. O. Walker, Edward B. Stewart, C. W. Sanderson, DeBlois, and Juglariz. He first painted in the White Mountains . in June 1884, staying on Bear Mountain Road in Albany, NH. He returned to the area almost every summer of his long life. An extremely prolific painter, he completed 532 oils, 357 watercolors, and 69 pencil sketches during his lifetime. He exhibited at the Boston Art Club in 1899 and later.
Information courtesy of Rolf Kristiansen.
CHOCORUA. S/L.
>Watercolor.
>11½ x 14½ (29.3 x 36.8).
>Private collection (1974).
CHOCORUA. S/L.
>Oil.
>12 x 15½ (30.5 x 39.4).
>Private collection (1974).
MOUNT WASHINGTON ROAD (copy of Harry Fenn's engraving). S/L/L.
>Oil.
>20 x 13 (50.8 x 33).
>Private collection (1974).
NORTHERN RAVINE OF CHOCORUA MOUNTAIN; THE. . .
>Boston Art Club (1899), #201.

PATTISON, ROBERT J.
G&W, N
Born New York, NY, 1838.
Died Brooklyn, NY, Sept. 13, 1903.
Pattison began exhibiting at the NAD at the age of 20 and continued to do so until 1886.
WHITE MOUNTAINS FROM SHELBOURE [sic].
>Pre-1877; Yale School of the Fine Arts, New Haven, CT (1867).

PEARSON, WILLIAM
Ce, F(sup), G&W
Active 1857-60.
Nothing is presently known of this artist except that he lived in New York City in 1859.
HILLSIDE PASTURE, VIEW IN NEW HAMPSHIRE.
>NAD, 1859, #301.
VIEW IN NEW HAMPSHIRE.
>NAD, 1857, #174.

PERKINS, GRANVILLE
A, F, G&W, K, N, R, S
Born Baltimore, MD, Oct. 16, 1830.
Died New York, NY, April 18, 1895.
Perkins was primarily an illustrator and scenery painter who studied under James Hamilton. About 1855 he moved to New York City and began to work for Frank Leslie's Illustrated Newspaper. About five years later he started a long engagement with Harper and Brothers. He exhibited his work at the NAD and the Brooklyn Art Association from 1862 to 1889. He illustrated The Heart of the White Mountains *in 1882. A fine watercolorist, Perkins exhibited a painting in that medium in 1881 at the Boston Art Club for $200.*
Bibliography:
Aldine #2 (Feb. 1872), p. 48.
EAGLE CLIFF AND THE ECHO HOUSE.
>1882. Illustration.
>Drake, Samuel Adams. *The Heart of the White Mountains: Their Legend and Scenery.* New York: Harper and Brothers, 1882.
ECHO LAKE, WHITE MOUNTAINS. S/L/L.
>Oil.
>18 x 14 (45.7 x 35.6).
>Old Print Shop.
FRANCONIA IRON WORKS AND NOTCH.
>1882. Illustration.
>Drake. *Heart of the White Mountains,* p. 248.

New Hampshire Scenery

MOUNT WASHINGTON.
    Watercolor.
    Aldine 8:11 (Nov. 1876-77), p. 335.
MOUNT WASHINGTON.
    Watercolor.
    Boston Art Club (1881), #107.
MOUNTAIN RAILWAY STATION IN STAGING TIMES.
    1882. Illustration.
    Drake. *Heart of the White Mountains*, p. 305.
REMINISCENCES OF THE WHITE MOUNTAINS.
    Harper's Weekly (Sept. 8, 1877), pp. 704-705.

PERRY, ENOCH WOOD, JR.
Born Boston, MA, July 31, 1831.
Died New York, NY, Dec. 14, 1915.
Perry went to Europe at the age of 21 and studied under Emanuel Leutze and Thomas Couture. First known as a portraitist, he settled in New York City in 1866. He traveled widely in the American West and Hawaii. Returning to the East, he exhibited for many years at the NAD and turned more and more to genre painting. His paintings became extremely popular and were widely reproduced as chromolithographs.
PEMIGEWASSET COACH; THE. . . (unfinished).
    C. 1899. Oil on canvas.
    42½ x 66½ (108 x 169).
    Shelburne Museum (1980); University Art Gallery catalog, University of New Hampshire (1980), #27.
PEMIGEWASSET COACH; THE. . . (finished).
    Unlocated.
    Information courtesy of Douglas A. Philbrook.
Attributed:
BEEDE FALLS, SANDWICH, NH.
    Oil on canvas.
    14 x 18 (35.6 x 45.7).
    Private collection (1983).

PHELPS, W.H.
THE WHITE HILLS.
    1889. Oil on canvas.
    34 x 56 (86.4 x 142.2).
    New Hampshire Historical Society.

PHELPS, WILLIAM PRESTON
C&H, F, N, S
Born Chesham (now Dublin), NH, March 6, 1848.
Died Chesham (now Harrisville), NH, 1923.
Phelps moved to Lowell, MA, by the age of 20 where he worked as a sign painter and painted landscapes. His self-taught talent was recognized, and in 1875 he was sent to study in Paris and Munich for three years where he was a pupil of Velten. In the late 1880s he began to exhibit, primarily Mount Monadnock views in Boston. He exhibited twice at the NAD and after years of travel from a base in Lowell returned to Chesham, where he devoted himself to depictions of Mount Monadnock.
Bibliography:
Allison, Hildreth M. "Some Painters of the Grand Monadnock." *Appalachia* 34 (1962-63), pp. 441-453.
The Lowell Book. Boston, 1899.
MONADNOCK.
    Oil.
    Keene (NH) Public Library.
MONADNOCK AND DUBLIN LAKE.
    Oil.
    9 x 12 (22.9 x 30.5).
    Vose Galleries.
MONADNOCK AT DAWN, DUBLIN.
    Oil.
    26 x 42 (66 x 106.7).
    Vose Galleries (1918); North Conway Library Exhibition (1965).
MONADNOCK AT SUNSET, WINTER.
    Oil.
    14 x 22 (35.6 x 55.9).
    Vose Galleries (sold Aug. 15, 1915).
MONADNOCK AUTUMN, AFTER THE SHOWER.
    Oil.
    12 x 18 (30.5 x 45.7).
    Storrs Museum, University of Connecticut; Vose Galleries (sold Feb. 28, 1972).
MONADNOCK IN WINTER.
    Oil.
    14 x 22 (35.6 x 55.9).
    Vose Galleries (sold March 11, 1977).
MONADNOCK MEADOW WITH SNOW.
    Oil.
    42¼ x 26½ (107.3 x 67.3).
    Private collection (1974); NMAA Inventory.

MOUNT MONADNOCK FROM DUBLIN.
North Conway Library Exhibition (1965).

MOUNT WASHINGTON FROM THE VALLEY OF CONWAY (after Kensett).
1889.
Private collection.

NEW HAMPSHIRE MOUNTAIN LANDSCAPE. S/L/R.
Oil on canvas.
14 x 20 (35.6 x 50.8).
Richard Bourne, Inc., catalog (Nov. 1980), #90.

SUNSET, MONADNOCK.
Oil.
9 x 12 (22.9 x 30.5).
Vose Galleries (sold Aug. 18, 1917).

VIEW ON MONADNOCK BROOK, NEW HAMPSHIRE.
Leonard Auction (Nov. 23, 1888), #5.

WINTER, MONADNOCK, OLD DESERTED HOUSE.
Oil.
14 x 22 (35.6 x 55.9).
Vose Galleries (sold April 18, 1972).

WOODS; THE...S/D
1881.
Oil on canvas.
66 x 84 (167.6 x 213.4).
New Hampshire Historical Society.

PIERCE, CHARLES FRANKLIN

F, S
Born Sharon, NH, April 26, 1844.
Died Brookline, MA, Feb. 27, 1920, or March 5, 1920.
It is not known where Pierce received his training as a landscapist. He apparently was involved with the Boston art world, for he was a member of the Paint and Clay Club of that city about 1884 and the Boston Art Club in 1886, where he had exhibited an oil as early as 1875. He evidently enjoyed painting winter landscapes.

Bibliography:
Archives of American Art. Roll 1406.
Sharf, Jean S. and Frederic. "Charles Franklin Pierce, Painter of Rural New England." *Antiques* (Vol. 102), pp. 899-903.

AUTUMN IN NEW HAMPSHIRE.
1874. Oil.
10 x 16 (25.4 x 40.6).
Private collection; NMAA Inventory; *Antiques* (Nov. 1972).

CHARCOAL SKETCH AT CAMPTON, NEW HAMPSHIRE.
Boston Art Club (1879), #50.

KIDDER MOUNTAIN, NEW IPSWICH, NH.
C. 1880. Oil on canvas.
12 x 18 (30.5 x 45.7).
Currier Gallery (1981).

MOUNT MADISON AND GLEN ELLIS FALLS WITH SAWMILL. Signed.
1874. Oil.
Private collection.

NEW HAMPSHIRE SNOW SCENE.
1874. Oil.
10 x 15 (25.4 x 38.1).
Old Print Shop; *Antiques* (May 1975).

WILLEY MOUNTAIN, NEW HAMPSHIRE.
Oil.
Boston Art Club (1876), #118.

WINTER SCENE IN NEW HAMPSHIRE.
1874. Oil.
14 x 25 (35.6 x 63.5).
Old Print Shop *Portfolio* 25:6, p. 140.

PIETERSZ, BERTUS L.

F
Born Amsterdam, Holland, 1869.
Died 1938.
Almost nothing is known of this Dutch artist, who seems to have spent much time around the Monadnock region. He exhibited at the Jordan Marsh Art Gallery (Boston) from 1894 to 1896.

GRAND MONADNOCK OVER THE MIST.
Oil on canvas.
24¼ x 30 (61.6 x 76.2).
High Museum (1975).

OCTOBER IN NEW HAMPSHIRE.
Jordan Marsh Art Gallery (1894-95).

VIEW OF CROTCHED MOUNTAIN.
Antiques (Sept. 1975).

PIXLEY, M. A.

Nothing is presently known of this artist.
SCENE IN THE WHITE MOUNTAINS.
1853. Oil.
Private collection (1976); NMAA Inventory.

PLUMMER, W. H.

Active 1899.
Nothing is presently known of this artist.
OLD MAN WITH HALF A FULL MOON BEHIND THE PROFILE. S/D/L/L.
1899. Oil.

New Hampshire Scenery

20 x 24 (50.8 x 61).
Division of Parks and Recreation, Concord, NH.

POPE, JOHN
A, Ce, F(sup), G&W, N, R, T
Born Gardiner, ME, March 2, 1820.
Died New York, NY, Dec. 29, 1880.
Pope moved from the farming town of Gardiner about 1836 to study art in Boston. He exhibited at the Boston Athenaeum from 1843 through 1869. After joining the gold rush of 1849 he went to Europe for further study and returned to New York City about 1857 when he first exhibited at the NAD. He was made an associate member of the NAD in 1859. He also exhibited at the PAFA and the Brooklyn Art Association.

CHICORUA [sic] MOUNTAINS, NEW HAMPSHIRE.
   Pre-1877; Cincinnati Industrial Exposition (1875) (see Cincinnati Art Museum for information).

LANDSCAPE, WHITE MOUNTAINS.
   Pre-1877; Utica (NY) Art Association (1868).

LANDSCAPE, WHITE MOUNTAINS CASCADE.
   Pre-1877; Utica (NY) Art Association, Mechanics Hall (1868).

OSSIPEE MEADOWS.
   Boston Art Association (1877), #138.

WHITE MOUNTAIN STUDY.
   Boston Athenaeum (1867), #239; PAFA.

WHITE MOUNTAINS.
   Brooklyn Art Association (1865), #157; Pre-1877 (3).

WHITE MOUNTAINS FROM BETHEL, ME.
   Boston Art Association (1875), #262.

PORTE CRAYON
See Strother, David Hunter.

PRATT, HENRY CHEEVER (or CHEEVES)
A, Ce, F, G&W, K, Ka, R, S
Born Orford, NH, June 13, 1803.
Died Wakefield, MA, Nov. 27, 1880.
Pratt's talent was discovered by Samuel F. B. Morse when, as a boy of 15, Pratt was painting scenes on barn doors. The portrait artist took him to Boston as an errand boy and gave him lessons. Pratt assisted Morse in his work in Charleston, SC, and also sketched in portrait heads for Morse's large painting of the House of Representatives. Probably through work in the early days of the NAD, Pratt and Thomas Cole, two years his senior, met and became friends. They journeyed through the White Mountains in October 1828 gathering sketches for studio paintings. Temperamentally, the two men were very different: Cole was poetic in feeling and wished through his paintings to convey the grandeur of nature as the visible hand of God, while Pratt was factual and pragmatic. These traits are seen in both their paintings and their writings. Pratt was appointed official draftsman to the U.S.-Mexican Boundary Commission, and his works reflect his topographical approach to landscape.

Bibliography:
Campbell, Catherine H. "Two's Company: The Diaries of Thomas Cole and Henry Cheever Pratt in Their Walk Through Crawford Notch, 1828." *Historical New Hampshire* 33:4 (Winter 1978), pp. 309-333.
Hodgson, Alice Doan. "Henry Cheever Pratt (1803-1880)." *Antiques* (Nov. 1972), pp. 842-847.

1828 SKETCHBOOK.
   1828. Pencil.
   4¾ x 7⅝ (12.1 x 19.4).
   Boston Museum of Fine Arts (1983).

A VIEW IN THE NOTCH OF THE WHITE MOUNTAINS.
   Boston Athenaeum (1827), #91.

MOUNT WASHINGTON.
   Boston Athenaeum (1829), #93.

NEW HAMPSHIRE MOUNTAIN SCENE.
   Private collection (1981); *Art and Antiques* (May-June 1981), p. 71; BIAP.

Attributed to Pratt, A. (probably H. C.?).
NOTCH IN THE WHITE MOUNTAINS.
   Pre-1877; Western Art-Union exhibition, Cincinnati, OH, 1849.

ON THE AMMONOOSUC RIVER. S/Reverse.
   1828. Oil on canvas.
   25¼ x 30¼ (64.1 x 76.8).
   Boston Museum of Fine Arts, Karolik collection (1980); University Art Gallery catalog. University of New Hampshire (1980), #36.

RAPIDS IN THE AMMONOOSUCK [sic] RIVER AT LITTLETON.
   C. 1866. Oil.
   38 x 31 (96.5 x 78.7).
   Orford (NH) Museum; *Antiques* (Nov. 1972).

ROCKS NEAR THE SUMMIT OF CHOCORUA MOUNTAIN.
   Boston Athenaeum (1829), #180.

SILVER CASCADE IN THE WHITE MOUNTAINS;
THE . . .
  Boston Athenaeum (1829), #60.
SUMMIT OF CHOCORUA MOUNTAIN.
  Boston Athenaeum (1829), #157.
VIEW OF LITTLETON, NEW HAMPSHIRE.
  Leonard Auction (Dec. 29, 1864), #91.
VIEW AT THE FRANCONIA NOTCH, NH.
  Pre-1877: 1st exhibition of Boston Artists'
  Association, Hardings Gallery (1842).
VIEW IN THE NOTCH IN THE WHITE
MOUNTAINS.
  Pre-1877; Boston Athenaeum (1827), #117;
  (1829), #97.
VIEW IN WHITE MOUNTAINS.
  NAD, 1829, #70.
VIEW NEAR THE NOTCH OF THE WHITE
MOUNTAINS.
  Boston Athenaeum (1829), #63.
VIEW OF LITTLETON, NEW HAMPSHIRE.
  1866. Oil.
  29 x 35 (73.7 x 88.9).
  Private collection; *Antiques* (Nov. 1972).
VIEW OF THE WHITE MOUNTAINS AFTER THE
LATE SLIDE.
  1828. Engraving.
  Kilbourne, p. 111; *Token* (1828).
WHITE MOUNTAINS, FROM TAMWORTH, IN-
CLUDING CHOCORUA PEAK, POND, AND THE
SEA.
  Boston Athenaeum (1834), #45.
Attributed:
ORFORD, NEW HAMPSHIRE.
  C. 1831.
  Private collection; NMAA Inventory.

PRESTON, WILLIAM GIBBONS
Born Boston, MA, 1844.
Died Boston, MA, April 26, 1910.
*Preston was a well-known Boston architect who
studied with his father and later at the Ecole des
Beaux-Arts in Paris. Among the many notable
buildings that he designed in Boston is the
Massachusetts Charitable Mechanic Building.
Preston illustrated the Pemigewasset Peram-
bulators, a humorous book, to commemorate
a visit made to the White Mountains in July
1866, describing the adventures of a group of
his friends.*
PEMIGEWASSET PERAMBULATORS (7).
  July 18-27, 1866. Lithograph.
  Private collection.

PRITCHARD, J. AMBROSE
S
Born Boston, MA, April 11, 1858.
Died Roxbury, MA, Feb. 5, 1905.
*Pritchard devoted most of his talents to water-
color landscapes. He apparently lived in and
around Boston and exhibited at the
Massachusetts Charitable Mechanic Association
in 1881 and the Boston Art Club in 1882 and
1899.*
CLEARING OFF, FRANCONIA NOTCH.
  Watercolor.
  MA Charitable (1881), #393.
IN THE WOODS, NORTH WOODSTOCK, NH.
  Watercolor or black and white.
  Boston Art Club (1899), #89.
MOOSILAUKE [sic] GLEN.
  Watercolor.
  MA Charitable (1881), #381.
MOUNT WASHINGTON FROM THE SACO.
  Watercolor.
  Boston Art Club (1882), #223.
SHOWERY WEATHER, FRANCONIA VALLEY.
  Watercolor.
  MA Charitable (1881), #392.
SOUVENIR OF NORTH CONWAY (Kearsarge and
the Saco).
  Aug. 29, 1888. Watercolor.
  Goodspeed's Gallery (1977).

Half Way Up Mt. Washington
Edward Moran, 1868
Oil on canvas, 30" x 50" / Collection: Ira Spanierman Galleries,
*   New York / Ref. page 119*

R

RAWSTORNE, EDWARD (or EDWIN)

C, F(sup), G&W, N
Active 1858-99.
Rawstorne lived in New York City in 1859 and exhibited at the NAD from 1858 to 1862 and at the Brooklyn Art Association in 1862.

ROCKY BROOK, BARTLETT, NEW HAMPSHIRE.
    NAD, 1859, #743.

RICE, HENRY WEBSTER

Born 1853. Died 1933.
Nothing else is known of this watercolorist.

MANADNOCK [sic].
    Watercolor.
    20⅜ x 14⅜ (51.8 x 36.5).
    Private collection (1978).

MOUNT WASHINGTON IN SNOW.
    Watercolor.
    Portland Museum of Art (1977).

PINKHAM NOTCH, (NH) IN WINTER.
    Watercolor.
    Portland Museum of Art (1977).

RICHARDS, MARY F.

Nothing is presently known of this artist.

MOUNT LAFAYETTE.
    Pre-1877; Providence artists' sale (May 5, 1888) at Leonard Auction Rooms, Boston.

RICHARDS, THOMAS ADDISON

B, C, C&H, DAB, F, G&W, N, S, T
Born London, England, Dec. 3, 1820.
Died Annapolis, MD, June 28, 1900.

Richards arrived in the U.S. with his family at the age of 11 and eventually settled in South Carolina before moving on to Georgia. He published a book on flower painting in Charleston, SC, in 1836 and Georgia Illustrated in 1842 while gradually gaining a reputation as a good portraitist. He moved to New York City to study at the NAD and became an associate in 1848, a full member in 1851, and acted as the corresponding secretary until 1892. He illustrated landscapes for Orion Magazine, Harper's Magazine, and Appleton's, and taught at New York University and the School of Design for Women at Cooper Institute. The Crayon wrote in 1855 that he was at Campton, NH, and again in 1858 that he painted "Brook Scene" in the valley of Pemigewasset, NH.

Bibliography:
Richards, T. Addison. *The Romance of American Landscape*. New York: Leavitt and Allen, 1855.

AT WEST CAMPTON, NEW HAMPSHIRE.
    NAD, 1857, #211.

AUTUMN MEMORIES OF LAKE WINNIPISEOGEE [sic].
    NAD, 1851, #122.

BROOK SCENE IN THE VALLEY OF PEMIGEWASSET, NEW HAMPSHIRE.
    Crayon (1858), p. 147; NAD, 1858, #66.

BROOK SCENE, FRANCONIA MOUNTAINS.
    NAD, 1862, #113.

EVENING ON THE AMMANOOSUCK [sic], NEW YORK [New Hampshire].
    NAD, 1862, #453.

FRANCONIA HILLS.
    Pre-1877; Derby Athenaeum, N.Y.C. (1868).

FRANCONIA MOUNTAINS, NEW HAMPSHIRE.
    NAD, 1857, #203.

FRANCONIA MOUNTAINS; THE . . .
    NAD, 1859, #710.

LAKE SCENE, NEW HAMPSHIRE.
    NAD, 1846, #236.

LAKE WINNIPISEOGEE [sic].
    NAD, 1873, #171; C&H, p. 208 (see Standard Source Reference List).

MEADOW SCENE IN THE VALLEY OF THE PEMIGEWASSET.
    NAD, 1858, #385.

ON LAKE WINNIPISEOGEE [sic], NEW HAMPSHIRE.
    NAD, 1868, #248.

PEMIGEWASSET RIVER; THE . . .
    NAD, 1859, #357.

RIVER SCENE, NEW HAMPSHIRE.
    NAD, 1846, #2.

SCENE ON THE PEMIGEWASSET RIVER, NEW HAMSPHIRE (3).
    NAD, 1858, #448, #449, #482.

THOUGHTS OF THE WHITE MOUNTAINS.
    NAD, 1851, #137.

VALLEY OF THE PEMIGEWASSET; THE . . .
    NAD, 1857, #245.

VILLAGE OF WEST CAMPTON IN THE VALLEY OF THE PEMIGEWASSET; THE . . .
    NAD, 1858, #60.

WELSH [sic] MOUNTAIN FROM WEST CAMPTON.
    NAD, 1858, #91.

RICHARDS, WILLIAM TROST

B, C&H, DAB, F, G&W, K, Ka, N, S, T
Born Philadelphia, PA, Nov. 14, 1833.
Died Newport, RI, Nov. 8, 1905.
Richards was one of the foremost proponents of the American Pre-Raphaelite movement, which was fostered in the 1850s, his formative years, by The Crayon, The New Path, and the Craftsman, all influential art publications of the period. Meticulously faithful factual rendering was deemed essential, and throughout his life, Richards practiced the tenet. His views of the White Mountains are almost photographically identifiable, yet he imbues them with a delicacy and atmospheric quality which makes them extraordinarily beautiful. Though he was proficient in oils, many of his most appealing works are executed in watercolor. Richards was about 20 when he received a commission to have Mount Vernon engraved for the AAU to be completed in 1854. Unfortunately, this was never carried out, as the AAU was dissolved in 1853. His first publicly shown work was exhibited at the Bierstadt Exhibition, in New Bedford in 1858, and in 1859 he painted the THE GREAT STONE FACE. In 1872, 1874, and 1876 he produced a number of watercolor views of the White Mountains of consummate beauty, several of which were presented to the Metropolitan Museum of Art by Rev. Elias Magoon. He exhibited at the NAD from 1861 to 1899 and at the Brooklyn Art Association from 1863 to 1885. It is interesting to note that he used photography as an aid in obtaining his extraordinary realism. In later years Richards

New Hampshire Scenery

almost exclusively painted translucent water-colors of the sea.

Bibliography:
Ferber, Linda S. *William Trost Richards, American Landscape and Marine Painter, 1833-1905.* New York. The Brooklyn Museum, 1973.

AUTUMN AFTERNOON (or MOUNT WASHINGTON FROM ABOVE THE GLEN HOUSE). S/D/L/R.
    1865. Oil on canvas.
    25 x 36 (63.5 x 91.4).
    Kenneth Lux Gallery; *Antiques* (1983).

CRAWFORD NOTCH.
    C. 1872. Pencil on paper.
    10⅞ x 14⅞ (27.6 x 37.8).
    Private collection (1980); University Art Gallery catalog, University of New Hampshire (1980), #118.

EAGLE'S NEST, FRANCONIA NOTCH. S/D/L/R.
    1873. Watercolor.
    12 ¹⁵/₁₆ x 9½ (32.9 x 24.1).
    Metropolitan Museum of Art.

FRANCONIA MOUNTAINS FROM COMPTON [sic], NH. S/D/L/R.
    1872. Watercolor.
    8 ³/₁₆ x 14 ³/₁₆ (20.8 x 36).
    Metropolitan Museum of Art.

FROM THE FLUME HOUSE, FRANCONIA. S/D/L/R.
    1872. Watercolor.
    8 x 14⅛ (20.3 x 35.9).
    Metropolitan Museum of Art.

GATE OF THE NOTCH OF THE WHITE MOUNTAINS.
    C. 1865. Pencil.
    Boston Museum of Fine Arts, Stebbins collection.

GATE OF THE NOTCH, WHITE MOUNTAINS.
    Watercolor.
    Pre-1877; American Society of Painters in Watercolors, N.Y.C. (1873).

LAKE SQUAM AND THE SANDWICH MOUNTAINS. S/D/L/R.
    1872. Watercolor.
    8½ x 14⅜ (21.6 x 36.5).
    Metropolitan Museum of Art.

LAKE SQUAM FROM RED HILL. S/D/L/R.
    1874. Watercolor.
    8⅞ x 13⅝ (22.6 x 34.6).
    Metropolitan Museum of Art (1973).

MOONLIGHT ON MOUNT LAFAYETTE, NH. S/D/L/L.
    1873. Watercolor.
    8⅜ x 14⅛ (21.3 x 35.9).
    Metropolitan Museum of Art.

MOUNT CHOCORUA AND LAKE. S/D/L/L.
    1873. Watercolor.
    8⅛ x 14¼ (20.6 x 36.2).
    Metropolitan Museum of Art.

MOUNT JEFFERSON AND MOUNT ADAMS.
    Watercolor.
    Vose Galleries (1975).

MOUNT WASHINGTON FROM THE GLEN ROAD (formerly CONWAY, N.H.).
    Oil on canvas.
    14½ x 24¼ (36.8 x 61.6).
    Private collection (1983); Vose Galleries (1975).

MOUNT WASHINGTON RANGE FROM MOUNT KEARSARGE. S/D/L/R.
    1872. Watercolor.
    8 x 14⅛ (20.3 x 35.9).
    Metropolitan Museum of Art; Pre-1877.

MT. CHICORUA [sic].
    Watercolor.
    Pre-1877; American Society of Painters in Watercolors, N.Y.C. (1873).

PULPIT ROCK S/L/L.
    1876. Watercolor.
    13 x 10¾ (33 x 27.3).
    Museum of Fine Arts, Springfield, MA.

SQUAM LAKE, NEW HAMPSHIRE, 1876. S/D/L/L.
    1876. Watercolor.
    12⅞ x 10¾ (32.7 x 27.3).
    Museum of Fine Arts, Springfield, MA (1972).

SUNDOWN AT CENTRE HARBOR. S/D/L/R.
    1874. Watercolor.
    8⅝ x 13½ (22 x 34.3).
    Metropolitan Museum of Art.

SUNSET ON MOUNT CHOCORUA, NH. S/D/L/R.
    1872. Watercolor.
    8 x 14 (20.3 x 35.6).
    Metropolitan Museum of Art (1973).

VIEW IN THE WHITE MOUNTAINS (CRAWFORD NOTCH). S/D/L/L.
    1876. Watercolor.
    12¾ x 10⅝ (32.4 x 27).
    Museum of Fine Arts, Springfield, MA (1972).

WHITE MOUNTAIN NOTCH.
Pre-1877; NAD, watercolor show (March 5, 1873).

RITTER, PAUL

Born 1829. Died 1907.
There is presently no further information on this artist.

MOUNT WASHINGTON. S/L/R.
Oil.
30 x 46¼ (76.2 x 117.5).
Vose Galleries (sold Nov. 12, 1946); Ferdinand's Restaurant, Cambridge, MA.

NEW ENGLAND WINTER.
Oil.
28 x 38 (71.1 x 96.5).
Knoedler; Vose Galleries (sold Aug. 11, 1943).

NEW HAMPSHIRE LANDSCAPE.
Oil.
30 x 46 (76.2 x 116.8).
Old Print Shop *Portfolio* 13:8, p. 191.

ROAD COACH IN NEW HAMPSHIRE.
Oil.
30 x 40 (76.2 x 101.6).
Old Print Shop *Portfolio*, 13:8, p. 191.

ROBBINS, HORACE WOLCOTT, JR.

B, C, C&H, F, G&W, N, S, T
Born Mobile, AL, Oct. 21, 1842.
Died New York, NY, Dec. 14, 1904.
Robbins moved to New York City after college, studied under James M. Hart, and opened his own studio in 1860. In 1864 he was elected an associate of the NAD, a full member in 1878, and the recording secretary four years later. He accompanied Frederic Church to Jamaica in 1864 and continued his studies in England and France for two years. He was elected a member of the Century Association in 1863 and exhibited frequently at the NAD and the Brooklyn Art Association from 1863 to 1883. He painted in both oil and watercolor.

A NEW HAMPSHIRE SCENE.
NAD, 1862, #427.

ANDROSCOGGIN RIVER; THE . . .
NAD, 1865, #453; Brooklyn Art Association (1865), #51.

MOUNT MADISON AND ADAMS.
1842. Oil.
Hirschl and Adler Gallery.

SUNSET ON THE ANDROSCOGGIN.
Boston Art Association (1863), #89.

VIEW OF THE PRESIDENTIAL RANGE OF THE WHITE MOUNTAINS, NEW HAMPSHIRE.
Oil.
30 x 53¾ (76.2 x 136.5).
Sotheby PB (1977).

WHITE MOUNTAIN SCENERY.
NAD, 1865. #387.

WHITE MOUNTAINS SCENERY.
Brooklyn Art Association (1863), #181.

WHITE MOUNTAINS.
PAFA, 1864.

ROBINSON, GODFREY HARDING

Active 1899.
Research has uncovered no information on this artist at present.

DECEMBER DAY, NORTH CONWAY.
Exhibited in watercolor or black and white section. Boston Art Club (1899), #87.

ROCK, J. F.

Active 1881.
There is presently no information on this artist.

ELLIS RIVER, JACKSON, NEW HAMPSHIRE.
MA Charitable (1881), #226.

ROGERS, WILLIAM ALLEN

A, F
Born Ohio, 1854. Died Washington, DC, 1931.
Rogers was predominately an illustrator, and many of his illustrations were placed in Samuel Adams Drake's Heart of the White Mountains. *He worked for Harper and Brothers Publishers with Thure de Thulstrup and exhibited at the Brooklyn Art Association in 1883. He was elected a member of the Century Association in 1894.*

Bibliography:
Drake, Samuel Adams. *The Heart of the White Mountains: Their Legend and Scenery.* New York: Harper and Brothers, 1882.
Rogers, W. A. *A World Worth While: A Record of 'Auld Acquaintance.'* New York: Harper and Brothers, 1922.

ALONE WITH ALL THOSE MEN.
Drake, Samuel Adams. *Heart of the White Mountains.*

BUCK-BOARD WAGON; THE . . .
Drake. *Heart of the White Mountains.*

ROADSIDE SPRING; THE . . .
Drake. *Heart of the White Mountains.*
SLIDING DOWN KEARSARGE.
Drake. *Heart of the White Mountains.*

RONDEL, FREDERICK
A, G&W, N, S
Born Paris, France, 1826. Died 1892.
Rondel moved to the U.S. by 1855 and lived in Boston and its vicinity until 1869. He exhibited at the Boston Athenaeum from 1855 to 1869 and was elected an associate of the NAD, where he exhibited from 1861 to his death. He also sent pictures to the PAFA. NEW HAMPSHIRE SCENERY, which came up at the Leonard Auction Rooms in 1864, was described as a picture "with a general view of the White Mountains in the distance; a very fine sketch from Nature."
NEW HAMPSHIRE SCENERY.
Watercolor.
Leonard Auction (Dec. 29, 1864), #12.
NEW HAMPSHIRE SCENERY.
Sketch.
Leonard Auction (Dec. 29, 1864), #111.

ROPES, JOSEPH C.
A, C, F, G&W, N, S, T
Born Salem, MA., 1812.
Died New York, NY, 1885.
Ropes studied at the NAD in the 1840s and under John R. Smith. He worked as a miniaturist, a landscapist, and a teacher of art, and used crayon as well as the more conventional techniques. A peripatetic man, he moved about, starting in New York City, settling in Hartford, CT, for 14 years, then traveling abroad for 11 years, returning in 1876 to Philadelphia, and finally going back to New York City for his final years.
Bibliography:
Ropes, Joseph C. *Linear Perspective.* Portland, ME, 1849.
Ropes, Joseph C. *Progressive Steps in Landscape Painting.* Hartford, CT, 1853.
BEECHER'S FALLS.
1883. Charcoal drawing.
8 $^{11}/_{16}$ x 10⅝ (22 x 27).
Dartmouth College Art Galleries (1983).
MOUNT WASHINGTON FROM NORTH CONWAY.
Oil on canvas.
7 x 11 (17.8 x 27.9).
Bowdoin College Museum of Art (1972).

MOUNTAIN STREAM, JACKSON, NEW HAMPSHIRE; THE . . .
Brooklyn Art Association (1878), #278.
SCENE IN NORTH CONWAY.
Brooklyn Art Association (1879), #546.

RUGGLES, EDWARD
C, F, G&W, T
Active 1848-65. Died c. 1866.
Ruggles, a physician, could technically be classified as an amateur painter, as he was made an honorary member of the NAD from 1851 to 1860. He was elected to the Century Association in 1848 (and apparently resigned in 1851), a group whose members were all practitioners of the arts. He exhibited at the NAD from 1851 to 1860, and Prang lithographic firm of Boston published nine of his New Hampshire views, titled RUGGLES' GEMS.
MOUNT WASHINGTON.
Chromolithograph.
Leonard Auction (May 22, 1864), #15. See McClinton, p. 153.
RUGGLES' GEMS (9 views).
Lithographs.
McClinton.
WHITE MOUNTAINS.
Leonard Auction (May 22, 1863), #188.

RUSSELL, G. D.
Active 1874.
Nothing is presently known of this artist.
NORTH CONWAY.
Oil.
Boston Art Club (Jan. 1874), #70.

RYDER, HENRY ORNE
N
Active 1897-98.
Ryder exhibited at the NAD in 1897 and at the Boston Art Club in 1898. There is no further information on this artist.
OLD ROAD TO FRANCONIA NOTCH.
Boston Art Club (1898), #252.

S

SCHAFER, FREDERICK FERDINAND
Born 1839. Died 1927.
There is presently no information on this artist.
AFTER A STORM IN THE WHITE MOUNTAINS.
   C. 1880. Oil.
   22 x 36 (55.9 x 91.4).
   John H. Garzoli, Gallery, San Francisco, CA
   (1975).

SCHROFF, ALFRED HERMANN
F
Born Springfield, MA, 1863.
Schroff was a pupil of DeCamp and the Cowles Art School. He taught at the University of Oregon.

Information courtesy of Vose Galleries.

SKATING SCENE ON LAKE SUNAPEE, NH, AT SUNSET.
   1889. Oil.
   14 x 20 (35.6 x 50.8).
   Private collection.
THREE RICKER GIRLS (NH MOUNTAINS IN THE BACKGROUND); THE... S/D.
   1886. Oil on canvas.
   Lion Gallery (1976).
Signed S., A. (F.?) (probably Alfred Hermann Schroff).

SCOLLAY, CATHERINE
A, G&W
Born Boston, MA, 1783. Died 1863.
Scollay exhibited at the Boston Athenaeum from 1827 to 1848. A landscape and figure painter, Scollay produced a series of Trenton Falls, NY, which were lithographed by the Boston firm of John B. Pendleton (brother of William S.).

OLD MAN OF THE MOUNTAINS.
   Boston Athenaeum (1837), #35.

SCOTT, JOHN WHITE ALLEN
A, F, G&W
Born Roxbury, MA, 1815.
Died Cambridge, MA, March 4, 1907.
Scott began his artistic career as an apprentice to the lithographer, William S. Pendleton (brother of John B.), in his native Boston. Nathaniel Currier worked in the same shop. In the mid-1840s, Scott and Fitz Hugh Lane formed a business partnership to make and publish lithographs in Boston. Beginning about 1842, Scott exhibited his paintings at the Boston Athenaeum and other local galleries. He was a member of the Boston Art Club and, by 1905, had outlived all its other original members. Scott painted and sketched until the end of his long life.

Bibliography:
Allison, Hildreth M. "Some Painters of the Grand Monadnock." *Appalachia* 34 (1962-63), pp. 441-453.

BANKS OF A COLD STREAM, WHITE MOUNTAINS, NEW HAMPSHIRE. S/D/L/R.
   1874. Oil on canvas.
   22 x 36 (55.9 x 91.4).
   Old Print Shop *Portfolio* 32:3 (Oct. 1972), p. 71.
CONWAY VALLEY. S/D/L/L.
   1869. Oil on canvas.
   12 x 20 (30.5 x 50.8).
   Old Print Shop *Portfolio* (March 1973), p. 168.
DIXVILLE NOTCH. S/L/L.
   Oil on canvas.
   12 x 20 (30.5 x 50.8).
   Kennedy Galleries (1978).
FRANCONIA NOTCH.
   Leonard Auction (May 22, 1863), #147.
IN THE NOTCH. S/D/L/R.
   1857. Oil on canvas.
   24 x 36 (61 x 91.4).
   New Hampshire Historical Society (1980); University Art Gallery catalog, University of New Hampshire (1980), #119.
KEARSARGE. S/D.
   1876.
   20 x 30 (50.8 x 76.2).
   Private collection (1980).
KEARSARGE AND THE SACO. S/D/L/R.
   1880. Oil on canvas.
   14 x 20 (35.6 x 50.8).
   Elizabeth R. Daniel, dealer (1979); *Antiques* (May 1979).

New Hampshire Scenery

MOUNT CHOCORUA, NEW HAMPSHIRE, SUMMER VIEW.
> Oil on board.
> 5¾ x 12¾ (14.6 x 32.4).
> Private collection; Richard Bourne, Inc., catalog (1977), #128.

MT. CHOCORUA, N.H.
> Oil.
> 30 x 50 (76.2 x 127).
> Sold at Sotheby's, Apr. 1976.

MOUNT MONADNOCK, NEW HAMPSHIRE, IN SUMMER.
> 1876. Oil.
> 15 x 30 (38.1 x 76.2).
> Private collection (1974).

MOUNT MONADNOCK, NEW HAMPSHIRE, IN WINTER.
> Oil.
> 12 x 20 (30.5 x 50.8).
> Private collection (1974).

MOUNT WASHINGTON FROM CONWAY, NEW HAMPSHIRE. S/D/L/R/Center.
> 1866. Oil on canvas.
> 30 x 50 (76.2 x 127).
> Kenneth Lux Gallery catalog (Oct. 1980).

MOUNT WASHINGTON, N.H. S/L/L.
> 11¾ x 9¾ (29.9 x 24.9).
> Signal Co. (1983).

MT. MONADNOCK.
> Mid-19th century. Oil.
> 10 x 14 (25.4 x 35.6).
> Vose Galleries.

NEAR MOUNT MONADNOCK, NEW HAMPSHIRE.
> 1869. Oil.
> 12 x 22 (30.5 x 55.9).
> Sotheby PB (1970).

NEW HAMPSHIRE LANDSCAPE.
> 1866. Oil.
> 30 x 50 (76.2 x 127).
> Richard Bourne, Inc., catalog (Aug. 6, 1974).

SCENE IN THE PEMIGEWASSET RIVER VALLEY, LOOKING NORTH. S/D/L/R.
> 1871. Oil on canvas.
> 21 x 36 (53.3 x 91.4).
> Goodspeed's Gallery catalog, 39:8 (May 1968), p. 201.

SCENE IN THE PEMIGEWASSET VALLEY, PROSPECT MOUNTAIN IN THE BACKGROUND. S/L/L.
> Oil on canvas.
> 30 x 50 (76.2 x 127).

Goodspeed's Gallery catalog, 39:8 (May 1968), p. 201.

SLIP MOUNTAIN, NORTH CONWAY. Signed.
> 21 x 13 (53.5 x 33).
> Private collection (1983).

SPORTSMEN'S CAMP IN NEW HAMPSHIRE.
> C. 1860. Oil.
> 18 x 30 (45.7 x 76.2).
> Old Print Shop *Portfolio* 18:8, p. 215.

VIEW FROM TOP OF JACKSON FALLS, OCTOBER MORNING, N.H., LANDSCAPE. S/L/L.
> Oil on canvas.
> 13½ x 19⅝ (34.5 x 50).
> Signal Co. (1983).

VIEW OF CONWAY VALLEY, NEW HAMPSHIRE.
> C. 1865. Oil.
> 30 x 50 (76.2 x 127).
> Butler Institute of American Art; Old Print Shop *Portfolio* 27:7.

WHITE MOUNTAINS.
> Oil.
> 20 x 32 (50.8 x 81.3).
> Stepping Stones Gallery, Great Neck, NY; *Antiques* (July 1977).

SEAGER, EDWARD

A
Born Maidstone, Kent, England, April 8, 1809. Died Washington, DC, Jan. 23, 1886.
Seager came to Canada about 1832 and was living on Tremont Row in Boston in 1838. He made his first trip to the White Mountains in 1839 and exhibited at the Boston Athenaeum in 1847 and 1848 after a brief visit to Europe. He became the first professor of drawing and drafting at the U.S. Naval Academy, a post which he held from 1850 to 1867. He also taught drawing at the English High School in Boston. He made further sketching trips to New Hampshire in 1861, 1863, and the 1870s.

Bibliography:
The Drawings of Edward Seager. Hirschl and Adler Gallery catalog.

MOUNT WASHINGTON, NEW HAMPSHIRE. S/D/L/R.
> 1862.
> 13 x 17½ (33 x 44.5).
> Hirschl and Adler Gallery catalog, #58.

NOTCH OF THE WHITE MOUNTAINS, NH. S/L/L.
   C. 1848. Pencil on white paper.
   12 x 17⅛ (30.5 x 43.5).
   Hirschl and Adler Gallery catalog, #29.

SANDWICH HILLS, SQUAM LAKE, NEW HAMPSHIRE. S/L/R.
   C. 1848. Pencil on white paper.
   9¼ x 12⅝ (23.5 x 32.1).
   Hirschl and Adler Gallery catalog, #32.

WATERFALL IN THE FRANCONIA NOTCH, NH.
   Pencil on white paper.
   8 x 10¼ (20.3 x 26).
   Hirschl and Adler Gallery catalog, #11.

SEAVEY, GEORGE M.

Seavey was an artist who pursued his vocation between Florida and the Maplewood Hotel in Bethlehem, NH, where he kept a summer studio. No New Hampshire views have yet been found.

Bibliography:
New Hampshire Historical Society, Shapleigh exhibition catalog (1982), p. 9.

SELINGER, JEAN PAUL

F, N, S
Born Boston, MA, June 24, 1850.
Died Boston, MA, Sept. 12, 1909.
Selinger was a pupil of Wilhelm Lieble in Munich and also attended the Lowell Institute. He was a friend of Frank Shapleigh and took over Shapleigh's studio at the Crawford House in 1894 when the latter went to Europe. He exhibited at the NAD in 1880 and at the Paint and Clay Club in Boston in 1889.

Bibliography:
Vogel, Charles and Gloria. "Jean Paul Selinger." *Historical New Hampshire* 34:2 (Summer 1979), pp. 125-142.

CRAWFORD NOTCH, CRAWFORD HOUSE.
   Crawford House Auction (July 1976).

LOOKING DOWN THE NOTCH FROM WEBSTER. S/L/R.
   Crawford House Auction (July 1976).

PRESIDENTIAL RANGE AND CRAWFORD HOUSE FROM MOUNT AVALON.
   Crawford House Auction (July 1976).

VIEW OF ELEPHANT'S HEAD.
   Crawford House Auction (July 1976).

WATERFALL.
   Crawford House Auction (July 1976).

SEYMOUR, SAMUEL

F, G&W, R
Born possibly England. Died 1832?
Seymour worked as an engraver and landscapist in Philadelphia from 1796 to 1823. He was a draftsman for Major H.S. Long's expeditions into the Rocky Mountains and the Mississippi River in 1830.

INDIANS, SALMON FALLS, NEW HAMPSHIRE.
   Whitney Museum of Art, N.Y.C.; Carnegie Institute exhibition (March-April 1939), #52.

SHAPLEIGH, FRANK HENRY

A, B, C&H, F, N, R, S
Born Boston, MA, March 7, 1842.
Died Jackson, NH, May 30, 1906.
Shapleigh was one of the most prolific painters of New Hampshire mountain scenery. Born in Boston, he studied at the Lowell Institute of Drawing around 1860. When the Civil War broke out, he enlisted as a volunteer and served from 1862 to 1863. After the war he began traveling, visiting the White Mountains in 1866, then California and Europe, where he studied in Paris with Emile Lambinet. Returning to his Boston studio in 1870, he became a member of the Boston Art Club and frequently exhibited there. From 1877 to 1894, Shapleigh spent his summers at the Crawford House, living in a cozy studio near the big hotel, taking in pupils and painting hundreds of mountain scenes to sell to tourists. He was very successful and, according to Champney, who knew him well, "happy with his success." A two-year trip to Europe from 1894 to 1896 ended his tenure at the Crawford House, and when he returned he built a home in Jackson called Maple Knoll behind the Jackson Falls House. He turned to watercolor painting almost exclusively in the 1890s and died in Jackson in 1906. Shapleigh had the happy faculty, for art historians, of signing, dating, and identifying the subject of his paintings on the reverse in almost every case. As with the works of Benjamin Champney, it is impossible to list here more than a representative sample of his paintings.

Bibliography:
Full of Facts and Sentiment: The Art of Frank H. Shapleigh. New Hampshire Historical Society catalog, Concord, NH (Oct. 15-Nov. 28, 1982).

ARTIST'S BROOK, NORTH CONWAY.
   12 x 18 (30.5 x 45.7).
   Vose Galleries (1974).

Franconia Mountains from Compton (sic) N. H.
William Trost Richards, 1872
Watercolor, 8 3/16" x 14 3/16" / Collection: The Metropolitan Museum of Art,
*   gift of Reverend Elias L. Magoon, 1880 / Ref. page 133*

BRIDAL VEIL FALLS, #1.
   Oil.
   18 x 12 (45.7 x 30.5).
   Vose Galleries (sold May 6, 1962, to J. McGrath, dealer).

BRIDAL VEIL FALLS, #2.
   Oil.
   18 x 12 (45.7 x 30.5).
   Vose Galleries (sold Sept. 15, 1962, to J. McGrath, dealer).

BRIDGE AT JACKSON, NEW HAMPSHIRE.
   Oil.
   20 x 14 (50.8 x 35.6).
   Vose Galleries (sold Oct. 24, 1972, to the Shapleigh Foundation).

CARTER NOTCH AND OLD MILL AT JACKSON, NH. S/D.
   1879. Oil on canvas.
   10 x 16 (25.6 x 40.6).
   Eden Gallery, Salem, NY (1976).

CARTER NOTCH AND SACO RIVER.
   Private collection (1974).

CARTER NOTCH FROM JACKSON, NEW HAMPSHIRE.
   Oil on canvas.
   14 x 24 (35.6 x 61).
   Baridoff Gallery (April 4, 1981), #66.

CARTER NOTCH FROM THORN HILL.
   Vose Galleries.

CHOCORUA. S/D/R.
   1866. Oil.
   17½ x 29 (44.4 x 73.7).
   Private collection.

CONWAY INTERVALE (Mount Washington and White Horse Ledge).
   1871. Oil.
   29 x 46 (73.7 x 116.8).
   Private collection (1976).

CONWAY MEADOWS FROM JACKSON, NEW HAMPSHIRE.
   Leonard Auction (June 5, 1874), #75.

CRAWFORD NOTCH.
   1882. Oil.

Dictionary of Painters

Frederic A. Sharf, dealer; *Antiques* (Nov. 1961).

CRAWFORD NOTCH.
   24 x 36 (61 x 91.4).
   Old Print Shop *Portfolio* (May 1965).

CRAWFORD NOTCH FROM CRAWFORD HOUSE; THE... S/D/L/L.
   1883. Oil on canvas.
   22 x 36 (55.9 x 91.5).
   New Hampshire Historical Society exhibition (1982); Frederic A. Sharf, dealer.

CRAWFORD NOTCH FROM MOUNT WILLARD. S/D/L/R.
   1883. Oil on canvas.
   22⅛ x 36⅛ (56.1 x 91.6).
   Private collection (1983); New Hampshire Historical Society exhibition (1982); Crawford House Auction (July 1976).

CRAWFORD NOTCH FROM WILLARD – VIEW FROM RIGHT.
   1889.
   13⅞ x 23⅞ (35.2 x 60.6).
   Robert Goldberg.

CRAWFORD NOTCH RAILWAY STATION.
   Oil.
   25 x 15 (63.5 x 38.1).
   Private collection (1974).

CRAWFORD NOTCH, WHITE MOUNTAINS, NEW HAMPSHIRE.
   1879. Oil.
   24 x 60 (61 x 101.6).
   Kennedy *Quarterly* 8:4 (Jan. 1969), p. 225.

CRAWFORD VALLEY FROM MOUNT WILLARD. S/L/R and Reverse.
   1877. Oil on canvas.
   21 x 36 (53.3 x 91.4).
   Private collection (1980); University Art Gallery catalog, University of New Hampshire (1980), #22; NMAA Inventory.

CRYSTAL CASCADE NEAR THE GLEN HOUSE. S/L/R.
   Oil on composition board.
   16¾ x 10⅝ (42.5 x 27).
   Private collection (1979).

DIXVILLE NOTCH, FROM COLEBROOK ROAD.
   Leonard Auction (April 22-23, 1875), #85.

DIXVILLE NOTCH, NEW HAMPSHIRE. S/L/R.
   37 x 26 (94 x 66).
   Private collection; *Antiques* (Jan. 1974).

DIXVILLE NOTCH, NH.
   C. 1880. Oil on canvas.
   25⅜ x 36⅝ (64.5 x 93).
   Signal Co. (1983).

DIXVILLE NOTCH, NORTHERN NEW HAMPSHIRE.
   Leonard Auction (April 11, 1873), #79.

ECHO LAKE, NEW HAMPSHIRE, FRANCONIA NOTCH.
   1879. Oil.
   25½ x 39½ (64.8 x 100.3).
   Jack Havrahan, Inc. (1973).

ELLIS RIVER AT JACKSON, NEW HAMPSHIRE.
   Oil.
   16 x 10 (40.6 x 25.4).
   Vose Galleries (sold Oct. 12, 1979).

EMERALD POOL.
   Oil on canvas.
   14 x 24 (35.6 x 61).
   Kennedy Galleries (Nov. 1978).

EMERALD POOL NEAR GLEN HOUSE.
   Oil.
   14 x 24 (35.6 x 61).
   Vose Galleries (sold Feb. 1, 1969).

FRANCONIA AVALANCHE (6 illustrations in a pamphlet).
   1883.
   Published by Henry M. Burt, who edited the newspaper *Among the Clouds*, Mount Washington, NH.

FRANCONIA MOUNTAINS FROM WEST CAMPTON.
   Leonard Auction (June 5, 1874), #25.

FRANCONIA MOUNTAINS AND VALLEY OF THE PEMIGEWASSET RIVER FROM WEST CAMPTON, NH; THE... S/D/L/R.
   1872. Oil on canvas.
   22⅛ x 36¼ (56.1 x 92).
   Private collection; New Hampshire Historical Society (1982).

GATE OF THE NOTCH. Signed.
   Before 1875.
   Robert Goldberg (1974).

GIANT'S STAIRS, WHITE MOUNTAINS; THE...
   Oil.
   Boston Art Club (Jan. 10-Feb. 10, 1877), #80, and (Jan. 15-Feb. 8, 1879), #140.

GLEN ELLIS FALLS.
   Leonard Auction (April 22-23, 1875), #31.

GOODRICH FALLS, NEW HAMPSHIRE.
   1886. Oil.
   10 x 16 (25.4 x 40.6).
   Frank S. Schwarz, dealer (1977).

New Hampshire Scenery

JACKSON AND WILDCAT VALLEY. Signed.
  1885. Oil.
  22 x 36 (55.9 x 91.4).
  Private collection.

JACKSON FALLS AND OLD MILL.
  Leonard Auction (Dec. 11, 1874), #11.

LANDSCAPE FROM CRAWFORD HOUSE, NEW
HAMPSHIRE.
  1878. Oil.
  27¼ x 39½ (69.2 x 100.3).
  Private collection (1975).

LANDSCAPE FROM EAGLE CLIFF AT
CRAWFORD NOTCH.
  1884. Oil.
  29 x 19 (73.7 x 48.3).
  Private collection (1975).

LOOKING DOWN THE NOTCH.
  1888.
  Crawford House Auction (1976).

MOAT MOUNTAIN FROM CONWAY LAKE.
  Private collection.

MOTT [sic] MOUNTAIN FROM JACKSON FALLS,
NEW HAMPSHIRE.
  1877. Oil on canvas.
  24 x 14 (61 x 35.6).
  Dartmouth College Art Galleries (1984).

MOUNT ASCUTNEY FROM CLAREMONT, NEW
HAMPSHIRE.
  Oil.
  28 x 50 (71.1 x 127).
  Vose Galleries (sold Oct. 12, 1979).

MOUNT CHOCORUA.
  1850.
  Private collection (1973).

MOUNT CHOCORUA AND SACO RIVER FROM
FRYEBURG, ME. S/L/L.
  Oil on canvas.
  7⅝ x 12⅝ (19.2 x 32).
  Private collection; New Hampshire
  Historical Society exhibition (1982).

MOUNT CHOCORUA FROM FRYEBURG, ME.
S/R.
  7 x 12¼ (17.8 x 31.1).
  Robert Goldberg (sold).

MOUNT CHOCORUA FROM TAMWORTH, NEW
HAMPSHIRE. S/D/L/R.
  1875. Oil on canvas.
  20¼ x 30¼ (51.3 x 76.7).
  New Hampshire Historical Society exhibition
  (1982).

MOUNT KEARSARGE AND SACO RIVER. S/L/R.
  1880. Oil on canvas.
  18 x 30 (45.7 x 76.2).

Richard Bourne, Inc., catalog (Aug. 14,
1979), #131.

MOUNT KEARSARGE AND THE SACO FROM
FRYEBURG, ME. S/D/L/R.
  1872. Oil on board.
  9 x 13⅛ (22.6 x 33.2).
  Robert Goldberg; New Hampshire Historical
  Society catalog (1982).

MOUNT WASHINGTON. S/D/L/L.
  1881. Oil on canvas.
  16 x 10 (40.6 x 25.4).
  Baridoff Gallery (Nov. 7, 1981), #20.

MOUNT WASHINGTON AND CARTER NOTCH
FROM BARTLETT, NEW HAMPSHIRE.
  Leonard Auction (June 5, 1874), #58.

MOUNT WASHINGTON AND ELLIS RIVER.
S/D/L/R.
  1883. Oil on canvas.
  10 x 16 (25.4 x 40.6).
  Private collection (1979); Vose Galleries (sold
  Jan. 31, 1979).

MOUNT WASHINGTON AND ELLIS RIVER AT
JACKSON.
  1882. Oil.
  38 x 60 (96.5 x 152.4).
  Smith College Museum of Art (1973).

MOUNT WASHINGTON AND ELLIS RIVER AT
JACKSON, NEW HAMPSHIRE.
  1890. Oil.
  22 x 36 (55.9 x 91.4).
  Sotheby PB (1970).

MOUNT WASHINGTON AND ELLIS RIVER,
JACKSON, NEW HAMPSHIRE.
  Oil.
  8 x 12 (20.3 x 30.5).
  Richard Bourne, Inc., catalog (Aug. 29,
  1970).

MOUNT WASHINGTON AND THE AMMO-
NOOSUC. S/D/L/R.
  1891. Oil on canvas.
  30 x 20 (76.2 x 50.8).
  Private collection (1983).

MOUNT WASHINGTON AND WALKER'S POND
FROM OLD BARN IN CONWAY. S/D/L/R.
  1885. Oil on canvas.
  10 x 16 (25.4 x 40.6).
  Dartmouth College Art Galleries (1983);
  University Art Galleries catalog, University
  of New Hampshire (1980), #92.

MOUNT WASHINGTON FROM BROOK NEAR CRAWFORD HOUSE.
Kennedy Galleries.

MOUNT WASHINGTON FROM CONWAY. S/D and S/Reverse.
1870. Oil on canvas.
12 x 20 (30.5 x 50.8).
Elizabeth R. Daniel, dealer (1980); *Antiques* (Feb. 1980).

MOUNT WASHINGTON FROM ELLIS RIVER, JACKSON.
1874.
Antiques (Nov. 1961); Leonard Auction (April 11, 1873), #65.

MOUNT WASHINGTON FROM ELLIS RIVER MEADOWS, JACKSON, NH.
1882. Oil on canvas.
26⅛ x 45¼ (66.4 x 114.7).
Collection: William Nathaniel Banks.

MOUNT WASHINGTON FROM GLEN ROAD. S/D/L/R.
1879.
New Hampshire Historical Society exhibition (1982), #20; Richard Bourne, Inc., catalog (1974), #12.

MOUNT WASHINGTON FROM INTERVAL [sic] HOUSE, NORTH CONWAY, NH.
Leonard Auction (April 11, 1873), #68.

MOUNT WASHINGTON FROM IRON MOUNTAIN.
Leonard Auction (April 20-21, 1876), #35.

MOUNT WASHINGTON FROM JACKSON.
Leonard Auction (April 20-21, 1876), #16.

MOUNT WASHINGTON FROM JACKSON. S/D/L/R.
1885. Oil on canvas.
22 x 36 (55.9 x 91.5).
University Art Galleries catalog, University of New Hampshire (1980), #67.

MOUNT WASHINGTON FROM JACKSON. S/D/L/R.
1888. Oil on board.
7⅜ x 12¼ (18.7 x 31.1).
Christie's (Jan. 30, 1981), #36A.

MOUNT WASHINGTON FROM PORTER'S FARM, CONWAY CENTRE.
Leonard Auction (April 20-21, 1876), #79.

MOUNT WASHINGTON FROM THE GLEN ROAD AT JACKSON. S/Reverse.
Oil on board.
7½ x 12¼ (19.1 x 31.1).

Private collection (1983); Blackwell Antiques, San Francisco, CA (1974).

MOUNT WASHINGTON FROM THE SACO RIVER.
Oil.
18 x 30 (45.7 x 76.2).
Vose Galleries (sold Feb. 23, 1979).

MOUNT WASHINGTON RANGE AND AMMONOOSUC RIVER.
1869. Oil.
10 x 16 (25.4 x 40.6).
Private collection (1971).

MOUNT WASHINGTON, JACKSON, NEW HAMPSHIRE.
1883. Oil.
10 x 6 (25.4 x 15.2).
Parke-Bernet (1954).

NEW HAMPSHIRE FARMYARD. S/L/Center.
Oil on tin.
10⅛ x 7½ (25.7 x 19.1).
Richard Bourne, Inc. (Nov. 26, 1983).

NEW HAMPSHIRE HILLS.
1885. Oil.
Frederic A. Sharf, dealer; *Antiques* (Nov. 1961).

NOTCH HOUSE, CRAWFORD NOTCH; THE... S/D/L/R.
1879. Oil on canvas.
18 x 30 (45.8 x 76).
New Hampshire Historical Society exhibition (1982).

OLD BARN IN JACKSON, NEW HAMPSHIRE.
1883 or 1893. Oil.
10 x 16 (25.4 x 40.6).
Old Print Shop *Portfolio* 28:7, p. 168; *Antiques* (Dec. 1969).

OLD BARN, NORTH CONWAY.
Oil.
Boston Art Club (1880), #77.

OLD BRIDGE AT JACKSON, NEW HAMPSHIRE.
Oil.
7½ x 12½ (19.1 x 31.8).
New Bedford (MA) Free Library (1971).

OLD FARM HOUSE AND CINNAMON ROSES, JACKSON, NH. S/D/L/L.
1887. Oil.
16 x 10 (40.6 x 25.4).
Old Print Shop *Portfolio* 21:4 (Nov. 1971), p. 94.

OLD HANSON TAVERN, UPPER BARTLETT, NEW HAMPSHIRE.
Leonard Auction (April 20-21, 1876), #32.

New Hampshire Scenery

OLD MAN OF THE MOUNTAINS. Signed.
Oil on wood bowl.
11 (27.9). Round.
Private collection (1983); Franconia Bicentennial Art Show (1972).

OLD MILL AT JACKSON, NEW HAMPSHIRE (GOODRICH FALLS). S/D/L/L.
1877. Oil on canvas.
14 x 24 (35.6 x 61).
Private collection (1980); University Art Gallery catalog, University of New Hampshire (1980), #33.

OLD WELL SWEEP, JACKSON.
Oil.
10 x 16 (25.4 x 40.6).
Vose Galleries (sold Oct. 25, 1980).

ON THE BROOK, JACKSON, NEW HAMPSHIRE.
Leonard Auction (Dec. 11, 1874), #20.

ON THE ELLIS RIVER, JACKSON, NEW HAMPSHIRE.
1878. Oil.
10 x 18 (25.4 x 45.7).
Adam Weschler and Sons (Feb. 22-28, 1971).

ON THE ELLIS RIVER, JACKSON, NH.
1875. Oil on canvas.
12 x 22¼ (30.5 x 56.5).
Unlocated.

ON THE ELLIS RIVER, JACKSON, NH. S/D.
14 x 24 (35.6 x 61).
Private collection.

ON THORN MOUNTAIN ROAD, JACKSON. S/D/L/R.
1894. Oil on canvas.
10 x 16 (25.4 x 40.6).
Old Print Shop (1973).

ON WILDCAT BROOK, JACKSON. S/D/L/L.
1884. Oil on board.
7½ x 12½ (19.1 x 31.8).
Skinner catalog (1977).

PRESIDENTIAL RANGE AND AMMONOOSUC RIVER.
1885. Oil.
40½ x 26 (102.9 x 67.3).
Sporting Gallery; *Antiques* (June 1968).

PRESIDENTIAL RANGE AND AMMONOOSUC RIVER NEAR FABYAN'S, NH; THE...S/D/L/R.
S
1881. Oil on canvas.
14⅛ x 24 (35.8 x 61.0).
Gift of the W. N. Banks Foundation to the New Hampshire Historical Society.

PRESIDENTIAL RANGE FROM THE MOUNT PLEASANT HOUSE. S/D/L/R.
1888.
20 x 30 (50.8 x 76.2).
Vose Galleries.

PRESIDENTIALS FROM COOS.
17⅞ x 30 (45.4 x 76.2).
Private collection.

RED BARN BY THE BRIDGE.
13¾ x 15¼ (34.9 x 38.7).
Richard Bourne, Inc., catalog (1976), #1.

SAW MILL AT JACKSON, NEW HAMPSHIRE.
1874. Oil on panel.
7½ x 12½ (19.1 x 31.8).
Kennedy Galleries (1980); University Art Gallery catalog, University of New Hampshire (1980), #89.

SMALL POND BACK OF THE CRAWFORD HOUSE.
Private collection.

THROUGH THE BARN (THE HATCH PLACE).
3rd Art of Northern New England Show (1975).

VIEW OF MOUNT WASHINGTON THROUGH A BARN. Signed.
Conway Historical Society.

WELL SWEEP, JACKSON.
Oil.
12 x 7½ (31.8 x 19.1).
Vose Galleries (sold Oct. 25, 1962, to J. McGrath, dealer).

WHITE MOUNTAIN LANDSCAPE.
12 x 22½ (30.5 x 57.2).
Private collection.

WHITE MOUNTAINS FROM MOUNT PLEASANT HOUSE; THE...
George Kent, dealer, Rumney, NH (pamphlet on the hotel).

WHITE MOUNTAINS FROM WALKER'S POND, CONWAY, NH. S/D/L/R.
1874. Oil on canvas.
23¾ x 37¾ (60.3 x 95.9).
Private collection (1976).

WILD CAT RIVER.
George Kent, dealer, Rumney, NH (1975); private collection (1973).

WILDCAT FROM THORN HILL IN JACKSON.
1874. Oil.
Private collection; *Antiques* (Nov. 1961).

SHATTUCK, AARON DRAPER

A, Ce, C&H, DAB, F, G&W, N, R, S, T
Born Francestown, NH, March 9, 1832.
Died Granby, CT, July 30, 1928.

Until recently, Aaron Shattuck's success and popularity in the 19th century as a painter of portraits, landscapes, and animals had been forgotten. Shattuck was raised in Francestown, NH, and Lowell, MA, and was one of nine children. He sought portrait and landscape painting instruction from Alexander Ransom in Boston. A year later, in 1852, Shattuck moved to New York City and enrolled in antique and life classes at the NAD. Ransom followed his student to New York City where they boarded together and recommenced painting lessons. In 1854 Shattuck painted Mount Chocorua, Tuckerman Ravine, and Mount Washington, and sold his first paintings. His first exhibit at the NAD followed in 1855 when he was 23 years of age. Shattuck enjoyed increasing recognition and popularity, exhibiting his work at the Boston Athenaeum, the PAFA, the Brooklyn Art Association, and the NAD. His paintings sold well, and many were reproduced in wood engravings and illustrations. He was elected an associate member of the NAD in 1859 and a full member in 1861. He kept a studio in the 10th Street Studio Building (N.Y.C.) from 1859 until 1896. Shattuck married Marian Colman, sister of the painter and illustrator, Samuel Colman. In 1870 he moved to a farm in Granby, CT, where he lived until his death in 1928. He stopped painting in 1886 after a serious illness, reported to have been measles complicated by pneumonia. Thereafter, he lived on the profits made from sales of his patented designs for canvas stretcher keys, produced a new method for ventilating tobacco barns, and made violins.

Select Bibliography:
Agar, Eunice. "Aaron Draper Shattuck." *Art and Antiques* (Sept.-Oct. 1982), pp. 48-55.
Aaron Draper Shattuck, 1832-1928: A Retrospective Exhibition. New Britain Museum of American Art catalog (1970).
Ferguson, Charles B. "Aaron Draper Shattuck, White Mountain School Painter." *American Art Review* 3:3 (May-June 1976), pp. 68-81.

ACROSS INTERVALE TO MOUNT WASHINGTON.
1858.
10 x 18 (25.4 x 45.7).
Chapellier Gallery (1975).

ALONG THE SACO RIVER. S/D.
1858. Oil.
15 x 14 (38.1 x 35.6).
Anthony Schmidt (1983).

AUTUMN LANDSCAPE AND MOUNT WASHINGTON.
1859. Oil.
10 x 17 (25.4 x 43.2). Oval.
New Britain Museum of American Art (1981), #31; Chapellier Gallery (1975).

AUTUMNAL SNOW ON MOUNT WASHINGTON. S/L/L.
1856. Oil.
10 x 15¾ (25.4 x 40).
Vassar College Art Gallery (1980); New Britain Museum of American Art (1970), plate 3.

AUTUMNAL VIEW OF ANDROSCOGGIN AND WHITE MOUNTAINS.
Before 1859.
10 x 17 (25.4 x 43.2).
Emigh, Eugene and Katherine, dealers (sold 1981); T; C&H, p. 250 (see Standard Source Reference List).

BLUE SHADOWS OVER MOUNT WASHINGTON.
1856. Oil.
4½ x 6½ (11.4 x 16.5).
Emigh, Eugene and Katherine, dealers.

BOULDER IN FOREST, CONWAY, NEW HAMPSHIRE.
1861. Oil on canvas.
11¾ x 19⅞ (29.8 x 50.5).
Hirschl and Adler Gallery (1978).

CASCADE, JULY, 1858.
1858. Pencil and ink.
Emigh, Eugene and Katherine, dealers.

CASCADES, PINKHAM NOTCH, MOUNT WASHINGTON; THE...
1858 or 1859. Oil on canvas.
15¼ x 19 (38.7 x 48.3).
Smithsonian Bicentennial Tour (1976), #143.

CATHEDRAL LEDGE, CONWAY, NEW HAMPSHIRE.
1854. Oil.
5½ x 9 (14 x 22.9).
Hirschl and Adler Gallery (1978); Emigh, Eugene and Katherine, dealers.

CHERRY LAKE, WHITE MOUNTAINS, AUG. 29, '59.
1859. Pencil and ink.
Emigh, Eugene and Katherine, dealers.

CHOCORUA LAKE AND MOUNTAIN. S/L/L.
1855. Oil.

New Hampshire Scenery

Dixville Notch
John White Allen Scott
Oil on canvas, 12" x 20" / Courtesy of Kennedy Galleries,
New York / Ref. page 136

10 ¹/₁₆ x 19⅝ (25.7 x 49.8).
Vassar College Art Gallery; University Art Gallery catalog, University of New Hampshire (1980), #59.

CHOCORUA PEAK, AUG. 8, '54. Signed.
1854. Sketch.
Emigh, Eugene and Katherine, dealers (sold May 1980).

CLOUDS OVER MOUNT WASHINGTON, AUTUMN COLORS.
1858. Oil.
7 x 11½ (17.8 x 29.2). Arch.
Emigh, Eugene and Katherine, dealers (sold Jan. 1981).

CONWAY – CLOUD STUDY, MOUNT WASHINGTON AND COG RAILWAY.
1856. Oil.
14 x 10 (35.6 x 25.4).
Emigh, Eugene and Katherine, dealers.

CONWAY – HAYING NEAR MOAT MOUNTAIN.
1854. Oil.
9½ x 14 (24.1 x 35.6).
Emigh, Eugene and Katherine, dealers (sold Dec. 1982).

CONWAY – LEDGES IN SUMMER.
Aug. 22, 1856. Oil.
9 x 16 (22.9 x 40.6).
Emigh, Eugene and Katherine, dealers (1983).

CONWAY – MOAT MOUNTAIN – BOY HERDING CATTLE.
1859. Oil.
11 x 14 (27.9 x 35.6).
Emigh, Eugene and Katherine, dealers (1983).

CONWAY, JULY 11, '54.
1854. Sketch.
Emigh, Eugene and Katherine, dealers.

CONWAY, JULY 15, '54. Signed.
1854. Sketch.
Emigh, Eugene and Katherine, dealers.

CONWAY, MEADOW BROOK AND CARDINAL WILDFLOWER.
1854. Oil.
12 x 20 (30.5 x 50.8).
Emigh, Eugene and Katherine, dealers.

Dictionary of Painters

CONWAY, NEW HAMPSHIRE, GARDEN STUDY NEAR MOAT MOUNTAIN.
    1858. Oil on cardboard.
    10 x 7 (25.4 x 17.8).
    Sotheby PB (1980), #100.

ECHO LAKE, WHITE MOUNTAINS.
    Sketch.
    Emigh, Eugene and Katherine, dealers.

GIANT MULLENS, CONWAY, NEW HAMPSHIRE.
    1854. Oil.
    10 x 14 (25.4 x 35.6).
    Honolulu Academy (1983); Hirschl and Adler Gallery (1978).

GLEN STUDY.
    1857. Oil on canvas.
    13½ x 21½ (34.3 x 54.6).
    Private collection; New Britain Museum of American Art exhibition (1970), #50.

GORHAM, NH, AUG. 22, 1858.
    1858. Sketch.
    Emigh, Eugene and Katherine, dealers.

HAYING AT INTERVALE, CONWAY.
    1859. Oil.
    6 x 16 (15.2 x 40.6).
    Emigh, Eugene and Katherine, dealers.

HAYING SCENE NEAR MOAT MOUNTAIN, CONWAY, NH.
    1859. Oil on cardboard.
    9 x 14 (22.9 x 35.6).
    University Art Gallery catalog, University of New Hampshire (1980), #121; Baridoff Gallery (Nov. 10, 1979).

HILLSIDE VIEW OF MOUNT WASHINGTON.
    1864. Oil.
    10 x 15½ (25.4 x 39.4).
    Emigh, Eugene and Katherine, dealers.

INDIAN GUIDE, MOUNT CHOCORUA, NEW HAMPSHIRE; THE . . . S/L/L.
    1858. Oil on canvas.
    10 x 18 (25.4 x 45.7).
    New Britain Museum of American Art exhibition (1970), plate 12.

INDIAN SUMMER IN THE WHITE MOUNTAINS.
    NAD, 1857, #171.

INTERVALE, MOUNT WASHINGTON BEHIND CLOUDS.
    1859. Oil.
    10 x 17 (25.4 x 43.2). Oval.
    Emigh, Eugene and Katherine, dealers.

INTERVALE, NH. Signed.
    1854. Pencil and ink.
    5½ x 9 (14 x 22.9).
    Emigh, Eugene and Katherine, dealers (sold June 1979).

LAKE WINNEPESAUKEE [sic].
    Danforth Museum.

LANCASTER, NH, SEPT. 6, 1860.
    1860. Sketch.
    Emigh, Eugene and Katherine, dealers.

LANDSCAPE AND LAKE SCENE – MOUNTAIN SCENERY IN AUTUMN.
    Leonard Auction (Dec. 29, 1864), #56.

LANDSCAPE AND RIVER, CONWAY, NH. S/D/Reverse.
    1854. Oil on paper.
    14 x 18 (35.6 x 45.7). Oval.
    Emigh, Eugene and Katherine, dealers; New Britain Museum of American Art exhibition (1970), #38.

LEAD MINE FALLS, SHELBOURNE [sic], NH. Signed.
    Sketch.
    Emigh, Eugene and Katherine, dealers.

MADISON BOULDER, CONWAY, NEW HAMPSHIRE.
    C. 1858. Oil on canvas.
    11 ¹³/₁₆ x 19⅞ (30.1 x 50.5).
    Brooklyn Museum.

MEADOW BROOK, CONWAY, NEW HAMPSHIRE.
    Brooklyn Art Association (1869), #191.

MOAT MOUNTAIN AND NEW MOON FROM CONWAY MEADOWS.
    Oil on board.
    4½ x 9½ (11.4 x 24.1).
    Private collection (1983); Baridoff Gallery (Nov. 1979).

MOAT MOUNTAIN AND SUMMER CLOUDS.
    9 x 14 (22.9 x 35.6).
    Emigh, Eugene and Katherine, dealers.

MOUNT CHOCORUA, CONWAY, NH.
    1859. Pencil and ink.
    Emigh, Eugene and Katherine, dealers.

MOUNT CHOCORUA FROM CONWAY (Moat Mountain from Intervale).
    Pencil on paper.
    12⅜ x 19⅜ (31.4 x 49.2).
    Hirschl and Adler Gallery (1976).

MOUNT CHOCORUA, CONWAY.
    1854. Oil.
    6 x 10 (15.2 x 25.4).

New Hampshire Scenery

Emigh, Eugene and Katherine, dealers (sold May 1980).

MOUNT CHOCORUA, NH. S/D/L/L.
   1858. Oil on canvas.
   9 x 17 (22.9 x 43.2).
   Private collection; New Britain Museum of American Art exhibition (1970), #59.

MOUNT MOOSILAUKEE, RAVINE AND BAKER RIVER, BENTON, NH. S/L/R.
   1864. Oil on wood.
   5 x 15 (12.7 x 38.1).
   Emigh, Eugene and Katherine, dealers (1983).

MOUNT WASHINGTON AND JEFFERSON FROM SHELBOURNE [sic], NH.
   Aug. 1858. Sketch.
   Emigh, Eugene and Katherine, dealers.

MOUNT WASHINGTON AND THE PRESIDEN-TIAL RANGE.
   1858. Oil on board.
   10¼ x 17⅞ (26 x 45.4).
   Richard Bourne, Inc., catalog (Oct. 1976); New Britain Museum of American Art (1970), #67.

MOUNT WASHINGTON AND THE SACO RIVER.
   1858. Oil on masonite.
   10¼ x 20⅞ (or 19⅞) (26 x 53).
   Emigh, Eugene and Katherine, dealers (1978); Hirschl and Adler Gallery (1976).

MOUNT WASHINGTON FROM GREEN HILL STUDIO, JACKSON.
   1858. Oil on canvas.
   12 x 17 (30.5 x 43.2).
   Emigh, Eugene and Katherine, dealers (1973).

MOUNT WASHINGTON FROM NORTH CON-WAY. S/L/L.
   10½ x 16½ (26.7 x 41.9).
   Vose Galleries.

MOUNT WASHINGTON, ADAMS AND DOUBLEHEAD – SUMMER, 1858.
   1858. Oil.
   10 x 18 (25.4 x 45.7).
   New Britain Museum of American Art exhibition (1981), #30; Emigh, Eugene and Katherine, dealers.

MOUNT WASHINGTON, AUTUMN GLORY. S/L/R.
   1864. Oil on cardboard.
   9 x 15 (22.9 x 38.1).
   Private collection (1980); University Art Gallery catalog, University of New Hampshire (1980), #42.

MOUNT WASHINGTON, JULY 22 '59.
   1859. Pencil and ink.

Emigh, Eugene and Katherine, dealers.

MOUNT WASHINGTON, NEW HAMPSHIRE.
   1854.
   5½ x 9 (14 x 22.9).
   Chapellier Gallery (1976).

MOUNT WASHINGTON, PRESIDENTIAL RANGE. S/L/L.
   1858. Oil on canvas.
   12¼ x 17 (31.1 x 43.2).
   New Britain Museum of American Art exhibition (1970), plate 11; Emigh, Eugene and Katherine, dealers.

MOUNTAIN STREAM, JULY, 1858, WHITE MOUNTAINS; THE. . .S/D/L/L.
   July 1858. Pencil on paper.
   12 x 9 (30.5 x 22.9).
   Emigh, Eugene and Katherine, dealers (1980); University Art Gallery catalog, University of New Hampshire (1980), #120.

NEAR GORHAM, NEW HAMPSHIRE.
   Brooklyn Art Association (1863), #183.

NEAR LANCASTER, NEW HAMPSHIRE. S/D/L/L.
   1862. Oil.
   7½ x 12 (19.1 x 30.5).
   Sotheby PB (June 24, 1980); Oakland Museum; Berry Hill Galleries (1983).

NEW HAMPSHIRE SCENERY.
   14 x 23 (35.6 x 58.4).
   NAD, 1857, #114.

NO. 4 IN THE WHITE MOUNTAINS, NH.
   C. 1854. Oil on cardboard.
   5 x 9¼ (12.7 x 23.5).
   Private collection; New Britain Museum of American Art exhibition (1970), #40.

NORTH CONWAY. S/D/L/L.
   10½ x 16½ (26.7 x 41.9).
   Vose Galleries.

NORTH CONWAY, AUG. 1854 (Echo Lake and Eagle Cliff).
   1854. Sketch.
   Emigh, Eugene and Katherine, dealers.

ON MT. MORIAH, JULY 7, 1858, MOTE [sic] MOUNTAIN IN DISTANCE.
   1858. Sketch.
   Emigh, Eugene and Katherine, dealers.

ON THE GLEN ROAD.
   C. 1854. Pencil.
   10¾ x 15 (27.3 x 38.1).
   Emigh, Eugene and Katherine, dealers; New Britain Museum of American Art exhibition (1970), #39.

OSSIPEE VALLEY AND BEARCAMP RIVER, NH.
S/L/L.
   1854 or 1859.
   10 x 16 (25.4 x 40.6).
   Emigh, Eugene and Katherine, dealers;
   Chapellier Gallery (1975).

PINES ON MOAT MOUNTAIN, NEW
HAMPSHIRE.
   C. 1860. Oil on canvas.
   13 x 19½ (33 x 49.5).
   Private collection (1983).

PRESIDENTIAL RANGE AND CENTRAL VALLEY,
NH. S/L/L.
   1859. Oil.
   10 x 18 (25.4 x 45.7).
   Emigh, Eugene and Katherine, dealers.

PRESIDENTIAL RANGE, AUTUMN.
   1856.
   Lion Gallery (1976).

RED CLOUDS OVER DARK INTERVALE LEDGES.
   1854.
   10 x 16 (25.4 x 40.6).
   Chapellier Gallery (1975).

REMINISCENCE OF THE ANDROSCOGGIN.
   NAD, May 1859, p. 153.

SACO RIVER, CONWAY (Mount Washington, Jefferson, Adams).
   1854.
   9½ x 13 (24.1 x 33).
   Emigh, Eugene and Katherine, dealers.

SANDWICH RANGE FROM OSSIPEE LAKE, NH.
S/L/R.
   1856. Oil on canvas.
   12 x 20 (30.5 x 50.8).
   Shore Gallery, Boston (1970).

SUNSET AT LANCASTER, NEW HAMPSHIRE.
S/L/L.
   1859. Oil.
   8½ x 14 (21.6 x 35.6). Arch.
   Vassar College Art Gallery (1973); New Britain Museum of American Art (1970), plate 17.

SUNSET ON MOAT MOUNTAIN. S/L/R.
   1859. Oil.
   13 x 20 (33 x 50.8).
   Vassar College Art Gallery (1973); New Britain Museum of American Art exhibition (1970), #62.

SUNSET OVER MOUNT THORN, NORTH CONWAY, NH.
   1854. Oil on board.
   9 x 13 (22.9 x 33).
   Baridoff Gallery (July 11, 1981).

VALLEY SCENE IN THE WHITE MOUNTAINS.
   C. 1860. Oil on cardboard.
   10 x 17 (25.4 x 43.2). Oval.
   Emigh, Eugene and Katherine, dealers; New Britain Museum of American Art exhibition (1970), #71.

WHITE HILLS IN OCTOBER. S/L/L.
   1868. Oil on cardboard.
   48 x 72 (121.9 x 182.9).
   University of Utah, Art Galleries, Salt Lake City, UT; Brooklyn Art Association (1873), #214; C&H, (see Standard Source Reference List).

WHITE MOUNTAIN SCENERY.
   22 x 37 (55.9 x 94).
   Leeds Gallery Auction Sale (April 1859), p. 126.

WHITE MOUNTAINS.
   Oil.
   Leonard Auction (Dec. 6, 1861).

WHITE MOUNTAINS, NH, SACO RIVER.
   C. 1858. Oil on paper.
   10¼ x 20 (26 x 50.8).
   Emigh, Eugene and Katherine, dealers; New Britain Museum of American Art exhibition (1970), #58.

WOODS AND WATERFALL.
   1859.
   North Conway Library Exhibition (1965).

Attributed:
COMING STORM, CONWAY MEADOWS.
   Oil on canvas.
   15½ x 23½ (39.4 x 59.7).
   Private collection (1983).

SHEARER, CHRISTOPHER H.
F(sup), G&W, N
Born Reading, PA?, 1840.
Died Reading, PA, April 29, 1926.
Shearer exhibited at the NAD in 1881 and at the Brooklyn Art Association in 1874 and 1882. He also sent paintings to the Massachusetts Charitable Mechanic Association in Boston, exhibiting landscapes.

FLUME, WHITE MOUNTAINS; THE. . .S/L/L.
   Oil on canvas.
   24¼ x 14 (61.6 x 35.6).
   Richard Bourne, Inc., catalog (Oct. 1976).

New Hampshire Scenery

JUNE IN THE WHITE HILLS. S/D/L/R.
  1871 or 1875. (possibly two paintings).
  Oil on canvas.
  36 x 29 (91.4 x 73.7).
  Richard Bourne, Inc., catalog (Aug. 6, 1974).
SCENE IN THE WHITE MOUNTAINS.
  MA Charitable (1878), #19.
SCENE IN THE WHITE MOUNTAINS.
  MA Charitable (1878), #60.

SHED, C. D.

*The Providence, RI, city directory for 1884
listed him as a miniature and ornamental
painter.*

Information courtesy of Vose Galleries.

HIGH PEAK, NORTH CONWAY, NEW
HAMPSHIRE.
  Pre-1877; San Francisco Art Association
  (1874) (see New York Public Library for
  information).

SHERMAN, G. B.

Active 1887.
There is presently no information on this artist.
BROADS, LAKE WINNEPESAUKEE [sic].
  1887. Oil.
  21 x 36 (53.3 x 91.4).
  NMAA Inventory.
LAKE CHOCORUA WITH MOUNTAIN IN
BACKGROUND.
  C. 1887. Oil.
  24 x 36 (61 x 91.4).
  NMAA Inventory.

SHINDLER, ANTONIO ZENO

F, G&W, K, Ka, R, S
Born Germany, c. 1813 or 1823.
Died Washington, DC, 1899.
*Shindler's real name was Antonio Zeno, but he
adopted the name of Shindler from a person he
admired. A pastelist, he taught drawing in
Philadelphia in the 1850s, during which time he
exhibited at the PAFA. In 1876 he was employed
by the United States National Museum working
as an artist and colorist of exhibits. He was
respected for the accuracy of his work.*
FRANCONIA MOUNTAINS, THE POOL.
  PAFA, 1859.
FRANCONIA, CATARACT.
  PAFA, 1854.
FRANCONIA, ECHO LAKE.
  PAFA, 1860.

GREAT STONE FACE.
  PAFA, 1854.
PAMASAWASEE [sic] RIVER.
  PAFA, 1860.
PLYMOUTH, NEW HAMPSHIRE.
  PAFA, 1857.
PROFILE MOUNTAIN.
  PAFA, 1854.

SILSBEE, MARTHA

Co, F
Born Salem, MA, 1858. Died after 1899.
*Silsbee was a watercolorist who belonged to the
Boston Water Color Club and exhibited at the
Boston Art Club in 1899.*
MONADNOCK.
  Boston Art Club (1899), #193.

SLAYTON, M. E.

Nothing is presently known about this artist.
PRESIDENTIAL RANGE, NH.
  1899. Oil on canvas.
  28 x 36 (71.1 x 91.4).
  Private collection (1975); BIAP.

SMILLIE, GEORGE HENRY

A, C&H, DAB, F, G&W, K, N, R, S
Born New York, NY, Dec. 29, 1840.
Died Bronxville, NY, Nov. 10, 1921.
*Smillie first studied under his father, James
Smillie, and then with James M. Hart in 1861.
The following year he exhibited at the NAD and
was elected an associate in 1864. He shared a
studio for many years with his brother, James
David Smillie, and his wife, the artist Nellie
Sheldon Jacobs. In 1868 he exhibited at the
Boston Athenaeum and, in the 1860s and 1870s,
visited the White Mountains. He became a full
member of the NAD in 1882 and was very ac-
tive in the institution, acting as treasurer and
recording secretary. He was also a member of
the American Society of Painters in Water
Colors.*
VIEW OF THE ARTIST'S BROOK, CONWAY.
  Boston Athenaeum (1868), #314.

SMILLIE, JAMES

B, Ce, C&H, DAB, E, F, G&W, N, T
Born Edinburgh, Scotland, Nov. 23, 1807.
Died Poughkeepsie, NY, Dec. 4, 1885.

Smillie was apprenticed to a silver engraver at a very early age and worked with his father in the jewelry business as well as doing engravings for his brother. He moved to Quebec with his family in 1821 and, after a brief visit to England, moved to New York City in 1829 where he was able to find work as an engraver with the help of Asher B. Durand. Although he did some work in watercolor, he was best known for his bank note and fine steel engravings, among them Thomas Cole's *VOYAGE OF LIFE* and John Kensett's *MOUNT WASHINGTON FROM THE VALLEY OF CONWAY* as well as others by Hart, Tait, Bierstadt, Shattuck, and Casilear. He exhibited at the NAD from 1832 to 1881. He was elected an associate member of the NAD in 1832 and a full member in 1853, one of the few engravers to receive such an honor. He was considered the best engraver in the U.S.

A GLIMPSE IN NEW HAMPSHIRE.
    NAD, 1858, #247.

MOUNT WASHINGTON FROM THE VALLEY OF CONWAY (after Kensett).
    NAD, 1852, #266; C&H (see Standard Source Reference List).

ON THE SACO, NEAR NORTH CONWAY.
    Watercolor.
    Brooklyn Art Association (1877), #337.

SMILLIE, JAMES DAVID
DAB, F, G&W, Ka, N, R, S
Born New York, NY, Jan. 16, 1833.
Died New York, NY, Sept. 14, 1909.
Smillie was a son of the engraver, James Smillie, and learned his trade from his father with whom he worked until he visited Europe in 1864. He also practiced etching, lithography, aquatint, drypoint, and landscape painting. He was a founder of the American Society of Painters in Water Colors and the New York Etching Club, and an officer of the NAD, to which he was elected in 1876. He exhibited at the NAD from 1864 to 1898 and at the PAFA, and was a member of the Century Association from 1877 to 1909. He was particularly fond of depicting mountain scenery.

MOAT MOUNTAIN FROM WHITE HORSE LEDGE, NEW HAMPSHIRE.
    NAD, 1868, #319.

ON THE SACO NEAR CRAWFORD'S [sic] NOTCH, NEW HAMPSHIRE.
    NAD, 1868, #67.

STUDY, NORTH CONWAY (Moat Mountain) (or UNFINISHED STUDY). S/D/L/L.
    1867. Oil on canvas.
    15 x 26 (38.1 x 66).
    Unlocated.

WHITE MOUNTAINS FROM RANDOLPH HILL (2).
    Watercolor.
    Pre-1877; NAD, Watercolor Show (1867-68); Utica (NY) Art Association (1868).

SMITH, FRANCIS HOPKINSON
A, B, C&H, DAB, F, G&W, N, S
Born Baltimore, MD, Oct. 23, 1838.
Died New York, NY, April 7, 1915.
Smith came from an old Baltimore family that had been reduced to poverty by the time Smith was in his teens. He began painting at the age of nine and was entirely self-taught. He was an iron merchant for a few years with his brother, then went into engineering, saving his artistic endeavors for his spare time. He exhibited at the NAD in 1868 and 1880 and at the Brooklyn Art Association from 1875 to 1891. He spent six weeks a summer in the White Mountains sketching in watercolors and charcoal from 1865 to 1880. He was once quoted as saying, "More than an hour spoils a charcoal sketch," and often finished three large pictures in a day and was thus able to illustrate numerous books of travel, poetry, and fiction. He belonged to the Tile Club in New York City and the Century Association from 1875 to 1909. He was well known in the many fields he attempted to explore: art, engineering, writing, and lecturing.
Bibliography:
Aldine 9:6, pp. 195-198.
Foster, Kathleen A. "The Watercolor Scandal of 1882: An American Salon des Réfuses." *Archives of American Art Journal* 19:2 (1979), pp. 19-25.
Sheldon, G. W. *American Painters.* New York: Appleton and Co., 1879, pp. 120-122.

A COOL SPOT (WALKER'S POND).
    1875.
    Private collection; C&H (see Standard Source Reference List).

A GLIMPSE OF FRANCONIA NOTCH, NH. S/D/L/L.
    Engraving.

Art Journal (1878), pp. 362-364; Sheldon, G. W. *American Painters* (1879), p. 122.

BALD MOUNTAIN ROCK, NEW HAMPSHIRE.
Watercolor.
Pre-1877; American Society of Painters in Watercolors exhibition (1879).

CANNON MOUNTAIN CLIFF – WHITE MOUNTAINS.
1879. Illustration.
Aldine 9:6, pp. 195-198.

EAGLE CLIFF, WHITE MOUNTAINS.
1879.
Aldine 9:6, pp. 195-198; Pre-1877; American Society of Painters in Water Colors exhibition (1879).

FRANCONIA MOUNTAINS, NEW HAMPSHIRE.
Watercolor.
Pre-1877; American Society of Painters in Water Colors exhibition (1879).

IN THE DARKLING WOOD (WHITE MOUNTAIN AUTUMN SCENE).
52 x 34 (132 x 86.4).
Private collection.

MOUNT LINCOLN FROM BLACK MOUNTAIN, FRANCONIA NOTCH.
Watercolor.
Pre-1877; American Society of Painters in Water Colors exhibition (1879).

OLD CEDARS, FRANCONIA MOUNTAINS.
American Society of Painters in Water Colors (1876); C&H (see Standard Source Reference List).

OLD MAN OF THE MOUNTAINS.
American Society of Painters in Water Colors (1874); C&H (see Standard Source Reference List).

OVER THE BRIDGE, FRANCONIA, NEW HAMPSHIRE.
Brooklyn Art Association (1876), #183; *Aldine* 9:6, pp. 195-198.

OVERLOOK FALLS AND WALKER'S FALLS, FRANCONIA NOTCH.
American Society of Painters in Water Colors (1875); C&H (see Standard Source Reference List); Pre-1877.

PROFILE NOTCH.
Charcoal.
American Society of Painters in Water Colors (1876); C&H (see Standard Source Reference List).

SUMMER IN THE WOODS, WHITE MOUNTAINS.
Watercolor.

American Society of Painters in Watercolors (1871); C&H (see Standard Source Reference List); Pre-1877.

WINTER IN THE WOODS, WHITE MOUNTAINS, NEW HAMPSHIRE.
Watercolor.
Pre-1877; American Society of Painters in Water Colors (1872).

SMITH, JOHN ROWSON

DAB, G&W, R
Born Boston, MA, May 11, 1810.
Died Philadelphia, PA, March 21, 1864.
Smith studied under his father, John Rubens Smith, whose pupils later included Sanford Robinson Gifford. The elder Smith was primarily an engraver and lithographer, but his son became a scenery painter, working after 1832 in Philadelphia, New Orleans, St. Louis, and other cities. About the end of the 1830s, John Rowson took up panoramic painting, and his most successful example, a panorama of the Mississippi River, was exhibited in both the U.S. and Europe. He went to Europe in 1848 and afterward settled in New Jersey, where he painted scenery for theaters in New York and the South.

Bibliography:
Smith, Edward S. "Recollections of John Rowson Smith." MS, New York Public Library.

WHITE MOUNTAINS SUNRISE WITH INDIANS.
S/D/L/Center.
1841. Oil on panel.
20 x 24 (50.8 x 61).
University Art Gallery catalog, University of New Hampshire (1980), #88; G&W (see Standard Source Reference List).

SMITH, L. L. (or C.)

Possibly **Letta Crapo Smith.**
N, R, S
Born Flint, MI, 1862.
Died Boston, MA, 1921.
L. L. Smith worked in oils and exhibited at the NAD in 1892.

MOUNT WASHINGTON FROM NORTH CONWAY.
Pre-1877; Utica (NY) Art Association (1867).

VIEW OF MOUNT WASHINGTON.
Pre-1877; Buffalo (NY) Fine Arts Academy (Dec. 23, 1866).

SMITH, [WILLIAM THOMPSON] RUSSELL

A, C, C&H, DAB, F, G&W, R, S, T
Born Glasgow, Scotland, April 26, 1812.
Died Glenside, PA, Nov. 8, 1898.

Russell Smith settled in western Pennsylvania with his family when he was seven and learned the trade of tool and cutlery manufacturing from his father. Painting instruction came from James Reid Lambdin of Pittsburgh in 1828. After three years of study, he began the serious pursuit of painting theater scenery and portraits. Throughout his life, Smith, who was known as just Russell Smith for most of his career, continued to paint scenery for theaters in Philadelphia, Boston, Washington, DC, and Baltimore. His summers were spent traveling and painting the mountain landscapes in New Hampshire and New York. Smith married Mary Priscilla Wilson, accomplished painter of flowers, in 1838. Their two children also became proficient painters. In 1851-52 he traveled with his family to Europe and painted a panoramic view of the Holy Land. Smith was elected a member of the Artist's Fund Society and of the PAFA, where he also served as a member of the board. He was elected to the Century Association in 1848 but resigned in 1855. He devoted his final years to landscape painting.

Bibliography:
Archives of American Art. Roll 2036, P23.
Lewis, Virginia E. *Russell Smith: Romantic Realist.* Pittsburgh: University of Pittsburgh Press, 1956.
New Hampshire Landscapes, 1848-1850 by Russell Smith (1812-1896). Boston: Vose Galleries, 1979.
Pennsylvania Landscapes, 1834-1892 by Russell Smith (1812-1896). Boston: Vose Galleries, 1979.

AT CRAWFORD'S [sic] NOTCH.
  1849.
  Lewis, Virginia. *Russell Smith: Romantic Realist*, pp. 124, seq.

CHOCORUA.
  Lewis. *Russell Smith*, pp. 124, seq.

CHOCORUA PEAK, NEW HAMPSHIRE.
  1851.
  8¼ x 12¼ (21 x 31.1).
  Parke-Bernet (1945); NMAA Inventory.

CRAWFORD HOUSE AND SACO LAKE.
  Tamworth (NH) Bicentennial Show.

IN THE FALLS OF THE SACO.
  Sept. 20, 1849. Watercolor sketch.
  7 x 9¾ (17.8 x 24.8).
  Private collection (1983); Vose Galleries (1978).

IN THE NOTCH.
  1895?
  Private collection.

LAKE OF AMMONOOSUCK [sic].
  1849.
  Lewis. *Russell Smith*, pp. 124, seq.

LAKE OF THE CLOUDS, MOUNT WASHINGTON.
S/L/L.
  1867. Oil on canvas.
  24 x 36⅜ (61 x 92.4).
  Private collection (1979).

LAKE WINNEPESAUKEE [sic].
  Lewis. *Russell Smith*, pp. 124, seq.

MOUNT FRANKLIN, WHITE MOUNTAINS.
S/D/L/L.
  Sept. 17, 1848. Oil on canvas.
  24 x 36 (61 x 91.4).
  Kennedy Galleries (1980); University Art Gallery catalog, University of New Hampshire (1980), #15.

MOUNT KEARSARGE.
  Lewis. *Russell Smith*, pp. 124, seq.; PAFA, 1849, 1851.

MOUNT LAFAYETTE FROM THE AMNOWOOSUCK [sic].
  1851. Oil.
  7⅝ x 11⅝ (19.4 x 29.5).
  Mead Art Gallery (1973); NMAA Inventory.

MOUNT WASHINGTON.
  PAFA, 1851, 1868.

MOUNT WASHINGTON.
  1848-85. Oil.
  12 x 18 (30.5 x 45.7).
  Parke-Bernet (1963); NMAA Inventory.

MOUNT WASHINGTON FROM THE SACO.
  1843. Oil on canvas.
  12 x 18 (30.5 x 45.7).
  Private collection (1976); NMAA Inventory.

NEAR BETHLEHEM
  PAFA, 1851.

NORTH CONWAY, NEW HAMPSHIRE.
  Private collection (1967); NMAA Inventory.

NOTCH, WHITE MOUNTAINS, NEW HAMPSHIRE; THE... S/D/L/L.
  1867. Oil on canvas.
  24 x 36⅜ (61 x 92.4).
  Private collection (1979).

New Hampshire Scenery

Mount Washington from Ellis River Meadows, Jackson, N.H.
Frank S. Shapleigh, 1882
Oil on canvas, 26 1/8" x 45 1/4" / Collection: William Nathaniel
    Banks / Ref. page 142

NOTCH, WHITE MOUNTAINS; THE...
    1848. Oil.
    11¼ x 16 (28.6 x 40.6).
    Private collection (1983); Vose Galleries
    (1979).
OLD MAN OF THE MOUNTAIN, FRANCONIA
NOTCH, NH.
    1864. Oil.
    38 x 51 (96.5 x 129.5).
    Sotheby PB (1974); NMAA Inventory.
OLD MAN OF THE MOUNTAINS. S/D/L/R.
    1864. Oil on canvas.
    55½ x 44 (141 x 109.2).
    Elizabeth R. Daniel, dealer (1977); NMAA
    Inventory; *Antiques* (April 1977).
OSSIPEE LAKE.
    Kennedy Galleries.
OSSIPEE MOUNTAIN FROM CENTRE HARBOR.
S/L/L.
    Oil.
    12 x 18 (30.5 x 45.7).
    Vose Galleries.

OSSIPEE MOUNTAIN, FROM THE LAKE, NEW
HAMPSHIRE.
    Oil.
    35 x 56 (88.9 x 142.2).
    Kennedy *Quarterly* 10:4 (1971); NMAA
    Inventory.
POND NEAR LAKE WINNIPESAUKEE, NEW
HAMPSHIRE.
    1869. Oil.
    24½ x 36 (62.2 x 91.4).
    Private collection (1960); NMAA Inventory.
SACO, MOOSE HILL.
    Lewis. *Russell Smith*, pp. 124, seq.
SQUAM LAKE FROM GARNET HILL. S/L/L.
    Oil on canvas.
    18 x 24 (45.7 x 61).
    Private collection; Kennedy Galleries.
SQUAM LAKE, NEW HAMPSHIRE.
    Oil.
    12 x 18 (30.5 x 45.7).
    Kennedy *Quarterly* 10:4 (1971); NMAA
    Inventory.

Dictionary of Painters

VIEW OF CHOCORUA.
C. 1848.
On the Boston Museum Theatre Curtain.

VIEW OF PEQUAWKET AND CHOCORUA PEAK,
NEW HAMPSHIRE.
C. 1867. Oil.
36 x 24 (91.4 x 61).
Vose Galleries (1979).

VIEW OF SQUAM LAKE, NEW HAMPSHIRE.
Oil on canvas.
11¼ x 17½ (28.6 x 44.6).
Private collection (1983); Kennedy Galleries
(1979).

WINNEPSAUKEE [sic] FROM NEAR CENTER
HARBOR.
Oil.
8 x 11 (20.3 x 27.9).
Vose Galleries (1979); *Antiques* (Feb. 1979).

SMITH, XANTHUS RUSSELL
DAB, G&W, S, T
Born Philadelphia, PA, Feb. 26, 1839.
Died Edgehill, PA, Dec. 2, 1929.
*Xanthus Smith was brought up in an artistic
household where both his mother, Mary, and
his father, Russell, were artists. Though he
studied medicine at the University of Pennsylvania for two years, he soon changed to
painting and took courses at the PAFA and at
the Royal Academy in London. He entered the
Civil War after his return from England
thereafter devoting himself to marines. He kept
a summer home on an island in Casco Bay, ME,
and a studio in Philadelphia.*

MOTE [sic] MOUNTAIN FROM ECHO LAKE, NEW
HAMPSHIRE.
1863? Oil.
12 x 20 (30.5 x 50.8).
Kennedy Galleries (1972).

SMYTH, EUGENE L.
Active 1891.
*No information is presently available on this
artist.*

MOUNT KEARSARGE . S/D.
1891.
Private collection.

SNELL, GEORGE
There is no information on this artist at present.

THE BROOK, NORTH CONWAY.
Boston Art Club (May 1874), #5.

SNOWE, W. FRANCIS
Active 1870-74.
Nothing is presently known about this artist.

CONWAY MEADOWS (MOTE [sic] MOUNTAIN).
S/D/L/L.
1870. Oil on canvas.
15 x 34½ (38.1 x 87.6).
Private collection (1979).

NEW HAMPSHIRE SCENERY.
Leonard Auction (June 5, 1874), #51.

VIEW NEAR WHITEFIELD, NEW HAMPSHIRE.
Leonard Auction (May 23, 1871), #69.

WHITE MOUNTAINS FROM GUILDHALL.
Leonard Auction (May 23, 1871), #45.

SOMMER (or SOMMERS), OTTO
A, F, N, T
*There is almost no information on this
obviously competent artist, but the name would
suggest a European background. Sommer exhibited at the NAD from 1862 to 1866 and at
the Boston Athenaeum in 1864. The titles all
seem to be American views, but none is of the
White Mountains. One of his works,
WESTWARD HO! or CROSSING THE
PLAINS, is in the Capitol in Washington, DC.
His first known landscape is of the Passaic River
and is dated 1860. One of his landscapes, sold
at auction in 1867, brought $150, a respectable
sum for the period. It is probable that he never
came to the White Mountains but used engravings as his guide. His view of Mount
Washington is a direct copy of Kensett's
MOUNT WASHINGTON FROM THE
VALLEY OF CONWAY, which was engraved
by James Smillie and widely circulated.*

VIEW OF CONWAY VALLEY (Mount Washington)
(after Kensett). S/L/R.
C. 1860-65. Oil on canvas.
31 x 46 (78.7 x 116.8).
Private collection (1980); University Art
Gallery catalog, University of New Hampshire (1980), #122; Old Print Shop (1970).

SONNTAG (or SONTAG), WILLIAM LOUIS
A, B, C, Ce, C&H, F, G&W, K, N, R, T
Born East Liberty (now part of Pittsburgh), PA,
March 2, 1822.
Died New York, NY, Jan. 22, 1900.
*Sonntag began his artistic career in 1842 in Cin-
cinnati and worked there until 1853, when he
first visited Europe, staying mainly in Florence.
He returned to the U.S. briefly, then recom-
menced study in Florence two years later, after*

New Hampshire Scenery

establishing himself as an artist in New York City. In 1861 the NAD elected him a member, and Sonntag exhibited there throughout his career. He spent his summers sketching in the mountains of New England and West Virginia, or abroad in Florence. Sonntag is best known today for his romantic Italian and American landscapes in the Hudson River School tradition, but, in fact, he never painted the Hudson River at all. His only son, William Sonntag, Jr., became an artist and illustrator as well, but died before he reached the age of 30. Sonntag outlived his son by a year.

Bibliography:
Moure, Nancy Dustin Wall. *William Louis Sonntag: Artist of the Ideal, 1822-1900.* Goldfield Galleries: Los Angeles, 1980.

A HILLSIDE, NEW HAMPSHIRE.
NAD, 1885, #563.

A MOUNTAIN STREAM FROM THE FOOT OF MOUNT CARTER, NEW HAMPSHIRE.
NAD, 1888, #348.

A STUDY FROM NATURE IN NEW HAMPSHIRE.
NAD, 1868, #173; 1869, #172.

A VIEW ON THE RATTLE RIVER, NH. S/L/L.
C. 1887. Oil on canvas.
24 x 36 (61 x 91.4).
Berkshire Museum, Pittsfield, MA (1983).

AMONG THE TANGLED WOODS OF NEW HAMPSHIRE.
NAD, 1880, #237.

AN ISLAND IN THE ANDROSCOGGIN, NEW HAMPSHIRE.
Boston Art Association (1871), #64.

AN OCTOBER DAY IN THE PEMIGEWASSET, PLYMOUTH, NEW HAMPSHIRE.
Oil.
16 x 24 (40.6 x 61).
Sotheby PB (1971); NMAA Inventory.

AUTUMN IN NEW HAMPSHIRE.
C. 1865. Oil.
20¼ x 36¼ (51.4 x 92.1).
Milwaukee (WI) Art Center (1976); NMAA Inventory.

BURBANKS LAKE NEAR SHELBURNE, NEW HAMPSHIRE.
NAD, 1884, #169.

CANNON MOUNTAIN FROM A POINT NEAR BETHLEHEM, NEW HAMPSHIRE.
NAD, 1887, #389.

CARTER DOME FROM CARTER LAKE. S/L/L.
C. 1880. Watercolor.
13⅝ x 14⅛ (34.6 x 35.9).

Cooper-Hewitt Museum; University Art Gallery catalog, University of New Hampshire (1980), #65.

CLEARING, A MOUNTAIN FOREST. S/L/L.
Oil on canvas.
20 x 31 (50.8 x 78.7).
Richard Bourne, Inc., catalog (Oct. 1976).

CLEARING UP – A VIEW NEAR BERLIN FALLS.
NAD, 1889, #177.

CLEMENT'S BROOK, NEW HAMPSHIRE – AN OUTDOOR STUDY.
NAD, 1878, #683; C&H (see Standard Source Reference List).

CLEMENT'S FALLS, NEW HAMPSHIRE.
NAD, 1886, #264.

EAGLE CLIFF, NEW HAMPSHIRE.
Oil.
6¾ x 10¾ (17.1 x 27.3).
Sotheby PB (1977); NMAA Inventory.

EDGE OF A POND, NEW HAMPSHIRE.
Oil.
20 x 36 (50.8 x 91.4).
Hirschl and Adler Gallery (1978); Sotheby PB (1971 and 1977); NMAA Inventory.

FOG RISING OFF MOUNT ADAMS.
NAD, 1882, #44; F (see Standard Source Reference List).

GREY MORNING (the Ossipee Mountains).
1898. Oil on canvas.
20 x 31 (50.8 x 78.7).
Private collection (1975); BIAP.

IN THE NOTCH. S/D/L/R.
1899. Oil on panel.
19¼ x 30½ (48.9 x 77.5).
Oliver Auction, Kennebunk, ME (Nov. 6, 1981), #7.

IN THE NOTCH. S/D/L/R.
1899. Oil on canvas.
20 x 31½ (50.8 x 80).
Sotheby PB (1983), #151.

IN THE WHITE MOUNTAINS, NEW HAMPSHIRE. S/D.
1876. Oil on canvas.
23¼ x 37½ (59 x 95.3).
The White House, Washington, DC (1978); NMAA Inventory; *Antiques* (March 1976), p. 393.

IN THE WOODS, NEW HAMPSHIRE.
NAD, 1896, #44.

INGALL'S BROOK, NEW HAMPSHIRE.
NAD, 1886, #531.

MASCOT LAKE, NEW HAMPSHIRE.
NAD, 1885, #221.

MILLBROOK, NEAR SHELBOURNE [sic], NEW HAMPSHIRE (or ON MILLBROOK, NEW HAMPSHIRE). S/L/L.
Oil on canvas.
20 x 36 (50.8 x 91.4).
Baridoff Gallery auction (July 11, 1981); Vose Galleries (1978); Boston Art Association (1879), #159.

MORNING IN THE WHITE MOUNTAINS.
NAD, 1881, #375.

MOUNT ADAMS FROM RANDOLPH HILL, NEW HAMPSHIRE.
NAD, 1872, #204.

MOUNT HAYS [sic], NEW HAMPSHIRE.
NAD, 1886, #403.

MOUNT MORIAH FROM THE LEDGE NEAR SHELBURNE.
NAD, 1890, #372.

MOUNT SURPRISE FROM THE ANDROSCOGGIN.
NAD, 1893, #198.

MOUNT WILLARD, NH.
Oil on canvas.
21 x 35 (53.3 x 88.9).
Private collection (1973); BIAP.

MOUNTAIN CASCADE; THE... S/L/L.
Oil on canvas.
23¼ x 31¼ (59 x 79.5).
Signal Co. (1983).

MOUNTAIN LAKE. S/L/L.
Oil on canvas.
16 x 24 (40.6 x 61).
Baridoff Gallery auction (Nov. 1982), #45.

MOUNTAIN LANDSCAPE.
1854. Oil on canvas.
32 x 48 (81.3 x 121.9).
Hackley Art Museum, Muskegon, MI.

MOUNTAINS NEAR GORHAM, NEW HAMPSHIRE.
NAD, 1890 or 1893, #652.

MT. ADAMS.
Pre-1877; Louisville (KY) Industrial Exposition (1874).

NEAR LANCASTER, NEW HAMPSHIRE.
Boston Art Association (1871), #29.

NEAR PLYMOUTH, NEW HAMPSHIRE.
Oil on canvas.
12 x 17 (30.5 x 43.2).
Private collection (1983); Christie's (Nov. 3, 1977), #99; *Aldine* #4 (April 1874), p. 88.

NEW HAMPSHIRE HILLS.
Boston Art Association (1879), #333.

NEW HAMPSHIRE LANDSCAPE, WHITE MOUNTAINS.
18 x 26 (45.7 x 66).
Richard Bourne, Inc., catalog (1976), #98.

NEW HAMPSHIRE SCENE.
C. 1880.
Wellesley College.

NEW HAMPSHIRE SCENERY.
Brooklyn Art Association (1867), #111.

OCTOBER IN THE WHITE MOUNTAINS.
Brooklyn Art Association (1864), #29; Pre-1877.

OCTOBER MORNING IN NEW HAMPSHIRE.
1881. Oil.
16 x 26 (40.6 x 66).
Detroit Institute of Fine Arts (1965); NMAA Inventory.

OCTOBER, NEW HAMPSHIRE.
Boston Art Association (1879), #178.

ON THE ANDROSCOGGIN.
Boston Art Association (1866), #30; Boston Athenaeum (1869), #244.

ON THE ANDROSCOGGIN RIVER.
NAD, 1890, #390.

ON THE GLEN ROAD TO MOUNT WASHINGTON, NEW HAMPSHIRE.
NAD, 1886, #803.

ON WILD RIVER, NEW HAMPSHIRE.
NAD, 1867, #185.

OSSIPEE VALLEY, NEW HAMPSHIRE.
Oil.
20 x 31 (50.8 x 78.7).
Alexander Gallery (1978); NMAA Inventory.

PLYMOUTH MOUNTAIN. S/L/L.
Oil on canvas.
11¼ x 16½ (28.6 x 41.9).
Private collection (1978).

RAIN IN THE WHITE MOUNTAINS. S/L/L.
Portland Museum of Art, Percival Baxter collection; Frick Art Reference Library.

SCENE IN THE WHITE MOUNTAINS.
Oil on canvas.
16 ¹/₁₆ x 24 (40.8 x 61).
Brooklyn Museum (1976).

New Hampshire Scenery

SCENE IN THE WHITE MOUNTAINS. S/L/L.
Oil on canvas.
15½ x 23½ (39.4 x 59.7).
Brooklyn Museum.

STUDY OF A BIG POND IN NEW HAMPSHIRE.
12⅛ x 20¼ (30.8 x 51.2).
Christie's (1980).

SUMMER AFTERNOON, NEW HAMPSHIRE.
Boston Art Association (1878), #238.

SUNSET NEAR BETHLEHEM.
NAD, 1871, #379; C&H (see Standard Source Reference List).

TOP OF A MOUNTAIN, NEW HAMPSHIRE.
Boston Art Association (1879), #245.

VIEW IN NEW HAMPSHIRE, STUDY FROM NATURE.
Boston Art Association (1878), #314.

VIEW IN THE WHITE MOUNTAINS.
20¼ x 36⅛ (51.4 x 91.8).
Metropolitan Museum of Art; Frick Art Reference Library.

VIEW NEAR SHELBURNE, NEW HAMPSHIRE.
Boston Art Association (1886), #18.

VIEW OF THE WHITE MOUNTAINS (A NOTCH).
1866. Oil.
19¼ x 32¼ (48.9 x 81.9).
Sotheby PB (1975); NMAA Inventory.

VIEW TO GLEN HOUSE, NEW HAMPSHIRE.
Signed.
Oil on canvas.
10 x 12 (25.4 x 30.5).
Private collection (1976); NMAA Inventory; *American Art Review* (July-Aug. 1976).

WHITE MOUNTAIN LANDSCAPE.
Oil on canvas.
16 x 24 (40.6 x 61).
Portland Museum of Art (1983); NMAA Inventory.

WHITE MOUNTAIN LANDSCAPE.
1897. Oil.
20 x 31¼ (50.8 x 79.4).
Unlocated.

WHITE MOUNTAINS.
Jan. 1890. Watercolor.
8 x 11½ (20.3 x 29.2).
Private collection (1973); BIAP.

WHITE MOUNTAINS.
1891. Watercolor.
9 x 14 (22.9 x 35.6).
Private collection (1973); BIAP; Pre-1877.

WHITE MOUNTAINS.
Watercolor.

13 x 10 (33 x 25.4).
Vose Galleries (1970).

SOREN, JOHN JOHNSTON

A, C, G&W
Died Boston, MA, Feb. 20, 1889.
Soren is first known to have demonstrated his artistic abilities when he exhibited at the Boston Athenaeum in 1836. In 1841 he exhibited for the first time at the Apollo Association in New York City. During this time he was teller in a Boston bank. He continued as a cashier until 1875 but apparently did not exhibit after 1841.

FALLS OF THE SACO.
Boston Athenaeum (1836), #21.

NEW HAMPSHIRE MOUNTAIN SCENERY.
Boston Athenaeum (1836), #40; (1837), #21.

VIEW OF THE WILEY [sic] HOUSE, WHITE MOUNTAINS, NEW HAMPSHIRE.
AAU, 1841, #130.

VIEW ON THE SACO.
Boston Athenaeum (1841), #73.

SPEAR, THOMAS TRUMAN

A, F(sup), G&W
Born Massachusetts, 1803. Died c. 1882.
Spear was a New Englander who exhibited at the Boston Athenaeum between 1838 and 1856, and traveled to Charleston, SC, during that period. He seems to have worked as a portraitist, landscapist, miniaturist, and historical painter, and he exhibited a piece of sculpture in 1843.

MOUNT WASHINGTON FROM SUNSET HILL.
North Conway Library Exhibition (1965).

NEW HAMPSHIRE SCENERY.
Boston Athenaeum (1841), #91.

WHITE MOUNTAIN.
Pre-1877; Leeds Gallery (Feb. 7, 1870).

SPRAGUE, ISAAC

A, F(sup), G&W
Born Hingham, MA, Sept. 5, 1811.
Died Wellesley, MA, March 13, 1895.
Sprague was artist-assistant to John James Audubon in 1843 and produced many of the backgrounds in the ornithological plates. He accompanied Audubon on a trip to the Missouri

River, then settled in Cambridge and later moved to Needham, MA. He drew 15 plates for William Oakes's White Mountain Scenery, published in 1848. Many of his original drawings are at the Boston Athenaeum.

BASIN, IN LINCOLN, NEW HAMPSHIRE; THE...
1848. Lithograph.
11¼ x 8½ (28.6 x 21.6).
Oakes, William. White Mountain Scenery (1848), plate 11; Old Print Shop (1980).

CLIFFS OF THE FALLS OF THE AMONOOSUC [sic]; THE...(two views)
Lithograph.
5 x 8¾ (12.7 x 22.2).
Oakes. White Mountain Scenery, plate 7.

FALLS OF THE AMONOOSUCK [sic] NEAR THE MOUNT WASHINGTON HOUSE.
1848. Lithograph.
11¼ x 8½ (28.6 x 21.6).
Oakes. White Mountain Scenery, plate 6; Old Print Shop Portfolio 7:1, p. 5.

FLUME, IN LINCOLN, NEW HAMPSHIRE; THE...
1848. Lithograph.
11¼ x 8½ (28.6 x 21.6).
Oakes. White Mountain Scenery, plate 12; Old Print Shop Portfolio 7:1, p. 5.

FRANCONIA NOTCH WITH THE LAFAYETTE HOUSE.
1848. Lithograph.
8¼ x 11 (21 x 27.9).
Oakes. White Mountain Scenery, plate 8; Old Print Shop Portfolio 7:1, p. 5.

GATE OF THE NOTCH OF THE WHITE MOUNTAINS, WITH THE NOTCH HOUSE.
1848. Lithograph.
8½ x 11¼ (21.6 x 28.6).
Oakes. White Mountain Scenery, plate 5; Old Print Shop Portfolio 7:1, p. 5.

LOWER CASCADE IN THE NOTCH OF THE WHITE MOUNTAINS; THE...
1848. Lithograph.
11¼ x 8½ (28.6 x 21.6).
Oakes. White Mountain Scenery, plate 4; Old Print Shop Portfolio 7:1 p. 5.

MOUNT CRAWFORD FROM THE NOTCH.
1848. Lithograph.
5⅛ x 7½ (13.1 x 19.1).
Oakes. White Mountain Scenery, plate 14; Old Print Shop Portfolio 7:1, p. 5.

MOUNT CRAWFORD NEAR THE WHITE MOUNTAINS, WITH THE MOUNT CRAWFORD HOUSE.
1848. Lithograph.

8½ x 11¼ (21.6 x 28.6).
Oakes. White Mountain Scenery, plate 2; Old Print Shop Portfolio 7:1, p. 5.

MOUNT WASHINGTON FROM THE SUMMIT OF MOUNT PLEASANT.
1848. Lithograph.
5 x 9¾ (12.7 x 24.8).
Oakes. White Mountain Scenery, plate 15.

NANCY'S BRIDGE, NEAR THE WHITE MOUNTAINS.
1848. Lithograph.
11¼ x 8½ (28.6 x 21.6).
Oakes. White Mountain Scenery, plate 13; Old Print Shop Portfolio 7:1, p. 5.

NOTCH OF THE WHITE MOUNTAINS WITH WILLEY HOUSE; THE...
1848. Lithograph.
8½ x 11¼ (21.6 x 28.6).
Oakes. White Mountain Scenery, plate 3; Old Print Shop Portfolio 7:1, p. 5.

PROFILE MOUNTAIN AT FRANCONIA, NEW HAMPSHIRE.
1848. Lithograph.
11¼ x 8½ (28.6 x 21.6).
Oakes. White Mountain Scenery, plate 9; Old Print Shop Portfolio 7:1, p. 5.

PROFILE ROCK, 'OLD MAN OF THE MOUNTAIN' AT FRANCONIA, NEW HAMPSHIRE.
1848. Lithograph.
11¼ x 8½ (28.6 x 21.6).
Oakes. White Mountain Scenery, plate 10; Old Print Shop Portfolio 7:1, p. 5.

WHITE MOUNTAINS FROM BETHLEHEM, N.H.; THE...
Lithograph.
3½ x 9¾ (8.9 x 24.8).
Oakes. White Mountain Scenery, plate 15.

WHITE MOUNTAINS FROM THE GIANT'S GRAVE NEAR THE MOUNT WASHINGTON HOUSE; THE...
1848. Lithograph.
8½ x 11¼ (21.6 x 28.6).
Oakes. White Mountain Scenery, plate 1; Old Print Shop Portfolio 7:1, p. 5.

SPREAD, HENRY FENTON
C&H, F, S
Born Kinsdale, Ireland, 1844. Died after 1875. *Spread apparently traveled extensively in England, Germany, and Australia before he came to the U.S. in 1870, where he settled in Chicago.*

New Hampshire Scenery

MOUNT KEARSARGE, NEW HAMPSHIRE.
Pre-1877; Chicago Industrial Exposition (1875).

STANLEY, JOHN MIX
DAB, F(sup), G&W, R
Born Canandaigua, NY, Jan. 17, 1814.
Died Detroit, MI, April 10, 1872.
Stanley began his career as a portrait painter in the Northeast but by 1842 had been thoroughly engulfed by a consuming interest in the American Indian. Although most of his time was spent in the West, he was apparently in the White Mountains for a short time in the 1860s. Unfortunately, most of his paintings, with the years of careful research that went into them, were destroyed in the Smithsonian Institution fire of 1865.

MOUNT HAYES NEAR GORHAM, NEW HAMP-SHIRE. S/D.
1866.
36½ x 48½ (92.8 x 123.2).
Christie's (April 1981), Lot #24.

RASPBERRY PARTY, WHITE MOUNTAINS. S/L/L/Center.
1867.
Frick Art Reference Library.

WHITE MOUNTAINS.
Pre-1877; Detroit Art Association (Feb. 1876).

STANWOOD, FRANKLIN (or A.)
A
Born Portland, ME, March 15, 1852.
Died Gorham, ME, 1888.
Stanwood was born in the Portland Alms House and shortly thereafter was adopted by Capt. Gideon Stanwood. He was self-taught and developed a very linear style, which accorded well with the ship portraits for which he is best known. He also painted "house portraits" and landscapes. He was a sailor by profession and perhaps went to England at some time for he met Charles Dickens, whom he admired, either there or in this country at the time of the latter's visit in 1867. In the middle of the 19th century, Portland was an important commercial and cultural center, boasting such artists and writers as Charles Codman, Charles Octavius Cole, Harrison Brown, John Rollin Tilton, Nathaniel Hawthorne, and Nathaniel Willis. Stanwood died at the early age of 36 of consumption.

Bibliography:
Barry, William David. "Franklin Stanwood, Portland Marine Painter." *Antiques* (Oct. 1981), pp. 926-930.

CRAWFORD NOTCH. S/L/R.
1884. Oil on canvas.
39⅛ x 49 ³/₁₆ (99.5 x 125).
Signal Co. (1983).

MORNING IN THE WHITE MOUNTAINS (or COACH AT FULL SPEED). S/D/L/R.
1878.
12¼ x 18 (31.1 x 45.7).
Metropolitan Museum of Art (April 24-Oct. 29, 1939).

MOUNT LAFAYETTE IN WINTER.
Unlocated.

STETSON, SYLVIA C.
N
Active 1868-78.
Stetson exhibited at the NAD in 1868 and 1869 when she gave her address as Boston. She also exhibited at the Massachusetts Charitable Mechanic Association in 1878.

MEADOW – NORTH CONWAY.
MA Charitable (1878), #436.

STEVENS, JOHN CALVIN
Born Boston, MA, Oct. 8, 1855.
Died Portland, ME, Jan. 25, 1940.
A landscape painter and architect, Stevens spent most of his life in the Portland area.

OLD MAN OF THE MOUNTAIN. Signed.
C. 1885. Oil on canvas.
18 x 9½ (45.7 x 24.1).
Private collection (1983).

STEWART, EDWARD B.
Active 1883-85.
There is presently no information on this artist.
HILLSIDE, NEW HAMPSHIRE.
Oil.
Boston Art Club (1883), #32.

MONADNOC [sic].
Oil.
Boston Art Club (1885), #50.

STEWART, RONALD A.
There is no information presently available on this artist.
SACO RIVER.
MA Charitable (1874), #183.

STILLMAN, WILLIAM JAMES

A, Ce, DAB, F(sup), G&W, N, R
Born Schenectady, NY, June 1, 1828.
Died Surrey, England, July 6, 1901.
Stillman studied painting for a year under Frederic Church after graduating from Union College, Schenectady, NY, in 1848. He traveled to England and became a close friend of John Ruskin. On his return to the U.S. he became a major spokesman for the American Pre-Raphaelite Brotherhood. In 1855 he became the founder and editor of The Crayon, A Journal Devoted to the Graphic Arts, and Literature Related to Them, with John Durand (although he was forced by ill health to resign from the position a year later), and the same year he was elected to associate membership in the NAD where he exhibited from 1851 to 1859. He went on a trip to the White Mountains in 1856 and in 1857 exhibited at the Boston Athenaeum. He kept a studio at the 10th Street Studio Building (N.Y.C.) from 1858 to 1860 and in 1861 received a commission from J. M. Forbes of Boston for studies in the White Mountains (which are, at present, unlocated). Stillman enjoyed the outdoors, and James Bryce found him again in the White Mountains at Glen Ellis camping out on Sept. 4, 1870. He wrote many books on art and archeology and was a consul in Rome from 1861 to 1865 and in Crete from 1865 to 1868.

Bibliography:
Bradbury, John M., Edgar P. Richardson and James J. Rorimer. "William James Stillman," #12, *Union Worthies.* Union College, Schenectady, NY, 1957.

ON KEARSARGE BROOK, NORTH CONWAY.
NAD, 1857, #166; Boston Athenaeum (1857), #331.

STEPPING-STONES, KEARSARGE BROOK, NORTH CONWAY; THE. . .
NAD, 1857, #190.

STONE, BENJAMIN BELLOWS GRANT

A, Ce, F(sup), G&W, K, Ka, N, S
Born Watertown, MA, Jan. 21, 1829.
Died Catskill, NY, Aug. 11, 1906.
Stone entered Benjamin Champney's art classes in Boston in 1851 after several years of work in a Boston ship chandlery. In 1853 he moved to New York City and enrolled as a student with Jasper Cropsey. In 1856 he rented Thomas Cole's studio from Cole's widow and settled in Catskill, NY. All his life he kept in touch with

contemporary artists, corresponding with Frederic Church, whom he frequently visited, his old teachers, Champney and Cropsey, as well as Sanford Gifford, Sylvester Hodgdon, and many others. His early promise was curtailed by military service in the Civil War, and, after his return to Catskill, he turned out any work that came to hand—lithographs for Goupil (a 19th-century art dealer), stage sets, book and magazine illustrations—and was often ill-paid. His painting, HARVEST SCENE, a view taken in North Conway which he sold to Louis Prang for $50, was the most popular chromolithograph ever put out by that firm and netted Prang about $100,000 over the years it was in their catalog.

Bibliography:
Campbell, Catherine H. "Benjamin Bellows Grant Stone: A Forgotten American Artist." New-York Historical Society *Quarterly* 72 (Jan. 1978), pp. 22-42.

1857 SKETCHBOOKS.
Pencil.
Greene County Historical Society (1977).

EAGLE CLIFF AND ECHO LAKE.
Oil.
13½ x 18½ (34.3 x 47).
Greene County Historical Society (1977).

ECHO LAKE.
Lithograph.
12 x 17 (30.5 x 43.2).
Dartmouth Art Galleries, lithograph by J. E. Bufford.

GATE OF THE NOTCH.
1857-59. Oil on paper.
6⅞ x 9⅞ (17.5 x 25.1).
Greene County Historical Society (1980); University Art Gallery catalog, University of New Hampshire (1980), #43.

GLEN ELLIS FALLS.
1857. Oil.
12 x 10 (30.5 x 25.4).
Greene County Historical Society.

HARVEST SCENE, NORTH CONWAY.
Oil.
9¼ x 14 (23.5 x 35.6).
Greene County Historical Society (1977); NMAA Inventory; Prang chromolithograph.

IN THE MOUNTAINS AT NORTH CONWAY.
1853. Oil.
18 x 24 (45.7 x 61).
Greene County Historical Society (1977); NMAA Inventory.

Mount Monadnock
Mrs. H. E. Martin, 1884
Oil on canvas, 18" x 23 ³/₄" / Private collection, photograph courtesy of Old
     Sturbridge Village / Ref. page 114

IN THE WHITE MOUNTAINS, NORTH CONWAY.
  Oil.
     17½ x 13 (44.5 x 33).
     Greene County Historical Society (1977).
MOUNT JEFFERSON AT SUNRISE, WHITE
MOUNTAINS.
     1867. Oil.
     25 x 30 (63.5 x 76.2).
     Greene County Historical Society (1977);
     NMAA Inventory.
OLD MAN OF THE MOUNTAINS.
     1858. Lithograph.
     Starr King special edition, New Hampshire
     Historical Society, lithograph by C. Parsons.
SILVER CASCADE.
     1857. Lithograph.
     17 x 13½ (43.2 x 34.3).
     Greene County Historical Society,
     lithograph by Sabatier.
STUDY FOR ARTIST'S BROOK, NORTH CON-
WAY, NEW HAMPSHIRE.
     1851 or 1857. Oil.
     12 x 10¼ (30.5 x 26).

Greene County Historical Society (1977);
NMAA Inventory.
STUDY OF ELLIS FALLS, PINKHAM NOTCH,
NEW HAMPSHIRE.
     1851. Oil.
     14 x 12 (35.6 x 30.5).
     Greene County Historical Society (1977);
     NMAA Inventory.
STUDY OF YELLOW BIRCH, NORTH CONWAY.
     1854? Oil.
     16 x 12 (40.6 x 30.5).
     Greene County Historical Society (1977);
     NMAA Inventory.
SUMMIT OF MOUNT WASHINGTON, 6380 FEET
ABOVE SEA LEVEL.
     1858. Lithograph.
     13 x 16¾ (33 x 42.5).
     Old Print Shop *Portfolio* 38:3, p. 38,
     lithograph by Sabatier.
WHITE MOUNTAINS SCENERY.
     NAD, 1857, #376.

Dictionary of Painters

WHITE MOUNTAINS, NORTH CONWAY; THE...
    Oil.
    17½ x 13 (44.6 x 33).
    Unlocated.

STROTHER, DAVID HUNTER (PORTE CRAYON)

Ce, DAB, F, G&W, K, Ka, S
Born Martinsburg, VA (now WV), Sept. 26, 1816.
Died Charleston, WV, March 8, 1888.
Strother studied under Samuel F. B. Morse and continued his training in France and Italy, where he remained from 1840 to 1843. In 1844 he began to draw illustrations in New York and by 1853 had begun his long association with Harper's, serving as their most highly paid artist-correspondent. From a family of soldiers, he served in the Civil War for the North in the Topographic Corps and from 1879 to 1885 served as the U.S. consul general to Mexico. He was primarily a freelance illustrator and used the pseudonym "Porte Crayon" in many of the articles and illustrations he produced. A cousin described him as "a slight, elastic and somewhat gaunt gentleman, with a dark, concentrated eye, sunk deep beneath a marked and rugged brow.... [He] wears a beard, after the fashion of the middle ages...a green cloth cap, with a straight, projecting visor to it, like the European military caps. An old coat, with gray pantaloons, and a pair of tough boots with large red tops — these drawn on outside, complete his dress....This is our artist...a man who would laugh a bear in the face, and take particular pleasure in pitching a panther" (quoted from Karolik). Strother produced the series listed below in 1859, when he stayed in the barn of the newly constructed Crawford House. He exhibited at the NAD in 1838 and 1853 and at the PAFA in 1855.
Bibliography:
Eby, Cecil D., Jr. *"Porte Crayon": The Life of David Hunter Strother.* Chapel Hill, NC, 1960.
ASCENT OF MOUNT WASHINGTON.
    Harper's (July 1861), pp. 145-163.
CRYSTAL CASCADE.
    Harper's (July 1861), pp. 145-163.
GLEN ELLIS FALLS.
    Harper's (July 1861), pp. 145-163.

LAKE OF THE CLOUDS, TOWARDS CRAWFORD'S.
    Harper's (July 1861), pp. 145-163.
MONUMENT; THE...
    Harper's (July 1861), pp. 145-163.
SLEEPING QUARTERS IN THE BARN AT CRAWFORD'S.
    Harper's (July 1861), pp. 145-163.
SUMMIT OF MOUNT WASHINGTON.
    Harper's (July 1861), pp. 145-163.
VIEW OF MOUNT WASHINGTON.
    Harper's (July 1861), pp. 145-163.

SUYDAM, HENRY

A, G&W, K
Born c. 1802. Died after 1883.
Suydam, a brother of the artist, James Augustus Suydam, lived in New York City and exhibited at the Washington Art Association in 1859. Flexner, in his book, Wilder Image, wrote that Suydam painted "rather amateurish canvasses."
Bibliography:
Flexner, James Thomas. *That Wilder Image* (1970).
CONWAY MEADOWS. S/D.
    1874.
    Private collection.

SUYDAM, JAMES AUGUSTUS

A, Ba, Ce, C&H, F, G&W, N, R, T
Born New York, NY, March 27, 1819.
Died North Conway, NH, Sept. 15, 1865.
Suydam began his career as a businessman but turned to painting, studying under Minor C. Kellogg. At the age of 30 he was elected to the Century Association. One of the "regulars" who gathered to paint at North Conway, NH, he exhibited CONWAY MEADOWS at the Boston Athenaeum and opened his studio at the 10th Street Studio Building (N.Y.C.) in 1858. The following year he was elected an honorary professional member in the NAD, which granted him full membership in 1861. He died suddenly in North Conway at the age of 46.
Bibliography:
Baur, John I. H. "A Tonal Realist: James Suydam." *Art Quarterly* (Summer 1950).
CHOCORUA, WHITE MOUNTAINS.
    NAD, 1860, #371.
CONWAY MEADOWS.
    NAD, 1858, #551; Boston Athenaeum (1858), #67; *Crayon* (1858), p. 147.

New Hampshire Scenery

FROM NORTH CONWAY.
  NAD, 1856, #152.

MOAT MOUNTAIN.
  NAD, 1858, #204; *Crayon* (1858), p. 147.

STUDY NEAR NORTH CONWAY (Kearsarge).
  C. 1850. Oil.
  14 x 26¼ (35.6 x 66.7).
  NAD, 1971.

SWORD, JAMES BRADE
F, G&W, K, Ka, N, S
Born Philadelphia, PA, Oct. 11, 1839.

Died Philadelphia, PA, Dec. 1, 1915.
Sword began his adult life as an engineer but turned to art at about 25 years of age. He won medals for his watercolors and was a founder of the Philadelphia Art Club and president for a time of the Philadelphia Society of Artists as well as the Artist's Fund Society. He exhibited at the NAD from 1876 to 1892 and at the Brooklyn Art Association from 1873 to 1884.

MOUNTAIN VIEW. S/D/R.
  1873.
  17½ x 29¾ (44.5 x 75.6).
  Private collection.

T

TALBOT, JESSE
C, Ce, F(sup), G&W, K, N, R, S, T
Born probably New York, NY, 1806 or 1807. Died Brooklyn, NY, 1879.
Talbot began exhibiting at the NAD in 1838 and continued to do so until 1860. He also sent work to the Apollo Association (N.Y.C.) and in 1870 to the Brooklyn Art Association. He was elected an associate member of the NAD in 1842 or 1843. For much of his artistically active life he gave his address as New York University.

LANDSCAPE—WHITE MOUNTAINS SCENERY.
  Pre-1877; *Art Journal* Supplement (1858).

NEW HAMPSHIRE MILL. S/L/L.
  Oil on canvas.
  15 ¹⁵/₁₆ x 25⅝ (40.5 x 65).
  Signal Co. (1983).

SCENE IN THE WHITE MOUNTAINS, NEW HAMPSHIRE.
  Pre-1877; *Cosmopolitan Art Journal* 3:5 (Dec. 1859).

VIEW IN THE WHITE MOUNTAINS OF NEW HAMPSHIRE.
  NAD, 1844, #56; AAU, 1844, #3.

VIEW OF GRAND MONADNOCK, NEW HAMPSHIRE.
  AAU, 1841, #57.

VIEW ON THE SACO RIVER, MOUNT WASHINGTON IN DISTANCE.
  NAD, 1842, #84.

WHITE MOUNTAINS SCENERY.
  Pre-1877; *Art Journal* Supplement (1858).

TATE, ARTHUR
Nothing is presently known about this artist.

VIEW OF WINNIPISEOGEE [sic] FROM CENTRE HARBOR.
  Oil on canvas.
  Private collection.

THAYER, ABBOTT HENDERSON (or HANDERSON)
A, Ba, C&H, F, N, S
Born Boston, MA, Aug. 12, 1849. Died 1921.
After studying art in Boston, Brooklyn, and Paris, Thayer exhibited at the Brooklyn Art Association from 1866 to 1884. He summered in Dublin, NH, in the 1880s, finally moving there in 1901, and was a great influence in establishing an art colony there. He was very well known for his many views of Monadnock, but most were painted after 1900. He was very much interested in the properties of color, recognizing the protective coloring of animals. His theories were used to develop camouflage in World War I.

Bibliography:
Allison, Hildreth M. "Some Painters of the Grand Monadnock." *Appalachia* 34 (1962-63), pp. 441-453.
White, Nelson C. *Abbot H. Thayer, Painter and Naturalist* (1951).

MOUNT MONADNOCK.
  Boston Athenaeum (1897), #38; Carnegie Institute (PA) show, 1919.

THOMPSON, ALFRED (or ALBERT) WORDSWORTH (or WARDSWORTH or WADSWORTH)

B, C&H, DAB, F, G&W, K, Ka, N, R, S
Born Baltimore, MD, May 26, 1840.
Died Summit, NJ, Aug. 28, 1896.
Thompson trained as a lawyer but turned to painting shortly before the Civil War. He served as an illustrator of war scenes with Harper's Weekly *and* Illustrated London News *for the first year of the war. In 1861 he went to Paris for further study and returned to the U.S. in 1868, the same year he exhibited at the PAFA. He exhibited at the NAD from 1867 until his death and was elected an associate in 1873 and an academician in 1875. In 1876 one of his paintings was exhibited at the Leonard Auction Rooms in Boston. He traveled often throughout Europe and the U.S. during his career, searching for material to draw.*

A NEW HAMPSHIRE FARM HOUSE.
    NAD, 1888, #340.

In Leonard Auction records as Albert Thompson (probably Alfred).
ARTIST'S BROOK, NORTH CONWAY.
    Leonard Auction (April 20-21, 1876), #51.
MOUNT CHOCORUA.
    NAD, 1867, #238; Pre-1877.
ROAD TO FRANCONIA, WHITE MOUNTAINS, NEW HAMPSHIRE; THE...
    NAD, 1889, #427.

THOMPSON, HARRY IVES

F, G&W, N, S
Born West Haven, CT, Jan. 31, 1840.
Died West Haven, CT, 1906.
Trained as a merchant, Thompson turned his interest to painting at the age of 21. He studied under Benjamin Coe and exhibited at the NAD from 1877 to 1890. He taught drawing for many years in New Haven and painted portraits as well as landscapes.

PRESIDENTIAL RANGE FROM JEFFERSON, NEW HAMPSHIRE.
    Oil.
    29 x 48 (73.7 x 121.9).
    Kennedy Galleries (1978); Kennedy *Quarterly* 10:4 (1971).
QUIMBY BROOK, NEW HAMPSHIRE.
    NAD, 1882, #31.

THORNDIKE, GEORGE QUINCY

A, Ce, C&H, F, G&W, N, R, S, T
Born Boston, MA, Feb. 24, 1827.
Died Boston, MA, Dec. 27, 1886.
After graduating from Harvard at the age of 20, Thorndike went abroad to study art in Paris. In 1857 he exhibited both at the Boston Athenaeum and at the NAD, giving his address as New York City. The same year he took a studio in the 10th Street Studio Building (N.Y.C.), which he kept until 1869. In 1861 he was elected an associate of the NAD.

ECHO LAKE, FRANCONIA MOUNTAINS, NEW HAMPSHIRE.
    NAD, 1858, #405; Boston Athenaeum (1857), #315.
NEW HAMPSHIRE SCENERY.
    NAD, 1857, #169; Boston Athenaeum (1857), #264.
RECOLLECTIONS OF FRANCONIA.
    Boston Athenaeum (1858), #260.

THWAITES, WILLIAM H.

Ce, G&W, N
Active 1854-71.
Thwaites was primarily an engraver but also painted landscapes. He exhibited at the NAD in 1854, 1858, and 1860 and at the Brooklyn Art Association from 1868 to 1871. The Crayon in November 1856 noted: "Mr. W. H. Thwaites has returned from a tour of study in the White Mountains, and has brought with him a number of carefully studied drawings in watercolors and sepia, heightened with pencil. Mr. T's ability with watercolors should make his works much sought after as are his designs on wood."

CONWAY LEDGE.
    NAD, 1860, #134.
WHITE MOUNTAINS; THE...
    Pre-1877; NAD, watercolor show (1867-68).

THYNG, J. WARREN

A
Born Lakeport, NH, 1840.
Died North Woodstock, NH, July 9, 1927.
Thyng went to Boston to study under George Loring Brown and also at the NAD. He was "a welcome frequenter of studios of F. E. Church, George Innis [sic] and William Hart" (Granite Monthly, NH, 1897). A landscapist, he taught art in the Massachusetts State Normal Art School in Salem, MA, for 11 years and illustrated volumes of poetry and literature. He also worked in his native state, teaching in the

New Hampshire Scenery

Manchester Public Schools and at the normal school in Plymouth, NH, in 1874-75. The Boston Transcript noted on Aug. 20, 1875, that he was to "spend a vacation at Lake Village, NH." He moved briefly to Akron, OH, in 1883 and founded the Akron School of Design. John Greenleaf Whittier wrote to him: "I sympathize with thee in the love of the New Hampshire hills, and Chocorua is the most beautiful and striking of all. . . . Thy beautiful picture [of Winnipesaukee] is the best I have ever seen of our lake" (Musgrove, The White Hills in Poetry, p. 338). Thyng was interested in the difference between idealistic and realistic art. He was a 32nd-degree Mason.

Bibliography:
Baldwin, Maurice. "A New Hampshire Artist." Granite Monthly 22 (1897), pp. 31-40.
Musgrove, Eugene R., ed. The White Hills in Poetry: An Anthology. Boston, 1912.

LAKE WINNIPESAUKEE SHOWING THE EXCURSION STEAMER.
    Aquatint.
    12¾ x 16¼ (32.4 x 41.3).
    New Hampshire Historical Society exhibition (1965).

MOUNT WASHINGTON STEAMER – A SIDE WHEELER.
    1869. Oil on canvas.
    Private collection.

TIDD, MARSHALL M.

G&W
Born 1828. Died Woburn, MA, Aug. 1895.
Though Peters, in America on Stone, suggested that Tidd was English due to his use of British synonyms for certain words in his lithographs, he seems to have stayed his entire artistic career in and around Boston. Tidd was a lithographer and watercolorist. He drew the illustrations on woodblocks for wood engravings to illustrate Lucy Crawford's History of the White Mountains. He was apparently paid $49 for the job, but they were never cut. Tidd was also a civil engineer.

Bibliography:
Appalachia 32 (1958-59), pp. 45-65.
Morse, Stearns, ed. Lucy Crawford's History of the White Mountains. Reprint Boston: Appalachian Mountain Club, 1978.
Peters, Harry T. America on Stone (1931).
Tidd, Marshall M. "Up the Magalloway River in 1861." MS in Bangor (ME) Public Library.

CARRYING A LADY DOWN JACOB'S LADDER.
    1859. Woodblock.
    Dartmouth College Art Galleries.
CRAWFORD CARRYING A BEAR.
    1859. Woodblock.
    Dartmouth College Art Galleries.
FLUME AT DIXVILLE NOTCH.
    Appalachia 32 (1958-59), pp. 45-65.
GETTING A TEAM UP THE NOTCH AT THE ROCKS.
    1859. Woodblock.
    Dartmouth College Art Galleries.
HAMSTRINGING A MOOSE AT SAWYER'S ROCK.
    1859. Woodblock.
    Dartmouth College Art Galleries.
PEAKS AT DIXVILLE NOTCH.
    Appalachia 32 (1958-59), pp. 45-65.
ROSEBUD HOUSE [ROSEBROOK] NEAR FABYANS [sic].
    1859. Woodblock.
    Dartmouth College Art Galleries.
TWO CAMPS AFTER THE SLIDE.
    1859. Woodblock.
    Dartmouth College Art Galleries.
TWO CAMPS BEFORE THE SLIDE.
    1859. Woodblock.
    Dartmouth College Art Galleries.
VIEW OF DIXVILLE NOTCH.
    Appalachia 32 (1958-59), pp. 45-65.
WILLEY PLACE AFTER THE SLIDE.
    1859. Woodblock.
    Dartmouth College Art Galleries.
WILLEY PLACE BEFORE THE SLIDE.
    1859. Woodblock.
    Dartmouth College Art Galleries.

TILTON, GEORGE H.

Born Littleton, NH, 1860.
Died Littleton, NH, 1931.
Tilton studied under Edward Hill. He spent his entire life in the Franconia, NH, area.

Information courtesy of the artist's grandson, John H. Tilton.

DELL, LITTLETON, NEW HAMPSHIRE.
    C. 1880. Oil.
    32 x 21 (81.3 x 53.3).
    Private collection; NMAA Inventory.

EAGLE CLIFF, FRANCONIA, NEW HAMPSHIRE.
C. 1880. Oil.
14 x 20 (35.6 x 50.8).
Private collection; NMAA Inventory.

FLUME GORGE, FRANCONIA NOTCH.
C. 1880-83. Oil.
20 x 12 (50.8 x 30.5).
Private collection; NMAA Inventory.

GALE RIVER, FRANCONIA, NEW HAMPSHIRE.
1879. Oil.
12 x 20 (30.5 x 50.8).
Private collection; NMAA Inventory.

MOUNTAINS FROM FRANCONIA; THE. . .
1879.
Franconia Bicentennial Art Show (July 1972).

RIVER SCENE (NEAR LITTLETON).
C. 1880-90. Oil.
12½ x 11½ (31.8 x 29.2).
Private collection; NMAA Inventory.

SUNSET ON THE RIVER (AMMONOOSUC NEAR LITTLETON).
C. 1880. Oil.
8 x 10 (20.3 x 25.4).
Private collection; NMAA Inventory.

TILTON (or TILTEN), JOHN ROLLIN

A, C, C&H, DAB, F, G&W, N, R, S, T
Born Loudon, NH, June 8, 1828.
Died Rome, Italy, March 22, 1888.
Tilton was a largely self-taught watercolorist who also painted in oils. He went to live permanently in Italy in 1852, where he catered to European and American tourists' artistic desires. He maintained ties with the American art world, however, and sent paintings to the NAD in 1861 and 1874 and to the Boston Athenaeum.

VIEW IN THE WHITE MOUNTAINS.
Boston Athenaeum (1851), #181.

TITCOMB, MARY BRADISH

F
Born New Hampshire. Died 1927.
Titcomb studied at the Boston Museum of Fine Arts School under Tarbell, Benson, and Hale. She was a member of the Copley Society in 1895, the New York Water Color Club, and the National Society of Women Painters and Sculptors.

WINTER IN NEW HAMPSHIRE.
Oil.
NMAA Inventory.

TITCOMB (or TITCOMBE), WILLIAM H.

A, F(sup), G&W
Born Raymond, NH, Sept. 24, 1824.
Died Boston, MA, Feb. 11, 1888.
Titcomb's rather naïve, extremely individual style would seem to indicate little training. After a career in merchandising, he apparently started painting professionally about 1860. He was successful as an artist and teacher in the Boston area until his death in 1888. At one time he acted as principal and director of the art department of the Academy of Art in that city. Many of Titcomb's works are New Hampshire views.

CENTER HARBOR FROM OLD MEREDITH ROAD.
C. 1865 or c. 1855. Oil on canvas.
26⅜ x 35⅜ (67 x 89.9).
Private collection (1983); NMAA Inventory; Boston Public Library, Brockton catalog, p. 54.

CHOCORUA. Signed.
24 x 28 (61 x 71.1).
Private collection.

CONWAY VALLEY IN AUTUMN.
C. 1860. Oil.
14 x 20 (35.6 x 50.8).
Childs Gallery (Fall 1970); NMAA Inventory.

Records attribute to William B. Titcomb (probably William H.).

COUNTRY SCENE (Mount Chocorua).
Oil on canvas.
14 x 30 (35.6 x 76.2).
Private collection; Old Print Shop.

ECHO LAKE, NEW HAMPSHIRE.
C. 1865. Oil on canvas.
20½ x 27½ (52.1 x 69.9).
Old Print Shop *Portfolio* 26:4 (1973), p. 95.

LAKE WINNEPESAUKEE [sic].
Oil on canvas.
20 x 30 (50.8 x 76.2).
Private collection (1983); Fine Art Gallery, San Francisco, CA (1974).

MOUNT CHOCORUA.
Oil on canvas.
22½ x 30½ (57.2 x 77.5).
Private collection

MOUNT MONADNOCK, NEW HAMPSHIRE.
C. 1860. Oil.
22 x 30⅛ (55.9 x 76.5).
NMAA Inventory.

MOUNT WASHINGTON AND CONWAY VALLEY.
  Lion Gallery (1976).
MOUNT WASHINGTON VALLEY. S/Stretcher.
  12 x 18 (30.5 x 45.7).
  Richard Bourne, Inc., catalog (Aug. 6, 1974), #26.
NEAR LAKE WINNIPESAUKEE. S/D/L/L/Center.
  1851. Oil on canvas.
  22¼ x 30⅜ (55.7 x 76.6).
  University Art Gallery catalog, University of New Hampshire (1980), #123.
NEW HAMPSHIRE LANDSCAPE.
  Oil.
  18 x 24 (45.7 x 61).
  Richard Bourne, Inc., catalog (Aug. 7, 1973).
NEW HAMPSHIRE LANDSCAPE (probably Chocorua). Signed.
  C. 1870. Oil on canvas.
  14 x 18½ (35.6 x 47).
  Private collection (1983); Old Print Shop (1977).
NEW HAMPSHIRE LANDSCAPE, MOUNT MONADNOCK.
  C. 1870. Oil on canvas.
  14 x 20 (35.6 x 50.8).
  Old Print Shop *Portfolio* 26:4 (1973).
PARKER MOUNTAIN, LITTLETON, NEW HAMPSHIRE. Signed.
  Oil on canvas.
  30 x 42 (76.2 x 106.7).
  Kennedy Galleries.
SUMMER IN NEW HAMPSHIRE.
  C. 1850-59. Oil.
  18 x 26 (45.7 x 66).
  NMAA Inventory.
VIEW IN NEW HAMPSHIRE.
  C. 1860. Oil.
  18 x 23 (45.7 x 58.4).
  Childs Gallery (Fall 1970); NMAA Inventory.
WHITE MOUNTAINS.
  Oil on canvas.
  8 x 13¼ (20.3 x 33.7).
  Amherst College (sold March 1979); BIAP.
WINTER IN NEW HAMPSHIRE – SKATING.
  Oil.
  11½ x 15½ (29.2 x 39.4). Oval.
  Richard Bourne, Inc., catalog (Aug. 7, 1973); NMAA Inventory.

WINTER LANDSCAPE IN NEW HAMPSHIRE.
  1856.
  22 x 30 (55.9 x 76.2).
  Parke-Bernet (1952); NMAA Inventory.
Attributed:
CONWAY VALLEY.
  Oil.
  18 x 24 (45.7 x 61).
  Richard Bourne, Inc., catalog (Aug. 1973); NMAA Inventory.
NEW HAMPSHIRE SUMMER EVENING.
  Oil on canvas.
  11½ x 15¾ (29.2 x 40). Oval.
  Richard Bourne, Inc., catalog (Aug. 7, 1973); NMAA Inventory.
SUMMER IN NEW HAMPSHIRE.
  Oil.
  18 x 26 (45.7 x 66).
  Richard Bourne, Inc., catalog (Aug. 7, 1973); NMAA Inventory.

TRISCOTT, SAMUEL PETER ROLT
F, Ka, S
Born Gosport, England, 1847.
Died Monhegan Island, ME, 1925.
Triscott studied both civil engineering and painting in England and came to the U.S. in 1871. He eventually settled in Boston and during the 1880s and 1890s frequently exhibited New England and Canadian coastal scenes. A teacher of watercolor painting, he was a member of the Boston Society of Water-Color Painters and served as its vice-president in 1896. He worked in both oils and watercolors.

LAKE WINNIPISEOGEE [sic] – LOOKING TOWARD MOUNT BELKNAP.
  Boston Art Club (1881), #32.

TRYON, BENJAMIN FRANKLIN
A, C&H, F, G&W, N, S
Born New York, NY, 1824. Died 1896.
Tryon studied under Richard Bengough and James Cafferty and spent most of his life in Boston. He exhibited at the NAD from 1866 to 1873.

CONWAY VALLEY AND MOAT MOUNTAIN.
  NAD, 1870, #307; C&H (see Standard Source Reference List).
WHITE MOUNTAINS; THE... (Emerald Pool).
  Oil on canvas.
  34 x 59 (86.4 x 149.9).
  Anthony Schmidt (1979); *Antiques* (June 1979).

TUCKER, ALLEN
F, S
Born Brooklyn, NY, June 29, 1866.
Died Jan. 26, 1939.
Tucker studied at Columbia University. He was both an architect and a painter. He had residences in New York City and Castine, ME.
MOUNT CHOCORUA.
    Oil on canvas.
    29½ x 33½ (74.9 x 85.1).
    Amherst College (1973); BIAP.

TWOMBLY, HELEN M. (MRS. JOHN H.)
Active before 1877.
There is presently no other information on this artist.

SACO RIVER LANDSCAPE, NEW HAMPSHIRE.
    Mid-19th century. Oil.
    15 x 24 (38.1 x 61).
    NMAA Inventory.
WHITE MOUNTAINS FROM CONWAY VALLEY; THE...
    Oil.
    Pre-1877; Philadelphia Women's Pavilion (1876).

TYLER, WILLIAM RICHARDSON
N
Born 1825. Died 1896.
This artist exhibited at the NAD from 1863 to 1867 and in 1878.
NORTH CONWAY.
    Oil.
    NMAA Inventory.

U

UNDERWOOD, GEORGE L.
Active 1882.
There is presently no other information on this artist.
BALD MOUNTAIN, NEW HAMPSHIRE.
    Watercolor.
    Boston Art Club (1882), #202.

UNKNOWN
See end of this section.

URQUHART, A. C.
There is presently no information on this artist.
CONWAY VALLEY. S/L/R.
    Oil on canvas.
    27¾ x 40 (70.5 x 101.6).
    Robert Goldberg (lost in the fire of his store in 1979).

V

VAN ELTEN, HENDRICK DIRK KRUSEMAN
A, C&H, F, R, S, T
Born Alkmaar, Holland, 1829.
Died Paris, France, 1904.
Van Elten is often listed as Van Elten Kruseman. He came to the U.S. in 1865. He settled in New York City and kept a studio in the 10th Street Studio Building (N.Y.C.) from 1867 to 1897. He exhibited at the NAD from 1866 to 1900 and became an academician in 1883. He also exhibited at the Boston Athenaeum and the PAFA. He was elected a member of the Century Association in 1889 and resigned in 1896.
AUTUMN IN THE WHITE MOUNTAINS (3).
    Watercolor.
    C&H (see Standard Source Reference List), centennial exhibition; Pre-1877; American Society of Painters in Watercolors (Feb. 1875).

New Hampshire Scenery

Lake Winnepesaukee [sic]
William H. Titcomb
Oil on canvas, 20" x 30" / Collection of the author / Ref. page 166

WADSWORTH, DANIEL
G&W
Born New Haven, CT, 1771.
Died Hartford, CT, July 28, 1848.
Wadsworth was an amateur artist, an art col-
lector, a close friend and patron of Thomas
Cole, and a founder of the Wadsworth
Atheneum. He was the brother-in-law of
Benjamin Silliman, editor of the American Jour-
nal of Science and the Arts *who published some*
of Wadsworth's drawings. He painted in water-
colors and may have done lithography.

Bibliography:
Parry, Elwood C., III. "Recent Discoveries in
the Art of Thomas Cole." *Antiques* (Nov. 1981),
p. 1162.

Dictionary of Painters

COROWAY [sic] PEAK FROM THE WINIPICIOGEE
[sic] LAKE, N. HAMPSHIRE.
  June 1826. Lithograph.
  New Hampshire Historical Society; drawn
  on stone by William Browne.

WALKER, CHARLES ALVAH
F, N, S
Born Loudon, NH, 1848.
Died Brookline, MA, 1925.
Walker was a versatile artist who used oils, etch-
ing, wood and steel engraving, and monotype
as media for expression. He exhibited at the
NAD from 1884 to 1892 as well as at the Boston
Art Club and the Massachusetts Charitable
Mechanic Association.

A SUMMER AFTERNOON, CAMPDEN [sic], NEW HAMPSHIRE.
>Oil.
>MA Charitable (1884), #85.

HILL-SIDE PASTURE IN JUNE, CAMPDEN [sic], NEW HAMPSHIRE; THE...
>NAD, 1885, #524.

MIDSUMMER, CAMPTON, NEW HAMPSHIRE.
>NAD, 1884, #510.

MILL POND, CAMPTONVILLE, NEW HAMPSHIRE; THE...
>NAD, 1885, #230.

WOOD INTERIOR – WATERVILLE, NEW HAMPSHIRE.
>Black and white.
>Boston Art Club (1882), #93.

WALL, WILLIAM GUY

C, F, G&W, Ka, R, S
Born Dublin, Ireland, 1792. Died after 1864.
When Wall arrived in the U.S., on Sept. 1, 1818, he was already a well-trained artist. He was a member and founder of the NAD, elected in 1826, exhibiting there from 1826 to 1856, and also at the Boston Athenaeum in 1828, 1830, and 1836 and the Apollo Association (N.Y.C.), the AAU, and the PAFA from 1838 to 1840. After living in various places in New York and New England, he returned to Ireland for some years, coming back to the U.S. in 1856, then returning to Ireland in 1862.

LANDSCAPE (WHITE MOUNTAINS).
>Pre-1877; Yale College exhibition gallery (April 1859).

WHITE MOUNTAINS SCENERY.
>Pre-1877; Yale College exhibition, Alumni Building (1858).

WARREN, ASA COOLIDGE

A, F, G&W, S
Born Boston, MA, March 25, 1819.
Died New York, NY, Nov. 22, 1904.
Warren studied engraving with George Girdler Smith and worked for the Boston publisher Tichnor and Fields. He also engraved bank notes and drew illustrations for current publications.

CONFLUENCE OF SACO AND SWIFT RIVERS, CONWAY.
>*Appleton's Journal* (March 11, 1871), p. 289.

LAKE WINNEPISEOGEE [sic].
>*Appleton's Journal* (July 20, 1872), p. 72.

MONADNOCK MOUNTAIN FROM NORTH PETERBOROUGH.
>*Appleton's Journal* (March 11, 1871), p. 288.

MOUNT KEARSARGE.
>*Appleton's Journal* (March 11, 1871), p. 288.

SPRAGUE'S POND AND MOUNT MONADNOCK, DUBLIN, NEW HAMPSHIRE.
>Lithograph.
>Stinson House, Rumney, NH; Tappan and Bradford's Lithography, Boston.

SQUAM LAKE.
>*Appleton's Journal* (July 20, 1872), p. 73.

WARREN, HAROLD BRADFIELD (or BROADFIELD)

F, N, S
Born Manchester, England, 1859. Died 1934.
Warren studied under Charles H. Moore and Charles Eliot Norton in Boston. He was a landscape painter and illustrator who was an instructor in watercolor at Harvard University's Department of Architecture. He exhibited at the NAD in 1884 and became a member of the Copley Society in 1891.

CLEARING AFTER RAIN, WILDCAT VALLEY, JACKSON, NEW HAMPSHIRE.
>Boston Art Club (1898), #370.

WATERMAN, MARCUS S.

Nothing is presently known of this artist.

MOUNT WASHINGTON.
>Oil on board.
>The Homestead, Sugar Hill, NH.

WATERS, GEORGE W.

Ce, F, G&W, N, S
Born Coventry, NY, 1832.
Died Elmira, NY, 1912.
Waters studied art in New York City and also in Dresden and Munich. He was chairman of the art department at Elmira College for many years. He exhibited at the NAD from 1855 to 1891 and kept a studio in the 10th Street Studio Building (N.Y.C.) in 1881-82 and again in 1886.

A LAKE IN THE WHITE MOUNTAINS (Mount Washington and the Saco). S/D.
>1872. Oil on canvas.
>26¼ x 43¾ (66.7 x 111.1).
>Arnot Art Gallery, Elmira, NY; Frick Art Reference Library.

FRANCONIA NOTCH.
>1876.
>F (see Standard Source Reference List).

New Hampshire Scenery

WAY, C. J.
Possibly **A. J. H. Way.**
C&H, N
Born Washington, DC, 1826.
A J. H. Way studied under John P. Frankenstein in Cincinnati. When he exhibited at the NAD in 1863, he gave his address as Montreal.
ANDROSCOGGIN, THE WHITE MOUNTAINS.
    Pre-1877; Society of Canadian Artists, 2nd exhibition, Montreal (Feb. 7, 1870).
SCENE IN THE WHITE MOUNTAINS (2).
    Pre-1877; Art Association exhibition, Mechanic's Hall, Montreal (1865).

WEBB, CHARLES K.
There is presently no information on this artist.
MOUNT WASHINGTON, WHITE MOUNTAINS.
    Pre-1877; Louisville (KY) Industrial Exposition (1878).

WEBBER, WESLEY
F, N, S
Born Gardiner, ME, 1841.
Died Boston, MA, 1914.
Webber exhibited at the NAD in 1890, at which time his address was Boston, and at the Leonard Auction Rooms in 1873 and 1876.
ANDROSCOGGIN RIVER, NEAR GORHAM, NEW HAMPSHIRE.
    Leonard Auction (Jan. 28, 1873), #120.
AUTUMN IN THE WHITE MOUNTAINS.
    Leonard Auction (Feb. 11, 1876), #33.
AUTUMN ON ARTIST [sic] BROOK, NORTH CONWAY.
    Leonard Auction (Feb. 18, 1876), #61.
OUTLET OF WINNIPISEOGEE [sic] LAKE.
    Leonard Auction (Feb. 11, 1876), #39.
SUMMER ON ARTIST [sic] BROOK, NORTH CONWAY.
    Leonard Auction (Feb. 18, 1876), #77.
VIEW ON THE SACO RIVER.
    Leonard Auction (Feb. 18, 1876), #58.

WEBER, PAUL CARL
A, Ce, C&H, F, G&W, N, R, S, T
Born Darmstadt, Germany, 1823.
Died Philadelphia, PA, 1916.
Weber studied art in Frankfurt, Germany, and came to the U.S. at the age of 25. He began exhibiting at the PAFA in 1849. He also exhibited at the NAD from 1850 to 1893, the Boston Athenaeum in 1864, and the Brooklyn Art Association. He returned to Darmstadt in 1860 and was appointed court painter. He traveled once again to the U.S., probably about 1870, certainly by 1881, when he gave his address as Philadelphia. An expert technician, he taught Edward Moran, William Stanley Hazeltine, and William Trost Richards.
Bibliography:
Ferber, Linda. "Ripe for Revival: Forgotten American Artists." *Artnews* (Dec. 1980), p. 68.
A MORNING AT NORTH CONWAY, NEW HAMPSHIRE.
    NAD, 1881, #649.
BLUE RIDGE MOUNTAIN LANDSCAPE (Mount Washington). S/D/L/L.
    1854. Oil on canvas.
    25½ x 37 (64.8 x 94).
    Pennsylvania State University, Vessel collection; Sporting Gallery; *Antiques* (Dec. 1976).
OLD MAN OF THE MOUNTAIN.
    Boston Athenaeum (1864), #257.

WEISMAN, W. H.
Nothing is presently known about this artist.
FRANCONIA FALLS. S/R.
    Oil on board.
    9 x 5 (22.9 x 12.7).
    Private collection (1983).

WENZLER, HENRY ANTONIO, JR. (or A. H. WENZLER)
A, Ce, F, G&W, N, R, S, T
Born Denmark. Died New York, NY, 1871.
Wenzler immigrated to the U.S. and began exhibiting at the NAD in 1838, a practice he continued until 1867. He was made an associate member of the NAD in 1849 and a full member in 1860. He lived in New York City during his active years.
A STUDY OF NORTH CONWAY.
    NAD, 1860, #232.
ARTIST'S BROOK, NORTH CONWAY.
    NAD, 1859, #688.
MOTE [sic] MOUNTAIN, NORTH CONWAY.
    NAD, 1859, #705.

WESTON, MARY BARTLETT PILLSBURY (MRS.)
Co, F, G&W
Born Hebron, NH, Jan. 5, 1817.
Died Lawrence, KS, May 1894.

Weston seems to have gone to Hartford, CT, to study painting. She worked as a miniaturist, then turned to oil portraits, landscapes, and religious paintings.

VIEW OF KEARSARGE AND RAGGED MOUNTAIN.
C. 1849-50. Oil on canvas.
39½ x 60¼ (100.3 x 153).
Private collection (1976); NMAA Inventory.

WHEELER, WILLIAM RUTHVEN

F, G&W, S
Born Scio, Washington County, MI, 1832.
Died c. 1894.
Wheeler was basically a portrait painter but did produce some landscapes. His first instruction came at an early age from an itinerant miniature painter, and he began his profession at the age of 15. At the age of 28 he studied for a short time in Detroit under Alvan Bradish. He moved to Hartford, CT, about 1862 and kept a studio there until 1893. A painting of Mount Washington was listed in the first annual exhibition of the Hartford Art Association in 1872, but he had added landscape to his repertoire as early as 1866.

Bibliography:
Connecticut Historical Society *Bulletin* 39:4.

CHOCORUA LAKE AND MOUNTAIN.
Pre-1877; Detroit Art Association, 1st exhibition (Feb. 1876).

MOUNT CHOCORUA.
1866. Oil on canvas.
20 x 30 (50.8 x 76.2).
Private collection (1974); BIAP.

MOUNT WASHINGTON #2. S/L/L.
1873. Oil on canvas.
12 x 18 (30.5 x 45.7).
Connecticut Historical Society *Bulletin* 39:4; owned by Wheeler's descendants.

MOUNT WASHINGTON (from North Conway) #3.
C. 1872. Oil on canvas.
Hartford Art Association, 1st annual exhibition (1872). Unlocated.

MT. KEARSARGE SUMMIT.
Pre-1877; Detroit Art Association, 1st exhibition (Feb. 1876).

NEW HAMPSHIRE LANDSCAPE (Mount Chocorua).
1866. Oil on canvas.
19 x 29 (48.3 x 73.7).
Antiques (Nov. 1974), p. 782; NMAA Inventory.

VIEW OF MOUNT WASHINGTON. S/L/R.
1868. Oil on canvas.
26 x 41 (66 x 104.1).
Lyman Allyn Museum, New London, CT.

VIEW ON THE ANDROSCOGGIN FROM MILAN.
Boston Athenaeum (1859), #51.

WHITE MOUNTAINS #1. S/L/L.
1869. Oil on canvas.
26¼ x 40¼ (66.7 x 102.2).
Connecticut Historical Society *Bulletin* 39:4; owned by Wheeler's descendants.

WHITE MOUNTAINS #2, S/L/L.
1883. Oil on canvas.
10 x 16 (25.4 x 40.6).
Connecticut Historical Society *Bulletin* 39:4; owned by Wheeler's descendants.

WHITE MOUNTAINS. S/L/R.
1883. Oil on canvas.
11¾ x 14½ (29.8 x 36.8).
Private collection.

WHITE MOUNTAINS FROM GIANT'S GRAVE.
Boston Athenaeum (1859), #53.

WHITE MOUNTAINS FROM JEFFERSON HILL.
Boston Athenaeum (1859), #50.

WHITE MOUNTAINS FROM LANCASTER.
Boston Athenaeum (1859), #52.

WHEELOCK, MERRILL GREENE

A, F, G&W, K, Ka, T
Born Calais, VT, 1822.
Died and was buried Chelsea, MA, 1866.
In his short life, Wheelock was a popular and sought-after illustrator. He was a practicing architect in Boston from 1847 to 1859, but when he enlisted in the Union Army in 1860 he gave his occupation as "painter." He produced 57 drawings for Starr King's The White Hills, *published in Boston in 1866, and exhibited a group of White Mountain views at the Boston Athenaeum in 1859 and 1860. The Crayon, in Dec. 1859, noted that "Wheelock has also been in the White Mountains region but later in the season. His studies are in watercolor, and chiefly of autumnal scenery. They are remarkable works, showing great command over his materials, and a sound and healthy perception. He draws admirably and with delicacy, coupled with which is a fine feeling for color."*

Bibliography:
Information courtesy of Dr. Jere Daniel, Professor of History, Dartmouth College.
King, Thomas Starr. *The White Hills: Their Legends, Landscape, and Poetry.* Boston: Crosby and Ainsworth, 1866.

New Hampshire Scenery

ANDROSCOGGIN RIVER.
Black and white.
Boston Art Club (Jan. 17-Feb. 10, 1874), #43.

CHOCORUA.
1860.
King, Thomas Starr. *The White Hills.*

LAKE WINNEPESAUKEE [sic].
Boston Athenaeum (1860), #80.

LAKE WINNEPESAUKEE [sic], FROM CENTRE HARBOR.
Boston Athenaeum (1859), #49.

MOUNT WASHINGTON.
Pre-1877; MA Charitable (1874).

MOUNT WASHINGTON FROM GREEN HILL, JACKSON.
Lion Gallery (1976); North Conway Library Exhibition (1965).

SUMMITS OF MOUNTS WASHINGTON, CLAY AND JEFFERSON FROM THE RIDGE OF MOUNT ADAMS.
Watercolor.
Boston Athenaeum (1860), #43; Leonard Auction (Dec. 6, 1861).

VIEW ON THE ANDROSCOGGIN.
Boston Athenaeum (1859), #51.

WHITE MOUNTAINS FROM BETHEL, ME.
Boston Athenaeum (1859), #54.

WHITE MOUNTAINS FROM GIANT'S GRAVE.
Boston Athenaeum (1859), #53.

WHITE MOUNTAINS FROM JEFFERSON HILL.
Boston Athenaeum (1859), #50.

WHITE MOUNTAINS FROM LANCASTER.
Boston Athenaeum (1859), #52.

WHITE MOUNTAINS; THE . . .
Watercolor.
Crayon (June 16, 1858).

WHISTLER, JAMES ABBOTT MCNEILL
B, C&H, DAB, F, G&W, N, S, T
Born Lowell, MA, July 10, 1834.
Died London, England, July 17, 1903.
Though Whistler has no presently known paintings or sketches of the White Mountains, he was a friend of the Gambles (of Proctor & Gamble) who summered in Intervale, NH, and in 1852, while a cadet at West Point, he visited at the Pendexter Mansion in Intervale.
Information courtesy of Phyllis F. Greene.

WHITAKER, (EDWARD H.?)
A, G&W
Born New Hampshire, c. 1808.
Died after 1862.

Whitaker exhibited at the Boston Athenaeum in 1830 and 1831 and seems to have been active in the area until 1862. He was listed as a fresco painter.

CRAWFORD NOTCH FROM MOUNT WILLARD.
Pre-1877; Leonard Auction, Providence artists' sale (May 9, 1888).

WHITE, GABRIELLA EDDY
Born 1843. Died 1932.
White was a friend of Benjamin Champney and Albert Bierstadt and painted with them in North Conway. She exhibited at the Brooklyn Art Association in 1878 and at the Boston Museum of Fine Arts Contemporary Exhibit in April 1879.
Information courtesy of Phyllis F. Greene.

MOUNTAIN SCENES (5).
North Conway Library Exhibition (1965).

WHITEFIELD, EDWIN
A, Ce, Ka
Born East Lulworth, Dorset, England, 1816.
Died Dedham, MA, 1892.
Whitefield was a rather naïve flower and landscape painter and lithographer. He came to the U.S. about 1840 and lived in New York City in 1844. Moving frequently, he was in Canada, where he taught school for a short while and married, then traveled to Minnesota (1856-59). He lived in Boston, MA, and vicinity in the 1880s. While in Minnesota he wrote and illustrated articles on the area for Harper's *and the New York* Tribune. *He exhibited at the NAD from 1852 to 1854 and, late in life, published a series of books entitled* The Homes of Our Forefathers, *illustrating early New England houses. He never stopped traveling, returning to Britain for a while, before continuing his travels in America. His aim was to leave an accurate pictorial record of the areas he visited.*

VIEW OF LAKE WINNEPESAUKEE [sic].
1867. Oil on canvas.
19 x 27½ (48.3 x 69.9).
Boston Athenaeum (1983); High Voltage Engineering Corp.

WHITNEY, JOSIAH DWIGHT
DAB, G&W
Born Northampton, MA, Nov. 23, 1819.
Died Lake Sunapee, NH, Aug. 19, 1896.
Whitney developed a deep interest in chemistry while studying at Yale, and he joined Charles

Dictionary of Painters

T. Jackson as an unpaid assistant in the summer of 1840. He acted as a topographical artist who executed lithographs in 1841 for Jackson's Final Report (published in 1844), as well as engravings for Views and Maps Illustrative of the Scenery and Views of New Hampshire. His work with Jackson drew out an interest in geology, and he went abroad to study chemistry and geology for several years beginning in 1842. He returned to the U.S. in 1847, worked at various geologic jobs, and served as California's state geologist from 1860 to 1874. The final years of his life were spent teaching science at Harvard.

DIXVILLE NOTCH.
    1841. Lithograph.
    New Hampshire Historical Society, Jackson's Final Report.

FLUME, FRANCONIA.
    1841. Lithograph.
    New Hampshire Historical Society, Jackson's Final Report.

PROFILE MOUNTAIN, FRANCONIA NOTCH.
    1841. Lithograph.
    New Hampshire Historical Society, Jackson's Final Report.

SLIDE AT THE WILLEY HOUSE.
    1841. Lithograph.
    New Hampshire Historical Society, Jackson's Final Report.

VIEW ON WINNIPISSEOGEE [sic].
    1841. Lithograph.
    New Hampshire Historical Society, Jackson's Final Report.

WILBRAHAM, CAPTAIN C.

Active c. 1850.
There is presently no other information on this artist.

NOTCH OF THE WHITE MOUNTAINS.
    General Services Administration, FDR Library, Hyde Park, NY (1975); BIAP.

SCENE IN THE WHITE MOUNTAINS.
    C. 1850. Watercolor.
    9¾ x 14 (24.8 x 35.6).
    General Services Administration, FDR Library, Hyde Park, NY (1975); BIAP.

WILDE (or WILD), HAMILTON GIBBS

A, Ce, G&W, N, R
Born 1827. Died 1884.

Wilde was a portrait, genre, and landscape painter in Boston. Though there are no known works of New Hampshire by Wilde, he was with Benjamin Champney in North Conway in 1852 according to Kilbourne.

WILKIE, ROBERT DAVID

A, F(sup), G&W, K, Ka
Born Halifax, Nova Scotia, Feb. 23, 1827 (or 1828).
Died Swampscott, MA, 1903.
Wilkie exhibited his first paintings in Halifax at the age of 21. He moved to Massachusetts soon thereafter and had a prolific career as a landscapist and illustrator. By 1853 he was contributing work to Gleason's Pictorial Drawing Room Companion. He exhibited at the Boston Athenaeum in 1856. From 1863 to 1865 he served as an artist-correspondent for Frank Leslie's Illustrated Weekly. By 1868 he was working for Prang Lithographic Company of Boston. Through his wife's relatives, he made visits to New Hampshire from 1869 to 1872 and again in 1876 and painted landscapes, many of which were chromolithographed by Prang.

Bibliography:
Information courtesy of the painter's granddaughter, Ruth Kimball Wilkie.
See Prang's "Gems of the White Mountains" listed in McClinton.
Vose Galleries catalog. The Rediscovery of a 19th-Century Boston Painter (Boston, 1948).

BAKER RIVER VALLEY.
    After 1868. Lithograph.
    McClinton, Prang's "Gems of the White Mountains," #4.

CENTRE HARBOR AND OSSIPEE MOUNTAINS.
    After 1868. Lithograph.
    McClinton, Prang's "Gems of the White Mountains"; Boston Public Library.

CHOCORUA LAKE.
    After 1868. Lithograph.
    McClinton, Prang's "Gems of the White Mountains"; Boston Public Library.

FLOATING TIMBER, MEREDITH.
    After 1868. Lithograph.
    McClinton, Prang's "Gems of the White Mountains"; Boston Public Library.

LAKE ELSWORTH AND THE WELSH [sic] RANGE, ELSWORTH, NEW HAMPSHIRE.
    Oil.
    30 x 15 (76.2 x 38.1).
    Private collection.

LIVERMORE FALLS.
After 1868. Lithograph.
McClinton, Prang's "Gems of the White Mountains"; Boston Public Library.

LOON POND.
After 1868. Lithograph.
McClinton, Prang's "Gems of the White Mountains"; Boston Public Library.

MEREDITH BAY.
After 1868. Lithograph.
McClinton, Prang's "Gems of the White Mountains"; Boston Public Library.

MOONLIGHT ON LAKE WINNIPISEOGEE [sic].
After 1868. Lithograph.
McClinton, Prang's "Gems of the White Mountains"; Boston Public Library.

MOONLIGHT ON THE LAKE, HEBRON, NEW HAMPSHIRE (NEWFOUND LAKE).
Oil.
15⅛ x 30¼ (38.4 x 76.8).
Private collection.

OSSIPEE FALL.
After 1868. Lithograph.
McClinton, Prang's "Gems of the White Mountains"; Boston Public Library.

PASSACONAWAY MOUNTAIN.
After 1868. Lithograph.
McClinton, Prang's "Gems of the White Mountains"; Boston Public Library.

PLYMOUTH INTERVALE.
After 1868. Lithograph.
McClinton, Prang's "Gems of the White Mountains"; Boston Public Library.

PLYMOUTH MOUNTAIN.
After 1868. Lithograph.
McClinton, Prang's "Gems of the White Mountains"; Boston Public Library.

PLYMOUTH VALLEY.
After 1868. Lithograph.
McClinton, Prang's "Gems of the White Mountains"; Boston Public Library.

RED HILL, CENTRE HARBOR.
After 1868. Lithograph.
McClinton, Prang's "Gems of the White Mountains"; Boston Public Library.

SANDWICH RANGE.
After 1868. Lithograph.
McClinton, Prang's "Gems of the White Mountains"; Boston Public Library.

SQUAM LAKE.
After 1868. Lithograph.
McClinton, Prang's "Gems of the White Mountains"; Boston Public Library.

SUNSET, MEAD VALLEY, NEW HAMPSHIRE.
Watercolor.
9½ x 12½ (24.1 x 31.8).
Private collection.

TWIN BELKNAPS: THE...
After 1868. Lithograph.
McClinton, Prang's "Gems of the White Mountains"; Boston Public Library.

WAKAWAN [sic] LAKE.
After 1868. Lithograph.
McClinton, Prang's "Gems of the White Mountains"; Boston Public Library.

WELSH [sic] MOUNTAIN, NEW HAMPSHIRE; THE...
Private collection.

WILLARD

Nothing is presently known about this artist.

VIEWS IN NEW HAMPSHIRE (2).
Leonard Auction (June 16, 1865), #59 and #60.

WILLIAMS, FREDERICK DICKINSON

A, C&H, F, G&W, N, S
Born Boston, MA, 1829.
Died Brookline, MA, Jan. 27, 1915.
For the first part of his adult life, Williams taught drawing in Boston public schools and exhibited at the Boston Athenaeum as well as at the NAD and the Boston Art Club. About 1870 he went to Paris for further study and exhibited at the Paris Salon in 1878. Later, he returned to Boston and remained there the rest of his life.

ANDROSCOGGIN AT SHELBURNE, NEW HAMPSHIRE; THE...
Boston Athenaeum (1860), #302.

BANKS OF THE ANDROSCOGGIN; THE...
Boston Athenaeum (1860), #300.

CHOCORUA PEAK.
Boston Athenaeum (1856), #114.

MONADNOCK, DUBLIN, NEW HAMPSHIRE.
Boston Athenaeum (1859), #181.

MOUNT WASHINGTON.
Boston Athenaeum (1856), #122.

NEW HAMPSHIRE SCENERY.
Leonard Auction (Jan. 28, 1873), #56.

OLD TANNERY ON THE ROAD TO FRANCONIA; THE...
Boston Athenaeum (1867), #258; NAD, 1867, #485.

VIEW IN COMPTON [sic], NEW HAMPSHIRE.
Boston Athenaeum (1855), #176.

WHITE MOUNTAINS FROM JACKSON, NEW HAMPSHIRE.
Pre-1877; Cincinnati (OH) Industrial Exposition (1873).

WHITE MOUNTAINS SHOWING AFTERNOON.
Boston Athenaeum (1860), #272.

WILLIAMS, ISAAC L.

A, C, C&H, F, G&W, N, R, S
Born Philadelphia, PA, June 24, 1817.
Died Philadelphia, PA, April 23, 1895.
Williams was trained under John Neagle and John R. Smith. He exhibited at the PAFA and also at the NAD and in Boston. In 1852 he taught oil painting at the Burlington (VT) Female Seminary and made a trip to Lake Superior with Thomas Moran in 1860.

GREAT STONE FACE.
PAFA, 1859.

PROFILE MOUNTAIN.
PAFA, 1859.

WILLIAMS, VIRGIL

B, G&W
Born Taunton, MA, 1830.
Died near Mt. St. Helena, CA, Dec. 18, 1886.
Williams went to Europe to study art about 1856. He returned to Boston before 1862 and exhibited at the Leonard Auction Rooms in 1863 and again in 1871. He moved permanently to California that year.

MORNING, WINNEPISEOGEE [sic].
Leonard Auction (May 24, 1871), #95.

NEW HAMPSHIRE LANDSCAPE.
C. 1880. Watercolor.
5 x 15 (12.7 x 38.1).
Private collection; BIAP.

WHITE MOUNTAINS.
Leonard Auction (May 22, 1863), #11.

WILLIAMSON, JOHN

A, C, C&H, F, G&W, N, S
Born Toll Cross, Scotland, April 10, 1826.
Died Glenwood-on-Hudson, NY, May 25, 1885.
Williamson was brought to the U.S. at an early age and lived in the area of New York City. He exhibited at the AAU in 1852 and 1853 and at the NAD from 1850 to the end of his life. In 1861 he was elected an associate of the NAD.

OLD MAN OF THE MOUNTAIN.
Boston Athenaeum (1856), #101.

SCHOOL-HOUSE, NEAR SQUAM LAKE, NEW HAMPSHIRE.
Boston Athenaeum (1861), #60.

SHADY BROOK ON THE SACO.
Boston Athenaeum (1858), #625.

SUMMIT OF CHOCORUA.
C&H (see Standard Source Reference List).

WILSON, E. T.

Possibly the E. Wilson listed in G&W as an itinerant painter. On the reverse of the painting of Percy Peaks is written in pencil: "Given to Emma Chamberlain by E. T. Wilson," and on the frame, "Percy Peaks in the [?] of Hark [or "Hart"] Stratfor [sic] and Milan."

PERCY PEAKS. S/L/L.
Oil on board.
14¼ x 7¾ (36.2 x 19.7).
Private collection (1975); Dufty (1975).

WOLCOTT, JOSIAH

G&W
Active 1835-57.
This artist exhibited at the Boston Athenaeum in 1837.

MOUNT KEARSARGE FROM RATTLESNAKE HILLS.
Oil.
18 x 24 (45.7 x 61).
Private collection (1960); NMAA Inventory.

WOODWARD, LAURA (or LANA)

N
Active 1872-89.
Woodward exhibited at the NAD from 1872 to 1889, giving her address as New York City.

AFTERNOON ON THE ELLIS RIVER.
NAD, 1878, #691; Pre-1877.

SCENE IN THE WHITE MOUNTAINS.
Pre-1877; Louisville (KY) Industrial Exposition (1878) (see Library of Congress for information).

SILVER CASCADE AT BETHLEHEM, WHITE MOUNTAINS.
Pre-1877; Louisville (KY) Industrial Exposition (1878).

WOTHERSPOON, WILLIAM WALLACE

C, Ce, F(sup), G&W, N, R
Born 1821. Died 1888.

New Hampshire Scenery

Scene in the White Mountains
Alexander H. Wyant
Oil on canvas, 32 1/2" x 54 1/2" / Collection: Vose Galleries,
     Boston / Ref. page 178

Wotherspoon sent his first painting to the NAD in 1844, giving his address as New York City. He continued to do so until 1883. He was elected an associate member in 1849. Many of his paintings were of White Mountains subjects. A comment about Wotherspoon found in the Frick Art Reference Library noted: "the landscape painter in New York, who after demonstrating to his friends his proper calling, left reluctantly his first love for a mercantile pursuit. His union with trade was successful."

ECHO LAKE, NEW HAMPSHIRE.
     AAU, 1847, #192.
FRANCONIA   NOTCH   WITH   MOUNT
LAFAYETTE.
     NAD, 1848, #237.
MOUNT WASHINGTON FROM JACKSON.
     NAD, 1848, #314.
OUTLET OF WINNIPISEOGEE [sic] LAKE.
     AAU, 1846, #107.
SQUAM LAKES, NEW HAMPSHIRE.
     NAD, 1847, #89.

STUDY FROM NATURE, SHELBURNE, NEW HAMPSHIRE.
     NAD, 1870, #237.
VIEW OF NORTH EAST LAKE, MOUNT WASHINGTON.
     NAD, 1844, #148; AAU, 1844, #23.

WUST, FERDINAND ALEXANDER
A, Ce, G&W, K, Ka, N, R, T
Born Dortrecht, Netherlands, 1836 or 1837.
Died Antwerp, Belgium, 1876 (or after 1881).
Wust came to the U.S. in the 1850s and opened a studio in New York City. He began exhibiting at the NAD in 1859, continuing to do so until 1881, and was elected an associate member in 1861. He also exhibited at the Brooklyn Art Association and the PAFA. The Crayon in February 1861 noted that Wust was "engaged on a View of the White Mountains." There is some confusion as to his date of death, for G&W stated that he returned to Europe and died there, though his work was exhibited at the NAD as late as 1881.

Bibliography:
Archives of American Art. Roll DDU1, Frames 861-862.

IN THE WHITE MOUNTAINS.
   PAFA, 1861, #148.

MOUNT WASHINGTON.
   C. 1861. Oil on canvas.
   51 x 86 (129.5 x 218.4).
   Merchants National Bank, Burlington, VT (1973).

MOUNT WASHINGTON (5).
   Pre-1877; Yale School of the Fine Arts, 1867, 1871, 1872, 1875.

SUNSET, LAKE WINNIPISEOGEE [sic].
   Brooklyn Art Association (March 1867), #224.

VIEW OF THE WHITE MOUNTAINS.
   Crayon (Jan. 1861), p. 44; Pre-1877.

WYANT, ALEXANDER HELWIG

A, B, Ba, C&H, DAB, F, G&W, N, R, S
Born Evans Creek, OH, Jan. 11, 1836.
Died New York, NY, Nov. 29, 1892.
Wyant was apprenticed to a harness maker at an early age but decided to become a painter about 1857. He was advised by George Inness and successfully applied to Nicholas Longworth for funds to study art. He studied at the NAD, where he began to exhibit in 1865, and in Düsseldorf, Germany, briefly in 1865. He was elected a full member of the NAD in 1869. In 1873 he suffered a stroke paralyzing his right hand. He switched to the left hand and changed his entire style of painting from linear to impressionist. In 1875 he was elected a member of the Century Association.

Bibliography:
Clark, Eliot. *Alexander Wyant.* New York: Frederick Fairchild Sherman, 1916 (privately printed).
Sears, Clara Endicott. *Highlights Among the Hudson River Artists.* Boston: Houghton Mifflin, 1947, pp. 200-204.

CHOCORUA.
   C. 1860. Oil on canvas.
   23 x 32 (58.4 x 81.3).
   Sotheby PB (Nov. 1977), #291.

LANDSCAPE (possibly New Hampshire).
   C. 1880. Oil on canvas.
   18⅛ x 30 (46 x 76.2).
   Art Institute of Chicago.

SCENE IN THE WHITE MOUNTAINS (Mount Washington from Jackson).
   Oil on canvas.
   32½ x 54½ (82.6 x 138.4).
   Vose Galleries (July 1980).

WHITE MOUNTAINS.
   Oil on canvas.
   14½ x 22½ (36.8 x 57.2).
   Adam Wechsler and Sons (May 23, 1976).

WHITE MOUNTAINS OF NEW HAMPSHIRE.
   C. 1860. Oil.
   23 x 32 (58.4 x 81.3).
   Sotheby PB (1977); Los Angeles County Museum (1973); BIAP.

WHITE MOUNTAINS; THE... S/D/L/L.
   C. 1867. Oil on canvas.
   20 x 35 (50.8 x 88.9).
   Old Print Shop.

WHITEFACE MOUNTAIN, NEW HAMPSHIRE.
   Boston Public Library, special clippings file.

YOUNG, HENRY DE MERRITT

Active 1892-96.
Young worked out of Boston.
Information courtesy of the New Hampshire Historical Society.

CRAWFORD NOTCH. S/L/Center.
   Pencil and white guache.

   10 x 13 (25.4 x 33).
   Private collection; Burlwood Antiques, Meredith, NH (July 1981).

MOUNT CARDIGAN AND NEWFOUND LAKE FROM BRIDGEWATER HILLS.
   1896. Watercolor.
   17 x 13 (43.2 x 33).
   New Hampshire Historical Society exhibition (July 5-Sept. 1, 1965).

New Hampshire Scenery

WHITE MOUNTAINS.
    1892. Watercolor.
    15 x 21½ (38.1 x 54.6).
    New Hampshire Historical Society.

YOUNG, W. S.

Active 1866-67.
Nothing else is presently known about this artist.
MOUNT JEFFERSON.
    Pre-1877; Crosby Art House Art Association, Eastern and Western Galleries (Chicago, 1866).
MOUNT KEARSARGE.
    C. 1866.
    39 x 27 (99.1 x 68.6).
    Berry Hill Galleries (Sept. 1973); BIAP.
VIEW ON AMMONOUSUC [sic] AT LISBON.
    1867.
    North Conway Library Exhibition.
WHITE MOUNTAINS; THE . . .
    C. 1867.
    20 x 35 (50.8 x 88.9).
    Old Print Shop *Portfolio* (May 1962), p. 214.

UNKNOWN

AN AMERICAN FISHING IDYLL – A VIEW TOWARDS MOUNT MONADNOCK.
    C. 1835.
    30 x 40 (76.2 x 101.6).
    Old Print Shop (1973).
CENTRE HARBOR, NEW HAMPSHIRE.
    16 x 20 (40.6 x 50.8).
    Parke-Bernet (1945); NMAA Inventory.
CONWAY VALLEY.
    Oil on canvas.
    26 x 42 (66 x 106.7).
    Old Print Shop (1973 and 1980).
CONWAY VALLEY (after Kensett and Sommer).
    26 x 38 (66 x 96.5).
    Kennedy Galleries.
CRAWFORD NOTCH IN THE WHITE MOUNTAINS.
    1860-80. Oil.
    Private collection; *Antiques* (Aug. 1974); NMAA Inventory.
HAYING IN CONWAY VALLEY.
    Oil.
    12 x 18 (30.5 x 45.7).
    Richard Bourne, Inc., catalog (Aug. 7, 1973); NMAA Inventory.

IN THE HEART OF NEW HAMPSHIRE.
    Oil on canvas.
    30 x 27½ (76.2 x 69.9).
    Fruitlands Museum. Illustrated in Sears (see Section III).
INTERVALE, NEW HAMPSHIRE.
    Oil on canvas.
    14 x 24 (35.6 x 61).
    New Hampshire Historical Society (1983).
IRON MOUNTAIN, JACKSON, NEW HAMPSHIRE.
    Oil on canvas.
    12 x 9 (30.5 x 22.9).
    Dartmouth College Art Galleries (1983).
LANDSCAPE, JACKSON, NEW HAMPSHIRE.
    14 x 23½ (35.6 x 59.7).
    Private collection (1975); BIAP.
LANDSCAPE, WHITE MOUNTAINS.
    Mid-19th century. Oil.
    18 x 31 (45.7 x 78.7).
    Colonel Town Community House (1979); NMAA Inventory.
MILL ON LAKE WINNIPESAUKEE [sic].
    Watercolor.
    10 1/16 x 16⅞ (25.6 x 42.9).
    Boston Museum of Fine Arts, Karolik collection (1980); University Art Gallery catalog, University of New Hampshire (1980), #37.
MOUNT CHOCORUA.
    Oil on canvas.
    12½ x 17½ (31.8 x 44.5).
    Private collection (1973); NMAA Inventory.
MOUNT WASHINGTON.
    Oil on canvas.
    26 x 36 (66 x 91.4).
    Northeastern University, Wheaton Holden collection, Boston.
MOUNT WASHINGTON AND THE SACO.
    1865. Oil on canvas.
    25⅝ x 39¾ (60 x 101).
    Signal Co. (1983).
MOUNT WASHINGTON FROM NORTH CONWAY.
    C. 1870. Oil on canvas.
    30 x 44 (76.2 x 111.8).
    Private collection (1975); BIAP.
MOUNT WASHINGTON FROM NORTH CONWAY (after Kensett).
    The Homestead, Sugar Hill, NH.

MOUNT WASHINGTON FROM WALKER'S POND.
C. 1890. Oil on canvas.
7½ x 16 (19.1 x 40.6).
Private collection (1983).

MOUNT WASHINGTON, NEW HAMPSHIRE.
Dartmouth College Art Galleries.

NEW HAMPSHIRE FARM SCENE.
1845. Oil.
24¾ x 31¼ (62.9 x 79.4).
Abby Aldrich Rockefeller Folk Art Collection, Williamsburg, VA (1969); NMAA Inventory.

NEW HAMPSHIRE LANDSCAPE.
Mid-19th century. Oil.
27½ x 43⅜ (69.9 x 110.2).
Old Sturbridge Village (1974).

NEW HAMPSHIRE LANDSCAPE.
19th century.
19½ x 29½ (49.5 x 74.9).
Parke-Bernet (1947); NMAA Inventory.

NEW HAMPSHIRE LANDSCAPE, WHITE MOUNTAINS.
19th century. Oil on canvas.
21 x 29 (53.3 x 73.7).
Private collection (1973); BIAP.

NORTH CONWAY.
19th century. Oil.
11¼ x 23¼ (28.6 x 59.1).
Private collection (1973); NMAA Inventory.

NOTCH HOUSE (after Bartlett).
Oil on canvas.
10½ x 16½ (26.7 x 41.9).
Private collection (1983).

PEMIGEWASSET MOUNTAIN FROM WEST CAMPTON.
C. 1880. Oil on canvas.
24½ x 30¼ (62.2 x 76.8).
New Hampshire Historical Society (1983).

RIVER SCENE, WHITE MOUNTAINS.
Oil on canvas.
24 x 30 (61 x 76.2).
New Hampshire Historical Society (1983).

SAWYER POND (2, SPRING AND AUTUMN).
Oil on metal after Bricher.
4 x 9 (10.2 x 22.9).
Private collection (1983).

SILVER LAKE, NEW HAMPSHIRE.
C. 1830. Oil on canvas (?).
30 x 25 (76.2 x 63.5).
Fruitlands Museum. Illustrated in Sears (see Section III).

SQUAM LAKE FROM RED HILL.
Vose Galleries.

SWIFT RIVER AND MOAT MOUNTAIN.
1868-75. Oil on canvas.
10 x 15 (25.4 x 38.1).
Private collection (1974); BIAP.

VIEW IN THE WHITE MOUNTAINS.
Pre-1877; Utica (NY) Art Association (1867).

VIEW OF MEREDITH, NEW HAMPSHIRE.
C. 1840. Oil.
19 x 24 (48.3 x 61).
Private collection (1966); NMAA Inventory.

New Hampshire Scenery

VIEW OF MONADNOCK.
C. 1890. Oil on canvas.
23¾ x 35¾ (60.3 x 90.8).
New Hampshire Historical Society (1983).

VIEW OF WINNEPESAUKEE [sic] FROM BELOW MEREDITH.
Harvard Willoughby, Fine Art Gallery, San Francisco, CA.

WHITE MOUNTAINS.
1826?
9 x 12.4 (22.9 x 31.5).
Private collection.

WHITE MOUNTAINS. S/D (but illegible).
1879? Oil on canvas.
12 x 14 (30.5 x 35.6).
Private collection (1983).

WHITE MOUNTAINS SCENERY.
Pre-1877.

WILLEY BROOK BRIDGE; THE . . .
C. 1880.
15½ x 20½ (39.4 x 52.1).
Vose Galleries.

UNKNOWN – POSSIBLE PAINTERS

Possibly **Charles Beckett:**

ALPINE HOUSE, GORHAM, NH.
Wood engraving with black ink.
Boston Athenaeum.

Possibly **Thomas Doughty:**

MAIN STREET, NORTH CONWAY.
1853. Oil on canvas.
9 x 13½ (22.9 x 34.3).
Private collection (1980); University Art Galleries catalog, University of New Hampshire (1980), #124.

Possibly **Doughty** or **Fisher:**

PROFILE LAKE AND OLD MAN OF THE MOUNTAIN.
C. 1835. Oil on canvas.
17½ x 23½ (44.5 x 59.7).
Private collection (1983); 3rd Art of Northern New England Show.

Possibly **Harry Fenn:**

MOUNT WASHINGTON.
Oil on canvas.
9 x 13 (22.9 x 33).
Private collection; Nick's Antiques, Sandwich, NH (1971).

Possibly **Greeve** or **Griever:**

VIEW OF WINNEPESAUKEE [sic] FROM ABOVE THE WEIRS. S/D. (but signature unintelligible).
189? Watercolor.
10 x 27½ (25.4 x 69.9).
Private collection (1980).

Possibly **William McLeod:**

LAFAYETTE FROM FRANCONIA FIELDS.
1852. Oil on canvas.
14½ x 24½ (36.8 x 62.2).
Private collection (1983); Burlwood Antiques, Meredith, NH (1976).

Signed **Y. M.?:**

WHITE MOUNTAINS.
1868-75. Oil on canvas.
10 x 12 (25.4 x 30.5).
Private collection (1974); BIAP.

Saco River, North Conway
Benjamin Champney, 1874
Oil on canvas, 24" x 36" / Collection: New Hampshire Historical
Society / Ref. page 31

SECTION II

List

---

of Paintings

---

by Subject

White Mountain Scenery
John F. Kensett, 1859
Oil on canvas, 45" x 36" / The New-York Historical Society:
The Robert L. Stuart Collection, on permanent loan from the
New York Public Library / Ref. page 105

The following is a list of paintings by subject arranged in alphabetical order by painter. For more information on the paintings see the individual artist's paintings list.

Index of Subjects

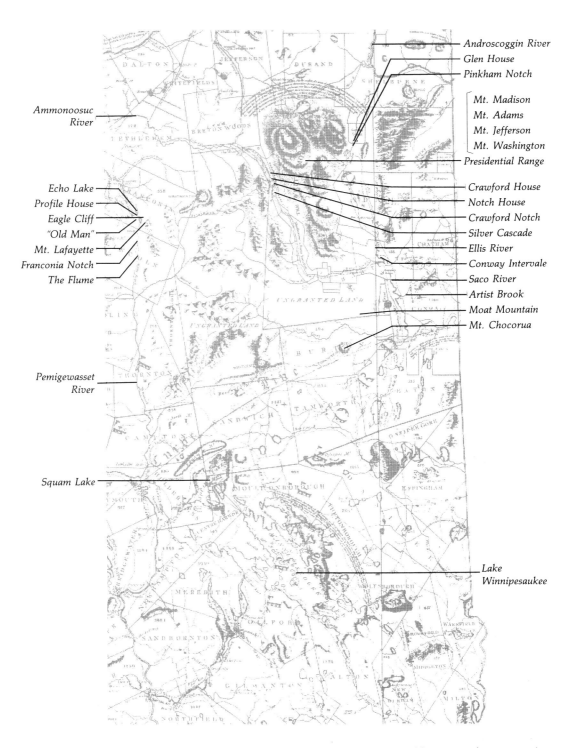

Androscoggin River
Glen House
Pinkham Notch

Mt. Madison
Mt. Adams
Mt. Jefferson
Mt. Washington
Presidential Range

Ammonoosuc
River

Crawford House
Notch House
Crawford Notch
Silver Cascade
Ellis River
Conway Intervale
Saco River
Artist Brook
Moat Mountain
Mt. Chocorua

Echo Lake
Profile House
Eagle Cliff
"Old Man"
Mt. Lafayette
Franconia Notch
The Flume

Pemigewasset
River

Squam Lake

Lake
Winnipesaukee

Location of landmark scenery painted by nineteenth-century artists.
The map is Philip Carrigain's 1816 "Map of New Hampshire."

New Hampshire Scenery

AMMONOOSUC RIVER

Bayne, Walter McPherson.
  AMMONOOSIC [sic] FALLS, NEAR THE WHITE MOUNTAINS.

Hill, Edward.
  ON THE AMMONUSAC [sic] RIVER. 1882.

Lanman, Charles.
  ON THE AMMANUSUC [sic]. Before 1870.

Lewis, Edmund Darch.
  VALLEY OF THE AMONOOSUCK [sic] (or VALE OF THE AMONOOSUCK [sic]). 1875.

Morviller, Joseph.
  ON THE AMMONOOSUC.

Pratt, Henry Cheever.
  ON THE AMMONOOSUC RIVER. 1828.
  RAPIDS IN THE AMMONOOSUC [sic] RIVER AT LITTLETON, NH. C. 1866.

Richards, Thomas Addison.
  EVENING ON THE AMMANOOSUCK [sic], NEW YORK [New Hampshire].

Shapleigh, Frank Henry.
  MOUNT WASHINGTON RANGE AND AMMONOOSUC RIVER. 1869.
  PRESIDENTIAL RANGE AND AMMONOOSUC RIVER. 1885.

Sprague, Isaac.
  CLIFFS OF THE FALLS OF THE AMONOOSUC [sic]; THE...
  FALLS OF THE AMONOOSUCK [sic] NEAR THE MOUNT WASHINGTON HOUSE. 1848.

Tilton, George H.
  SUNSET ON THE RIVER (AMMONOOSUC NEAR LITTLETON). C. 1880.

Young, W. S.
  VIEW ON AMMONOUSUC [sic] AT LISBON. 1867.

ANDROSCOGGIN RIVER

Bellows, Albert Fitch.
  AUTUMN ON THE ANDROSCOGGIN.

Birch, Thomas.
  (Attributed):
  EAST WHITE MOUNTAINS, ANDROSCOGGIN RIVER AT SEAGER. 1850.

Bricher, Alfred Thompson.
  AUTUMN ON THE ANDROSCOGGIN, SHELBURNE, NH.

Brown, George Loring.
  HAZY MORNING, HEAD OF THE ANDROSCOGGIN.

Brown, Harrison Bird.
  ON THE ANDROSCOGGIN.

Coleman, Charles Caryl.
  VIEW ON THE ANDROSCOGGIN.

Coombs, Delbert Dana.
  LANDSCAPE (Androscoggin).

Darley, Felix Octavius Carr.
  ANDROSCOGGIN RIVER.

Enneking, John Joseph.
  A SUMMER AFTERNOON ON THE ANDROSCOGGIN.

Fairman, Colonel James.
  MOUNTS MADISON AND JEFFERSON, AND ANDROSCOGGIN RIVER, NEAR GORHAM, NH.
  VALLEY OF THE ANDROSCOGGIN AT BETHEL, MAINE (DISTANT VIEW OF WHITE MOUNTAINS).

Fisher, D. A. (or D. H.?).
  ANDROSCOGGIN RIVER NEAR BETHEL, MAINE. 1895.

Frost, Francis Shedd.
  VIEW OF THE ANDROSCOGGIN.

Gerry, Samuel Lancaster.
  ANDROSCOGGIN FROM LEAD-MINE BRIDGE, SHELBURNE; THE...
  VALLEY OF THE ANDROSCOGGIN, MOUNTS MADISON AND WASHINGTON IN THE DISTANCE; THE...

Hart, William M.
  ON THE ANDROSCOGGIN.
  VIEW FROM ANDROSCOGGIN. 1859.

Higgins, George F.
  ON THE ANDROSCOGGIN.

Hill, J. W. (probably John William).
  ANDROSCOGGIN NEAR SHELBURNE, 1857.

Hill, John Henry.
  MOONLIGHT ON ANDROSCOGGIN.

Hill, John William.
  VALLEY OF ANDROSCOGGIN AT BIRBANKS FERRY, NEW HAMPSHIRE. 1859.

Johnson, David.
  VIEW ON THE ANDROSCOGGIN RIVER, MAINE (possibly New Hampshire). 1869-70.

Knapp, Charles W., Sr.
  VIEW ON THE ANDROSCOGGIN.

Lanman, Charles.
  ON THE ANDROSCOGGIN. Before 1870.

Martin, Homer Dodge.
  MORNING ON THE ANDROSCOGGIN.

Parker, John Adams.
  ON THE ANDROSCOGGIN.
Robbins, Horace Wolcott.
  ANDROSCOGGIN RIVER; THE...
  SUNSET ON THE ANDROSCOGGIN.
Shattuck, Aaron Draper.
  AUTUMNAL VIEW OF ANDROSCOGGIN
  AND WHITE MOUNTAINS. Before 1859.
  REMINISCENCE OF THE ANDROSCOGGIN.
Sonntag, William Louis.
  AN ISLAND IN THE ANDROSCOGGIN, NEW
  HAMPSHIRE.
  ON THE ANDROSCOGGIN.
  ON THE ANDROSCOGGIN RIVER.
Way, C. J.
  ANDROSCOGGIN, THE WHITE MOUNTAINS.
Webber, Wesley.
  ANDROSCOGGIN RIVER, NEAR GORHAM,
  NEW HAMPSHIRE.
Wheeler, William Ruthven.
  VIEW ON THE ANDROSCOGGIN FROM
  MILAN.
Wheelock, Merrill Greene.
  ANDROSCOGGIN RIVER.
  VIEW ON THE ANDROSCOGGIN.
Williams, Frederick Dickinson.
  ANDROSCOGGIN AT SHELBURNE, NEW
  HAMPSHIRE; THE...
  BANKS OF THE ANDROSCOGGIN; THE...

ARTIST FALLS AND BROOK

Ayer, Clara Dwight McMillan.
  ARTIST'S FALL, CONWAY, NH, FALL.
  C. 1875.
  ARTIST'S FALL, CONWAY, NH, SPRING.
  C. 1875.
Bellows, Albert Fitch.
  ARTIST'S BROOK, CONWAY.
  ARTIST'S BROOK, NH.
  ARTIST'S BROOK, NORTH CONWAY.
Bricher, Alfred Thompson.
  ARTISTS BROOK, NORTH CONWAY.
Champney, Benjamin.
  ARTIST'S BROOK.
  ARTIST'S BROOK, CONWAY, NH.
  ARTIST'S BROOK, CONWAY MEADOWS.
  1881.
  ARTIST'S BROOK, NORTH CONWAY. 1871.
  ARTIST BROOK, NORTH CONWAY, N.H.
  1878.

ARTIST'S BROOK, NORTH CONWAY, NH.
  ON ARTIST'S BROOK, NORTH CONWAY,
  NH.
Colman, Samuel, Jr.
  ARTIST'S BROOK, NORTH CONWAY.
Gerry, Samuel Lancaster.
  ARTIST'S BROOK, NORTH CONWAY, NEW
  HAMPSHIRE. C. 1857.
Griggs, Samuel W.
  ON THE ARTIST'S BROOK, WEST CAMPTON,
  NEW HAMPSHIRE.
Hill, Thomas.
  ARTIST'S BROOK.
Hilliard, William Henry.
  ARTIST'S BROOK, NORTH CONWAY, NEW
  HAMPSHIRE.
Hubbard, Richard William.
  ARTIST'S BROOK, NORTH CONWAY.
Inness, George.
  ARTIST'S BROOK, NORTH CONWAY. 1875.
Kensett, John Frederick.
  ARTIST'S BROOK, NORTH CONWAY, NEW
  HAMPSHIRE.
  ON THE ARTIST'S BROOK, NORTH CONWAY.
Mackey, Annie E.
  ARTIST'S BROOK.
Maxwell, Carrie C.
  RAMBLE ON ARTIST'S BROOK; THE... 1889.
Niles, George E.
  CAMPTON, ARTIST'S BROOK.
Ordway, Alfred T.
  ARTIST'S BROOK, NORTH CONWAY.
Shapleigh, Frank Henry.
  ARTIST'S BROOK, NORTH CONWAY.
Smillie, George Henry.
  VIEW OF THE ARTIST'S BROOK, CONWAY.
Stone, Benjamin.
  STUDY FOR ARTIST'S BROOK, NORTH CON-
  WAY, NEW HAMPSHIRE. 1851 or 1857.
Thompson, Albert (or Alfred Wadsworth).
  ARTIST'S BROOK, NORTH CONWAY.
Webber, Wesley.
  AUTUMN ON ARTIST BROOK, NORTH
  CONWAY.
  SUMMER ON ARTIST BROOK, NORTH
  CONWAY.
Wenzler, A. H. (or Henry Antonio).
  ARTIST'S BROOK, NORTH CONWAY.

CONWAY INTERVALE AND MEADOWS

Abbat, Agnes Dean.
  INTERVALE ROAD, NORTH CONWAY;
  THE...

Bierstadt, Albert.
  CATHEDRAL LEDGE. C. 1860-62.
  CONWAY MEADOWS, HAYING. 1864.
  CONWAY VALLEY, NEW HAMPSHIRE.
  MOAT MOUNTAIN, INTERVALE. 1860-62.
  VIEW FROM INTERVALE [,] MOAT, WHITE
  MOUNTAINS, NH.

Boutelle, DeWitt Clinton.
  CONWAY VALLEY.
  VALLEY OF CONWAY. 1860.

Champney, Benjamin.
  BROOK AND FALL SCENE (Albany, NY or
  Intervale).
  CONWAY MEADOWS. 1858.
  CONWAY MEADOWS. 1873.
  CONWAY MEADOWS.
  CONWAY MEADOWS.
  CONWAY MEADOWS.
  CONWAY MEADOWS AND MOAT MOUN-
  TAIN.
  CONWAY MEADOWS AND MOUNT WASH-
  INGTON. 1872.
  CONWAY MEADOWS AT MOUNT WASH-
  INGTON.
  CONWAY MEADOWS, SUMMER AFTER-
  NOON.
  CONWAY VALLEY. 1855-57.
  CONWAY VALLEY. 1857.
  HUMPHREY'S LEDGES, INTERVALE.
  INTERVALE.
  INTERVALE, 1852.
  INTERVALES OF NORTH CONWAY.
  LANDSCAPE, NEW ENGLAND (Conway Mead-
  ows?)
  NORTH CONWAY MEADOWS. After 1870.
  NORTH CONWAY MEADOWS.
  ON THE INTERVALE AT NORTH CONWAY.
  ON THE MEADOWS, NORTH CONWAY.
  PICNIC ON ARTIST'S LEDGE, OVERLOOKING
  CONWAY MEADOWS, NH. 1874.

Church, Frederic Edwin.
  AUTUMN LANDSCAPE, COWS AND STREAM.
  C. 1850.
  AUTUMN LANDSCAPE (WASHINGTON AND
  CONWAY MEADOWS). C. 1850.
  INTERVALE AT NORTH CONWAY. C. 1856.

Colman, Samuel, Jr.
  CONWAY MEADOWS.

Conway Valley.
  HARVEST SCENE (Mount Washington and Con-
  way Meadows).
  MOUNT WASHINGTON, CONWAY VALLEY.
  SUMMER LANDSCAPE (Conway Meadows and
  Moat Mountain).

Cropsey, Jasper Francis.
  WINTER (Conway Valley, New Hampshire).
  1859.

Fenn, Harry.
  WHITE MOUNTAINS, FROM CONWAY
  MEADOWS; THE...

Fisher, Alvan.
  VIEW IN LOWER BARTLETT, NH OF THE IN-
  TERVALE, LEDGES, AND MOTE [sic] MOUN-
  TAIN.

Frerichs, William Charles Anthony.
  MOUNT WASHINGTON, CONWAY VALLEY,
  NEW HAMPSHIRE. C. 1865.

Gauley, Robert David.
  LANDSCAPE, INTERVALE, NEW HAMP-
  SHIRE. 1894.

Gay, Winckworth Allan.
  CONWAY MEADOWS (looking south?).
  LEDGES; THE...

Gerry, Samuel Lancaster.
  GRASSY POOL WITH COWS AND AN ART-
  IST SKETCHING, NH. 1857.
  INTERVALE MEADOWS WITH COWS (look-
  ing south).
  LANDSCAPE WITH COWS AND PLOUGH-
  MAN (North Conway Meadows and Kearsarge).
  1852.
  ON CONWAY INTERVALE, MOUNTAINS
  AND MEADOW.
  ON CONWAY MEADOWS, BROOK VISTA.
  ON THE INTERVALE, NORTH CONWAY.

Gifford, Sanford Robinson.
  CONWAY VALLEY (with Mount Washington).
  CONWAY VALLEY FROM CATHEDRAL
  LEDGE.
  CONWAY VALLEY, NEW HAMPSHIRE. Before
  1867.
  MOUNTAIN VALLEY (Conway Meadows from
  Cathedral Ledge). C. 1854.
  Attributed:
  Pair: MOUNT CHICHOURA [sic], NEW HAMP-
  SHIRE, and INTERVALE, NEW HAMPSHIRE.

Griggs, Samuel W.
  CONWAY MEADOWS.

Hart, William M.
  CONWAY VALLEY AND MOUNT WASHING-
  TON. 1850-60.
  VALLEY OF CONWAY.

List of Paintings by Subject

Hidley, Joseph Henry.
CONWAY INTERVALE (Moat Mountain and Ledges).

Hilliard, William Henry.
KEARSARGE AND THORN MOUNTAINS, INTERVALE, NEW HAMPSHIRE. June 14, 1895.

Hotchkiss, Thomas Hiram.
MEADOWS OF NORTH CONWAY, NEW HAMPSHIRE.
SUMMER, CONWAY VALLEY.

Hubbard, Richard William.
PATH TO THE MEADOWS, NORTH CONWAY.

Inness, George.
CONWAY MEADOWS (or SUMMER SQUALL ON MOAT MOUNTAIN). 1876.
CONWAY VALLEY. 1875.
CONWAY VALLEY (or LATE SUMMER AFTERNOON). 1882.
NORTH CONWAY, WHITE HORSE LEDGE... C. 1875.
SACO FORD, CONWAY MEADOWS. 1872.

Insley, Albert B.
INTERVALE, NEW HAMPSHIRE. 1881.

Johnson, David.
CONWAY VALLEY, NEW HAMPSHIRE. 1859.

Keith, William.
CONWAY MEADOWS. 1881.

Kensett, John Frederick.
CLIFFS AT NORTH CONWAY.
CLIFFS, NEW HAMPSHIRE; THE...
CONWAY BLUFFS.
CONWAY VALLEY. 1851.
CONWAY VALLEY. 1854.
CONWAY VALLEY. 1854.
CONWAY VALLEY, NEW HAMPSHIRE. 1854.
CONWAY VALLEY, NH.
CONWAY VALLEY, NH. 1854.
CONWAY VALLEY, NH (or RANGE OF THE CATSKILLS). 1859.
FOOT OF THE CLIFFS, NORTH CONWAY, NEW HAMPSHIRE.
MOUNT WASHINGTON AND CONWAY VALLEY. 1867.
NORTH CONWAY (CLIFFS AND ROCKS).

Lanman, Charles.
CONWAY VALLEY. Before 1870.

Lewin, James Morgan.
CONWAY MEADOWS WITH MOAT MOUNTAIN AND CATHEDRAL LEDGE. 1859-60.

Lewis, Edmund Darch.
CONWAY VALLEY, NEW HAMPSHIRE. 1870.
INTERVALE, NEW HAMPSHIRE. 1863.
INTERVALE, NORTH CONWAY, MOUNT WASHINGTON.

Meade, J.
INTERVALE FROM NORTH CONWAY. C. 1860.

Morrison, William.
CONWAY VALLEY. 1853.

Ochtman, Leonard.
NORTH CONWAY INTERVALE TOWARDS ATTITASH.

Parker, John Adams.
CONWAY'S [sic] MEADOW.

Scott, John White Allen.
CONWAY VALLEY. 1869.
VIEW OF CONWAY VALLEY, NEW HAMPSHIRE. C. 1865.

Shapleigh, Frank Henry.
CONWAY INTERVALE (Mount Washington and White Horse Ledge). 1871.
CONWAY MEADOWS FROM JACKSON, NEW HAMPSHIRE.

Shattuck, Aaron Draper.
ACROSS INTERVALE TO MOUNT WASHINGTON. 1858.
CATHEDRAL LEDGE, CONWAY, NEW HAMPSHIRE. 1854.
CONWAY – LEDGES IN SUMMER. Aug. 22, 1856.
HAYING AT INTERVALE, CONWAY. 1859.
HAYING SCENE NEAR MOAT MOUNTAIN, CONWAY, NH. 1859.
INTERVALE, MOUNT WASHINGTON BEHIND CLOUDS. 1859.
INTERVALE, NH. 1854.
MEADOW BROOK, CONWAY, NEW HAMPSHIRE.
RED CLOUDS OVER DARK INTERVALE LEDGES. 1854.
Attributed:
COMING STORM, CONWAY MEADOWS.

Snowe, W. Francis.
CONWAY MEADOWS (MOTE [sic] MOUNTAIN). 1870.

Stetson, Sylvia C.
MEADOW – NORTH CONWAY.

Suydam, Henry.
CONWAY MEADOWS. 1874.

Suydam, James Augustus.
CONWAY MEADOWS.

Titcomb, William H.
  CONWAY VALLEY IN AUTUMN. C. 1860.
  MOUNT WASHINGTON AND CONWAY
  VALLEY.
  MOUNT WASHINGTON VALLEY.
  Attributed:
  CONWAY VALLEY.

Tryon, Benjamin Franklin.
  CONWAY VALLEY AND MOAT MOUNTAIN.

Unknown.
  CONWAY VALLEY.
  CONWAY VALLEY.
  CONWAY VALLEY (after Kensett and Sommer).
  HAYING IN CONWAY VALLEY.
  INTERVALE, NEW HAMPSHIRE.

Urquhart, A. C.
  CONWAY VALLEY.

EAGLE CLIFF

Bierstadt, Albert.
  EAGLE CLIFF, WHITE MOUNTAINS, NEW
  HAMPSHIRE. C. 1858.

Burnham, Thomas M.
  EAGLE ROCK, WHITE MOUNTAINS.

Cropsey, Jasper Francis.
  EAGLE CLIFF.
  EAGLE CLIFF, FRANCONIA NOTCH, 1852.
  Sept. 13, 1852.
  EAGLE CLIFF, FRANCONIA NOTCH, NEW
  HAMPSHIRE. 1858.
  EAGLE CLIFF, NEW HAMPSHIRE. 1850.
  EAGLE CLIFF, NEW HAMPSHIRE (AUTUMN
  SCENE). 1851.
  PIONEER'S HOME, EAGLE CLIFF, WHITE
  MOUNTAINS. 1859.
  SUNSET, EAGLE CLIFF, NEW HAMPSHIRE.
  1867.
  SUNSET, EAGLE CLIFF, NEW HAMPSHIRE.
  1851.
  SUNSET, EAGLE CLIFF, NEW HAMPSHIRE.

Duggan, Peter Paul.
  EAGLES [sic] CRAG, WHITE MOUNTAINS.

Ferguson, Henry A.
  FRANCONIA NOTCH, EAGLE CLIFF. C. 1870.

Gerry, Samuel Lancaster.
  ECHO LAKE AND EAGLE CLIFF. C. 1875.
  ECHO LAKE WITH EAGLE CLIFF.

Hill, Edward.
  EAGLE CLIFF AND EAGLE PASS.
  EAGLE CLIFF AND ECHO LAKE. 1881.
  EAGLE CLIFF, ECHO LAKE. 1878.

EAGLE CLIFF FROM PROFILE LAKE. 1897.
ECHO LAKE AND EAGLE CLIFF.
WHITE MOUNTAINS LANDSCAPE, EAGLE
CLIFF, ECHO LAKE.

Johnson, David.
  EAGLE CLIFF.
  EAGLE CLIFF, FRANCONIA NOTCH, NEW
  HAMPSHIRE. 1869.

Kensett, John Frederick.
  EAGLE CLIFF FROM DEVIL'S PASS.
  EAGLE CLIFF FROM LAKE PEMIGEWASSET,
  FRANCONIA NOTCH.

Martin, Homer Dodge.
  WHERE TROUT ABIDE (Eagle Cliff, Franconia,
  New Hampshire).

McEntee, Jervis.
  EAGLE CLIFF, FRANCONIA, NEW HAMP-
  SHIRE. 1866.

McLeod, William.
  EAGLE CLIFF. 1852.

Parker, John Adams.
  EAGLE CLIFF AT SUNSET.
  EAGLE CLIFF, FRANCONIA.
  EAGLE CLIFF, WHITE MOUNTAINS.

Perkins, Granville.
  EAGLE CLIFF AND THE ECHO HOUSE. 1882.

Richards, William Trost.
  EAGLE'S [sic] NEST, FRANCONIA NOTCH.
  1873.

Shattuck, Aaron Draper.
  NORTH CONWAY, AUG. 1854 (Echo Lake and
  Eagle Cliff).

Smith, Francis Hopkinson.
  EAGLE CLIFF, WHITE MOUNTAINS. 1879.

Sonntag, William Louis.
  EAGLE CLIFF, NEW HAMPSHIRE.

Stone, Benjamin.
  EAGLE CLIFF AND ECHO LAKE.

Tilton, George H.
  EAGLE CLIFF, FRANCONIA, NEW HAMP-
  SHIRE. C. 1880.

ECHO LAKE, CONWAY AND FRANCONIA

Bierstadt, Albert.
  ECHO LAKE, FRANCONIA MOUNTAINS,
  NEW HAMPSHIRE (or WILDERNESS LAKE).
  1861.

Bricher, Alfred Thompson.
  ECHO LAKE, FRANCONIA. 1868.
  ECHO LAKE, NEW HAMPSHIRE. C. 1860s.

List of Paintings by Subject

Brown, George Loring.
ECHO LAKE, SUNSET (FLUME HOUSE, WHITE MOUNTAINS, SUNSET, 1862). 1862.

Browne, Robert.
ECHO LAKE, WHITE MOUNTAINS.

Champney, Benjamin.
ECHO LAKE AND FRANCONIA NOTCH. 1853.

Cropsey, Jasper Francis.
AUSABLE CHASM (ECHO LAKE, FRANCONIA). 1875.

Dickerman, A.
ECHO LAKE.

Doughty, Thomas.
ECHO LAKE (FRANCONIA). 1836.

Fennimore, T. J.
HART'S LEDGE, ECHO LAKE, NEAR NORTH CONWAY, NEW HAMPSHIRE. 1867.

Frost, Francis Shedd.
ECHO LAKE.

Gay, Winkworth Allan.
EAGLE CLIFF ON ECHO LAKE, FRANCONIA.
ECHO LAKE, FRANCONIA.

Gerry, Samuel Lancaster.
ECHO LAKE AND EAGLE CLIFF. C. 1875.
ECHO LAKE WITH EAGLE CLIFF.
ECHO LAKE, FRANCONIA NOTCH.
LAKE IN THE WHITE MOUNTAINS (ECHO LAKE).

Gifford, Sanford Robinson.
A SKETCH OF ECHO LAKE IN THE FRANCONIA MOUNTAINS, NH.
ECHO LAKE, WHITE MOUNTAINS.

Gignoux, Marie-François Regis.
AUTUMN LANDSCAPE (Echo Lake?).

Hill, Edward.
COMING STORM, ECHO LAKE; THE... C. 1877.
EAGLE CLIFF AND ECHO LAKE. 1881.
EAGLE CLIFF, ECHO LAKE. 1878.
ECHO LAKE AND EAGLE CLIFF.
ECHO LAKE AND PROFILE HOUSE. 1887.
FRANCONIA NOTCH, THE WHITE MOUNTAINS, ECHO LAKE AND PROFILE HOUSE. 1887.
LAKE AND MOUNTAINS (Echo Lake). 1877.
WHITE MOUNTAINS LANDSCAPE, EAGLE CLIFF, ECHO LAKE.

Hill, Thomas.
ECHO LAKE, FRANCONIA NOTCH.

Hodgdon, Sylvester Phelps.
ECHO LAKE, MORNING.
ECHO LAKE, FRANCONIA.
ECHO LAKE, FRANCONIA, NEW HAMPSHIRE.
ECHO LAKE, FRANCONIA, NEW HAMPSHIRE. 1886.
ECHO LAKE, NEW HAMPSHIRE.

Hunting, Charles.
ECHO LAKE. C. 1880.

Johnson, David.
ECHO LAKE, FRANCONIA NOTCH, NEW HAMPSHIRE. 1867.
ECHO LAKE, WHITE MOUNTAINS.

Kensett, John Frederick.
MOONRISE, ECHO LAKE.

Kurtz, Henry.
ECHO LAKE, WHITE MOUNTAINS.

Lewis, Edmund Darch.
CANOEING ON THE LAKE, WHITE MOUNTAINS (Echo Lake, Conway). 1865.
ECHO LAKE, FRANCONIA.

McIlvaine, William, Jr.
ECHO POND, NEW HAMPSHIRE.

Parker, John Adams.
ECHO LAKE.
ON ECHO LAKE.

Perkins, Granville.
ECHO LAKE, WHITE MOUNTAINS.

Shapleigh, Frank Henry.
ECHO LAKE, NEW HAMPSHIRE, FRANCONIA NOTCH. 1879.

Shattuck, Aaron Draper.
ECHO LAKE, WHITE MOUNTAINS.
NORTH CONWAY, AUG. 1854 (Echo Lake and Eagle Cliff). 1854.

Shindler, Antonio Zeno.
FRANCONIA, ECHO LAKE.

Stone, Benjamin.
EAGLE CLIFF AND ECHO LAKE.
ECHO LAKE.

Thorndike, George Quincy.
ECHO LAKE, FRANCONIA MOUNTAINS, NEW HAMPSHIRE.

Titcomb, William H.
ECHO LAKE, NEW HAMPSHIRE. C. 1865.

Wotherspoon, William Wallace.
ECHO LAKE, NEW HAMPSHIRE.

EMERALD POOL

Bierstadt, Albert.
EMERALD POOL.
EMERALD POOL. 1871.
STUDY OF FERNS, WHITE MOUNTAINS, EMERALD POOL. 1869.
WHITE MOUNTAINS, STUDY OF FERNS ABOVE EMERALD POOL. C. 1860.

Fenn, Harry.
EMERALD POOL, PEABODY-RIVER GLEN. Before 1872.

Lewis, Edmund Darch.
EMERALD POOL, WHITE MOUNTAINS.

Shapleigh, Frank Henry.
EMERALD POOL.
EMERALD POOL NEAR GLEN HOUSE.

Tryon, Benjamin Franklin.
WHITE MOUNTAINS; THE... (Emerald Pool).

THE FLUME

Bierstadt, Albert.
FLUME, WHITE MOUNTAINS; THE... 1869.

Blakelock, Ralph Albert.
BOULDER AND THE FLUME; THE... C. 1878.

Chambers, Thomas.
FLUME, WHITE MOUNTAINS, NH; THE... 1696.

Cole, Thomas.
FLUME IN THE WHITE MOUNTAINS. 1827.
FLUME IN THE WHITE MOUNTAINS (another view).

Farr, Ellen B.
FLUME, NEW HAMPSHIRE.

Fenn, Harry.
FLUME; THE...

Gerry, Samuel Lancaster.
FLUME; THE...

Gibson, William Hamilton.
FALL OF THE BOWLDER [sic] (Flume). 1883.

Happel, Carl.
FLUME (several versions). Before 1864.

Herrick, Henry, W.
FLUME AT FRANCONIA, NEW HAMPSHIRE.

Hill, Thomas.
FLUME, FRANCONIA NOTCH, WHITE MOUNTAINS; THE...

Hodgdon, Sylvester Phelps.
FLUME; THE... 1856.

FLUME; THE... 1856.

Kensett, John Frederick.
FLUME, FRANCONIA MOUNTAINS; THE...
FLUME, FRANCONIA MOUNTAINS; THE...
FLUME, FRANCONIA NOTCH – A STUDY; THE...
FLUME, FRANCONIA NOTCH, NEW HAMPSHIRE; THE... C. 1850.
FLUME, NEW HAMPSHIRE; THE...
FLUME, NEW HAMPSHIRE; THE...

McLeod, William.
FLUME; THE... 1852.

Shearer, Christopher H.
FLUME, WHITE MOUNTAINS; THE...

Sprague, Isaac.
FLUME, IN LINCOLN, NEW HAMPSHIRE; THE... 1848.

Tilton, George H.
FLUME GORGE, FRANCONIA NOTCH. C. 1880-83.

Whitney, Josiah Dwight.
FLUME, FRANCONIA. 1841.

HOTELS

Beckett, Charles E.
GLEN HOUSE. 1852.
PLEASANT MOUNTAIN HOUSE NEAR BRIDGTON. C. 1851.
VALLEY HOUSE IN CRAWFORD NOTCH; THE...

Brown, George Loring.
ECHO LAKE, SUNSET (or FLUME HOUSE, WHITE MOUNTAINS, SUNSET, 1862).

Cabot, James Elliot.
LAFAYETTE HOUSE, FRANCONIA NOTCH, SEPTEMBER 1, 18[45]. 1845.
NOTCH HOUSE, AUGUST 30, 1845.
OLD CRAWFORD'S, NOTCH, WHITE MOUNTAINS. 1845-46.

Champney, Benjamin.
GLEN HOUSE FROM MOUNT WASHINGTON CARRIAGE ROAD.

DeFrees, T.
JACKSON ROAD TO BLACK MOUNTAIN (Christman Farm Inn). 1880.

Durand, Asher Brown.
NOTCH HOUSE, WHITE MOUNTAINS, NH, JULY 3, 1839.

Hill, Edward.
ECHO LAKE AND PROFILE HOUSE. 1887.

List of Paintings by Subject

FRANCONIA NOTCH, THE WHITE MOUN-
TAINS, ECHO LAKE AND PROFILE HOUSE.
1887.
LAFAYETTE AND PROFILE HOUSE. 1892.

Inness, George.
RIGOUR OF THE GAME, KEARSARGE HALL,
NH (or CROQUET, CONWAY, NH). C. 1875.

Perkins, Granville.
EAGLE CLIFF AND THE ECHO HOUSE. 1882.

Selinger, Jean Paul.
PRESIDENTIAL RANGE AND CRAWFORD
HOUSE FROM MOUNT AVALON.

Shapleigh, Frank Henry.
NOTCH HOUSE, CRAWFORD NOTCH;
THE. . . 1879.
OLD HANSON TAVERN, UPPER BARTLETT,
NEW HAMPSHIRE.

Smith, [William Thompson] Russell.
CRAWFORD HOUSE AND SACO LAKE.

Sonntag, William Louis.
VIEW TO GLEN HOUSE, NEW HAMPSHIRE.

Sprague, Isaac.
FRANCONIA NOTCH WITH THE LAFAYETTE
HOUSE. 1848.
GATE OF THE NOTCH OF THE WHITE
MOUNTAINS, WITH THE NOTCH HOUSE.
1848.
MOUNT CRAWFORD NEAR THE WHITE
MOUNTAINS, WITH THE MOUNT CRAW-
FORD HOUSE. 1848.

Strother, David Hunter.
SLEEPING QUARTERS IN THE BARN AT
CRAWFORD'S.

Tidd, Marshall M.
ROSEBUD HOUSE [Rosebrook] NEAR FAB-
YANS [sic]. 1859.

Unknown (possibly Charles Beckett).
ALPINE HOUSE, GORHAM, NH.

MOUNTAINS

Chocorua

B., S. E. (possibly Blackwell).
CHOCORUA MOUNTAIN, NH. 1875.

Bierstadt, Albert.
CHICOURA [sic] MOUNTAIN, NEW HAMP-
SHIRE.
CHICOURA [sic] MOUNTAIN, NEW HAMP-
SHIRE. C. 1857-58.
MOUNT CHOCORUA. C. 1857-58.
MOUNT CHOCORUA, NEW HAMPSHIRE.
MOUNT CHOCORUA, NEW HAMPSHIRE.

MOUNT CHOCORUA, NEW HAMPSHIRE
(previously titled WYOMING). C. 1860-62.
MOUNT CHOCORUA, NEW HAMPSHIRE. C.
1860-62.

Bricher, Alfred Thompson.
MOUNT CHOCORUA.
MOUNT CHOCORUA AND LAKE.
MOUNT CHOCORUA, N.H. 1865.
MOUNT CHOCURA [sic] AND MOUNT
MOAT FROM INTERVALE, NEW HAMP-
SHIRE. C. 1860-65.

Brown, John Appleton.
CHOCORUA PEAK. 1864.

Carpenter, Ellen Maria.
MOUNT CHOCORUA WITH AUTUMN
FOLIAGE.
MOUNT CHOCORUA, N.H.

Casilear, John William.
ANOCORUA [sic] PEAK, NH. Before 1871.
CHOCORUA PEAK. C. 1859.

Champney, Benjamin.
BACK OF CHOCORUA, SPRING.
CHICORUA [sic].
CHICORUA [sic].
CHOCORUA.
CHOCORUA.
CHOCORUA, SOUTHERN APPROACH. 1876.
MOTE [sic] MOUNTAIN AND CHOCORUA –
A VIEW FROM SUNSET HILL, NORTH CON-
WAY.
MOUNT CHOCORUA.
MOUNT CHOCORUA.
MOUNT CHOCORUA.
MOUNT CHOCORUA FROM CHOCORUA
LAKE.
MOUNT CHOCORUA, NEW HAMPSHIRE.
1858.
NEW HAMPSHIRE LAKE SCENERY – MOUNT
CHOCORUA IN DISTANCE.
PEAK OF CHOCORUA.
PUMPKIN TIME (Chocorua). 1871.

Church, Frederic Edwin.
LANDSCAPE WITH MOUNTAINS AND LAKE
(Chocorua). C. 1850.

Cole, Thomas.
AUTUMN TWILIGHT, VIEW OF CORWAY
PEAK (Chocorua). 1834.
CHOCORUA'S CURSE. 1827-29.
CORWAY PEAK, NH (Chocorua). 1844.
LAST OF THE MOHICANS (Chocorua); THE. . .
1827.
MOUNT CHOCORUA. C. 1827-28.

New Hampshire Scenery

PIC-NIC (Chocorua in Background); THE . . . 1846.

VIEW OF CORROWAY [sic] PEAK, NH. Before 1828.

WHITE MOUNTAINS, MOUNT CHOCORUA.

Colman, Samuel, Jr.
CHOCORUA.
CHOCORUA.
CHOCORUA POND AND MOUNTAIN.

Cropsey, Jasper Francis.
CHOCORUA MOUNTAIN. Sept. 28, 1852.
CHOCORUA PEAK, 1855. Oct. 8, 1855.
MOUNT CHOCORUA AND RAILROAD TRAIN, NEW HAMPSHIRE. 1869.
MOUNT CHOCORUA, NEW HAMPSHIRE. 1863.
MOUNT CHOCORUA, NEW HAMPSHIRE. 1873.
MOUNT CHOCORUA, NEW HAMPSHIRE, AUTUMN. C. 1872.
WINTER, CHOCORUA PEAK, WHITE MOUNTAINS.

Darrah, Ann Sophia Towne.
MOUNT CHOCORUA.

Doughty, Thomas.
RIVER SCENE WITH HUNTER AND FISHER-MAN (Chocorua). C. 1832.

Dunning, Robert Spear.
MOUNT CHOCORUA. 1864.

Durand, Asher Brown.
CHOCORUA. 1859.
CHOCORUA PEAK. 1855.
MOUNT CHOCORUA. 1855.
MOUNT CHOCORUA, NEW HAMPSHIRE.
MOUNT CHOCORUA, NEW HAMPSHIRE. Aug. 22, 1855.
MOUNT CHOCORUA, WHITE MOUNTAINS, NH (or CHOCORUA, WHITE MOUNTAIN SCENE). 1855.
SUNSET ON CHOCORUA. 1876.

Edwards, Thomas.
VIEW AT CHOCORUA.

Enneking, John Joseph.
MOUNT CHOCORUA.
MOUNT CHOCORUA. 1894.

Fairman, James.
MOUNT CHICOURA [sic], NEW HAMPSHIRE.
YOUTH OF CHICOURA [sic]; THE . . .

Fennimore, T. J.
MOUNT CHOCORUA.

Fisher, Alvan.
CHOCORUA PEAK, POND AND ADJACENT SCENERY AS SEEN TOWARDS EVENING. MOUNT CHOCORUA. 1855.
MOUNT CHOCORUA, FROM SANDWICH, NH, A VIEW FROM THE ROAD LEADING TO YOUNG MOUNTAIN.

Frost, Francis Shedd.
CHOCORUA. 1858.
MOUNT CHOCORUA, TAMWORTH. 1861.

Gallison, Henry Hammond.
CHOCORUA. (Untitled).

Gerry, Samuel Lancaster.
MOUNT CHOCORUA. 1849.

Gifford, Sanford Robinson.
A SKETCH OF MOUNT CHICORUA [sic]. Before 1863.
CHOCORUA. Before 1870.
CHOCORUA PEAK.
MOUNT CHOCORUA.
MOUNT CHICORUA [sic], NEW HAMPSHIRE. Before 1863.
SUMMER AFTERNOON (Chocorua). 1853.
Pair: MOUNT CHICHOURA [sic], NEW HAMP-SHIRE, and INTERVALE, NEW HAMPSHIRE.

Hart, William M.
AUTUMN VIEW OF MOUNT CHOCORUA.
CHOCORUA MOUNTAIN, NEW HAMPSHIRE.
CHOCORUA MOUNTAIN, NEW HAMPSHIRE.
MOUNT CHOCORUA.

Hill, Thomas.
NEW HAMPSHIRE MOUNTAIN SCENE (Chocorua).

Hinkley, Thomas Hewes.
STAG AT BAY, MOUNT CHOCORUA IN WINTER. 1851.

Hoit, Albert Gallatin.
CHOCORUA. 1835.
MOUNT CHOCORUA FROM SANDWICH, NEW HAMPSHIRE.

Hopkin, Robert.
MOUNT CHOCORUA, NEW HAMPSHIRE, FROM WALKER'S POND. 1880.

Hubbard, Richard William.
CHOCORUA.
NEW HAMPSHIRE SCENERY (Chocorua?).

Huntington, Daniel.
CHICORUA [sic] POND AND MOUNTAIN (or CHOCORUA FROM CARA'S POND). Sept. 28, 1854.
CHOCORUA FROM HILL TO RIGHT OF ALBANY ROAD. Sept. 12, 1854.

List of Paintings by Subject

CHOCORUA PEAK IN NEW HAMPSHIRE. 1860.
STUDY OF FIGURES FOR CHOCORUA.

Johnson, David.
A STUDY, MOUNT CHOCORUA. 1851.
CHOCORUA PEAK. 1856.
MOUNT CHACOROA [sic].
MOUNT CHOCORUA, NEW HAMPSHIRE. 1851.
TAMWORTH SCENERY (Chocorua and Lake).

Kensett, John Frederick.
CHICORUA [sic] FROM FRIBURG [sic], MAINE.
CHICORUA [sic] FROM FRIBURGH [sic], MAINE.
CHICORUA [sic] MOUNTAIN, NEW HAMPSHIRE (study for a picture in the Century Association).
CHICORUA [sic], NEW HAMPSHIRE.
CHICORUA [sic], NEW HAMPSHIRE AT SUNSET.
CHICORUA [sic], WHITE MOUNTAINS.
CHOCORUA FROM CONWAY MEADOW.
CHOCORUA, NEW HAMPSHIRE. 1864.
CHOCORUA, NEW HAMPSHIRE, WHITE MOUNTAINS (or WHITE MOUNTAIN SCENERY). 1864.
COMING STORM, CHICORUA [sic], NEW HAMPSHIRE; THE . . .
COMING STORM, CHICORUA [sic], NEW HAMPSHIRE; THE . . .
MOUNT CHICORUA [sic].
MOUNT CHOCORUA. 1857.
MOUNT CHOCORUA. 1857.
MOUNT CHOCORUA, NEW HAMPSHIRE. 1856.
MOUNT CHOCURA [sic], NEW HAMPSHIRE. 1873.
OCTOBER DAY IN THE WHITE MOUNTAINS (Chocorua). 1854.
SKETCH OF CHOCORUA.

Knapp, Charles W., Sr.
MOUNT CHOCORUA, SILVER LAKE, NEW HAMPSHIRE. 1863.

Lanman, Charles.
MOUNT COCOURA [sic]. Before 1870.

Lansil, Walter F.
MOUNT KEARSARGE AND MOUNT CHOCORUA.

Law, Ralph.
MOUNT CHOCORUA.

Lewis, Edmund Darch.
CHOCORUA MOUNTAIN.

Lowell, Lemuel L.
CHICORUA [sic] PEAK, WHITE MOUNTAINS.

Merrill, George N.
CHOCORUA AND THE SANDWICH RANGE.

Ordway, Alfred T.
MOUNT CHOCORUA AND LAKE.
MOUNT CHOCORUA, NEW HAMPSHIRE.

Osgood, Charles.
MOUNT CHOCORUA.

Owen, George.
MOUNT CHOCORUA.

Parker, John Adams, Jr.
CHICORUA [sic] PEAK.
CHO-COR-UA [sic] PEAK.
MORNING MISTS – FROM CHICORUA [sic].
MOUNT CHOCORUA.

Paskell, William Frederick.
CHOCORUA.
CHOCORUA.
NORTHERN RAVINE OF CHOCORUA MOUNTAIN; THE . . .

Pope, John.
CHICORUA [sic] MOUNTAINS, NEW HAMPSHIRE.

Pratt, Henry Cheever.
ROCKS NEAR THE SUMMIT OF CHOCORUA MOUNTAIN.
SUMMIT OF CHOCORUA MOUNTAIN.
WHITE MOUNTAINS FROM TAMWORTH INCLUDING CHOCORUA PEAK, POND, AND THE SEA.

Richards, William Trost.
MOUNT CHOCORUA AND LAKE. 1873.
MT. CHICOURA [sic].
SUNSET ON MOUNT CHOCORUA, NH. 1872.

Scott, John White Allen.
MOUNT CHOCORUA, NEW HAMPSHIRE, SUMMER VIEW.

Shapleigh, Frank Henry.
CHOCORUA. 1866.
MOUNT CHOCORUA. 1850.
MOUNT CHOCORUA AND SACO RIVER FROM FRYEBURG, ME.
MOUNT CHOCORUA FROM FRYEBURG, ME.
MOUNT CHOCORUA FROM TAMWORTH, NEW HAMPSHIRE. 1875.

Shattuck, Aaron Draper.
CHOCORUA LAKE AND MOUNTAIN. 1855.
CHOCURUA [sic] PEAK, Aug. 8, '54. 1854.
INDIAN GUIDE, MOUNT CHOCORUA, NEW HAMPSHIRE; THE . . . 1858.

New Hampshire Scenery

MOUNT CHOCORUA – CONWAY, NH. 1859.
MOUNT CHOCORUA, CONWAY. 1854.
MOUNT CHOCORUA, NH. 1858.

Sherman, G. B.
LAKE CHOCORUA WITH MOUNTAIN IN BACKGROUND. C. 1887.

Smith, [William Thompson] Russell.
CHOCORUA.
CHOCORUA PEAK, NEW HAMPSHIRE. 1851.
VIEW OF CHOCORUA. C. 1848.
VIEW OF PEQUAWKET AND CHOCORUA PEAK, NEW HAMPSHIRE. C. 1867.

Suydam, James Augustus.
CHOCORUA, WHITE MOUNTAINS.

Thompson, Alfred Wordsworth.
MOUNT CHOCORUA.

Titcomb, William H.
COUNTRY SCENE (Mount Chocorua).
CHOCORUA.
MOUNT CHOCORUA.
NEW HAMPSHIRE LANDSCAPE (probably Chocorua). C. 1870.

Tucker, Allen.
MOUNT CHOCORUA.

Unknown.
MOUNT CHOCORUA.

Wheeler, William Ruthven.
CHOCORUA LAKE AND MOUNTAIN.
MOUNT CHOCORUA. 1866.
NEW HAMPSHIRE LANDSCAPE (Mount Chocorua). 1866.

Wheelock, Merrill Greene.
CHOCORUA. 1860.

Williams, Frederick Dickinson.
CHOCORUA PEAK.

Williamson, John.
SUMMIT OF CHOCORUA.

Wyant, Alexander Helwig.
CHOCORUA. C. 1860.

Kearsarge

Boardman, William G.
INDIAN MAID'S TOILET (TAKEN FROM KEWASARGE [sic] MOUNTAINS, NH); THE...

Bricher, Alfred Thompson.
ON THE SACO (Kearsarge).

Champney, Benjamin.
HAYING IN CONWAY – LOOKING AT KEARSARGE. 1871.

KEARSARGE. 1870.
KEARSARGE. 1870.
KEARSARGE. 1878.
KEARSARGE MOUNTAIN.
MILL POND, KEARSARGE MOUNTAIN, NORTH CONWAY.
MOUNT CHOCORUA (Kearsarge). 1881.
MOUNT KEARSARGE. 1870.
MOUNT KEARSARGE.
MOUNT KEARSARGE, NORTH CONWAY.
SACO AND KEARSARGE. 1890.

Durand, Asher Brown.
MOUNT KEARSARGE, NORTH CONWAY, NEW HAMPSHIRE.

Fisher, Alvan.
VIEW IN NORTH CONWAY FROM THE WEST SIDE OF THE SACO RIVER (Kearsarge).

Frankenstein, Godfrey Nicholas.
SCENE IN THE WHITE MOUNTAINS (Kearsarge and the Saco).

Fueschel, Herman Traugott Louis.
ON THE TOP OF MOUNT KIARSARGE [sic], NORTH CONWAY.

Gerry, Samuel Lancaster.
LANDSCAPE WITH COWS AND PLOUGHMAN (North Conway Meadows and Kearsarge). 1852.

Gibson, William Hamilton.
KEARSARGE IN WINTER.

Gritten, Henry.
KEARSARGE MOUNTAIN.

Hart, William M.
SACO AT NORTH CONWAY AND MOUNT KEARSARGE. Before 1869.

Haseltine, Elizabeth Stanley.
STUDY NEAR COTTAGE ROCK, KEARSARGE MOUNTAIN.

Hay, DeWitt Clinton.
KEARSARGE MOUNTAIN, NH. 1863.

Heade, Martin Johnson.
Attributed:
WHITE MOUNTAINS LANDSCAPE (Kearsarge). 1871.

Hilliard, William Henry.
KEARSARGE AND THORN MOUNTAINS, INTERVALE, NEW HAMPSHIRE. June 14, 1895.

Hunting, Charles.
KEARSARGE AND SACO RIVER. C. 1880.

Knapp, Charles W., Sr.
SACO AND KEARSARGE.

Lansil, Walter F.
  MOUNT KEARSARGE AND MOUNT CHOCORUA.
Lewis, Edmund Darch.
  MT. KEARSARGE, NORTH CONWAY, NEW HAMPSHIRE.
Loveridge, Clinton.
  KEARSARGE AND THE SACO.
Montalant, Julius O.
  VIEW FROM MOUNT KEARSARGE.
Moore, Charles Herbert.
  MOUNT KEARSARGE. C. 1869-70.
Ordway, Alfred T.
  KEARSAGE [sic].
Prichard, J. Ambrose.
  SOUVENIR OF NORTH CONWAY (Kearsarge and the Saco). Aug. 29, 1888.
Rogers, William Allen.
  SLIDING DOWN KEARSARGE.
Scott, John White Allen.
  KEARSARGE. 1876.
  KEARSARGE AND THE SACO. 1880.
Shapleigh, Frank Henry.
  MOUNT KEARSARGE AND SACO RIVER. 1880.
  MOUNT KEARSARGE AND THE SACO FROM FRYEBURG [sic], ME. 1872.
Smith, [William Thompson] Russell.
  MOUNT KEARSARGE.
Smythe, Eugene C.
  MOUNT KEARSARGE. 1891.
Spread, Henry Fenton.
  MOUNT KEARSARGE, NEW HAMPSHIRE.
Suydam, James Augustus.
  STUDY NEAR NORTH CONWAY (Kearsarge). C. 1850.
Warren, Asa Coolidge.
  MOUNT KEARSARGE.
Weston, Mary Bartlett Pillsbury.
  VIEW OF KEARSARGE AND RAGGED MOUNTAIN. C. 1849-50.
Wheeler, William Ruthven.
  MOUNT KEARSARGE SUMMIT.
Wolcott, Josiah.
  MOUNT KEARSARGE FROM RATTLESNAKE HILLS.
Young, W. S.
  MOUNT KEARSARGE. C. 1866.

Lafayette

Barrow, John Dobson.
  MOUNT LAFAYETTE.
Bellows, Albert Fitch.
  FRANCONIA NOTCH AND MOUNT LAFAYETTE.
  MOUNT LAFAYETTE.
Bierstadt, Albert.
  MOUNT LAFAYETTE.
Champney, Benjamin.
  LAFAYETTE MOUNTAIN.
  LAFAYETTE MOUNTAIN FROM FRANCONIA, NH.
  SUMMIT OF MOUNT LAFAYETTE, A SUMMER HOUSE.
  VIEW OF LA FAYETTE [sic] MOUNTAIN, FROM LITTLETON, AUTUMN EFFECT.
Cobb, Cornelia Drake.
  MOUNT LAFAYETTE.
Doughty, Thomas.
  LANDSCAPE, MOUNT LAFAYETTE, NEW HAMPSHIRE.
Durand, Asher Brown.
  MOUNT LAFAYETTE FROM FRANCONIA IRONWORKS, NEW HAMPSHIRE. 1855.
Ferguson, Henry A.
  FRANCONIA VALLEY AND MOUNT LAFAYETTE.
  MOUNT LAFAYETTE.
Fisher, Alvan.
  MOUNT LAFAYETTE AND FRANCONIA NOTCH, VIEW FROM WEST OF FRANCONIA VILLAGE.
Gay, Michael.
  MOUNT LAFAYETTE, FRANCONIA, NH. 1877.
Gay, Miriam.
  MOUNT LAFAYETTE.
  MOUNT LAFAYETTE, FRANCONIA, NEW HAMPSHIRE.
Gerry, Samuel Lancaster.
  NORTHERN SLOPES OF MOUNT LAFAYETTE; THE . . .
Gibson, William Hamilton.
  MOUNT LAFAYETTE FROM BETHLEHEM.
Giles, Horace P.
  LAFAYETTE FROM FRANCONIA.
Griggs, Samuel W.
  MOUNT LAFAYETTE FROM ORE HILL. 1879.
  MOUNT LAFAYETTE FROM ORE HILL. 1870.

New Hampshire Scenery

Hill, Edward.
LAFAYETTE AND PROFILE HOUSE. 1892.
LAKE OF THE CLOUDS, MOUNT LAFAYETTE.

Hill, Thomas.
IN THE WOODS, NEW TRAIL, MOUNT LAFAYETTE.

Hubbard, Richard William.
MOUNT LAFAYETTE FROM NEWBURY, VT.

Johnson, David.
LAFAYETTE FROM THE LOWER AMMONOOSUC. 1874-75.
MOUNT LAFAYETTE.
MOUNT LAFAYETTE FROM FRANCONIA, NEW HAMPSHIRE. 1874.
MOUNT LAFAYETTE FROM MILL POND, FRANCONIA. 1871.
MOUNT LAFAYETTE, NEW HAMPSHIRE. 1871.

Kensett, John Frederick.
MOUNT LAFAYETTE.
MOUNT LAFAYETTE. Oct. 22, 1850.

Key, John Ross.
CLOUDY MORNING, MOUNT LAFAYETTE.

Lanman, Charles.
MOUNT LAFAYETTE. Before 1870.

McEntee, Jervis.
SUMMIT OF MOUNT LAFAYETTE.

McLeod, William.
VIEW OF MOUNT LAFAYETTE FROM FRANCONIA VALLEY.

Miles, John C.
MOUNT LAFAYETTE FROM SUGAR HILL, NH.

Niles, George E.
LAFAYETTE FROM SUNSET HILL. C. 1860.
MOUNT LAFAYETTE. 1870.

Richards, Mary F.
MOUNT LAFAYETTE.

Richards, William Trost.
MOONLIGHT ON MOUNT LAFAYETTE, NH. 1873.

Smith, [William Thompson] Russell.
MOUNT LAFAYETTE FROM THE AMNOWOOSUCK [sic]. 1851.

Stanwood, Franklin.
MOUNT LAFAYETTE IN WINTER.

Unknown (probably William McLeod).
LAFAYETTE FROM FRANCONIA FIELDS. 1852.

Wotherspoon, William Wallace.
FRANCONIA NOTCH WITH MOUNT LAFAYETTE.

Miscellaneous Identified Mountains

Adams, Willis Seaver.
MOOSILAUK [sic] MOUNTAIN. Before 1876.

Bacon, Julia.
CHERRY MOUNTAIN, JEFFERSON, NH.
EAGLE MOUNTAIN.

Baker, Charles.
Attributed:
UPPER SANDWICH RANGE FROM THE SOUTH (after Cole).

Bartlett, William Henry.
MOUNT JEFFERSON FROM MOUNT WASHINGTON.
VIEW FROM MOUNT WASHINGTON.

Beckett, Charles E.
IMP; THE . . . 1852.
MOUNT JEFFERSON AND ADAMS, FROM THOMPSON'S MILL. 1852.
MOUNT MORIAH FROM LARY'S. 1852.

Beckett, Maria.
CARTER MOUNTAIN. July 1859.
FOOT OF CARTER MOUNTAIN.

Bellows, Albert Fitch.
FRANCONIA MOUNTAINS.

Bierstadt, Albert.
ASCUTNEY MOUNTAIN FROM CLAREMONT, NEW HAMPSHIRE. 1862.
MOUNT ADAMS BY MOONLIGHT.
MOUNT ADAMS, NEW HAMPSHIRE. C. 1857-58.
MOUNTAIN TOPOGRAPHY (formerly TUCKERMAN'S RAVINE, WHITE MOUNTAINS, NH). C. 1869.

Bradley, Susan H.
MOUNT BARTLETT FROM INTERVALE.

Brenner, Carl C.
GLIMPSE FROM WILDCAT MOUNTAIN.

Bricher, Alfred Thompson.
MOUNT ADAMS. 1871.
MOUNT ADAMS AND JEFFERSON. 1870.
MOUNT ADAMS FROM JEFFERSON, NEW HAMPSHIRE.

Brown, George Loring.
STORMY DAY, MOUNT LIBERTY. 1876.

Brown, Harrison Bird.
MOAT MOUNTAIN RANGE.

List of Paintings by Subject

MOUNT JEFFERSON AND ADAMS FROM THE GLEN, NH. 1861.
VIEW OF WELCH MOUNTAIN. 1863.

Brown, W. Warren.
MOUNT ADAMS FROM THE GLEN HOUSE, NEW HAMPSHIRE.

Cabot, Edward Clarke.
JEFFERSON, AUGUST, '82. 1882.

Casilear, John William.
TWILIGHT, SANDWICH MOUNTAINS, NH.

Champney, Benjamin.
MOUNT ADAMS AND MADISON FROM MOUNT WASHINGTON CARRIAGE ROAD. 1853.
MOUNT CLINTON.
MOUNT JEFFERSON. 1853.
VIEW IN THE WHITE MOUNTAINS.

Cole, Charles Octavius.
IMPERIAL KNOB AND GORGE, WHITE MOUNTAINS OF NH (or WHITE MOUNTAINS OF NEW HAMPSHIRE). 1853.
MOUNT CARTER.
VIEW OF MOUNT MORIAH FROM STATION HOUSE AT GORHAM, NH. 1850.

Cole, Robert.
MOUNT CARTER.

Cole, Thomas.
LANDSCAPE (UPPER SANDWICH RANGE). C. 1839.
WHITEFACE MOUNTAIN, NEW HAMPSHIRE.

Colman, Samuel, Jr.
FRANCONIA MOUNTAINS, NH.

Cropsey, Jasper Francis.
MOUNT JEFFERSON. 1868.
MOUNT JEFFERSON, NEW HAMPSHIRE.
MOUNT MONROE, WHITE MOUNTAINS. 1872 or 1873.
VIEW FROM MOUNT WILLARD. Sept. 1852.
WHITE MOUNTAINS SCENERY (Mount Jefferson?).

Dolph, John Henry.
FRANCONIA MOUNTAIN.

Dunning, Robert Spear.
STUDY FROM NATURE, WELCH MOUNTAIN. 1864.

Edson, Allan.
MOUNT MADISON, WHITE MOUNTAINS.

Eldred, Leander D.
MOUNT MADISON, VIEW FROM LEAD MINE BRIDGE. 1878.
NEW ENGLAND AT DUSK (Madison). 1878.

Fairman, James.
MOUNTS MADISON AND JEFFERSON, AND ANDROSCOGGIN RIVER, NEAR GORHAM, NH.

Fenn, Harry.
CANNON MOUNTAIN CLIFF – WHITE MOUNTAINS. Before 1872.

Fisher, Alvan.
MOUNT JEFFERSON ON THE ROUTE FROM GORHAM TO THE GLEN HOUSE, NH.
SUGAR LOAF MOUNTAIN. 1821.

Fraser, J. (perhaps John A.)
STORM ON MOUNT JEFFERSON.

Frost, George Albert.
MOUNT SURPRISE.

Garigle, William.
FRANCONIA MOUNTAINS. 1858.

Garnier, Hippolyte Louis.
MOUNT JEFFERSON FROM MOUNT WASHINGTON (after Bartlett). C. 1845.

Gay, Winkworth Allan.
FRANCONIA MOUNTAINS, FROM WEST CAMPTON, NEW HAMPSHIRE.
MOUNT MADISON.
SANDWICH RANGE MOUNTAINS FROM WEST CAMPTON.
WELCH MOUNTAIN FROM WEST CAMPTON, NEW HAMPSHIRE. 1858.
WELCH MOUNTAIN FROM WEST CAMPTON, NEW HAMPSHIRE. 1856.

Gerry, Samuel Lancaster.
FRANCONIA MOUNTAINS NEAR THORNTON, NEW HAMPSHIRE. 1857.
MOUNT ISRAEL FROM RED HILL (or NORTH CONWAY AREA). 1856.
STARR KING VIEW, WEST CAMPTON, NEW HAMPSHIRE.
WELCH MOUNTAIN, A VIEW AT CAMPTON ON THE PEMIGEWASSET.
WHITEFACE IN THE WHITE MOUNTAINS. 1849.

Gibson, William Hamilton.
WELCH MOUNTAIN FROM MAD RIVER.

Gifford, Sanford Robinson.
MOUNT HAYES. C. 1860-70.

Griggs, Samuel W.
HAYING TIME IN NEW ENGLAND (Whiteface?). 1876.

Hammond, George F.
MOUNT ADAMS AND MADISON FROM SHELBURNE.

New Hampshire Scenery

Hart, William M.
MOONLIGHT ON MOUNT CARTER, GORHAM. 1859.
MOUNT MADISON.

Hill, Edward.
VIEW FROM MOUNT WILLARD. C. 1877.

Hill, John Henry.
IMP AND CARTER MOUNTAINS.
MOUNT JEFFERSON.

Hilliard, William Henry.
FRANCONIA MOUNTAINS, NEW HAMP-SHIRE. 1876.

Hoit, Albert Gallatin.
MOUNT CONWAY, NEW HAMPSHIRE BY TWILIGHT.

Hows, John Augustus.
STARR KING'S RAVINE, WHITE MOUNTAINS.

Hubbard, Richard William.
HIGH PEAK, NORTH CONWAY, NEW HAMPSHIRE.

Huntington, Daniel.
AN AUTUMN VIEW OF KUHN MOUNTAIN.

Johnson, David.
FRANCONIA MOUNTAINS. 1867.
FRANCONIA MOUNTAINS.
STARR KING MOUNTAIN, LANCASTER, NH. 1869.
STUDY OF FRANCONIA MOUNTAINS FROM WEST COMPTON [sic]. C. 1860-65.

Kensett, John Frederick.
EARLY AUTUMN IN THE FRANCONIA MOUNTAINS.
FRANCONIA MOUNTAINS.
MOUNT JEFFERSON.
SACO, WHITEFACE IN THE DISTANCE.

Key, John Ross.
CHERRY MOUNTAIN.
CHERRY MOUNTAIN FROM JEFFERSON, NH.
CHERRY MOUNTAIN, WHITE MOUNTAINS. 1873.
MOONLIGHT, CHERRY MOUNTAIN, NEW HAMPSHIRE.

Linsley, Wilford.
MOUNT MORIAH FROM THE ANDROSCOG-GIN RIVER.
STUDY, MOUNT WINTHROP, SHELBURNE, NEW HAMPSHIRE.

Lowell, Abner.
MOUNT WASHINGTON AND OTHER SUM-MITS IN THE WHITE MOUNTAINS RANGE FROM...PORTLAND. 1874.

Martin, Homer Dodge.
WHITE MOUNTAINS, MOUNT MADISON AND MOUNT ADAMS; THE...

Matthews, Ferdinand Schuyler.
CRYSTAL HILLS; THE...

Metcalf, Willard Leroy.
BLACK MOUNTAIN FROM CAMPTON VILLAGE. Sept. 1875.

Nichols, Edward West.
JEFFERSON MOUNT, WHITE MOUNTAINS.
MOUNT OSCEOLA.
MOUNTS JEFFERSON AND ADAMS, FROM THE GLEN.

Parker, John Adams.
MOUNT JEFFERSON FROM PEABODY RIVER.

Parkhurst, Daniel S.
FRANCONIA MOUNTAINS FROM CRAW-FORD NOTCH. 1860 or 1840.

Pierce, Charles Franklin.
KIDDER MOUNTAIN, NEW IPSWICH, NH. C. 1880.
MOUNT MADISON AND GLEN ELLIS FALLS WITH SAWMILL. 1874.
WILLEY MOUNTAIN, NEW HAMPSHIRE.

Pietersz, Bertus L.
VIEW OF CROTCHED MOUNTAIN.

Richards, Thomas Addison.
FRANCONIA MOUNTAINS, NEW HAMP-SHIRE.
FRANCONIA MOUNTAINS; THE...
WELSH [sic] MOUNTAIN FROM WEST CAMPTON.

Richards, William Trost.
FRANCONIA MOUNTAINS FROM COMPTON [sic], NH. 1872.
MOUNT JEFFERSON AND MOUNT ADAMS.

Robbins, Horace Wolcott.
MOUNT MADISON AND ADAMS. 1842.

Scott, John White Allen.
SCENE IN THE PEMIGEWASSET VALLEY, PROSPECT MOUNTAIN IN THE BACK-GROUND.
SLIP MOUNTAIN, NORTH CONWAY.

Seager, Edward.
SANDWICH HILLS, SQUAM LAKE, NEW HAMPSHIRE. C. 1848.

Shapleigh, Frank Henry.
FRANCONIA MOUNTAINS AND VALLEY OF PEMIGEWASSET RIVER FROM WEST CAMP-TON, NH; THE... 1872.
FRANCONIA MOUNTAINS FROM WEST CAMPTON.

List of Paintings by Subject

MOUNT ASCUTNEY FROM CLAREMONT, NEW HAMPSHIRE.

Shattuck, Aaron Draper.

MOUNT MOOSILAUKEE, RAVINE AND BAKER RIVER, BENTON, NH. 1864.

ON MOUNT MORIAH, JULY 7, 1858, MOTE [sic] MOUNTAIN IN DISTANCE.

SANDWICH RANGE FROM OSSIPEE LAKE, NH. 1856.

SUNSET OVER MOUNT THORN, NORTH CONWAY, NEW HAMPSHIRE. 1854.

Shed, C. D.

HIGH PEAK, NORTH CONWAY, NEW HAMP-SHIRE.

Smith, Francis Hopkinson.

BALD MOUNTAIN ROCK, NEW HAMPSHIRE.

CANNON MOUNTAIN CLIFF — WHITE MOUNTAINS. 1879.

FRANCONIA MOUNTAINS, NEW HAMP-SHIRE.

MOUNT LINCOLN FROM BLACK MOUN-TAIN, FRANCONIA NOTCH.

Smith, [William Thompson] Russell.

MOUNT FRANKLIN, WHITE MOUNTAINS. Sept. 17, 1848.

OSSIPEE MOUNTAIN, FROM CENTRE HAR-BOR.

OSSIPEE MOUNTAIN, FROM THE LAKE, NEW HAMPSHIRE.

VIEW OF PEQUAWKET AND CHOCORUA PEAK, NEW HAMPSHIRE. C. 1867.

Sonntag, William Louis.

CANNON MOUNTAIN FROM A POINT NEAR BETHLEHEM, NEW HAMPSHIRE.

CARTER DOME FROM CARTER LAKE. C. 1880.

FOG RISING OFF MOUNT ADAMS.

GREY MORNING (The Ossipee Mountains). 1898.

MOUNT ADAMS FROM RANDOLPH HILL, NEW HAMPSHIRE.

MOUNT HAYS [sic], NEW HAMPSHIRE.

MOUNT MORIAH FROM THE LEDGE NEAR SHELBURNE.

MOUNT SURPRISE FROM THE ANDROS-COGGIN.

MOUNT WILLARD, NH.

PLYMOUTH MOUNTAIN.

Sprague, Isaac.

MOUNT CRAWFORD FROM THE NOTCH. 1848.

MOUNT CRAWFORD NEAR THE WHITE MOUNTAINS, WITH THE MOUNT CRAW-FORD HOUSE. 1848.

Stanley, John Mix.

MOUNT HAYES NEAR GORHAM, NEW HAMPSHIRE. 1866.

Stone, Benjamin.

MOUNT JEFFERSON AT SUNRISE, WHITE MOUNTAINS. 1867.

Titcomb, William H.

PARKER MOUNTAIN, LITTLETON, NEW HAMPSHIRE.

Underwood, George L.

BALD MOUNTAIN, NEW HAMPSHIRE.

Unknown.

IRON MOUNTAIN, JACKSON, NEW HAMP-SHIRE.

PEMIGEWASSET MOUNTAIN FROM WEST CAMPTON. C. 1880.

Wadsworth, Daniel.

COROWAY [sic] PEAK FROM THE WINIPICIO-GEE [sic] LAKE, N. HAMPSHIRE. June 1826.

Wilkie, Robert David.

CENTRE HARBOR AND OSSIPEE MOUN-TAINS. After 1868.

LAKE ELSWORTH AND THE WELSH [sic] RANGE, ELSWORTH, NEW HAMPSHIRE.

PASSACONAWAY MOUNTAIN. After 1868.

PLYMOUTH MOUNTAIN. After 1868.

SANDWICH RANGE. After 1868.

TWIN BELKNAPS; THE. . . After 1868.

WELSH [sic] MOUNTAIN, NEW HAMPSHIRE; THE. . .

Wilson, E. T.

PERCY PEAKS.

Wyant, Alexander Helwig.

WHITEFACE MOUNTAIN, NEW HAMPSHIRE.

Young, Henry de Merritt.

MOUNT CARDIGAN AND NEWFOUND LAKE FROM BRIDGEWATER HILLS. 1896.

Young, W. S.

MOUNT JEFFERSON.

Moat

Bierstadt, Albert.

MOAT MOUNTAIN, INTERVALE. C. 1860-62.

Bricher, Alfred Thompson.

MOUNT CHOCURA [sic] AND MOUNT MOAT FROM THE INTERVALE. C. 1860-65.

Brown, George Loring.

MOAT MOUNTAIN FROM GOODRICH FALLS.

MOAT MOUNTAIN RANGE; THE. . .

Brown, Harrison Bird.
NORTH MOAT, NORTH CONWAY.

Champney, Benjamin.
CONWAY MEADOWS AND MOAT MOUN-
TAIN.
MOAT MOUNTAIN FROM INTERVALE.
C. 1870.
MOAT MOUNTAIN RANGE.
MOTE [sic] MOUNTAIN AND CHOCORUA –
A VIEW FROM SUNSET HILL, NORTH CON-
WAY.
MOUNT MOAT RANGE FROM LOCUST
LANE. 1858.
MOUNT WASHINGTON AND MOORE POND
FROM CONWAY, NH (Moat Mountain and the
Saco).
SACO AND MOAT MOUNTAIN.
SACO RIVER AND MOAT MOUNTAIN,
NORTH CONWAY.
SACO RIVER AND MOTE [sic] MOUNTAIN,
NORTH CONWAY.

Colman, Samuel, Jr.
SUMMER LANDSCAPE (Conway Meadows and
Moat Mountain).

Defrees, T.
MIDSUMMER MORNING, MOAT MOUN-
TAIN FROM HILLSIDE PASTURE, JACKSON,
NH. 1887.

Fisher, Alvan
VIEW IN LOWER BARTLETT, NH, OF INTER-
VALE, LEDGES AND MOTE [sic] MOUNTAIN.

Gay, Winckworth Allan.
MOAT MOUNTAIN.

Gerry, Samuel Lancaster.
VIEW IN CONWAY, MOAT MOUNTAIN IN
THE DISTANCE.

Gifford, Sanford Robinson.
A SKETCH OF MOTE [sic] MOUNTAIN. Before
1863.
MOAT MOUNTAIN FROM ECHO LAKE. 1863.
MOTE [sic] MOUNTAIN, NEW HAMPSHIRE.
1868.

Griggs, Samuel W.
MOAT MOUNTAIN AND WASHINGTON –
SACO RIVER.

Hidley, Joseph Henry.
CONWAY INTERVALE (Moat Mountain and
Ledges).

Inness, George.
CONWAY MEADOWS (or SUMMER SQUALL
ON MOAT MOUNTAIN). 1876.
FORD OF THE SACO (MOTE [sic] MOUNTAIN
IN BACKGROUND); THE...

LEDGE, MORTE [Moat] MOUNT, NORTH
CONWAY.

Johnson, David.
MOAT MOUNTAIN, NEW HAMPSHIRE. 1851.

Kensett, John Frederick.
MOAT MOUNTAIN.

Lewin, James Morgan.
CONWAY MEADOWS WITH MOAT MOUN-
TAIN AND CATHEDRAL LEDGE. 1859-60.

Lewis, Edmund Darch.
MOAT MOUNTAIN.

Moore, Charles Herbert.
MOUNT WASHINGTON (Moat Mountain).
C. 1870.

Shapleigh, Frank Henry.
MOAT MOUNTAIN FROM CONWAY LAKE.
MOTT [sic] MOUNTAIN FROM JACKSON
FALLS, NEW HAMPSHIRE. 1877.

Shattuck, Aaron Draper.
CONWAY – HAYING NEAR MOAT MOUN-
TAIN. 1854.
CONWAY – MOAT MOUNTAIN – BOY HERD-
ING CATTLE. 1859.
HAYING SCENE NEAR MOAT MOUNTAIN,
CONWAY, NH. 1859.
MOAT MOUNTAIN AND NEW MOON FROM
CONWAY MEADOWS.
MOAT MOUNTAIN AND SUMMER CLOUDS.
MOUNT CHOCORUA FROM CONWAY (Moat
Mountain from Intervale).
PINES ON MOAT MOUNTAIN, NEW HAMP-
SHIRE. C. 1860.
SUNSET ON MOAT MOUNTAIN. 1859.

Smillie, James David.
MOAT MOUNTAIN FROM WHITE HORSE
LEDGE, NEW HAMPSHIRE.
STUDY, NORTH CONWAY (Moat Mountain)
(or UNFINISHED STUDY). 1867.

Smith, Xanthus Russell.
MOTE [sic] MOUNTAIN FROM ECHO LAKE,
NEW HAMPSHIRE. 1863?

Snowe, W. Francis.
CONWAY MEADOWS (MOTE [sic] MOUN-
TAIN). 1870.

Suydam, James Augustus.
MOAT MOUNTAIN.

Tryon, Benjamin Franklin.
CONWAY VALLEY AND MOAT MOUNTAIN.

Unknown.
SWIFT RIVER AND MOAT MOUNTAIN.
1868-75.

List of Paintings by Subject

Wenzler, A. H.
MOTE [sic] MOUNTAIN, NORTH CONWAY.

Monadnock

Alexander, Maria B.
WINTER SCENE OF MOUNT MONADNOCK.
Late 19th century.

Baker, Annie D.
MOUNT MONADNOCK, NEW HAMPSHIRE.
1863.

Beaman, Gamaliel W.
MOUNT MONADNOCK FROM MOUNT
WACHUSETT.

Champney, Benjamin.
MOUNT MONADNOCK, NH. 1859.

Dolbear, Amos Emerson.
MOUNT MONADNOCK. 1860-64.

Eddy, Gabriella F.
MOUNT MONADNOCK.

Fisher, Alvan.
MONADNOC [sic] MOUNT FROM DUBLIN,
NEW HAMPSHIRE – PAINTED DIRECTLY
FROM NATURE.

Hallett, Hendricks A.
MOUNT MONADNOCK, NEW HAMPSHIRE.

Hinkley, Thomas Hewes.
VIEW OF MOUNT MONADNOCK. 1858.

Jackson, Charles Thomas.
MONADNOCK MOUNTAIN FROM JAFFREY.
1844.

Leighton, Nicholas Winfield Scott.
MOUNT MONADNOCK.

Martin, H. E. (Mrs.).
MOUNT MONADNOCK. 1884.

Miles, John C.
MONADNOCK MOUNTAIN FROM JAFFREY.
MONADNOCK MOUNTAIN IN A STORM.

Moran, Edward Percy.
MONADNOCK.

Phelps, William Preston.
MONADNOCK.
MONADNOCK AND DUBLIN LAKE.
MONADNOCK AT DAWN, DUBLIN.
MONADNOCK AT SUNSET, WINTER.
MONADNOCK AUTUMN, AFTER THE
SHOWER.
MONADNOCK IN WINTER.
MONADNOCK MEADOW WITH SNOW.
MOUNT MONADNOCK FROM DUBLIN.
SUNSET, MONADNOCK.

WINTER, MONADNOCK, OLD DESERTED
HOUSE.

Pierersz, Bertus L.
GRAND MONADNOCK OVER THE MIST.

Rice, Henry Webster.
MANADNOCK [sic].

Scott, John White Allen.
MOUNT MONADNOCK, NEW HAMPSHIRE,
IN SUMMER. 1876.
MOUNT MONADNOCK, NEW HAMPSHIRE,
IN WINTER.
MT. MONADNOCK.

Silsbee, Martha.
MONADNOCK.

Stewart, Edward B.
MONADNOC [sic].

Talbot, Jesse.
VIEW OF GRAND MONADNOCK, NEW
HAMPSHIRE.

Thayer, Abbott Henderson.
MOUNT MONADNOCK.

Titcomb, William H.
MOUNT MONADNOCK, NEW HAMPSHIRE.
C. 1860.
NEW HAMPSHIRE LANDSCAPE, MOUNT
MONADNOCK. C. 1870.

Unknown.
AN AMERICAN FISHING IDYLL – A VIEW
TOWARDS MOUNT MONADNOCK. C. 1835.
VIEW OF MONADNOCK. C. 1890.

Warren, Asa Coolidge.
MONADNOCK MOUNTAIN FROM NORTH
PETERBOROUGH.
SPRAGUE'S POND AND MOUNT MONAD-
NOCK, DUBLIN, NEW HAMPSHIRE.

Williams, Frederick Dickinson.
MONADNOCK, DUBLIN, NEW HAMPSHIRE.

Old Man of the Mountains

Cabot, James Elliot.
OLD MAN OF THE MOUNTAINS, FRAN-
CONIA NOTCH, SEPT. 1, 1845; THE...

Cass, George Nelson.
PROFILE LAKE (or PROFILE MOUNTAIN) AT
FRANCONIA NOTCH. C. 1870.

Champney, Benjamin.
OLD MAN OF THE MOUNTAIN.

Cropsey, Jasper Francis.
OLD MAN OF THE MOUNTAINS. Sept. 13,
1852.

New Hampshire Scenery

Enneking, John Joseph.
OLD MAN OF THE MOUNTAIN.
Fenn, Harry.
PROFILE MOUNTAIN.
Gerry, Samuel Lancaster.
OLD MAN.
OLD MAN OF THE MOUNTAINS. C. 1871.
Herrick, Henry W.
OLD MAN OF THE MOUNTAINS.
Hill, Edward.
ENTHRONED ABOVE THE CLOUDS (OLD MAN OF THE MOUNTAIN, FRANCONIA NOTCH). April 5, 1880.
OLD MAN OF THE MOUNTAINS. 1876.
OLD MAN OF THE MOUNTAINS. 1879 or 1874.
OLD MAN OF THE MOUNTAINS. Late 19th century.
Hill, Thomas.
CANNON MOUNTAIN AND FRANCONIA NOTCH.
OLD MAN OF THE MOUNTAINS.
Hodgdon, Sylvester Phelps.
OLD MAN OF THE MOUNTAINS. 1858.
Johnson, David.
OLD MAN IN THE MOUNTAIN (FRANCONIA NOTCH). 1876.
McLeod, William.
EASTERN FRONT OF PROFILE MOUNTAIN. 1852.
OLD MAN OF THE MOUNTAIN; THE... 1852.
PROFILE MOUNTAIN. 1852.
Parker, John Adams.
OLD MAN OF THE MOUNTAIN, WHITE MOUNTAINS, NEW HAMPSHIRE.
Plummer, W. H.
OLD MAN WITH HALF A FULL MOON BEHIND THE PROFILE. 1899.
Scollay, Catherine.
OLD MAN OF THE MOUNTAINS.
Shapleigh, Frank Henry.
OLD MAN OF THE MOUNTAINS.
Shindler, Antonio Zeno.
GREAT STONE FACE.
PROFILE MOUNTAIN.
Smith, Francis Hopkinson.
OLD MAN OF THE MOUNTAINS.
Smith, [William Thompson] Russell.
OLD MAN OF THE MOUNTAIN, FRANCONIA NOTCH, NH. 1864.
OLD MAN OF THE MOUNTAINS. 1864.

Sprague, Isaac.
PROFILE MOUNTAIN AT FRANCONIA, NEW HAMPSHIRE. 1848.
PROFILE ROCK, 'OLD MAN OF THE MOUNTAINS' AT FRANCONIA, NEW HAMPSHIRE. 1848.
Stone, Benjamin.
OLD MAN OF THE MOUNTAINS. 1858.
Unknown (possibly Doughty or Fisher).
PROFILE LAKE AND OLD MAN OF THE MOUNTAIN. C. 1835.
Weber, Paul Carl.
OLD MAN OF THE MOUNTAIN.
Whitney, Josiah Dwight.
PROFILE MOUNTAIN, FRANCONIA NOTCH. 1841.
Williams, Isaac L.
GREAT STONE FACE.
PROFILE MOUNTAIN.
Williamson, John.
OLD MAN OF THE MOUNTAIN.

Presidential Range

Bierstadt, Albert.
TURBULENT CLOUDS, PRESIDENTIAL RANGE, NEW HAMPSHIRE. C. 1858.
Brown, Harrison Bird.
PRESIDENTIAL RANGE FROM CONWAY MEADOWS. 1867.
PRESIDENTIAL RANGE, NH.
Casilear, John William.
PRESIDENTIAL RANGE.
Cropsey, Jasper Francis.
PRESIDENTIAL RANGE, NEW HAMPSHIRE. 1872.
PRESIDENTIAL RANGE, WHITE MOUNTAINS, NH.
Fisher, Alvan.
LANDSCAPE, PRESIDENTIAL RANGE.
Gay, Winckworth Allan.
PRESIDENTIAL RANGE IN EARLY AUTUMN.
Hart, James McDougal.
PRESIDENTIAL RANGE, WHITE MOUNTAINS, NEW HAMPSHIRE. Sept. 11, 1867.
Hart, William M.
PRESIDENTIAL MOUNTAINS, NEW HAMPSHIRE.
Hill, Edward.
PRESIDENTIAL RANGE (from Littleton?). 1886.
PRESIDENTIAL RANGE FROM MAPLEWOOD.

List of Paintings by Subject

Johnson, David.
PRESIDENTIAL RANGE, NEW HAMPSHIRE.

Kensett, John Frederick.
PRESIDENTIAL RANGE.

Key, John Ross.
PRESIDENTIAL RANGE FROM JEFFERSON.

Loomis, Otis Burr.
MOUNT WASHINGTON, JEFFERSON, ADAMS, AND MADISON FROM SURPRISE MOUNTAIN.

Robbins, Horace Wolcott.
VIEW OF PRESIDENTIAL RANGE OF WHITE MOUNTAINS, NEW HAMPSHIRE.

Selinger, Jean Paul.
PRESIDENTIAL RANGE AND CRAWFORD HOUSE FROM MOUNT AVALON.

Shapleigh, Frank Henry.
PRESIDENTIAL RANGE AND AMMONOO-SUC RIVER. 1885.
PRESIDENTIAL RANGE FROM THE MOUNT PLEASANT HOUSE. 1888.
PRESIDENTIALS FROM COOS.

Shattuck, Aaron Draper.
MOUNT WASHINGTON AND THE PRESIDENTIAL RANGE. 1858.
PRESIDENTIAL RANGE, AUTUMN. 1856.

Slayton, M. E.
PRESIDENTIAL RANGE, NH. 1899.

Thompson, Harry Ives.
PRESIDENTIAL RANGE FROM JEFFERSON, NEW HAMPSHIRE.

Washington

Ayer, Clara Dwight McMillan.
PANORAMA OF NORTH CONWAY, NH, WITH MOUNT WASHINGTON IN BACK-GROUND. 1884.

Babcock, Augusta.
MOUNT WASHINGTON.

Bartlett, William Henry.
MOUNT WASHINGTON AND THE WHITE HILLS.

Beckett, Charles E.
MOUNT WASHINGTON FROM PEABODY VALLEY. 1852.

Bierstadt, Albert.
AT THE SUMMIT.
DEER ON MOUNT WASHINGTON, WHITE MOUNTAINS, NEW HAMPSHIRE. 1871 or c. 1858.
MOUNT WASHINGTON. C. 1864.

MOUNT WASHINGTON FROM SHELBURNE, NEW HAMPSHIRE. 1859.
MOUNT WASHINGTON FROM THE SACO RIVER. 1871.
MOUNT WASHINGTON, WHITE MOUNTAINS, NEW HAMPSHIRE.
MOUNTAIN MOTIF (Mount Washington). C. 1858.
MOUNTAIN STREAM ON MOUNT WASHINGTON.
MOUNTAIN TOPOGRAPHY (formerly TUCKERMAN'S RAVINE, WHITE MOUNTAINS, N.H.). C. 1869.

Bradbury, Gideon
MOUNT WASHINGTON FROM CONWAY INTERVALE.

Bricher, Alfred Thompson.
MOUNT WASHINGTON. 1870.
MOUNT WASHINGTON AND THE SACO. 1864.
MOUNT WASHINGTON FROM WALKER'S POND.
NEW ENGLAND LANDSCAPE ("MOUNT KEARSARGE") (Mount Washington from the Saco). 1864.

Bristol, John Bunyan.
MOUNT WASHINGTON FROM LANCASTER, NH.

Brown, George Loring.
CROWN OF NEW ENGLAND. C. 1860.
CROWN OF NEW ENGLAND; THE... 1868.
VIEW OF MOUNT WASHINGTON.

Brown, Harrison Bird.
MOUNT WASHINGTON. 1864.
MOUNT WASHINGTON AND MOUNT MONROE FROM CONWAY VALLEY, NH. 1867.
MOUNT WASHINGTON FROM FRANKENSTEIN, MAINE CENTRAL RAILROAD. 1890
VIEW OF MOUNT WASHINGTON FROM CONWAY MEADOWS. 1866.
VIEW OF MOUNT WASHINGTON FROM THE CONWAY MEADOWS. 1863.

Brownell, Charles DeWolf.
MOUNT WASHINGTON.

Burdick, Horace Robbins.
MOUNT WASHINGTON FROM THE GLEN HOUSE. C. 1870.

Burgum, John.
MOUNT WASHINGTON FROM SEBAGO LAKE. 1897.

Carr, R. (?) P. (?) R.
MOUNT WASHINGTON AND TUCKERMAN'S RAVINE FROM THE SACO RIVER. 1873.

New Hampshire Scenery

Champney, Benjamin.
CONWAY MEADOWS AND MOUNT WASH-INGTON. 1872.
MOUNT WASHINGTON. 1853.
MOUNT WASHINGTON.
MOUNT WASHINGTON.
MOUNT WASHINGTON.
MOUNT WASHINGTON.
MOUNT WASHINGTON AND THE ELLIS RIVER. 1890.
MOUNT WASHINGTON FROM GOULD'S POND.
MOUNT WASHINGTON FROM HIGHLAND FARM ABOVE JACKSON, NH. 1834.
MOUNT WASHINGTON FROM HIGHLAND FARMS, CARTER NOTCH. 1881.
MOUNT WASHINGTON FROM NORTH CON-WAY.
MOUNT WASHINGTON FROM SUNSET HILL. C. 1856-84.
MOUNT WASHINGTON FROM THE GLEN ROAD (or THE MOUNTAIN).
MOUNT WASHINGTON FROM THE MEAD-OWS IN NO [rth] CONWAY.
MOUNT WASHINGTON FROM THE SACO RIVER, NH. 1865.
MOUNT WASHINGTON, NORTH CONWAY MEADOWS. 1870.
MOUNTAIN STREAM, NH (Mount Washington).
NORTH CONWAY, MOUNT WASHINGTON IN THE DISTANCE.
WHITE MOUNTAINS [Mount Washington]; THE. . . 1856 or 1858.

Christie, E. A. (Mrs.).
MOUNT WASHINGTON.

Church, Frederic Edwin.
INTERVALE AT NORTH CONWAY (formerly A CATSKILL LANDSCAPE). C. 1856.

Codman, John Amory.
VIEW OF MOUNT WASHINGTON FROM NORTH CONWAY.

Cole, Thomas.
LANDSCAPE, VIEW OF MOUNT WASHING-TON.
Attributed:
MOUNT WASHINGTON FROM THE UPPER SACO INTERVALE.
STORM NEAR MOUNT WASHINGTON. 1828.
VIEW FROM THE SUMMIT OF MOUNT WASHINGTON.
VIEW OF THE WHITE MOUNTAINS, NH (Mount Washington). Spring 1827.

Colman, Samuel, Jr.
HARVEST SCENE (Mount Washington and Con-way Meadows).
MOUNT WASHINGTON, CONWAY VALLEY.

Coombs, Delbert Dana.
NEW HAMPSHIRE MOUNTAINS (Mount Washington).

Craig, William.
MOUNT WASHINGTON.

Crawford, Emma.
VIEW OF MOUNT WASHINGTON, WHITE MOUNTAINS.

Crocker, V. B.
MOUNT WASHINGTON. 1864.

Cropsey, Jasper Francis.
AUTUMN IN AMERICA (Mount Washington).
EARLY MORNING ON MOUNT WASHING-TON.
MOUNT WASHINGTON. Sept. 18, 1852.
MOUNT WASHINGTON.
MOUNT WASHINGTON FROM CONWAY VALLEY.
MOUNT WASHINGTON FROM LAKE SEBA-GO, MAINE. 1867.
MOUNT WASHINGTON FROM LAKE SEBA-GO, MAINE. 1871.
MOUNT WASHINGTON FROM SEBAGO LAKE, MAINE. 1867.
MOUNT WASHINGTON, NEW HAMPSHIRE. 1870.
MOUNTAIN SCENE, AUTUMN, 1881 (Mount Washington?).

Darrah, Ann Sophia Towne.
MOUNT WASHINGTON.

DeFrees, T.
EARLY MORNING, MOUNT WASHINGTON.

Doughty, Thomas.
TUCKERMAN'S RAVINE.

Durand, Asher Brown.
LONE TRAVELER (MOUNT WASHINGTON); THE. . .
MOUNT WASHINGTON FROM CONWAY VALLEY. 1855.
MOUNT WASHINGTON FROM THORNE [sic] HILL, NH, 1855. Sept. 25, 1855.
MOUNT WASHINGTON, NEW HAMPSHIRE. Before 1869.
VIEW ACROSS A VALLEY TO DISTANT MOUNTAINS, MOUNT WASHINGTON, NH. C. 1855.

Elkins, Henry Arthur.
VIEW OF MOUNT WASHINGTON FROM OAK HILL.

List of Paintings by Subject

Enneking, John Joseph.
  MOUNT WASHINGTON FROM BETHLEHEM.
  MOUNT WASHINGTON FROM GREENE'S HILL IN JACKSON, NEW HAMPSHIRE.

Fairman, Colonel James.
  BRIDLE PATH, MOUNT WASHINGTON.

Farrer, Thomas Charles.
  EVENING ON MOUNT WASHINGTON.
  MOUNT WASHINGTON AND ADAMS.
  MOUNT WASHINGTON UNDER THREE FEET OF SNOW.
  MOUNT WASHINGTON, NORTH CONWAY.

Fenn, Harry.
  DESCENT FROM MOUNT WASHINGTON; THE...
  MOUNT WASHINGTON FROM THE CONWAY ROAD.
  MOUNT WASHINGTON FROM THE TOP OF THOMPSON'S FALLS, PINKHAM PASS.
  MOUNT WASHINGTON ROAD; THE...
  TUCKERMAN'S RAVINE, FROM HERMIT'S LAKE.

Fennimore, T. J.
  MOUNT WASHINGTON. 1869.

Ferguson, Henry A.
  TUCKERMAN'S RAVINE AND MOUNT WASHINGTON. 1869.
  VIEW OF THE SACO AND MOUNT WASHINGTON.

Fisher, Alvan.
  GENERAL VIEW OF MOUNT WASHINGTON RANGE FROM THE NORTHERN PART OF THE TOWN OF NORTH CONWAY, NH.
  MOUNT WASHINGTON IN AUTUMN, AS SEEN FROM PINKHAM NOTCH, ELLIS RIVER IN FOREGROUND.

Fitch, John Lee.
  MOUNT WASHINGTON.

Foster, Samuel Birket.
  MOUNT WASHINGTON.

Frankenstein, George Leo.
  FROM THE SUMMIT OF MOUNT WASHINGTON. Aug. 1887.

Frankenstein, Godfrey Nicholas.
  MOUNT WASHINGTON OVER TUCKERMAN'S RAVINE. 1848.

Fraser, J.
  MOUNT WASHINGTON.

Frerichs, William Charles Anthony.
  MOUNT WASHINGTON, CONWAY VALLEY, NEW HAMPSHIRE. C. 1865.
  PANORAMIC LANDSCAPE (Mount Washington from Sunset Hill).

Frost, Francis Shedd.
  VIEW IN TUCKERMAN'S RAVINE, WHITE MOUNTAINS.

Fueschel, Herman Traugott Louis.
  ON THE SACO, MOUNT WASHINGTON IN THE DISTANCE.
  VIEW OF MOUNT WASHINGTON AT SUNSET, NORTH CONWAY, NEW HAMPSHIRE.

Gay, Winckworth Allan.
  AT NORTH CONWAY, MOUNT WASHINGTON.
  MOUNT WASHINGTON. 1861.

Gerry, Samuel Lancaster.
  MOUNT WASHINGTON FROM THE GLEN.
  MOUNT WASHINGTON FROM THORN HILL, THE GRANDEST VIEW OF THE MONARCH.
  MOUNT WASHINGTON VIEWED FROM JACKSON, NEW HAMPSHIRE.
  SNOW LINE, MOUNT WASHINGTON; THE... 1855.

Gibson, William Hamilton.
  MOUNT WASHINGTON FROM FABYAN'S.
  MOUNT WASHINGTON FROM THE SACO.
  TRAVELLERS IN A STORM, MOUNT WASHINGTON.

Gifford, Sanford Robinson.
  A SKETCH OF MOUNT WASHINGTON. 1859.
  A SKETCH OF MOUNT WASHINGTON FROM THE SACO RIVER. Before 1858.
  MOUNT WASHINGTON.
  MOUNT WASHINGTON. 1871.
  MOUNT WASHINGTON FROM THE SACO RIVER. 1858 or 1854-55.
  MOUNT WASHINGTON FROM THE SACO RIVER. C. 1854.
  SUNSET AT WHITE MOUNTAINS (Mount Washington).

Gignoux, Marie-François Regis.
  MOUNT WASHINGTON.

Griggs, Samuel W.
  NEW ENGLAND SUMMER LANDSCAPE (Mount Washington).

Halsall, William Formby.
  SUMMIT OF MOUNT WASHINGTON IN WINTER. 1889 or 1887.

Hammer, John J.
  MOUNT WASHINGTON. Before 1887.

Hart, William M.
  CONWAY VALLEY AND MOUNT WASHINGTON. 1850-60.
  MOUNT WASHINGTON FROM NORTH CONWAY.
  SACO AND WASHINGTON.

New Hampshire Scenery

Heine, Peter Bernard William.
  MOUNT WASHINGTON, NORTH CONWAY.

Hekking, J. Antonio.
  WARD HOMESTEAD (MOUNT WASHINGTON); THE... C. 1860.

Hidley, Joseph Henry.
  MOUNT WASHINGTON FROM THE VALLEY OF CONWAY (after Kensett). After 1851.

Hill, Edward.
  CARRIAGE ROAD ON MOUNT WASHINGTON, NH. 1887.
  CARRIAGE ROAD, MOUNT WASHINGTON, NH. 1892.
  HAYING BELOW MOUNT WASHINGTON.
  MOUNT WASHINGTON FROM NORTH CONWAY AND THE SACO. 1896.
  MOUNT WASHINGTON FROM PINKHAM NOTCH. 1892.
  SUMMIT OF MOUNT WASHINGTON IN WINTER. 1889.

Hill, John Henry.
  MOUNT WASHINGTON. Before 1867.
  MOUNT WASHINGTON.
  MOUNT WASHINGTON AND MADISON.
  MOUNT WASHINGTON FROM CONWAY.
  MOUNT WASHINGTON FROM GORHAM, NEW HAMPSHIRE.

Hill, John William.
  MOUNT WASHINGTON FROM SHELBURNE, NEW HAMPSHIRE.

Hill, Thomas.
  MOUNT WASHINGTON (study).
  MOUNT WASHINGTON – SNOW.

Hillyer, Henry Livingston.
  A SPUR, MOUNT WASHINGTON.
  MOUNT WASHINGTON.

Hodgdon, Sylvester Phelps.
  LADY ON HORSEBACK, TUCKERMAN'S RAVINE.
  MOUNT WASHINGTON FROM JACKSON ROAD.
  MOUNT WASHINGTON FROM THE SOUTH.
  MOUNT WASHINGTON FROM THORN HILL.
  MOUNT WASHINGTON FROM WILDCAT AND ELLIS RIVER. 1867.
  ON THE SACO, MOUNT WASHINGTON.

Hoit, Albert Gallatin.
  MOUNT WASHINGTON.
  MOUNT WASHINGTON FROM BARTLETT.

Holmes, George W.
  MOUNT WASHINGTON.

Homer, Winslow.
  COOLEST SPOT IN NEW ENGLAND, SUMMIT OF MOUNT WASHINGTON; THE... 1870.
  END OF THE BRIDLE PATH, MOUNT WASHINGTON.
  MOUNT WASHINGTON. 1869.
  STUDY FOR COOLEST SPOT IN NEW ENGLAND, SUMMIT OF MOUNT WASHINGTON. C. 1870.
  SUMMIT OF MOUNT WASHINGTON. 1869.

Hotchkiss, Thomas Hiram.
  MOUNT WASHINGTON. 1857.

Hubbard, Richard William.
  BOY FISHING (Mount Washington and the Saco). 1863.

Inness, George.
  APPROACHING STORM (overpainted Mount Washington). 1893.
  MOUNT WASHINGTON. 1875.
  MOUNT WASHINGTON. 1875.
  MOUNT WASHINGTON FROM NORTH CONWAY. 1875.
  MOUNT WASHINGTON, NEW HAMPSHIRE. C. 1877.
  MOUNT WASHINGTON, NORTH CONWAY, NEW HAMPSHIRE. 1875.
  NORTH CONWAY (Mount Washington). 1875.
  NORTH CONWAY, NEW HAMPSHIRE (Mount Washington). C. 1870.
  STORM ON MOUNT WASHINGTON. C. 1875.

Insley, Albert B.
  MOUNT WASHINGTON FROM THE CONWAY INTERVAL [sic].

Johnson, David.
  MOUNT WASHINGTON. 1853.
  NORTH CONWAY (Mount Washington). 1852.

Kensett, John Frederick.
  A GLIMPSE OF MOUNT WASHINGTON.
  EASTERN MOUNTAIN LAKE (probably Mount Washington and the Saco). 1869.
  MOUNT WASHINGTON.
  MOUNT WASHINGTON.
  MOUNT WASHINGTON. 1851.
  MOUNT WASHINGTON AND CONWAY VALLEY. 1867.
  MOUNT WASHINGTON AND JEFFERSON, NEW HAMPSHIRE.
  MOUNT WASHINGTON FROM THE CONWAY VALLEY.
  MOUNT WASHINGTON FROM THE VALLEY OF CONWAY. 1851.
  MOUNT WASHINGTON FROM THE VALLEY OF CONWAY.

List of Paintings by Subject

MOUNT WASHINGTON, NEW HAMPSHIRE IN OCTOBER.

MOUNTAIN LANDSCAPE (Mount Washington).

SKETCH OF MOUNT WASHINGTON. 1851.

STUDY OF MOUNT WASHINGTON.

WHITE MOUNTAINS, MOUNT WASHINGTON; THE ... 1869.

Key, John Ross.
IN THE WHITE MOUNTAINS (Mount Washington). 1872.
MOUNT WASHINGTON.
MOUNT WASHINGTON. 1873.
MOUNT WASHINGTON TOPPED WITH FIRST SNOW IN SEPTEMBER FROM ... NORTH CONWAY

Knapp, Charles W., Sr.
ON THE PEABODY RIVER, MOUNT WASHINGTON.

Lanman, Charles.
MOUNT WASHINGTON. Before 1870.
TUCKERMAN'S RAVINE. Before 1870.

Lewis, Edmund Darch.
DISTANT VIEW OF MOUNT WASHINGTON.
INTERVALE, NORTH CONWAY, MOUNT WASHINGTON.
LANDSCAPE, MOUNT WASHINGTON, WHITE MOUNTAINS.
MOUNT WASHINGTON.
MOUNT WASHINGTON IN THE VALLEY OF CONWAY. 1870.

Loomis, Otis Burr.
MOUNT WASHINGTON FROM ISRAEL RIVER.
MOUNT WASHINGTON FROM THE HILL BACK OF GLEN HOUSE.

Luethy, L.
WHITE MOUNTAINS (Mount Washington from Sunset Hill, North Conway). Probably 1854.

McConnell, George.
MOUNT WASHINGTON AND THE SACO.

McIlvaine, William, Jr.
MOUNT WASHINGTON NEAR FABYAN'S, NEW HAMPSHIRE.

Millard, H. T.
FLEECY CLOUDS, MOUNT WASHINGTON, U.S. OBSERVATORY.

Miller, F.
MOUNT WASHINGTON.

Montague, Fannie S.
MOUNT WASHINGTON – A SKETCH AT SUNSET.

Montalant, Julius O.
MOUNT WASHINGTON.

Moore, Charles Herbert.
MOUNT WASHINGTON. C. 1870.
WHITE MOUNTAINS (Mount Washington). C. 1870.
WHITE MOUNTAINS COUNTRY (Mount Washington). C. 1870.

Moran, Edward.
HALF WAY UP MOUNT WASHINGTON. 1868.

Moran, Thomas.
WHITE MOUNTAINS – MOUNT WASHINGTON FROM ONE OF THE MANY PASSES (Carter Notch?). 1874.

Nichols, Edward W.
MOUNT WASHINGTON FROM THORN HILL.
VIEW OF MOUNT WASHINGTON.

Ogilvie, Clinton.
MOUNT WASHINGTON FROM JACKSON. 1880.

Ordway, Alfred T.
MOUNT WASHINGTON.

Osgood, Charles.
Attributed:
MOUNT WASHINGTON FROM CARTER NOTCH (or VIEW OF MOUNT WASHINGTON).

Otter, Thomas Proudley.
MOUNT WASHINGTON.

Palmer, Fanny F.
MOUNT WASHINGTON AND THE WHITE MOUNTAINS FROM THE VALLEY OF CONWAY. 1860.

Parmalee, Elmer Eugene.
MOUNT WASHINGTON.

Paskell, William Frederick.
MOUNT WASHINGTON ROAD (after H. Fenn engraving).

Perkins, Granville.
MOUNT WASHINGTON.
MOUNT WASHINGTON.

Phelps, William Preston.
MOUNT WASHINGTON FROM THE VALLEY OF CONWAY (after Kensett). 1889.

Pratt, Henry Cheever.
MOUNT WASHINGTON.

Prichard, J. Ambrose.
MOUNT WASHINGTON FROM THE SACO.

Rice, Henry Webster.
MOUNT WASHINGTON IN SNOW.

Richards, William Trost.
    MOUNT WASHINGTON FROM THE GLEN
    ROAD.
    MOUNT WASHINGTON RANGE FROM
    MOUNT KEARSARGE. 1872.
Ritter, Paul.
    MOUNT WASHINGTON.
Ropes, Joseph C.
    MOUNT WASHINGTON FROM NORTH
    CONWAY.
Ruggles, Edward.
    MOUNT WASHINGTON.
Scott, John White Allen.
    MOUNT WASHINGTON FROM CONWAY,
    NEW HAMPSHIRE. 1866.
    MOUNT WASHINGTON, NH.
Shapleigh, Frank Henry.
    CONWAY INTERVALE (Mount Washington and
    White Horse Ledge). 1871.
    MOUNT WASHINGTON. 1881.
    MOUNT WASHINGTON AND CARTER
    NOTCH FROM BARTLETT, NEW HAMPSHIRE.
    MOUNT WASHINGTON AND ELLIS RIVER.
    1883.
    MOUNT WASHINGTON AND ELLIS RIVER AT
    JACKSON. 1882.
    MOUNT WASHINGTON AND ELLIS RIVER AT
    JACKSON, NEW HAMPSHIRE. 1890.
    MOUNT WASHINGTON AND ELLIS RIVER,
    JACKSON, NEW HAMPSHIRE.
    MOUNT WASHINGTON AND THE AMMO-
    NOOSUC. 1891.
    MOUNT WASHINGTON AND WALKER'S
    POND FROM OLD BARN IN CONWAY. 1885.
    MOUNT WASHINGTON FROM BROOK NEAR
    CRAWFORD HOUSE.
    MOUNT WASHINGTON FROM CONWAY.
    1870.
    MOUNT WASHINGTON FROM ELLIS RIVER,
    JACKSON. 1874.
    MOUNT WASHINGTON FROM ELLIS RIVER
    MEADOWS, JACKSON, NH. 1882.
    MOUNT WASHINGTON FROM GLEN ROAD.
    1879.
    MOUNT WASHINGTON FROM INTERVAL
    [sic] HOUSE, NORTH CONWAY, NH.
    MOUNT WASHINGTON FROM IRON MOUN-
    TAIN.
    MOUNT WASHINGTON FROM JACKSON.
    MOUNT WASHINGTON FROM JACKSON.
    1885.
    MOUNT WASHINGTON FROM JACKSON.
    1888.
    MOUNT WASHINGTON FROM PORTER'S
    FARM, CONWAY CENTRE.

MOUNT WASHINGTON FROM THE GLEN
ROAD AT JACKSON.
MOUNT WASHINGTON FROM THE SACO
RIVER.
MOUNT WASHINGTON RANGE AND AM-
MONOOSUC RIVER. 1869.
MOUNT WASHINGTON, JACKSON, NEW
HAMPSHIRE. 1883.
VIEW OF MOUNT WASHINGTON THROUGH
A BARN.
Shattuck, Aaron Draper.
    ACROSS INTERVALE TO MOUNT WASH-
    INGTON. 1858.
    AUTUMN LANDSCAPE AND MOUNT WASH-
    INGTON. 1859.
    AUTUMNAL SNOW ON MOUNT WASH-
    INGTON. 1856.
    BLUE SHADOWS OVER MOUNT WASH-
    INGTON. 1856.
    CLOUDS OVER MOUNT WASHINGTON,
    AUTUMN COLORS. 1858.
    CONWAY – CLOUDS STUDY, MOUNT
    WASHINGTON AND COG RAILWAY. 1856.
    HILLSIDE VIEW OF MOUNT WASHINGTON.
    1864.
    MOUNT WASHINGTON AND JEFFERSON
    FROM SHELBOURNE [sic], NH. Aug. 1858.
    MOUNT WASHINGTON AND THE PRESI-
    DENTIAL RANGE. 1858.
    MOUNT WASHINGTON AND THE SACO
    RIVER. 1858.
    MOUNT WASHINGTON FROM GREEN HILL
    STUDIO, JACKSON. 1858.
    MOUNT WASHINGTON FROM NORTH CON-
    WAY.
    MOUNT WASHINGTON, ADAMS AND DOU-
    BLEHEAD – SUMMER, 1858.
    MOUNT WASHINGTON, AUTUMN GLORY.
    1864.
    MOUNT WASHINGTON, JULY 22, '59.
    MOUNT WASHINGTON, NEW HAMPSHIRE.
    1854.
    MOUNT WASHINGTON, PRESIDENTIAL
    RANGE. 1858.
    SACO RIVER, CONWAY (Mount Washington,
    Jefferson, Adams). 1854.
Smillie, James.
    MOUNT WASHINGTON FROM THE VALLEY
    OF CONWAY (after Kensett).
Smith, L. L.
    MOUNT WASHINGTON FROM NORTH CON-
    WAY.
    VIEW OF MOUNT WASHINGTON.
Smith, [William Thompson] Russell.
    MOUNT WASHINGTON.
    MOUNT WASHINGTON. 1848-85.

List of Paintings by Subject

MOUNT WASHINGTON FROM THE SACO. 1843.

Sommers, Otto.
VIEW OF CONWAY VALLEY (Mount Washington) (after Kensett). C. 1860-65.

Spear, Thomas Truman.
MOUNT WASHINGTON FROM SUNSET HILL.

Sprague, Isaac.
MOUNT WASHINGTON, FROM THE SUMMIT OF MOUNT PLEASANT. 1848.
WHITE MOUNTAINS FROM THE GIANT'S GRAVE NEAR THE MOUNT WASHINGTON HOUSE; THE . . . 1848.

Stone, Benjamin.
SUMMIT OF MOUNT WASHINGTON, 6380 FEET ABOVE SEA LEVEL. 1858.

Strother, David Hunter.
ASCENT OF MOUNT WASHINGTON. 1859.
MONUMENT; THE . . . 1859.
SUMMIT OF MOUNT WASHINGTON. 1859.
VIEW OF MOUNT WASHINGTON. 1859.

Talbot, Jesse.
VIEW ON THE SACO RIVER, MOUNT WASHINGTON IN DISTANCE.

Titcomb, William H.
MOUNT WASHINGTON AND CONWAY VALLEY.

Unknown.
MOUNT WASHINGTON.
MOUNT WASHINGTON AND THE SACO. 1865.
MOUNT WASHINGTON FROM NORTH CONWAY. C. 1870.
MOUNT WASHINGTON FROM NORTH CONWAY (after Kensett).
MOUNT WASHINGTON FROM WALKER'S POND.
MOUNT WASHINGTON, NEW HAMPSHIRE.

Unknown (Harry Fenn?).
MOUNT WASHINGTON.

Waterman, Marcus S.
MOUNT WASHINGTON.

Waters, George W.
A LAKE IN THE WHITE MOUNTAINS (Mount Washington and the Saco). 1872.

Webb, Charles K.
MOUNT WASHINGTON, WHITE MOUNTAINS.

Weber, Paul Carl.
BLUE RIDGE MOUNTAIN LANDSCAPE (Mount Washington). 1854.

Wheeler, William Ruthven.
MOUNT WASHINGTON #2. 1873.
MOUNT WASHINGTON (from North Conway) #3. C. 1872.
VIEW OF MOUNT WASHINGTON. 1868.

Wheelock, Merrill Greene.
MOUNT WASHINGTON.
MOUNT WASHINGTON FROM GREEN HILL, JACKSON.
SUMMITS OF MOUNTS WASHINGTON, CLAY AND JEFFERSON FROM THE RIDGE OF MOUNT ADAMS.

Williams, Frederick Dickinson.
MOUNT WASHINGTON.

Wotherspoon, William Wallace.
MOUNT WASHINGTON FROM JACKSON.

Wust, Ferdinand Alexander.
MOUNT WASHINGTON. C. 1861.
MOUNT WASHINGTON (5).

Wyant, Alexander Helwig.
SCENE IN THE WHITE MOUNTAINS (Mount Washington from Jackson).

NOTCHES

Crawford Notch

Bartlett, William Henry.
PULPIT ROCK. C. 1839.

Beckett, Charles E.
CRAWFORD NOTCH. 1852.

Bierstadt, Albert.
WHITE MOUNTAINS, NH (or TWO BEARS IN CRAWFORD NOTCH). C. 1858.

Blunt, John Sherburne.
NOTCH IN THE WHITE MOUNTAINS; THE . . . C. 1826.

Brown, Harrison Bird.
HEART OF THE NOTCH, WHITE MOUNTAINS, MAINE CENTRAL; THE . . . 1890.

Cabot, James Elliot.
AT THE LOWER END OF THE NOTCH, WHITE MOUNTAINS, JULY, 1847.
NOTCH, WHITE MOUNTAINS, JULY, 1847.
WILLEY HOUSE, SEPTEMBER 8, 1843; THE . . .

Champney, Benjamin.
GATE OF THE NOTCH FROM NEAR CRAWFORD HOUSE.
NOTCH IN THE WHITE MOUNTAINS FROM ABOVE THE NOTCH HOUSE. 1839-40.
NOTCH OF THE WHITE MOUNTAINS.
WHITE MOUNTAIN NOTCH, FROM FRANKENSTEIN CLIFF, LOOKING SOUTH.

New Hampshire Scenery

Codman, Charles.
VIEW OF THE NOTCH IN THE WHITE MOUN-
TAINS.

Coffin, R. A.
NOTCH OF THE WHITE MOUNTAINS. 1816.

Cole, Thomas.
A VIEW OF THE PASS CALLED THE NOTCH
OF THE WHITE MOUNTAINS.
NOTCH OF THE WHITE MOUNTAINS; THE.
1839.
VIEW OF THE SLIDES THAT DESTROYED THE
WHILLEY [sic] FAMILY, WHITE MOUNTAINS.
1830-35.

Colman, Samuel, Jr.
WILLEY RAVINE.

Cropsey, Jasper Francis.
WHITE MOUNTAIN NOTCH. 1852.

Darrah, Ann Sophia Towne.
CRAWFORD NOTCH. 1870.

Fenn, Harry.
CRAWFORD NOTCH, NEW HAMPSHIRE. C.
1870.
ELEPHANT'S HEAD, CRAWFORD NOTCH.
Before 1872.
GATE OF THE NOTCH; THE . . . Before 1872.

Fisher, Alvan.
A SUNNY SPOT, PASS OF THE MOUNTAINS.
BOWL OF THE WHITE MOUNTAINS; THE . . .
GATE OF THE NOTCH OF THE WHITE
MOUNTAINS WITH THE SOURCE OF THE
SACO.
PULPIT ROCK (CRAWFORD NOTCH, NEW
HAMPSHIRE). 1862.
SCENE ON THE SACO RIVER AT THE NOTCH
OF THE WHITE MOUNTAINS.
THE NOTCH. 1834.
VIEW NEAR THE GATE OF THE NOTCH OF
THE WHITE MOUNTAINS.

Frankenstein, Godfrey Nicholas.
NOTCH OF THE WHITE MOUNTAINS FROM
MOUNT CRAWFORD.

Fraser, Charles.
LANDSCAPE, NOTCH IN THE WHITE
MOUNTAINS.

Gibson, William Hamilton.
ELEPHANT'S HEAD, WINTER. 1882.

Grunewald, Gustavus.
THE NOTCH. 1857.

Herzog, Herman.
ELEPHANT'S HEAD, CRAWFORD HOUSE.
Before 1885.
NOTCH NEAR CRAWFORD HOUSE, NEW
HAMPSHIRE.

Hill, Edward.
CRAWFORD NOTCH FROM MOUNT
WILLARD.
LOOKING DOWN CRAWFORD NOTCH. C.
1880.
WATERFALL, CRAWFORD NOTCH. 1887.
WOODLAND SCENE IN THE NOTCH.

Hill, Thomas.
CRAWFORD NOTCH. 1872.
VIEW TO ELEPHANT'S HEAD FROM CRAW-
FORD HOUSE. 1869.
WHITE MOUNTAIN NOTCH, NEW HAMP-
SHIRE. 1865.

Hilliard, William Henry.
CRAWFORD NOTCH, WHITE MOUNTAINS.
1884.
GATES OF THE NOTCH.

Hillyer, Henry Livingston.
WHITE MOUNTAIN NOTCH.

Hodgdon, Sylvester Phelps.
CRAWFORD NOTCH.

Holmes, George W.
NOTCH; THE . . .

Howe, E. R.
ON THE ROAD TO THE NOTCH.

Kensett, John Frederick.
WHITE MOUNTAIN NOTCH. Aug. 5, 1851.

Lanman, Charles.
NOTCH IN THE WHITE MOUNTAINS. Before
1870.

Melrose, Andrew.
CRAWFORD NOTCH, NEW HAMPSHIRE.

Mussey, Osgood.
NOTCH IN THE WHITE MOUNTAINS.

Parker, John Adams.
PULPIT ROCK, WHITE MOUNTAIN NOTCH.

Pratt, Henry Cheever.
A VIEW IN THE NOTCH OF THE WHITE
MOUNTAINS.
VIEW IN THE NOTCH OF THE WHITE MOUN-
TAINS.
VIEW OF THE WHITE MOUNTAINS AFTER
THE LATE SLIDE. 1828.

Richards, William Trost.
CRAWFORD NOTCH. C. 1872.
GATE OF THE NOTCH OF THE WHITE
MOUNTAINS. C. 1865.
GATE OF THE NOTCH, WHITE MOUNTAINS.
PULPIT ROCK. 1876.
VIEW IN THE WHITE MOUNTAINS (CRAW-
FORD NOTCH). 1876.

List of Paintings by Subject

WHITE MOUNTAIN NOTCH.

Scott, John White Allen.
  IN THE NOTCH. 1857.

Seager, Edward.
  NOTCH OF THE WHITE MOUNTAINS, NH. C.
  1848.

Selinger, Jean Paul.
  CRAWFORD NOTCH, CRAWFORD HOUSE.
  LOOKING DOWN THE NOTCH FROM WEB-
  STER.
  VIEW OF ELEPHANT'S HEAD.

Shapleigh, Frank Henry.
  CRAWFORD NOTCH. 1882.
  CRAWFORD NOTCH.
  CRAWFORD NOTCH.
  CRAWFORD NOTCH FROM CRAWFORD
  HOUSE; THE . . . 1883.
  CRAWFORD NOTCH FROM MOUNT WIL-
  LARD. 1883.
  CRAWFORD NOTCH FROM WILLARD —
  VIEW FROM RIGHT. 1889.
  CRAWFORD NOTCH, WHITE MOUNTAINS,
  NEW HAMPSHIRE. 1879.
  CRAWFORD VALLEY FROM MOUNT WIL-
  LARD. 1877.
  GATE OF THE NOTCH. Before 1875.
  LOOKING DOWN THE NOTCH. 1888.
  NOTCH HOUSE, CRAWFORD NOTCH;
  THE . . . 1879.

Smith, [William Thompson] Russell.
  AT CRAWFORD'S NOTCH. 1849.
  IN THE NOTCH. 1895?
  NOTCH, WHITE MOUNTAINS, NEW HAMP-
  SHIRE; THE . . . 1867.
  NOTCH, WHITE MOUNTAINS; THE . . . 1848.

Sonntag, William Louis.
  IN THE NOTCH. 1899.

Soren, John Johnston.
  VIEW OF THE WILEY [sic] HOUSE, WHITE
  MOUNTAINS, NEW HAMPSHIRE.

Sprague, Isaac.
  NOTCH OF THE WHITE MOUNTAINS WITH
  WILLEY HOUSE; THE . . . 1848.

Stanwood, Franklin.
  CRAWFORD NOTCH. 1884.

Tidd, Marshall M.
  GETTING A TEAM UP THE NOTCH AT THE
  ROCKS. 1859.
  TWO CAMPS AFTER THE SLIDE. 1859.
  TWO CAMPS BEFORE THE SLIDE. 1859.
  WILLEY PLACE AFTER THE SLIDE. 1859.
  WILLEY PLACE BEFORE THE SLIDE. 1859.

Unknown.
  CRAWFORD NOTCH IN THE WHITE MOUN-
  TAINS. 1860-80.

Whitney, Josiah Dwight.
  SLIDE AT THE WILLEY HOUSE. 1841.

Wilbraham, Captain C.
  NOTCH OF THE WHITE MOUNTAINS.

Young, Henry de Merritt.
  CRAWFORD NOTCH.

Dixville Notch

Custer, Edward L.
  DIXVILLE NOTCH. 1864.

Fenn, Harry.
  COLUMN ROCK, DIXVILLE NOTCH. Before
  1872.

Lanman, Charles.
  IN THE DIXVILLE NOTCH. Before 1870.

McChesney, Clara Taggart.
  DIXVILLE NOTCH.

Scott, John White Allen.
  DIXVILLE NOTCH.

Shapleigh, Frank Henry.
  DIXVILLE NOTCH, FROM COLEBROOK
  ROAD.
  DIXVILLE NOTCH, NEW HAMPSHIRE.
  DIXVILLE NOTCH, NH. C. 1880.
  DIXVILLE NOTCH, NORTHERN NEW HAMP-
  SHIRE.

Tidd, Marshall M.
  PEAKS AT DIXVILLE NOTCH.
  VIEW OF DIXVILLE NOTCH.

Whitney, Josiah Dwight.
  DIXVILLE NOTCH. 1841.

Franconia Notch

Baker, Charles.
  VIEW IN FRANCONIA NOTCH.

Bellows, Albert Fitch.
  FRANCONIA NOTCH AND MOUNT LAFAY-
  ETTE.

Bierstadt, Albert.
  LAKE AT FRANCONIA NOTCH, NEW HAMP-
  SHIRE. C. 1860-62.

Brown, George Loring.
  FRANCONIA NOTCH, WHITE MOUNTAINS.
  PEMIGEWASSET VALLEY AND FRANCONIA
  NOTCH FROM WEST CAMPTON, NEW
  HAMPSHIRE. 1865.

New Hampshire Scenery

Brown, Harrison Bird.
FRANCONIA NOTCH.

Clough, D. A.
FRANCONIA NOTCH FROM WEST CAMP-
TON, NH.

Clough, George Lafayette.
A NOTCH IN THE WHITE MOUNTAINS (probably Franconia).

Codman, Charles.
FRANCONIA NOTCH.

Cropsey, Jasper Francis.
FRANCONIA NOTCH, WHITE MOUNTAINS.
1869.

Durand, Asher Brown.
FRANCONIA NOTCH.
NEW HAMPSHIRE SCENERY, FRANCONIA
NOTCH. 1857.
WHITE MOUNTAINS SCENERY, FRANCONIA
NOTCH. 1857.

Fisher, Alvan.
MOUNT LAFAYETTE AND FRANCONIA
NOTCH, VIEW FROM WEST OF FRANCONIA
VILLAGE.
NEW HAMPSHIRE LANDSCAPE, FRANCONIA
NOTCH. 1834.

Gay, Winckworth Allan.
FRANCONIA NOTCH, WHITE MOUNTAINS.
1857.

Gerry, Samuel Lancaster.
IN THE FRANCONIA NOTCH.

Hill, Edward.
FRANCONIA NOTCH AND EAGLE PASS.
FRANCONIA NOTCH FROM ARTIST'S
LEDGE. 1877.
FRANCONIA NOTCH FROM BALD MOUN-
TAIN. 1877.
FRANCONIA NOTCH, THE WHITE MOUN-
TAINS, ECHO LAKE AND PROFILE HOUSE.
1887.
MOUNTAINS AT SUNSET (Franconia Notch).
1888.

Hill, Thomas.
FRANCONIA NOTCH.
VIEW OF FRANCONIA NOTCH.
WHITE MOUNTAINS, FRANCONIA NOTCH.

Hilliard, William Henry.
FRANCONIA NOTCH AND BROOK.
ON THE ROAD TO THE NOTCH (Franconia).
July 14, 1877.

Hodgdon, Sylvester Phelps.
FRANCONIA NOTCH FROM NORTH WOOD-
STOCK.

Kensett, John Frederick.
FRANCONIA NOTCH. 1871.

Knapp, Charles W., Sr.
ENTRANCE TO FRANCONIA NOTCH. 1855.

Matthews, Ferdinand Schuyler.
FRANCONIA NOTCH FROM WOODSTOCK,
NEW HAMPSHIRE. Oct. 11, 1881.

McLeod, William.
FRANCONIA NOTCH. 1852.
MORNING IN THE FRANCONIA NOTCH.

Perkins, Granville.
FRANCONIA IRON WORKS AND NOTCH.
1882.

Pratt, Henry Cheever.
VIEW AT THE FRANCONIA NOTCH, NEW
HAMPSHIRE.

Prichard, J. Ambrose.
CLEARING OFF, FRANCONIA NOTCH.
SHOWERY WEATHER, FRANCONIA VALLEY.

Ryder, Henry Orne.
OLD ROAD TO FRANCONIA NOTCH.

Scott, John White Allen.
FRANCONIA NOTCH.

Smith, Francis Hopkinson.
A GLIMPSE OF FRANCONIA NOTCH, NEW
HAMPSHIRE.
PROFILE NOTCH.

Sprague, Isaac.
FRANCONIA NOTCH WITH THE LAFAYETTE
HOUSE. 1848.

Waters, George W.
FRANCONIA NOTCH. 1876.

Wotherspoon, William Wallace.
FRANCONIA NOTCH WITH MOUNT LAFAY-
ETTE.

Miscellaneous Notches

Bellows, Albert Fitch.
NOTCH AT LANCASTER. 1867.

Brown, Harrison Bird.
NEW HAMPSHIRE SCENE (Carter Notch?).

Brownell, Charles DeWolf.
PINKHAM NOTCH, WHITE MOUNTAINS.
1862.

Fraser, Charles.
GAP IN THE WHITE MOUNTAINS (2).

Gallison, Henry Hammond.
CARTER'S NOTCH FROM JACKSON, NEW
HAMPSHIRE.

List of Paintings by Subject

Gerry, Samuel Lancaster.
GLEN ELLIS RIVER AND PINKHAM NOTCH. C. 1855.

Hay, DeWitt Clinton.
WHITE MOUNTAINS (a notch).

Key, John Ross.
PINKHAM NOTCH, NEW HAMPSHIRE.

Rice, Henry Webster.
PINKHAM NOTCH, IN WINTER.

Shapleigh, Frank Henry.
CARTER NOTCH AND OLD MILL AT JACKSON, NH. 1879.
CARTER NOTCH AND SACO RIVER.
CARTER NOTCH FROM JACKSON, NEW HAMPSHIRE.
CARTER NOTCH FROM THORN HILL.
MOUNT WASHINGTON AND CARTER NOTCH FROM BARTLETT, NEW HAMPSHIRE.
MOUNT WASHINGTON AND CARTER NOTCH FROM BARTLETT, N.H.

Sonntag, William Louis.
VIEW OF THE WHITE MOUNTAINS (A NOTCH). 1886.

PEMIGEWASSET RIVER

Bierstadt, Albert.
ON THE PEMIGEWASSET. Before 1882.

Brown, George Loring.
OCTOBER, PEMIGEWASSET VALLEY.
ON THE PEMIGEWASSET.
PEMIGEWASSET VALLEY AND FRANCONIA NOTCH FROM WEST CAMPTON, NH. 1865.

Durand, Asher Brown.
ON THE PEMIGEWASSET.
PEMIGEWASSET SCENERY.

Frost, Francis Shedd.
VALLEY OF THE PEMIGEWASSET.

Gerry, Samuel Lancaster.
PEMIGEWASSET RIVER, THORNTON, NEW HAMPSHIRE. 1857.
VALLEY OF THE PEMIGEWASSET. 1858.
VIEW ON PEMIGEWASSET AT THORNTON, NEW HAMPSHIRE. 1857.

Griggs, Samuel W.
VALLEY OF THE PEMIGEWASSET, THORNTON, NEW HAMPSHIRE.
VIEW ON THE PEMIGEWASSET.

Hill, Edward.
ON THE PEMIGEWASSET RIVER. 1896.

Hill, Thomas.
PEMIGEWASSET VALLEY, NEW HAMPSHIRE.

Lanman, Charles.
ON THE PEMIGEWASSET. Before 1870.

Lewis, Edmund Darch.
VALLEY OF THE PEMIGEWASSET. 1863.

Matthews, Ferdinand Schuyler.
PEMIGEWASSET VALLEY; THE . . .

McLeod, William.
VIEW ON THE PEMIGEWASSET. 1852.

Miles, John C.
PEMIGEWASSET RIVER – NORTH WOODSTOCK.

Richards, Thomas Addison.
BROOK SCENE IN THE VALLEY OF PEMIGEWASSET, NEW HAMPSHIRE.
PEMIGEWASSET RIVER; THE . . .
SCENE ON THE PEMIGEWASSET RIVER, NEW HAMPSHIRE (3).
VALLEY OF THE PEMIGEWASSET; THE . . .

Scott, John White Allen.
SCENE IN THE PEMIGEWASSET RIVER VALLEY, LOOKING NORTH. 1871.
SCENE IN THE PEMIGEWASSET RIVER VALLEY, PROSPECT MOUNTAIN IN BACKGROUND.

Shindler, Antonio Zeno.
PAMASAWEE [sic] RIVER.

Sonntag, William Louis.
AN OCTOBER DAY IN THE PEMIGEWASSET, PLYMOUTH, NEW HAMPSHIRE.

SACO RIVER

Baker, Charles.
VIEW ON THE SACO RIVER.

Bierstadt, Albert.
ON THE SACO.

Blunt, John Sherburne.
VIEW ON THE SACO. 1826.

Boggs, William Benson.
VIEW ON SACO RIVER.

Bradbury, Gideon Elden.
ON SACO RIVER. 1877.
SUNSET ON THE SACO RIVER. 1891.
VIEW ON SACO AT SALMON FALLS, BUXTON. 1870.

Bradley, Susan H.
A NEW HAMPSHIRE SCENE (SACO IN THE NOTCH).

New Hampshire Scenery

Bricher, Alfred Thompson.
 HIDE-A-WAY PICNIC ALONG THE SACO RIVER. 1867.
 LATE AUTUMN IN THE WHITE MOUNTAINS. 1866.
 LATE AUTUMN, SACO RIVER.
 MOUNT WASHINGTON AND THE SACO. 1864.
 ON THE SACO (Kearsarge).
 ON THE SACO RIVER, NORTH CONWAY.
 SUMMER ON THE SACO. Before 1870.

Bristol, John Bunyan.
 SACO RIVER, NH.

Brown, Harrison Bird.
 PASTORAL, SACO VALLEY.

Champney, Benjamin.
 A QUIET STREAM (Saco). 1863.
 LANDSCAPE, SOURCE OF THE SACO.
 MOUNT WASHINGTON AND MOORE POND FROM CONWAY, NH (actually Moat Mountain and the Saco).
 ON THE SACO, NH, A STUDY FROM NATURE.
 SACO AND KEARSARGE. 1890.
 SACO AND MOAT MOUNTAIN.
 SACO RIVER ABOVE INTERVALE. 1863.
 SACO RIVER AND MOAT MOUNTAINS [sic], NORTH CONWAY.
 SACO RIVER AND MOTE [sic] MOUNTAIN, NORTH CONWAY.
 SACO RIVER, NORTH CONWAY. 1874.
 SACO VALLEY. 1855.
 SACO; THE . . . 1863.
 SWIMMERS AT SACO RIVER, NEAR NORTH CONWAY.
 THOMPSON'S FALLS AND THE SACO VALLEY. 1855.
 VALLEY OF THE SACO.
 VALLEY OF THE SACO, NEAR FRYEBURG, ME; THE . . .

Codman, John Amory.
 SACO RIVER, NORTH CONWAY, NH. October 1847.

Colman, Samuel, Jr.
 ON THE SACO, WHITE MOUNTAINS.
 SUMMER ON THE SACO.

Coulson, Nellie Magoon.
 SACO RIVER FROM INTERVALE. 1885.

DeHaas, William Frederick.
 ON THE SACO, NEW HAMPSHIRE.

Doughty, Thomas.
 VIEW ON THE SACO.

Durand, Asher Brown.
 SACO RIVER, NEW HAMPSHIRE. August 25, 1855.

Fennimore, T. J.
 SACO RIVER. 1867.
 SUNRISE ON THE SACO. 1866.

Ferguson, Henry A.
 VIEW ON THE SACO AND MOUNT WASHINGTON.

Fisher, Alvan.
 CROSSING THE SACO RIVER, CONWAY, NEW HAMPSHIRE.
 GATE OF THE NOTCH OF THE WHITE MOUNTAINS WITH THE SOURCE OF THE SACO RIVER.
 SCENE OF THE SACO RIVER AT THE NOTCH OF THE WHITE MOUNTAINS.

Frankenstein, Godfrey Nicholas.
 SACO RIVER. 1847.
 SCENE IN THE WHITE MOUNTAINS (Kearsarge and the Saco).
 WHITE MOUNTAINS AND THE SACO RIVER.

Fueschel, Herman.
 ON THE SACO, MOUNT WASHINGTON IN THE DISTANCE.
 ON THE SACO, NORTH CONWAY.

Gerry, Samuel Lancaster.
 SACO WITH MOUNTAINS. (Untitled).
 VIEW ON THE SACO RIVER, NEW HAMPSHIRE.

Griggs, Samuel W.
 MOAT MOUNTAIN AND WASHINGTON, SACO RIVER.

Hart, James McDougal.
 SACO RIVER. 1872.

Hart, William M.
 SACO AND WASHINGTON.
 SACO AT NORTH CONWAY AND MOUNT KEARSARGE. Before 1869.

Hill, Thomas.
 HEADWATERS OF SACO; THE . . .
 VIEW ON SACO RIVER.

Hillyer, Henry Livingston.
 EARLY AUTUMN ON THE SACO.
 SACO RIVER.

Hodgdon, Sylvester Phelps.
 ON THE SACO (or RIVER IN SPRING). 1863.
 ON THE SACO, MOUNT WASHINGTON.
 ON THE SACO, WHITE MOUNTAINS NOTCH. 1880 or 1850.

List of Paintings by Subject

Hubbard, Richard William.
GLIMPSE OF THE VALLEY OF THE SACO.

Hunting, Charles.
KEARSARGE AND SACO RIVER. C. 1880.

Huntington, Daniel.
SACO LOOKING NORTHWEST (JEFFERSON IN THE DISTANCE).

Inness, George.
FORD OF THE SACO (MOTE [sic] MOUNTAIN IN BACKGROUND); THE ... Before 1876.
SACO FORD, CONWAY MEADOWS. 1872.
SACO RIVER VALLEY (or IN THE WHITE MOUNTAINS or WHITE MOUNTAIN VALLEY). 1875-78.
SACO VALLEY, NORTH CONWAY. 1875.

Insley, Albert B.
ON THE SACO RIVER, NEW HAMPSHIRE.

Kensett, John Frederick.
EASTERN MOUNTAIN LAKE (probably Mount Washington and the Saco). 1869.
SACO, WHITEFACE IN THE DISTANCE.

Knapp, Charles W., Sr.
SACO AND KEARSARGE.
SCENE ON THE SACO RIVER.

Lanman, Charles.
ON THE SACO. Before 1870.

Loveridge, Clinton.
KEARSARGE AND THE SACO.

Matthews, Ferdinand Schuyler.
SACO VALLEY; THE ...

McConnell, George.
MOUNT WASHINGTON AND THE SACO.

Ordway, Alfred T.
SACO AND VALLEY.
VIEW ON THE SACO.

Parker, John Adams.
AUTUMN ON THE SACO.

Prichard, J. Ambrose.
SOUVENIR OF NORTH CONWAY (Kearsarge and the Saco). Aug. 29, 1888.

Scott, John White Allen.
KEARSARGE AND THE SACO. 1880.

Shapleigh, Frank Henry.
CARTER NOTCH AND SACO RIVER.
MOUNT CHOCORUA AND SACO RIVER FROM FRYEBURG, ME....
MOUNT KEARSARGE AND SACO RIVER. 1880.
MOUNT KEARSARGE AND THE SACO FROM FRYEBURG, ME. 1872.

Shattuck, Aaron Draper.
MOUNT WASHINGTON AND THE SACO RIVER. 1858.
SACO RIVER, CONWAY (Mount Washington, Jefferson, Adams). 1854.
WHITE MOUNTAINS, NH, SACO RIVER. C. 1858.

Smillie, James.
ON THE SACO, NEAR NORTH CONWAY.

Smillie, James David.
ON THE SACO NEAR CRAWFORD'S NOTCH, NEW HAMPSHIRE.

Smith, [William Thompson] Russell.
IN THE FALLS OF THE SACO. Sept. 20, 1849.
SACO, MOOSE HILL.

Soren, John Johnson.
FALLS OF THE SACO.
VIEW ON THE SACO.

Stewart, Ronald A.
SACO RIVER.

Talbot, Jesse.
VIEW ON THE SACO RIVER, MOUNT WASHINGTON IN DISTANCE.

Twombly, Helen M. (Mrs. John H.).
SACO RIVER LANDSCAPE, NEW HAMPSHIRE. Mid-19th century.

Unknown.
MOUNT WASHINGTON AND THE SACO. 1865.

Warren, Asa Coolidge.
CONFLUENCE OF SACO AND SWIFT RIVERS, CONWAY.

Waters, George W.
A LAKE IN THE WHITE MOUNTAINS (Mount Washington and the Saco). 1872.

Webber, Wesley.
VIEW ON THE SACO.

Williamson, John.
SHADY BROOK ON THE SACO.

SILVER CASCADE

Bartlett, William Henry.
SILVER CASCADE. C. 1839.

Bricher, Alfred Thompson.
SILVER CASCADES.

DeGrailley, Victor.
SILVER CASCADE.
SILVER CASCADE (after Doughty).
SILVER CASCADE. C. 1845.

New Hampshire Scenery

SILVER CASCADE, WHITE MOUNTAINS (after Doughty). C. 1845.

Doughty, Thomas.
SILVER CASCADE. Before 1835.
SILVER CASCADE. Before 1838.
SILVER CASCADE, NH FROM RECOLLECTION (or LANDSCAPE, SILVER CASCADE).
SILVER CASCADE, WHITE MOUNTAINS, NEW HAMPSHIRE. C. 1838.

Garnier, Hippolyte Louis.
SILVER CASCADE, WHITE MOUNTAINS.

McIlvaine, William, Jr.
SILVER CASCADE, WHITE MOUNTAINS, NEW HAMPSHIRE.

Parker, John Adams.
SILVER CASCADE, CRAWFORD NOTCH, WHITE MOUNTAINS.

Pratt, Henry Cheever.
SILVER CASCADE IN THE WHITE MOUNTAINS; THE . . .

Woodward, Laura.
SILVER CASCADE AT BETHLEHEM, WHITE MOUNTAINS.

SQUAM LAKE

Bartlett, William Henry.
SQUAM LAKE FROM RED HILL. C. 1839.

Boardman, William G.
SQUAM LAKE.
SQUAM LAKE ROAD, NH.
SUNSET ON SQUAM.

Bunce, William Gedney.
SQUAM LAKE, NEW HAMPSHIRE. Possibly 1860s.

Doughty, Thomas.
SCENE ON SQUAM LAKE.
SQUAM LAKE, NEW HAMPSHIRE.
SQUAM LAKE, NEW HAMPSHIRE, FROM RECOLLECTION.

Gerry, Samuel Lancaster.
HARVEST TIME, RED HILL, SQUAM LAKE, NH. C. 1857.
SQUAM LAKE FROM RED HILL.
SQUAM LAKE FROM SHEPHERD'S HILL.
SQUAM LAKE, SUNSET. C. 1850.
VIEW OF SQUAM LAKE (or VIEW FROM CENTER HARBOR WITH RED MOUNTAIN).

Griggs, Samuel W.
RED HILL, SQUAM LAKE, N.H.

Higgins, George F.
SQUAM LAKE – NEAR CENTER HARBOR.

Richards, William Trost.
LAKE SQUAM AND THE SANDWICH MOUNTAINS. 1872.
SQUAM LAKE FROM RED HILL. 1874.
SQUAM LAKE, NEW HAMPSHIRE. 1876.

Seager, Edward.
SANDWICH HILLS, SQUAM LAKE, NEW HAMPSHIRE. C. 1848.

Smith, [William Thompson] Russell.
SQUAM LAKE FROM GARNET HILL.
SQUAM LAKE, NEW HAMPSHIRE.
VIEW OF SQUAM LAKE, NEW HAMPSHIRE.

Unknown.
SQUAM LAKE FROM RED HILL.

Warren, Asa Coolidge.
SQUAM LAKE.

Wilkie, Robert David.
SQUAM LAKE. After 1868.

Wotherspoon, William Wallace.
SQUAM LAKES, NEW HAMPSHIRE.

LAKE WINNIPESAUKEE

Bartlett, William Henry.
LAKE WINNEPISAUKEE [sic] FROM RED HILL. C. 1839.

Blunt, John Sherburne.
VIEW OF LAKE WINIPISEOGEE [sic]. C. 1826.

Boggs, William Benson.
VIEW OF LAKE WINNIPISEOGEE [sic]. Before 1841.

Brown, Harrison Bird.
LAKE WINNIPISAUKEE [sic]. 1867.

Casilear, John William.
VIEW OF LAKE WINNIPESAUKEE. 1867.

Cole, Thomas.
ALTON BAY, WINNIPISSAGEE [sic]. 1839-44.
LAKE WINNIPESAUKEE, NH. C. 1827-28.
NORTHWEST BAY, LAKE WINNEPESAUKEE [sic]. 1828?
THREE LANDSCAPE VIEWS ON THE WINNIPISOGE [sic] LAKE.
VIEW ON LAKE WINNIPISEOGEE [sic]. 1828.

Danforth, C. A.
WINNIPISEOGEE [sic] LAKE.

Doughty, Thomas.
VIEW ON THE WINNEPISCOGE [sic] LAKE.

List of Paintings by Subject

Durand, Asher Brown.
   A PIONEER SETTLEMENT (Winnipesaukee?).
   1853.
   WINNIPISEOGEE [sic] LAKE (after Cole). C.
   1830.
Freeman, Bradford.
   LAKE WINNIPISEOGEE [sic].
Gerlach, Anthony.
   LAKE WINNIPESEOGEE [sic].
Gerry, Samuel Lancaster.
   BANKS OF THE WINNEPESAUKEE. [sic].
   EARLY MORNING IN WINTER, ON THE WIN-
   NIPISEOGEE [sic].
   LAKE WINNEPESAUKEE [sic]. 1848.
   LAKE WINNEPESAUKEE [sic]. C. 1850.
   LAKE WINNIPESAUKEE, NEW HAMPSHIRE.
   C. 1850.
   SURVEYING SCENE, LAKE WINNIPESAUKEE.
   WINNEPESAUKEE [sic] FROM DANE'S HILL,
   CENTRE HARBOR.
Gibson, William Hamilton.
   WINNIPISEOGEE [sic] FROM RED HILL. Before
   1882.
Gifford, Sanford Robinson.
   LAKE WINNIPISEOGEE [sic].
   LAKE WINNIPISEOGEE [sic]. Before 1858.
   LAKE WINNIPISEOGEE [sic]. Before 1858.
   LAKE WINNIPISEOGEE [sic] FROM RED HILL.

Greaves, Harry E.
   VIEW OF WINNEPESAUKEE [sic] FROM
   ABOVE THE WEIRS. Late 19th century.
Griggs, Samuel W.
   GLIMPSE OF LAKE WINNIPISEOGEE [sic],
   FROM SANDWICH, NH.
   LAKE WINNIPISEOGEE [sic].
   LAKE WINNIPISEOGEE [sic], FROM CENTER
   HARBOR.
Havell, Robert.
   VIEW OF LAKE WINIPISEOGEE [sic].
   WINNEPISSEGEE [sic] LAKE NEAR CENTRE
   HARBOR.
Higgins, George F.
   LAKE WINNIPESEOGEE [sic].
   RATTLESNAKE ISLAND, WINNEPISEOGEE
   [sic].
   WINNEPISEOGEE [sic].
   WINNEPISEOGEE [sic].
Hill, John Henry.
   LAKE WINNIPESAUKEE, NEW HAMPSHIRE.
   1868.
Johnson, David.
   LAKE WINNEPESAUKEE [sic]. 1867.
Kensett, John Frederick.
   LAKE WINNIPESEOGEE [sic].
Key, John Ross.
   MORNING STROLL, LAKE WINNIPISEOGEE
   [sic].
Lanman, Charles.
   LAKE WINNEPESOG [sic]. Before 1870.
Lewis, Edmund Darch.
   EVENING ON LAKE WINNIPESEOGEE [sic].
   LAKE WINNIPISEOGEE [sic].
   LAKE WINNIPISEOGEE [sic].

Morrison, William.
  LANDSCAPE WITH FERRYBOAT ON LAKE WINNIPESAUKEE.
Palmer, Fanny F.
  WINNEPISEOGEE [sic], CENTRE HARBOR. 1850.
Richards, Thomas Addison.
  AUTUMN MEMORIES OF LAKE WINNIPISOGEE [sic].
  LAKE WINNIPISEOGEE [sic].
  ON LAKE WINNIPISEOGEE [sic], NEW HAMPSHIRE.
Shattuck, Aaron Draper.
  LAKE WINNEPESAUKEE [sic].
Sherman, G. B.
  BROADS, LAKE WINNEPESAUKEE [sic]. 1887.
Smith, [William Thompson] Russell.
  LAKE WINNEPESAUKEE [sic].
  WINNEPESAUKEE [sic] FROM NEAR CENTER HARBOR.
Thyng, J. Warren.
  LAKE WINNIPESAUKEE SHOWING THE EXCURSION STEAMER.
  MOUNT WASHINGTON STEAMER – A SIDE WHEELER. 1869.
Titcomb, William H.
  LAKE WINNEPESAUKEE [sic].
Triscott, Samuel Peter Rolt.
  LAKE WINNIPISEOGEE [sic] – LOOKING TOWARD MOUNT BELKNAP.
Unknown.
  MILL ON LAKE WINNIPESAUKEE.
  VIEW OF WINNEPESAUKEE [sic] FROM BELOW MEREDITH.

Unknown (Greeve or Griever).
  VIEW OF WINNEPESAUKEE [sic] FROM ABOVE THE WEIRS. 189?.
Warren, Asa Coolidge.
  LAKE WINNEPISEOGEE [sic]. Before 1872.
Wheelock, Merrill Greene.
  LAKE WINNEPESAUKEE [sic].
  LAKE WINNEPESAUKEE [sic], FROM CENTRE HARBOR.
Whitefield, Edwin.
  VIEW OF LAKE WINNEPESAUKEE [sic]. 1867.
Whitney, Josiah Dwight.
  VIEW ON WINNIPISSEOGEE [sic]. 1841.
Wilkie, Robert David.
  MEREDITH BAY. After 1868.
  MOONLIGHT ON LAKE WINNIPISEOGEE [sic]. After 1868.
Williams, Virgil.
  MORNING – WINNEPISEOGEE [sic].
Wotherspoon, William Wallace.
  OUTLET OF WINNIPISEGEE [sic] LAKE. 1847 or 1846.
Wust, Ferdinand Alexander.
  SUNSET, LAKE WINNIPISEOGEE [sic].

List of Paintings by Subject

Echo Lake and Profile House
Edward Hill, 1887
Oil on canvas, 38" x 62" / Collection: New Hampshire
Historical Society / Ref. page 82

SECTION III

Location / Source

Reference

List

The Boulder and the Flume
Ralph Albert Blakelock,
c. 1878
Oil on canvas, 54" x 28"
Collection: The
Metropolitan Museum
of Art, gift of Mr. and Mrs.
Hugh J. Grant, 1974 / Ref.
page 13

The painting descriptions in Section I are followed by an abbreviated version of the location or information source name. The complete addresses or citations for the most commonly used sources may be found in the alphabetical list below.

1823 *Gazeteer*
John Farmer and Jacob B. Moore. *A Gazetteer of the State of New Hampshire, embellished with an accurate map of the state and several other engravings by Abel Bowen.* Concord: Jacob B. Moore, 1823.

3rd Art of Northern New England Show
Cardigan Mountain School, Canaan, New Hampshire.

Adams-Davidson Gallery, Inc.
3233 P St. N.W., Washington, DC 20007.

Albany Institute of History and Art
125 Washington Ave., Albany, NY 12210.

Aldine, The
A nineteenth-century periodical. New-York Historical Society.

Alexander Gallery
996 Madison Ave., New York, NY 10021.

Allen Memorial Art Museum
Oberlin, OH 44174.

America Illustrated
Williams, J. David, ed. *America Illustrated.* Boston: DeWolfe, Fiske and Co., Publishers, 1883.

American Antiquarian Society
Park and Salisbury Sts., Worcester, MA 01609.

American Art Journal
40 West 57th St., New York, NY 10019.

Amherst College
See Mead Art Gallery.

Anderson Auction Galleries
A nineteenth-century gallery and precursor to Parke-Bernet (now Sotheby Parke-Bernet).

Antiques
The Magazine Antiques. 551 Fifth Ave., New York, NY 10176.

Appalachia
5 Joy St., Boston, MA 02108.

Appleton's Journal
Appleton's Journal of Literature, Science and Art. Boston Public Library (see below).

Archives of American Art and ***Archives of American Art Journal***
8th and F Sts., N.W., Washington, DC 20560.

Argosy Book Stores
116 East 59th St., New York, NY 10022.

Art and Antiques
1515 Broadway, New York, NY 10036.

Austin Arts Center
Trinity College, Summit St., Hartford, CT 06106.

Babcock Gallery
New York, NY.

Baridoff Gallery
242 Middle St., Portland, ME 04101.

Berry Hill Galleries
743 Fifth Ave., New York, NY 10022.

BIAP — Bicentennial Inventory of American Paintings
National Museum of American Art, Smithsonian Institution, Washington, DC 20560.

Bierstadt Exhibition, New Bedford, 1858
"Catalog of the New-Bedford Art Exhibition commencing July 1st and closing Aug. 7th, 1858...," New Bedford (MA) Public Library.

Bliss, Elam. *American Landscape*

Esther Bloch, The Art Searcher
13 Leslie O. Johnson Rd., Gloucester, MA 01930.

Boston Art Club
Boston Public Library, Boston, MA (see below).

Boston Museum of Fine Arts
479 Huntington Ave., Boston, MA 02115.

Boston Public Library
P.O. Box 286, Boston, MA 02117.

Richard Bourne, Inc.
Corporation St., Hyannis, MA 02601.

Bowdoin College Museum of Art
Walker Art Building, Brunswick, ME 04011.

Brooklyn Art Association
Marlor, Clark S. *History of the Brooklyn Art Association with an Index of Exhibitions.* New York: James F. Carr, Inc., 1970.

Brooklyn Museum
188 Eastern Parkway, Brooklyn, NY 11238.

Buffalo Bill Historical Center
Cody, WY 82414.

Butler Institute of American Art
Youngstown, Ohio 44502.

Century Association
7 West 43rd St., New York, NY 10036.

Champney, Benjamin
Sixty Years of Memories of Art and Artists. Woburn, MA, 1899.

Chapellier Gallery
Formerly of New York, NY (22 East 80th St.).

Chicago Institute of Art
Michigan Ave. at Adams St., Chicago, IL 60603.

Childs Gallery
169 Newbury St., Boston, MA 02116.

Christie, Mason and Woods, International
502 Park Ave., New York, NY 10022.

Chrysler Museum
Norfolk, VA 23510.

Cleveland Museum
11150 East Blvd., Cleveland, OH 44126.

Coe Kerr Gallery
49 East 82nd St., New York, NY 10028.

Colonel Town Community House
Lancaster, NH 03584.

Thomas Colville
See Gallery 44.

Conway Historical Society
Conway, NH 03818.

Conway Public Library
Conway, NH 03818.

Cooper-Hewitt Museum
9 East 90th St., New York, NY 10028.

Corcoran Gallery
17th St. and New York Ave. N.W., Washington, DC 20006.

Crawford House Auction
Crawford Notch, NH, M. D. Straw, Jr., and Emory Sanders, Auctioneers, Seabrook and New London, NH (July 26-29, 1976).

Crayon
Durand, J., and W. J. Stillman. *The Crayon.* Reprint, New York: AMS Press, Inc., 1970.

Currier Gallery of Art
172 Orange St., Manchester, NH 03104.

Bernard Danenberg Gallery
945 5th Ave., New York, NY 10021.

Danforth Museum
123 Union Ave., Framingham, MA 01701.

Elizabeth R. Daniel, dealer
2 Gooseneck Rd., Chapel Hill, NC 27514.

Daring Young Men
Dickason, David Howard. *Daring Young Men.* Indiana University Press, 1953.

Darrah, William Culp
The World of Stereographs. Gettysburg, PA: Darrah, 1977.

Dartmouth College Art Galleries
Hanover, NH 03755.

Delaware Art Museum
Wilmington, DE 19806.

Denver Art Museum
100 West 14th Ave. Parkway, Denver, CO 80204.

Detroit Institute of Fine Arts
5200 Woodward Ave., Detroit, MI 48202.

M. H. de Young Memorial Museum
San Francisco, CA 94118.

Drake, Samuel Adams
Heart of the White Mountains: Their Legend and Scenery. New York: Harper and Brothers, 1882.

New Hampshire Scenery

Dufty
James Dufty, Art Dealer, 304 Washington, Ave., Albany, NY 12203.

Earle's Gallery
Out of business. Formerly of Philadelphia, PA.

Ebert, John and Katherine
Old American Prints for Collectors. New York, 1974.

Emigh, Eugene and Katherine, dealers
73 Harding St., New Britain, CT 06052.

Fine Arts Museum of San Francisco, M. H. de Young Memorial Museum (see above)
San Francisco, CA 94118.

Fine Arts Museum of the South at Mobile
Museum Dr., Langan Park, P.O. Box 8426, Mobile, AL 36608.

Robert Hull Fleming Museum
University of Vermont, Burlington, VT 05401.

Flexner, *Wilder Image*
Flexner, James Thomas. *That Wilder Image: The Paintings of America's Native School from Thomas Cole to Winslow Homer.* New York, 1970.

Franconia Bicentennial Art Show
Franconia, NH, 1972 (Franconia Public Library).

Frick Art Reference Library
10 East 71st St., New York, NY 10021.

Fruitlands Museum
Prospect Hill, Harvard, MA 01451.

Gallerie de Tours
559 Sutter St., San Francisco, CA 94102.

Gallery 44
Rt. 44, New Hartford, CT 06057.

John H. Garzoli Gallery
223 Masonic Ave., San Francisco, CA 94118.

Georgia Museum of Art
University of Georgia, Athens, GA 30602.

Thomas Gilcrease Institute of American History and Art
Rt. 6, Tulsa, OK 74127.

Robert Goldberg
North Conway, NH 03860.

Goodspeed's Gallery
Boston, MA 02108.

James Graham and Sons
1014 Madison Ave., New York, NY 10021.

Greene County Historical Society
Coxsackie, NY 12051.

Gussow, Alan
A Sense of Place: The Artist and the American Land. Friends of the Earth, San Francisco, CA. 1973.

Hardings Gallery
Boston, MA (a nineteenth-century gallery).

John D. Hatch Gallery
Lenox, MA 02140.

Jack Havrahan, Inc.
Portsmouth, NH.

High Museum
Atlanta, GA 30309.

High Voltage Engineering Corp.
101 South Bedford St., Burlington, MA 01803.

Hinton, John Howard
History and Topography of the United States of America. London: John Tallis and Co., 1830.

Hirschl and Adler Gallery
21 East 70th St., New York, NY 10021.

Hirshhorn Museum and Sculpture Garden
Smithsonian Institution, Washington, DC 20560.

The Homestead
Sugar Hill, NH 03585.

Jackson's *Final Report*
Jackson, Charles T., M. D. *Final Report of the Geology and Mineralogy of the State of New Hampshire...* Concord, NH: Carroll and Baker, State Printers, 1844.

Herbert F. Johnson Museum of Art
Cornell University, Ithaca, NY 14853.

Jordan Marsh Art Gallery
A nineteenth-century gallery. Boston, MA.

Kennedy Galleries and **Kennedy *Quarterly***
40 West 57th St., New York, NY 10019.

Kilbourne
Kilbourne, Frederick W. *Chronicles of the White Mountains.* Boston: Houghton Mifflin Co., 1916.

Location / Source Reference List

Starr King
King, Thomas Starr. *The White Hills; Their Legends, Landscape, and Poetry.* Boston: Crosby and Ainsworth, 1866.

Knoedler
M. Knoedler and Co., Inc., 19 East 70th St., New York, NY 10021.

Leeds Gallery
A nineteenth-century gallery (Boston Public Library).

Leonard Auction
Nineteenth-century auction rooms, Boston, MA (Boston Public Library).

Florence Lewison Gallery
Out of business. Formerly of New York, NY.

Lion Gallery
Out of business. Formerly of North Conway, NH.

Littleton Community Center
Littleton, NH 03561.

Littleton Public Library
Littleton, NH 03561.

Los Angeles County Museum
5905 Wilshire Blvd., Los Angeles, CA 90036.

Kenneth Lux Gallery
1021 Madison Ave., New York, NY 10021.

MA Charitable
Massachusetts Charitable Mechanic Association (Boston Public Library).

Maine Library *Bulletin*
Portland Public Library, Portland, ME 04101.

McClinton
McClinton, Katherine Morrison. *The Chromolithographs of Louis Prang.* New York: Clarkson N. Potter, Inc., 1973.

Mead Art Gallery
Amherst College, Amherst, MA 01002.

Merwin Gallery
New York, NY.

Metropolitan Museum of Art
5th Ave. at 82nd St., New York, NY 10028.

Mount Holyoke College
South Hadley, MA 01075.

Museum of Fine Arts, Springfield, MA
49 Chestnut St., Springfield, MA 01103.

Nassau County Museum of Fine Arts
P.O. Box D, Northern Blvd., Roslyn, NY 11516.

National Academy of Design
1083 5th Ave., New York, NY 10028.

National Museum of American Art
8th and G Sts. N.W., Washington, DC 20560.

New Atkins Museum of Art
4525 Oak St., Kansas City, MO 64111.

New Britain Museum of American Art
56 Lexington St., New Britain, CT 06051.

New Hampshire Historical Society
30 Park St., Concord, NH 03301.

New Path
The New Path, a nineteenth-century paper published by the Society for the Advancement of Truth in Art, New York, NY.

New-York Historical Society
170 Central Park West, New York, NY 10024.

New York Public Library
5th Ave. at 42nd St., New York, NY 10018.

Newark Museum
43-49 Washington St., Newark, NJ 07102.

NMAA Inventory
Inventory of American Paintings, NCFA (National Collection of Fine Arts) (now NMAA-National Museum of Fine Arts), Smithsonian Institution, Washington, DC 20560.

North Carolina Museum of Art
2110 Blue Ridge Blvd., Raleigh, NC 27607.

North Conway Library Exhibition
North Conway, NH 03860 (1965).

Oakes, *White Mountain Scenery*
Oakes, William. *White Mountain Scenery.* 1848.

Oakland Museum
1000 Oak St., Oakland, CA 94607.

Olana (Frederic Church Museum)
Olana, Catskill, NY 12414.

Olana Gallery
Drawer 9, Brewster, NY 10509.

Old Print Shop and **Old Print Shop** *Portfolio*
150 Lexington Ave., New York, NY 10016.

Old Sturbridge Village
Sturbridge, MA 01566.

New Hampshire Scenery

Parke-Bernet
See Sotheby PB.

Pennsylvania State University Museum of Art
All That Is Glorious Around Us: Paintings from the Hudson River School. 1981. Pennsylvania State University Museum of Art, University Park, PA 16802.

Peters, Harry T.
America on Stone. New York, 1931.

Peters, Harry T.
Currier and Ives: Printmakers to the American People. New York, 1942.

Picturesque America
Bryant, William Cullen, ed. *Picturesque America; or, The Land We Live In*...New York: D. Appleton and Co., 1872.

Pierce Galleries, Inc.
721 Main St., Hingham, MA 02043.

Portland Museum of Art
Portland, ME 04101.

Prang
See McClinton.

Pre-1877
NMAA [National Museum of American Art], Index of Pre-1877 Art Exhibition catalogs, summary of paintings by subject categories, Smithsonian Institution, 1981 (see listing for National Museum of American Art).

Princeton University Art Gallery
Princeton, NJ 08540.

Raydon Gallery
New York, NY.

Reading Public Museum and Art Gallery
500 Museum Rd., Reading, PA 19602.

Robinson, F. T.
Living New England Artists. Boston, 1888.

Lauren Rogers Library and Museum of Art
5th Ave. at 7th St., Laurel, MS 39440.

Rutgers University, Jane Voorhees Zimmerli Art Gallery
Hamilton St., New Brunswick, NJ 08903.

St. Louis Art Museum
Forest Park, St. Louis, MO 63110.

Santa Barbara Museum of Art
1130 State St., Santa Barbara, CA 93101.

Anthony Schmidt
Collingswood, NJ 08108.

Frank S. Schwarz and Sons
Dealer, 1806 Chestnut St., Philadelphia, PA 19103.

Schweitzer Gallery
958 Madison Ave., New York, NY 10021.

Sears, Clara Endicott
Highlights Among the Hudson River Artists. Boston: Houghton Mifflin Co., 1947.

Shelburne Museum
Shelburne, VT 05482.

Shreve, Crump, & Low, Inc.
Jewelers and Antiquarians. 330 Boylston St., Boston, MA 02116.

Signal Co.
Signal Companies, Inc., Engineered Products Group (attn: Spencer Stokes), Liberty Lane, Hampton, NH 03842.

Skidmore College
Saratoga Springs, NY 12866.

Robert W. Skinner, Inc.
585 Boylston St., Boston, MA 02116.

Sloan & Roman Gallery
Formerly of New York, NY.

Smith College Museum of Art
Elm St. at Bedford Terrace, Northampton, MA 01060.

Sotheby PB
Sotheby Parke-Bernet Gallery, 1334 York Ave., New York, NY 10021.

Ira Spanierman, Inc.
50 East 78th St., New York, NY 10021.

Victor D. Spark
1000 Park Ave., New York, NY 10028.

Sporting Gallery
Middlebury, VT 05753.

Stark Museum of Art
Orange, TX 77630.

Stauffer, *American Engraving*
Stauffer, David McNeely. *American Engraving on Copper and Steel.* 3 vols. New York: Burt Franklin.

Stinson House
George Kent, Proprietor, Rumney, NH 03266.

Strawbery Banke Museum
Portsmouth, NH 03801.

John H. Surovek, Fine Arts, Inc.
Palm Beach, FL 33480.

Location / Source Reference List

Ticknor & Co.
The White Mountains, a Handbook for Travellers. Boston: Ticknor and Co., 1858.

University Art Gallery, University of New Hampshire
The White Mountains: Place and Perception (1980). University Art Gallery, University of New Hampshire, Durham, NH 03824.

University of California at Los Angeles
405 Hilgard Ave., Los Angeles, CA 90024.

University of Michigan Museum of Art
Ann Arbor, MI 48109.

University of Notre Dame Art Gallery
Notre Dame, IN 46556.

University of Rochester (NY) Memorial Art Gallery
490 University Ave., Rochester, NY 14607.

University of Southern California
University Park, Los Angeles, CA 90007.

U.S. Sanitary Commission
Exhibition of Paintings and Sculpture at the Studio of Erastus Dow Palmer, February 1864, for the Benefit of the U.S. Sanitary Commission, Albany, NY (Boston Public Library).

Vassar College Art Gallery
Vassar College, Poughkeepsie, NY 12601.

Vose Galleries
238 Newbury St., Boston, MA 02116.

Wadsworth Atheneum
600 Main St., Hartford, CT 06103.

Washburn Gallery
42 East 57th St., New York, NY 10022.

Washington County Museum of Art
City Park, Box 423, Hagerstown, MD 21740.

Wellesley College
Jewett Art Center, Wellesley, MA 02181.

Adam Weschler and Sons
905-9 E St. N.W., Washington, DC 20004.

White Mountain Echo
Published in Littleton, NH.

Whitney Downtown Gallery
55 Water St., New York, NY 10041.

Wigmore Fine Arts
D. Wigmore Fine Art, Inc., American Paintings, 121 East 71st St., New York, NY 10021.

Willey Incidents
Rev. Benjamin G. *Incidents in White Mountain History. . .* Boston: Nathaniel Noyes, 1856.

Willis, N. P. *American Scenery; Or Land, Lake, and River. Illustrations of Transatlantic Nature from Drawings by W. H. Bartlett.* 2 vols. Published at various times and bound by George Virture in London, 1840.

Withington Auction
Richard W. Withington, Inc., Auctioneer and Appraiser, Hillsboro, NH.

Woburn Public Library
Woburn, MA 01801.

Worcester Art Museum
55 Salisbury St., Worcester, MA 01608.

Yale University Art Gallery
1111 Chapel St., New Haven, CT 06520.

SECTION IV

Stereographic Views

of the

White Mountains

A LIMITED SELECTION

Self portrait of Benjamin West Kilburn, famous for his stereoscopic views produced in Littleton, New Hampshire. Courtesy of the Littleton Area Historical Society.

The daguerreotype, the first type of photography, was discovered by William Fox-Talbot in England and Louis Daguerre in France in 1839, after much experimentation. The daguerreotype is a single mirror image of the object photographed, which cannot be reproduced. The method was extremely popular during the mid- and latter half of the nineteenth century as an inexpensive portrait medium. It was introduced to this country in 1840. The photograph, producing a negative from which many prints could be obtained, evolved from the daguerreotype and appeared about 1851. The stereograph is a card with two pictures, almost identical, taken three or four inches apart, which, when placed in a viewer, fuse and produce a three-dimensional picture. Literally millions of stereographs were produced between 1850 and 1940.

The authority on stereographs is William Culp Darrah. He noted methods for estimating the approximate date of stereographs in his book, *The World of Stereographs* (1977), which are briefly listed here.

1. Cards flat, not curved, 1857-90. Curved cards indicate a date of 1879-1940.

2. Square corners, 1857-70.

3. Color white, gray, or cream, 1857-63.

4. Yellow card, progressively darker, 1861-70. After 1866 many colors were introduced — lavender, green, blue, red.

5. Corners rounded for easier introduction into viewer, 1868-90.

6. Larger sizes, 1870-90.

7. Early cards often bore no number, and numbering in general was erratic and should not be used as proof of date.

*

For a full understanding of the impact of photography on art see:

Buckland, Gail. *Fox-Talbot and the Invention of Photography*. Boston: David R. Godine, publisher, 1980.

Darrah, William Culp. *The World of Stereographs*. Gettysburg, PA: W. C. Darrah, publisher, 1977.

Rudisill, Richard. *Mirror Image, The Influence of the Daguerreotype on American Society*. Albuquerque, NM: University of New Mexico Press, 1971.

ADAMS, STEPHEN F.

Born 1844.

Adams's earliest known work was with the Bierstadt Brothers at 39 Purchase Street, New Bedford, MA. He took over their business in 1866 or 1867, using many of their old negatives. His latest known work was done in 1876.

> Adams and Madison, Chandler's Point Carriage Road, Railroad, and Bridle Path.

#2811. Crawford House from the Notch.

 #758. Crawford House.

> Frost Work in Mount Washington. 1871-72.

#2797. Glen House from Mount Washington Carriage Road.

 #757. Glen House. C. 1866.

> Interior of Tip Top House.
>
> Jacob's Ladder, Mount Washington Railroad, 13½ inches in 3 feet.
>
> Just After Sunrise from Mount Washington, NH.
>
> Just Starting Up Mount Washington Railway.

 #688. Lizzie Bourne's Monument and Summit of Mount Washington. C. 1866.

> Running Gear, Mount Washington Engine.
>
> Tip Top House and Coach, 6285 Feet Above the Sea.
>
> Tip Top House, 6285 Feet Above Sea Level.
>
> Tip Top House, Distant View.
>
> Track Repairer Coming Down Jacob's Ladder.
>
> View From Top of Mount Washington.
>
> Winter View of Glen Ellis Falls.

ALDRICH, G. H.

Active 1870-80.

Worked in Littleton, NH. Took over F. G. Weller's negatives in 1873.

> Flume, The... After 1883.

#911. Frost Work on Mount Washington.

#921. Frost Work on Mount Washington.

AMERICAN VIEWS STANDARD SERIES

1866.

See Soule, John P.

> The Pool, White Mountains, NH.

BARNHUM, DELOS

Active 1859.

Barnhum worked in Boston, MA. His first known stereographs are dated 1857, and he continued working through the 1860s.

> Indian Camp, White Mountains. C. 1861.

BATCHELDER, JOHN

Active 1860s and 1870s.

Bathchelder worked in Andover, NH.

> Camping Group.

BECKFORD, C. A.

Active 1870s.

141 Essex Street, Salem, MA.

> #74. Profile House. Before 1883.

THE BEST SERIES

1870-80.

Boston, MA.

> Mount Washington Railroad Depot.
>
> Profile Lake, Franconia.

BIERSTADT BROTHERS

Active 1859-66 in New Hampshire.

Charles (1819-1903). Active 1859-90. Specialist on Niagara Falls.

Edward (1824-1907). Active 1859-60s. Moved to New York City.

Albert (1830-1902). Active 1859-60s.

Address on back of Bierstadt sterographs: c. 1860-62: China Hall, 39 Purchase St., New Bedford, MA.

Their earliest work was with glass stereographs. Issued the first self-contained stereobooks with eyepieces in the cover (1862 and 1875). Edward Bierstadt was considered the best albertypist on the East Coast.

#419. Above the Clouds, Mount Washington. 1865.

#408. Above the Clouds from the Summit of Mount Washington. 1865.

#222. Above the Flume Looking Down. 1865.

#218. Above the Flume. 1865.

#386. Alpine House, Gorham, NH. 1865.

New Hampshire Scenery

#420. Among the Clouds. 1865.

#223. Approaching the Flume from Above. 1865.

Approaching the Flume, from Above. 1860.

#309. Artist's Falls. 1865.

#310. Artist's Falls. 1865.

#227. At the Mouth of the Flume Looking Down. 1865.

Basin; The... 1860.

#238. Basin As Seen from the Road; The... 1865.

#240. Basin from Below; The... 1865.

#239. Basin Looking Towards the Notch; The... 1865.

#240. Basin, Franconia Mountains, NH; The...

#228. Below the Flume Looking Down. 1865.

#1038. Berlin Falls on the Androscoggin. 1865.

#425. Berlin Falls on the Androscoggin. 1865.

#45. Berlin Falls on the Androscoggin, Berlin, NH. 1860.

Boat Landing at Echo Lake, Franconia Mountains. 1860.

#1044. Boat Landing on Echo Lake. 1865.

#320. Boatman at the Pool. 1865.

#321. Boatman at the Pool. 1865.

#272. Boatman in the Pool, Franconia Mountains.

#417. Carriage Road Near the Ledge, Mount Washington. 1865.

Cascade Above the Basin, Franconia Notch. 1860.

Cascade Above the Flume. 1860.

#388. Cascade in the Flume. 1865.

#389. Cascade in the Notch (Dixville). 1865.

#390. Cascade in the Notch (Dixville). 1865.

#2780. Cascade on Crystal Stream Near Tuckerman's Ravine. 1865.

#241. Cascades above the Basin. 1865.

#219. Cascades above the Flume. 1865.

#212. Cascades below the Flume. 1865.

Cascades below the Flume, Franconia Mountains, NH. 1860.

#242. Cascades, Franconia Notch. 1865.

#305. Cathedral, Hart's Ledge. 1865.

Cave and Cascade above the Flume. 1860.

#220. Cave and Cascade above the Flume. 1865.

#422. Clouds from Summit of Mount Washington. 1865.

#2811. Crawford House from the Gate of the Notch. 1865.

#335. Crawford House, White Mountains, NH. 1865.

#2787. Crystal Cascade. 1865.

Crystal Cascade, Glen. 1860.

#360. Crystal Cascade, White Mountains, NH, Winter View. 1865.

#303. Diana's Baths. 1865.

#304. Diana's Baths. 1865.

#352. Diana's Baths. 1865.

#245. Down the Rapids. 1865.

Down the Stream Below the Flume. 1860.

#254. Eagle Cliff from Echo Lake. 1865.

#38. Eastman's Falls, Thompson's Cascade, Glen. 1860.

#259. Echo Lake Looking North. 1865.

#1011. Echo Lake, Franconia, NH.

Emerald Pool, Glen. 1865.

Entrance to the Flume. 1860.

#215. Entrance to the Flume. 1865.

Flume; The... 1860.

#216. Flume; The... 1865.

#356. Flume from Above, Winter View; The... 1865.

#357. Flume Under the Boulder, Winter View; The... 1865.

#358. Flume Under the Boulder, Winter View; The... 1865.

#359. Flume Under the Boulder, Winter View; The... 1865.

#387. Flume, Dixville Notch. 1865.

#354. Flume, from Above, Winter View; The... 1865.

#355. Flume, from Above, Winter View; The... 1865.

#353. Flume, Winter View; The... 1865.

#211. Foot of the Cascades on the Way to the Flume. 1865.

Stereographic Views of the White Mountains

Foot of the Cascades, Below the Flume, Franconia Mountains, NH. 1860.

#255. Franconia Notch from Echo Lake. 1865.

#260. Franconia Notch from Echo Lake. 1865.

#249. Franconia Notch from Lafayette House. 1865.

#328. Frost Work on Mount Washington. 1865.

#329. Frost Work on Mount Washington. 1865.

#411. Frost Work on Mount Washington, NH. 1865.

#5. Garnet Pool, Peabody River, White Mountains. 1860.

#1032. Garnet Pool on Peabody River. 1865.

#1033. Garnet Pool on Peabody River. 1865.

#316. Gibb's Falls (1st), White Mountain Notch, NH. 1865.

#317. Gibb's Falls (2nd), White Mountain Notch, NH. 1865.

#318. Gibb's Falls (3rd), White Mountain Notch, NH. 1865.

Glen Ellis Falls. C. 1860.

#1019. Glen Ellis Falls. 1865.

Glen Ellis Falls, White Mountains, NH. 1860.

#40. Glen Ellis Falls, White Mountains, NH. 1860.

#369. Glen Ellis Falls, Winter View. 1865.

#398. Glen House from Above the Ledge. 1865.

#2797. Glen House from the Mount Washington Carriage Road. 1865.

#2775. Glen House With Haying Party. 1865.

#312. Goodrich Falls, Jackson, NH. 1865.

#313. Goodrich Falls, Jackson, NH. 1865.

#41. Grinnell Cascade, Glen. 1860.

#2807. Group on Mount Willard. 1865.

#2808. Group on Mount Willard. 1865.

#308. Hart's Ledge, from Echo Lake. 1865.

#2800. Imp Mountain Near the Glen. 1865.

#323. Interior of Tip Top House. 1865.

#404. Interior of Tip Top House. 1865.

#416. Interior of Tip Top House. 1865.

#319. Lake Winnepesaukee [sic] from Centre Harbor. 1865.

#332. Leaving Tip Top House for the Winter, Mount Washington, NH. 1865.

#397. Ledge and Halfway House, Mount Washington, NH. 1865.

#399. Ledge and Mount Adams, from Carriage Road. 1865.

#315. Ledges, from Sunset Hill; The . . . 1865.

#206. Livermore Falls. 1865.

#208. Livermore Falls. 1865.

#209. Livermore Falls. 1865.

#201. Livermore Falls, below the Bridge. 1865.

#203. Livermore Falls, from under the Bridge. 1865.

Livermore Falls, Plymouth, NH. 1860.

#46. Lizzie Bourne's Monument on Mount Washington. 1860.

#2794. Lizzie Bourne's Monument on Mount Washington. 1865.

#2779. Looking Down Crystal Stream near Tuckerman's Ravine. 1865.

#221. Looking Down from the Cave above the Flume. 1865.

#418. Looking East from Summit of Mount Washington. 1865.

#224. Looking into the Flume from above. 1865.

#2784. Looking into the Snow Arch. 1865.

#271. Looking out of the Notch. 1865.

#2809. Looking out of the Notch. 1865.

Looking out of the Notch, White Mountains, NH. 1860.

#2785. Looking out of the Snow Arch. 1865.

#2781. Looking under Snow Arch, Tuckerman's Ravine. 1865.

#39. Major Roger's Bath, Thompson's Cascade, Glen. 1860.

#324. Mount Adams and Madison from Mount Washington, NH. 1865.

#2796. Mount Adams and Madison from the Glen House. 1865.

#300. Mount Kiarsarge [sic], from Diana's Baths. 1865.

#405. Mount Washington Carriage near the Summit. 1865.

#412. Mount Washington Carriage on the Summit. 1865.

New Hampshire Scenery

#2795. Mount Washington from the Glen House. 1865.

Mount Washington, NH, Tip Top House after a Snow Storm. 1865.

#230. Near the Cascade below the Flume. 1865.

Near the Flume. 1860.

#214. Near the Flume. 1865.

#423. Near the Summit of Mount Washington. 1865.

#256. North End of Echo Lake. 1865.

#257. North End of Echo Lake. 1865.

North End of Echo Lake, Franconia, NH. 1860.

#210. Old Court House Where Daniel Webster Sustained his First Argument, Plymouth, NH. 1860.

Old Man of the Mountain, Franconia, NH; The... 1860.

#250. Old Man of the Mountains. 1865.

#262. On the Pond near Profile Lake. 1865.

#263. On the Pond near Profile Lake. 1865.

#333. On the Summit of Mount Washington, NH. 1865.

On the Summit of Mount Washington. C. 1865.

On the Summit of Mount Washington. C. 1875.

On the Way to the Flume, Franconia Mountains, NH. 1860.

#204. Pemigewasset above Livermore Falls; The... 1865.

#336. Pemigewasset House. 1865.

#314. Poised Boulder, Lower Bartlett. 1865.

Pony Tram Coming Down the Mountain, NH. 1865.

#234. Pool From Below. 1865.

#233. Pool from Foot of the Stairs. 1865.

Pool from the Top of the Stairs. 1860.

Pool – Philosopher; The... C. 1860.

#231. Pool, Franconia Mountains, NH, from Top of Stairs. 1865.

Pool; The... C. 1860.

#2825. Profile House, Franconia Notch. 1865.

#391. Profile in the Notch (Dixville?). 1865.

#270. Pulpit Rock in the Notch. 1865.

Pulpit Rock, White Mountain Notch. 1860.

#243. Rapids and Cascades, Franconia Notch. 1865.

#244. Rapids and Cascades, Franconia Notch. 1865.

#25. Rapids and Cascades, Franconia Notch. 1860.

#1026. Rocks at Foot of Crystal Cascade. 1865.

#36. Rocks at Foot of Crystal Cascade, Glen, White Mountains. 1860.

Rocks below the Flume. 1860.

#2828. Senter House, Centre Harbor. 1865.

#37. Shelf Rock Cascade, Thompson's Cascade. 1860.

#229. Shelving Rock Below the Flume. 1865.

#2812. Silver Cascade after a Heavy Rain. 1865.

#1047. Silver Cascade in the Notch. 1865.

Silver Cascade in White Mountain Notch, NH. 1860.

#2782. Snow Arch, Tuckerman's Ravine. 1865.

#2786. Snow Arch, Tuckerman's Ravine. 1865.

Staircase at the Pool; The... 1860.

#232. Stairs at the Pool. 1865.

#2826. Steamboat "Lady of the Lake" at Weirs. 1865.

#1037. Summit House on Mount Washington. 1865.

#326. Summit House, After a Frost, Mount Washington, NH. 1865.

#327. Summit House, After a Frost, Mount Washington, NH. 1865.

#301. Summit House, Mount Kiarsarge [sic]. 1865.

#44. Summit House, Mount Washington. 1860.

#40. Sunrise from the Summit of Mount Washington, NH. 1860.

#409. Sunrise from the Summit of Mount Washington, NH. 1865.

#402. Sunset from Mount Washington, NH. 1865.

#403. Sunset from Mount Washington, NH. 1865.

#421. Sunset from Mount Washington. 1865.

Stereographic Views of the White Mountains

Suspended Boulder from Above; The... 1860.

#322. Suspended Boulder in the Flume. 1865.

#225. Suspended Boulder in the Flume from above. 1865.

#40. Sylvia's Rest, Thompson's Cascade, Glen. 1860.

#1027. Thompson's Cascade (1st). 1865.

#4081. Thompson's Cascade (2nd). 1865.

#1028. Thompson's Cascade (3rd). 1865.

#1029. Thompson's Cascade (4th). 1865.

#1030. Thompson's Cascade (5th). 1865.

#1031. Thompson's Cascade (6th). 1865.

Tip Top House. C. 1861-62.

Tip Top House. C. 1865.

Tip Top House. C. 1865.

#43. Tip Top House on the Summit of Mount Washington. 1860.

#213. To the Flume. 1865.

#426. Under the Bridge at Berlin Falls. 1865.

#207. Under the Bridge at Livermore Falls. 1865.

Under the Bridge, Livermore Falls, Plymouth, NH. 1860.

#246. Up the Rapids. 1865.

Up to 300 Different Views of Summit Groups Made Each Day of the 1863-64 Season.

#2815. Upper Falls of the Amonoosuc [sic]. 1865.

#2817. Upper Falls of the Amonoosuc [sic]. 1865.

View above Glen Ellis Falls. 1860.

#1022. View above Glen Ellis Falls. 1865.

#247. View Among the Cascades, Franconia Notch. 1865.

#370. View at Foot of Glen Ellis Falls, in Winter. 1865.

#372. View at Foot of Glen Ellis Falls, in Winter. 1865.

#361. View at the Foot of Crystal Cascade, Winter View. 1865.

#362. View at the Foot of Crystal Cascade, Winter View. 1865.

#363. View at the Foot of Crystal Cascade, Winter View. 1865.

#364. View at the Foot of Crystal Cascade, Winter View. 1865.

#365. View at the Foot of Crystal Cascade, Winter View. 1865.

#366. View at the Foot of Crystal Cascade, Winter View. 1865.

#367. View at the Foot of Crystal Cascade, Winter View. 1865.

#368. View at the Foot of Crystal Cascade, Winter View. 1865.

#2788. View from above the Ledge, Mount Washington. 1865.

View from Above the Flume. 1860.

#236. View from Below the Pool Looking Up. 1865.

#202. View from Livermore Falls. 1865.

#325. View from Mount Washington, Looking S.W. 1865.

#1. View from Pemigewasset House. C. 1860.

#385. View from Pemigewasset House. 1865.

View from Pemigewasset House, Plymouth, NH. 1860.

#205. View from the Bridge at Livermore Falls. 1865.

View from the Flume, Franconia Mountains, NH. 1860.

#267. View from the Gate of the Notch. 1865.

#237. View from the Pool looking down. 1865.

#247. View from the Rapids and Cascades, Franconia Notch. 1865.

#401. View from the Summit House, White Mountains, NH. 1865.

#2790. View from the Summit of Mount Washington, Looking Southwest. 1865.

#334. View from the Top of Mount Washington, NH. 1865.

#226. View from Under the Boulder looking out of the Flume. 1865.

#2773. View in Gorham from the Alpine House. 1865.

#392. View in the Notch (Dixville). 1865.

#393. View in the Notch (Dixville). 1865.

#396. View in the Notch (Dixville). 1865.

#268. View in the Notch. 1865.

#235. View in the Pool. 1865.

New Hampshire Scenery

#302. View near the Summit of Mount Kearsarge. 1865.

#1043. View of the Notch from the Crawford House. 1865.

View of the Notch, White Mountains, NH. 1860.

View of the Pool. 1860.

#1045. View on Echo Lake. 1865.

#258. View on Echo Lake. 1865.

#264. View on Profile Lake. 1865.

#394. View on the Mohawk River, Colebrook, NH. 1865.

#2827. Village of Centre Harbor. 1865.

#2774. Village of Gorham from the South. 1865.

#384. Village of Plymouth from the South. 1865.

#2822. Walker's Cascade (1st Fall). 1865.

#2823. Walker's Cascade (2nd Fall). 1865.

#2824. Walker's Cascade (3rd Fall). 1865.

Waterfall above the Rapids and Cascades (Franconia Notch). 1860.

#2771. Waumbek House, Jefferson, NH. 1865.

#306. White Horse Ledge. 1865.

#307. White Horse Ledge. 1865.

#2770. White Mountains from Waumbek House. 1865.

#1040. Willey House in the Notch. 1865.

#47. Willey House in White Mountain Notch; The... 1860.

#372. Winter View of Glen Ellis Falls. 1865.

Published in *Gems of American Scenery*, 1875:

Basin.

Cathedral, North Conway.

Crawford House from Notch.

Crystal Cascade.

Eagle Cliff.

Elephant's Head.

Emerald Pool.

Flume.

Gibb's Cascade.

Glen Ellis Falls.

Glen From Carriage Road.

Goodrich Falls.

Mount Adams from Glen.

Mount Kiarsarge [sic].

Mount Washington from Glen.

Mount Washington Railroad.

North Conway.

Old Man.

Plymouth.

Pool.

Profile Lake.

Silver Cascade.

Upper Falls of the Ammonusuc [sic].

Willey House.

BIERSTADT, CHARLES

#83. Echo Lake, North Conway.

CLIFFORD, D. A.

Active 1870s.

St. Johnsbury, VT.

Photographed Dartmouth College, 1870-72.

Lake Winnipeseogee [sic] (3 various views). C. 1868.

CLOUGH A. F.

Active 1870s.

Warren, NH.

Address 1870: Springfield, VT, and Oxford, NH.

#288. Mount Carr from Top of Cascades on Ellsworth Hill Brook. C. 1870.

CLOUGH & KIMBALL

Active 1870s.

Concord, NH.

Also see Kimball, H. A.

#43. Ammonoosuc Lower Falls. 1870-71.

#372. Berlin Falls from Foot Bridge. 1870s.

#37. Measuring Wind at 83 Miles per Hour, Mount Adams and Madison Beyond. 1870-71.

#9. Over the Alpine Stable, Lake Winnipiseogee [sic] in the Distance. 1870-71.

DESCRIPTIVE SERIES

Stereographs published under this title carry a full description of the picture on the back, taken from local guidebooks.

Crystal Cascade (from Eastman's White Mountains Series).

Stereographic Views of the White Mountains

FIFIELD, H. S.

Active 1867-83.

New Hampton, NH, during the winter. From July 1 to October 10 at the Flume House, Lincoln, NH. Fifield specialized in taking photographs of groups with the Flume's suspended boulder in the background. Though thousands of groups were taken over the years, each stereograph represented an individual, unduplicated scene of portraiture in nature. Fifield stopped taking such stereographs after the great boulder was washed away in a storm on July 14, 1883.

#18. Flume No. 115½ (railcar). 1877.

#149. Flume. C. 1863.

#73. Flume. 1872.

#226. Flume with People; The. . . 1876.

#217. The Flume. 1868.

HARRIMAN, M. C.

Active 1870s.

Fisherville, NH.

Interior of Tip Top House. 1870s.

HEYWOOD, JOHN B.

Active 1858-65.

335 Washington St., Boston.

#507. Tip Top House, Mount Washington. C. 1865.

HOAG, A. B.

Active 1870s.

Center Sandwich, NH.

Forest Road. (Untitled).

KILBURN, BENJAMIN WEST

Active from 1865. Died 1904.

Littleton, NH.

Kilburn often used larger-sized cards than was the norm in stereographs. He took over the business from Kilburn Brothers in 1877 and carried about 300 views of White Mountain subjects.

#7311. Falstaff on Skates. 1892.

#212. Flume above Boulder, Franconia Notch. Before 1883.

#26. Frost Feather on Signal Station, Mount Washington. 1877.

#886. Great Avalanche from Owls Head, Jefferson, NH, July 10, 1892.

#892. Great Avalanche from Owls Head, Jefferson, NH, July 10, 1892.

#888. House Destroyed by Avalanche from Owls Head, Jefferson.

#193. Mountaineer, Crawford Notch; The. . . After 1877.

#214. Pool, Franconia Notch, NH; The. . . C. 1878.

#393. Profile, Franconia Notch, NH. 1878.

#4093. When We Went Sleighing. 1886.

KILBURN BROTHERS

Littleton, NH.

Benjamin West Kilburn.

Active from 1865. Died 1904.

Edward Kilburn.

Active 1865-77. Died 1909.

Kilburn Brothers was probably the most prolific of the New Hampshire stereographers. Their subjects ranged world-wide. Edward was particularly interested in photographing the frost work on Mount Washington. Edward retired from the business in 1877 and started selling stereos through a canvassing system in 1879.

#148. 91st Psalm in Ice.

#3420. Among the Pines.

#70. Basin, Franconia. C. 1867.

#71. Basin, Franconia. C. 1867.

#91. Basin, Franconia. C. 1867.

#81. BC & MRR Bridge, Woodsville, NH. C. 1867.

#514. Beecher's Falls, Crawford Notch.

#493. Bethlehem. 1874.

#668. Bethlehem.

#626. Bethlehem, NH.

#141. Boat House, Profile Lake. C. 1867.

Boating on Lake Winnipeseogee [sic].

#76. Carriage Road to Mount Washington, the Ledge.

#49. Cascade, below the Flume, Franconia. C. 1867.

#150. Cloud Views from Mount Washington. C. 1867.

#139. Crawford House with Party for Mount Washington. C. 1867.

#136. Crawford House. C. 1867.

#138. Crawford House. C. 1867.

#189. Crawford House, from the Notch. C. 1867.

#569. Crawford Notch Road after a Storm.

#171. Crawford Notch. C. 1867.

#31. Crawford Notch. C. 1867.

#65. Crawford Notch. C. 1867.

#67. Crawford Notch. C. 1867.

#68. Crawford Notch. C. 1867.

#108. Crystal Cascade. C. 1867.

#362. Dismal Pool, Crawford Notch.

#172. Dixville Notch, NH. C. 1867.

#43. Eagle Cliff, from Echo Lake. C. 1867.

#26. Eagle Cliff, from Echo Lake, Franconia Notch. C. 1867.

#248. Eagle Cliff, Winter.

Echo Lake Boathouse. (Untitled). Before 1877.

#111. Echo Lake.

#504. Echo Lake, Franconia Notch.

#505. Echo Lake, Franconia Notch.

#506. Echo Lake, Franconia Notch.

#133. Echo Lake, Franconia. C. 1867.

Engine, Mount Washington; The... C. 1867.

#217. Elephant's Head, Crawford Notch. C. 1867.

#2558. Enthroned among the Clouds, White Mountains, NH. 1880.

#1787. Fabyan House and Railroad Train, White Mountains.

#1246. Fabyan House, White Mountains.

#9. Falls on the Ammonoosuc. C. 1867.

#17. Falls on the Ammonoosuc. C. 1867.

#18. Falls on the Ammonoosuc. C. 1867.

#20. Falls on the Ammonoosuc. C. 1867.

#21. Falls on the Ammonoosuc. C. 1867.

#22. Falls on the Ammonoosuc. C. 1867.

#121. Flume above the Boulder. C. 1867.

#122. Flume above the Boulder. C. 1867.

#46. Flume below the Boulder. C. 1867.

#47. Flume below the Boulder. C. 1867.

#48. Flume below the Boulder. C. 1867.

#64. Flume, Franconia. C. 1867.

#70. Flume, Franconia. C. 1867.

#90. Flume, Franconia. C. 1867.

#103. Flume, Franconia. C. 1867.

#174. Flume, Dixville Notch. C. 1867.

#3519. Flume; The... 1883.

#82. Franconia Notch. C. 1867.

#84. Franconia Notch from Echo Lake. C. 1867.

#85. Franconia Notch from Bald. C. 1867.

#545. Franconia Notch, Suspended Boulder.

#12. Franconia, NH. C. 1867.

#2041. Frankenstein Trestle, P&O Railroad.

#2170. Frankenstein Cliff, P&O Railroad, Franconia Notch.

#2135. Frankenstein Trestle. 1875-80.

#165. Frost Work. C. 1867.

#167. Frost Work. C. 1867.

#190. Frost Work. C. 1867.

#197. Frost Work. C. 1867.

#198. Frost Work. C. 1867.

#199. Frost Work. C. 1867.

#200. Frost Work. C. 1867.

#201. Frost Work. C. 1867.

#202. Frost Work. C. 1867.

#203. Frost Work. C. 1867.

#204. Frost Work. C. 1867.

#205. Frost Work. C. 1867.

#206. Frost Work. C. 1867.

#207. Frost Work. C. 1867.

#208. Frost Work. C. 1867.

#209. Frost Work. C. 1867.

#210. Frost Work. C. 1867.

#211. Frost Work. C. 1867.

#1250. Gates of Dixville Notch.

#27. Gates of the Crawford Notch. C. 1867.

#118. Georgianna Falls. C. 1867.

#105. Glen Ellis Falls. C. 1867.

#2331. Glen Ellis Falls.

#160. Glen Ellis Falls, Close Up. C. 1873.

#107. Glen House. C. 1867.

#42. Glen House. C. 1867.

#707. Glen House, White Mountains.

#1791. Government Signal Station, Mount Washington.

Stereographic Views of the White Mountains

#86. Graves of the Willey Family. C. 1867.

#2312. Gulf of Mexico.

#151. Half Way House, Carriage Road to Mount Washington. C. 1867.

#220. Head Waters of the Saco. C. 1867.

#3. Ice Jam on the Ammonoosuc. C. 1867.

#4. Ice Jam on the Ammonoosuc. C. 1867.

#1262. Interior of US Observatory, Mount Washington. Before 1877.

#2062. Lake Winnipeseogee [sic] from the Old Pine, Center Harbor. C. 1868.

#356. Lake Winnipeseogee [sic].

#352. Lake Winnipisseogee [sic] from the Weirs.

#128. Littleton, NH. C. 1867.

#83. Littleton, NH. C. 1867.

#2. Littleton, NH, State Quarry. C. 1867.

#95. Main St., Littleton, NH. C. 1867.

#991. McMillan House, North Conway. Before 1877.

#175. Mount Cannon, Franconia. C. 1867.

#176. Mount Cannon, Franconia. C. 1867.

#89. Mount Cannon, From Echo Lake. C. 1867.

#89. Mount Cannon, From Echo Lake. C. 1867.

Mount Lafayette. C. 1867.

#1. Mount Lafayette from Bald.

#355. Mount Lafayette from Littleton.

#2049. Mount Lafayette from Lonesome Lake.

#125. Mount Lafayette from Mount Cannon. C. 1867.

#1778. Mount Lafayette from Mount Canon [sic].

#8. Mount Lafayette, from Franconia. C. 1876.

#187. Mount Pleasant, from the Railroad. C. 1867.

#185. Mount Washington Railroad, Looking Down. C. 1867.

#184. Mount Washington Railroad, Looking Up. C. 1867.

#2219. Mount Washington Signal Station.

#623. Mount Washington.

#44. Mount Washington, from the Giant's Grave. C. 1867.

#183. Mount Washington, from the Railroad. C. 1867.

#28. Mount Webster, Crawford Notch. C. 1867.

#2171. Mount Willard and Willey Valley, P&O Railroad, Crawford Notch.

#69. Mount Willard, Crawford Notch. C. 1867.

#80. Mount Willard, Crawford Notch. C. 1867.

#221. Mount Willard, from the Saco. C. 1867.

#2167. Nancy's Brook and P&O Railroad. C. 1873-75.

#673. Nancy's Brook.

Observatory, Mount Agassiz. C. 1880.

#714. Old Man. 1880.

#73. On the Pemigewasset. C. 1867.

#77. On the Pemigewasset. C. 1867.

#2120. P&O Railroad Pass, Crawford Notch, NH.

#2181. Pass of Crawford Notch, P&O Railroad. 1875+.

#261. Pass of the Dixville Notch. C. 1867.

#262. Pass of the Dixville Notch. C. 1867.

#361. Pavilion Hotel, Wolfeborough.

#193. Pemigewasset House, Plymouth, NH. C. 1867.

#194. Pemigewasset House. Plymouth, NH. C. 1867.

#195. Pemigewasset House, Plymouth, NH. C. 1867.

#196. Pemigewasset House, Plymouth, NH. C. 1867.

#50. Pool, Franconia. C. 1867.

#52. Pool, Franconia. C. 1867.

#96. Pool, Franconia. C. 1867.

Post Office, Bethlehem.

#678. Profile House, Dining Hall, Franconia Notch.

#58. Profile House, Drawing Room. C. 1867.

#38. Profile House, Franconia Notch. C. 1867.

#526. Profile House, Franconia Notch.

#129. Profile House, Franconia. C. 1867.

#72. Profile House, Franconia. C. 1867.

#509. Profile Lake, Franconia Notch.

New Hampshire Scenery

#109. Profile Lake, Franconia. C. 1867.
#110. Profile Lake, Franconia. C. 1867.
#111. Profile Lake, Franconia. C. 1867.
#140. Profile Lake, Franconia. C. 1867.
#142. Profile Lake, Franconia. C. 1867.
#527. Profile, Franconia Notch, NH.
#131. Profile, Franconia. C. 1867.
#2177. Pulpit Rock and P&O Railroad. 1875+.
#518. Pulpit Rock.
#100. Railroad on to Mount Washington. C. 1867.
#101. Railroad on to Mount Washington. C. 1867.
#104. Railroad on to Mount Washington. C. 1867.
#2063. Red Hill, Center Harbor. C. 1868.
#1983. Reflections in Saco Lake.
#88. Ripley's Falls, Crawford Notch. C. 1867.
#358. Senter House, Centre Harbor. C. 1868.
Silver Cascade. C. 1870.
#160. Silver Cascade and Bridge.
#25. Silver Cascade, Crawford Notch. C. 1867.
#160. Silver Cascade, Crawford Notch. C. 1867.
#170. Silver Cascade, Crawford Notch. C. 1867.
#113. Sinclair House, Bethlehem, NH. C. 1867.
#772. Smile of the Great Spirit (Winnipiseogee [sic]).
#694. Summit of Mount Washington.
#545. Suspended Boulder, Franconia Notch.
#153. Tip Top House. C. 1867.
#535. Tuckerman's Ravine, Aug. 10, 1869.
#531. Under the Snow, Tuckerman's Ravine, Aug. 10, 1869.
#34. Valley of the Saco. C. 1867.
#132. View from Columnar Heights. C. 1867.
#92. View from Echo Lake. C. 1867.
#2137. View from Idlewild. C. 1870.
#114. View from Jefferson. 1866.
#2313. View from Mount Clay.

#188. View from Mount Washington Railroad Depot. C. 1867.
#363. View from Pavilion Hotel.
#106. View from Glen House. C. 1867.
#119. View in Franconia Notch. C. 1867.
#120. View in Franconia Notch. C. 1867.
View in Littleton, NH. C. 1867.
Walker's Falls, Franconia.
#5. Walker's Pond, Franconia Notch. C. 1867.
#836. Water Nymph's Lace Work.
#611. Water Nymph's Palace.
#612. Water Nymph's Palace.
#69. White Mountains, from Carroll, NH. C. 1867.
#27. White Mountains, from Littleton, NH. C. 1867.
#2087. Willey Brook Bridge with Wooden Trestle.
#2045. Willey House and Mount Willey. C. 1870.
#87. Willey House, Crawford Notch. C. 1867.
#219. Willey House, Crawford Notch. C. 1867.
#676. Willey House, White Mountains. C. 1868.
#216. Winter View of Pulpit Rock, Crawford Notch. C. 1867.
#212. Winter View, White Mountains. C. 1868.

KIMBALL, H. A.

Active 1870s and 1880s.
Concord, NH.
In 1881 Kimball printed photographs on silk and linen in the Platinotype process.
#108. Views of Masonic Encampment at Centre Harbor, Aug. 1869.

MOON, T. C., and MOULTON, F. J.

Active 1870s and 1880s.
Moon and Moulton set up the Weirs Photographic Company, Laconia and Weirs, NH.
South from Campground Bridge. C. 1880.

Stereographic Views of the White Mountains

MOULTON, J. S.

Active 1870s.
Amherst, NH.

#132. Thompson's Cascade, White Mountains, NH. 1870s.

MOULTON, J. W. and J. S.

Active 1870s.
Salem, MA.

#407. Bridge near Fabyan House. 1870s.

#403. Frankenstein Trestle Work. 1870s.

#404. Frankenstein Trestle Work. 1870s.

#412. P&O Railroad from Crawford Notch. 1870s.

#215. View in Crawford Notch. 1870s.

PARKER, J., JR.

Active 1870s.
Newport, NH.

Rear of Mountain House, Sunapee, NH. 1870s.

PEASE, NATHAN W.

Active 1860s and 1870s.
Born Cornish, ME.
Pease came to North Conway in 1858 and lived next to the Baptist Church. He was listed as a photographer in Carroll County, NH, in 1858 and was the first president of the North Conway Library Association, 1887. Pease was very civic-minded and connected with many local organizations. His early stereographic cards carried his name on the back; on later ones it was along the front sides.

#19. Artists' Brook and Meadows.

#11. Artists Brook.

Artists Brook and the Meadow, North Conway.

#27. Artists Brook, Bridge and Mill.

#5. Artists Falls.

#6. Artists Falls.

#7. Artists Falls.

#9. Artists Falls, North Conway, C. 1868.

#220. Basin, Franconia Notch; The . . .

#185. Beecher's Cascade.

#186. Beecher's Cascade.

#187. Beecher's Cascade.

#225. Berlin Falls.

#35. Big Pine, Enchanted Woods.

#88. Cascades Near Goodrich Falls.

#31. Cathedral Woods, North Conway.

#57. Cathedral, Hart's Ledge.

#195. Center Harbor and Ossipee Mountains.

#226. Centre Harbor and Ossipee Mountains.

#196. Centre Harbor and Red Hill.

Chocurua [sic] Lake and Mountain.

#61. Church's Falls.

#122. Crawford House and Cherry Mountain from Elephant's Head.

Crawford House, Distant. 1862-64.

#131. Crystal Cascade.

#149. Crystal Cascade. 1870s.

#59. Devils [sic] Den, Hart's Ledge, North Conway.

#47. Diana's Baths.

#48. Diana's Baths.

#49. Diana's Baths.

#50. Diana's Baths.

#51. Diana's Baths.

#52. Diana's Baths.

#54. Diana's Baths.

#56. Diana's Baths.

#224. Eagle Cliff from Profile House.

#113. Echo Lake.

#139. Echo Lake, Franconia Mountains. C. 1868.

#242. Echo Lake, Franconia Mountains. C. 1868.

#63. Echo Lake, North Conway.

#64. Echo Lake, North Conway.

#66. Echo Lake, North Conway.

#68. Echo Lake, North Conway.

#65. Echo Lake, White Horse Ledge, North Conway.

#82. Elevated Boulders, Bartlett. 1862-64.

Emerald Pool. (Untitled).

#146. Emerald Pool.

#67. Enchanted Woods, North Conway.

#256. Fabyan House.

#119. Fairview Cottage and Mote [sic] Mountain.

Flume from Above Boulder.

New Hampshire Scenery

Stereographic Views of the White Mountains

#218. Mount Willard, P&O Railroad.
North Conway and Ledges from Artists' Ledge.

#21. North Conway and Mote [sic] Mountain.

#1. North Conway and White Mountains.

#137. Old Man.

#53. On Diana's Baths.

#58. On Diana's Baths.

#164. On Mount Washington Carriage Road, Looking Down.

#189. Ossipee Falls. C. 1868.

#191. Ossipee Falls.

#192. Ossipee Falls.

#202. Ossipee Mountains from Center Harbor.

#184. P&O Railroad, White Mountain Notch.

#216. P&O Railroad, White Mountain Notch.

#152. Pass, White Mountain Notch, P&O Railroad.

#201. Pass, White Mountain Notch, P&O Railroad.
Pemigewasset House. C. 1870.

#211. Pemigewasset River and Welch Mountain.

#131. Pool; The...

#132. Pool; The...

#249. Profile House, Franconia Mountains.
Profile Lake.
Profile Lake and the Old Man.

#10. Pulpit Rock.

#101. Pulpit Rock, Looking Down.

#206. Saco River, Upper Bartlett.

#194. Senter House from Garden.

#193. Senter House, Center Harbor.

#84. Serpentine Tree, North Conway.

#180. Silver Cascade After a Storm.

#112. Silver Cascade. 1862-64.

#231. Snow Arch.

#232. Snow Arch.

#233. Snow Arch.

#228. Snow Arch, Tuckerman's Ravine.

#200. Squam Lake from Sunset Hill.

#188. Starting for Mount Washington from Crawford House.

#197. Steamboat Landing, Centre Harbor.

#29. Summer Rambles, North Conway.

#36. Summer Rambles, North Conway.

#37. Summer Rambles, North Conway.

#38. Summer Rambles, North Conway.

#40. Summer Rambles, North Conway.

#171. Summit from Chandler's Point.

#169. Summit House.

#120. Summit of Mount Washington, South of Tuckerman's.

#28. Sunset Pavillion, North Conway.

#70. Thompson's Falls, North Conway.

#141. Tip Top and Summit House.
Tip Top House.
Tip Top House. C. 1868.

#160. Tip Top House.

#170. Tip Top House.

#171. Tip Top House.

#161. Tuckerman's Ravine from Glen Notch.

#176. Tuckerman's Ravine.

#259. Twin Mountain House.
View above Glen Ellis Falls.

#173. View above the Clouds, Mount Washington.

#161. View from the Summit of Mount Washington.

#118. View from Mount Willard.

#98. View from Thorn Hill, Bartlett.

#97. View of Jackson Falls.

#165. View on Carriage Road, Looking Down.

#166. View on Carriage Road, Looking Up.
View on Diana's Baths.

#126. View on Mount Willard.

#25. View on road from Artists Falls.

#158. View on the Ledge, Mount Washington.

#130. Walker's Falls, Franconia Mountains.

#45. Washington Boulder.

#172. Where Lizzie Bourne Died.

#41. White Horse Ledge.

#114. White Mountain Notch; The...
C. 1868.

New Hampshire Scenery

#207. White Mountain Notch and P&O Railroad.

#204. White Mountain Notch From Elephants [sic] Head.

#110. White Mountain Notch Looking Towards Mount Webster.

#99. White Mountain Notch, Looking Down.

#116. White Mountain Notch, P&O Railroad.

#13. White Mountains and Kearsarge Village.

#111. Willey House.

#109. Willey House and Mount Willard.

#95. Winter View, North Conway.

SCRIPTURE, G. H.

Active 1860s and 1870s.
2 French's Block.
Peterborough, NH.
Scripture specialized in views of Mount Monadnock.

Half Way House, Monadnock. C. 1860.

#30. Monadnock Mountain, On the Tip Top. C. 1865.

SHACKFORD, A. W.

Farmington, NH.

Alton Bay. 1870s.

Alton Bay Campmeeting Boarding Tent. 1870s.

Alton Bay with Row Boat. 1870s.

STEREOSCOPIC VIEWS OF THE WHITE MOUNTAINS SCENERY PUBLISHED FOR THE MILLIONS

C. 1862.

#148. Thompson's Cascades.

Major Rogers [sic] Bath near Glen House.

SOULE, JOHN P.

1827-1904.
Soule's address in the 1860s and 1870s was 199 Washington St., Boston, MA. He became a professional photographer in 1859 and published *American Views* in 1866.

#520. Among the Clouds, Mount Washington.

#52. Artists Falls, North Conway. C. 1860.

#203. Ascending Mount Lafayette.

#185. Basin (side view); The...

#144. Berlin Falls Above the Bridge.

#513. Carriage Road at the Ledge.

#514. Carriage Road at the Ledge, Mount Washington.

#180. Cascade in the Flume.

#181. Cascade in the Flume.

#136. Centre Harbor. C. 1861.

#165. Crawford House, Near View.

#527. Crystal Cascade, Pinkham Notch.

#499. Dining Room, Glen House.

#199. Eagle Cliff and Part of Profile House. C. 1861.

#169. Echo Lake and Franconia Notch.

#168. Echo Lake and Mount Cannon.

#167. Echo Lake and Mount Lafayette.

#170. Echo Lake Near Outlet.

#155. Emerald Pool, Near Glen House.

#406. Full Moon.

#524. Glen Ellis Falls.

#525. Glen Ellis Falls.

#147. Glen House from Carriage Road.

#176. Goodrich Falls, Bartlett.

#504. Half Way House, Mount Washington.

#508. Half Way House, Mount Washington.

#509. Half Way House, Mount Washington.

#510. Half Way House, Mount Washington.

#158. In the Notch (Crawford's), Looking Up.

#159. In the Notch (Crawford's), Looking Up.

#177. Jackson Falls.

#210. Lake Winnepesaukee [sic] from Senter House, Centre Harbor.

#212. Lake Winnipesaukee from Senter House.

#218. Long Pond and Red Hill, Centre Harbor.

#175. Mount Chocorua and Lake.

#503. Mount Madison and Adams from Peabody Bridge.

#502. Mount Washington from Glen House. C. 1861.

#157. Mount Willard from Gate of the Notch.

#154. Near View of Glen House and Stages.

Stereographic Views of the White Mountains

#500. New Glen House; The...

#501. New Glen House; The...

North Conway and White Mountains from Sunset Hill. C. 1860.

#114. Old Man of the Mountains. C. 1861.

#174. On Artists Brook, North Conway.

#166. Profile House, Near View.

#192. Profile Lake.

#193. Profile Lake.

Red Hill from the Lake (Winnepesaukee [sic]).

#214. Red Hill from the Lake, Center Harbor.

#206. Senter House and Stages, Centre Harbor.

#216. Squam Lake from Sunset Hill, Centre Harbor.

#204. Summit of Mount Lafayette.

#205. Summit of Mount Lafayette.

#160. Summit of Mount Washington from Chandler's Point.

#31. Tip Top House. 1861.

#153. Tip Top House, Summit of Mount Washington. 1862.

#516. Tip Top House, Summit of Mount Washington. After 1862.

#171. Walker's Falls.

#172. Walker's Falls.

#530. White Mountains from Lead Mine Bridge, Shelburne; The...

#135. Winnipesaukee near Wolfeborough. C. 1861.

STIFF, C. W., and COOK

Active 1870s.
Danvers, MA.

#65. Franconia Notch From Echo Lake. C. 1866.

SUBSCRIPTION SERIES

Active 1880s.
The series bears no titles or numbers. On the back is a short description.

Boat Scene, Lake Winnipiseogee [sic]. C. 1880.

TOWLE, SIMON

Active 1860s and 1870s.
92 Merrimack St.
Lowell, MA.

Falls of Song, Ossipee Park, Moultonborough, NH. 1870s.

UNKNOWN

Across Winnipesaukee from Wolfboro [sic].

#112. Almost there, Lizzie Bourne's Monument.

#139. Androscoggin River at Berlin. 1862-64.

#149. Arctic Philosopher in the Pool. C. 1868.

#11. Artists Falls.

#126. Basin; The...

#154. Basin, Franconia Notch, NH.

#132. Cascade below the Flume, Franconia Notch, NH.

Cascade, Dixville Notch.

Courser Brook, Errol, NH.

Crawford Notch Cascade (Silver Cascade).

Eagle Cliff and Profile Lake.

#71. Elephants [sic] Head and Crawfords [sic] Gateway, White Mountains, NH. 1884.

New Hampshire Scenery

Franconia House, Franconia, NH. C. 1875.

Franconia House, Franconia, NH. C. 1875.

Gateway of Crawford Notch, White Mountains, NH. 1884.

Glen Ellis Falls.

Half Way House, Mount Washington Road.

#70. Headwater of Saco River and Crawford House, White Mountains, NH. 1884.

#69. Headwater of Saco River from Idlewild, White Mountains, NH. 1884.

Hotel Diamond Moved to Weirs.

#136. Ice Cavern. Before 1859.

Intervale, NH, Looking North.

#350. Lake Winnipiseogee [sic] from the Weirs. C. 1868.

#900. Mount Liberty, Franconia Notch.

#519. Mount Liberty, Franconia Notch. C. 1868.

Mountain Pool, Monadnock; The...

#84. Profile Cascade.

#38. Profile House, Franconia Notch, NH.

#421. Profile House, Franconia Notch, NH.

Pulpit Rock. C. 1869.

Silver Cascade, White Mountains.

#71. Thompson's Falls. C. 1861.

#120. View of Franconia Notch. C. 1868.

Winter Scene, NH.

WELLER, F. G.
Active 1867-73.
Littleton, NH.
Weller was known for his very fine, crisp views.

#259. All Aboard for Mount Washington. C. 1869.

#36. Crystal Cascade. C. 1867.

#247. Echo Lake. C. 1868.

#456. Fabyan House. C. 1867.

#219. Flume; The... C. 1867.

#141. Flume above the Boulder; The... C. 1867.

#130. Flume in October. C. 1867.

#75. Pool; The... C. 1867.

#81. Silver Cascade, Crawford Notch.

#211. View from Twin Mountain House. C. 1867.

#205. White Mountains from Bethlehem. C. 1867.

WHITE, FRANKLIN & COMPANY
Active 1859.
Lancaster, NH.
White had a studio in the attic of the Summit House on Mount Washington. He specialized in photographs of the Mount Washington summit and the Franconia range, probably the first American mountain photography.

Carriage Road and Half Way House. C. 1865.

#180. Cascades in Flume, Franconia Notch.

Lancaster (Percy Peaks?).

WILDER, W. L.
Active 1870s.
Laconia, NH.

Elliott's Cove, Lake Winnepesaukee [sic], NH. C. 1868.

Stereographic Views of the White Mountains

List of Plates and Illustrations